D0828242

UNLIMITED EMBRACE

UNLIMITED

A Canon of Gay Fiction, 1945–1995

EMBRACE

Reed Woodhouse

UNIVERSITY OF MASSACHUSETTS PRESS *Amherst*

Woodhouse, Reed, 1949–
Unlimited embrace : a canon of gay fiction, 1945–1995 / Reed Woodhouse.
p.   cm.
Includes bibliographical references and index.
ISBN 1-55849-132-5 (alk. paper)
1. American fiction — 20th century — History and criticism.
2. Homosexuality and literature — United States — History — 20th
century.   3. Literature and society — United States — History — 20th
century.   4. Gay men's writings, American — History and criticism.
5. Gay men — United States — Books and reading.   6. Gay men in
literature.   7. Canon (Literature)   I. Title.
PS374.H63W66   1998
813'.54099206642 — dc21   97-48588
CIP

British Library Cataloguing in Publication data are available.

For
Larey Allen

and in memory of
Tom Stehling and Karl Laubenstein

Contact of friend led to another friend,
Supple entwinement through the living mass
Which for all that I knew might have no end,
Image of an unlimited embrace.

Thom Gunn, "The Missing"

CONTENTS

         Michael Cunningham's *A Home at the End of
             the World*   174
         Ethan Mordden's Short Stories   184

PART FOUR   Imagining Death

7   A Wedding and Three Funerals: Four AIDS Novels   201
         John Weir's *The Irreversible Decline of
             Eddie Socket*   206
         Samuel R. Delany's *The Mad Man*   212
         Christopher Davis's *Valley of the Shadow*   221
         Dale Peck's *Martin and John*   228

PART FIVE   Looking Back

8   Boy's Life: Neil Bartlett's *Ready to Catch Him Should
             He Fall*   241

9   White Lies: Edmund White's Gay Fiction   263

         Afterword   297

         More Gay Fiction: An Appendix   301
         Nonce, Genre, and One-Handed Books   304

         Notes   307

         Index   329

ACKNOWLEDGMENTS

This book originated in a course I gave three times at the Cambridge Center for Adult Education with my friend Michael Schwartz. It was in this course that I began to formulate my canon of gay fiction. Throughout the writing of this book, Michael has been the reader I had most in mind, at once the most critical and the most generous. I hope it will not disappoint him.

I also owe a debt of gratitude to Professor Robert Bennett of the Classics department of Kenyon College for inviting me to give a lecture at Kenyon on gay fiction, an invitation which spurred me to put my thoughts down on paper for the first time. I am also indebted to Richard Schneider, editor of the *Harvard Gay and Lesbian Review,* who published this lecture ("Five Houses of Gay Fiction") in the inaugural issue of the *Review.* I am grateful to have had the chance to review many works of contemporary gay authors for the *Harvard Gay and Lesbian Review* and also for the *Boston Book Review,* whose editor, Theo Theoharis, has been a staunch supporter of this project and a kind friend.

I would like to thank Michael Denneny, David Bergman, and John Crowley for reading and commenting on earlier versions of the present book; their criticism was invaluable. They are not, of course, to be held accountable for the opinions I express.

Finally, I would like to acknowledge the assistance of the librarians of the New York Public Library for their help in finding rare periodical material from the early 1970s; the Writers' Room of New York for finding me a desk during my research in New York; and the Writers' Room of Boston for comradeship and the encouragement of high standards.

UNLIMITED EMBRACE

INTRODUCTION:

FIVE HOUSES OF GAY FICTION, REVISITED

The composer Virgil Thomson once remarked in my hearing that when he was working on a new piece he kept at it until (as he put it) the piece "composed itself the same way" three days in a row. Several years ago, my friend Michael Schwartz and I began teaching a course at the Cambridge Center for Adult Education called "Gay Male Fiction" — literature (as we put it) "by, for, and about gay men." When we first conceived of this course, we were faced in the most practical sense with the question of a "canon." Which books *had* to go on the syllabus? Which ones would be fun to teach if we had time? Which were irrelevant or bad? Further questions occurred to us: What was the essence of a "gay" fiction? Were the best books necessarily the gayest? Or did a book's "gay-density," so to speak, have little to do with its literary value? Our experience confirmed Thomson's, for the course composed itself in basically the same way three times. Each time, we came back to the same core of texts, around which we then situated certain others. This core I began calling "ghetto literature"; its satellites closet, proto-ghetto, assimilative, and transgressive. And my thrice-repeated experience with this "canon" formed the basis of an essay, "Five Houses of Gay Fiction,"[1] and eventually of the present book.

By "ghetto" fiction, I did not mean only the books whose authors lived in the gay ghettos of San Francisco, Los Angeles, or New York, nor those whose characters did. The more important reason for my choice of the word *ghetto* was that this core fiction seemed to occupy a place in literature analogous to the place occupied in the city by the gay ghetto; a place where homosexuality was both taken for granted (and thus invisible) and at the same time easily identifiable (and thus highly visible): a sort of parallel city, in fact. "Ghetto fiction," then, *was* literature "by, for, and about gay men." These were not books, in other words, whose characters "just happened to be gay," any more than the ghetto was a place whose residents "just happened to be gay." Its characters (whether truly or mistakenly, comically or disastrously) saw their sexuality as a key to their lives. These books, like the gay ghetto itself, represented the gay world at its furthest point of self-definition, and were an expression of homosexuality at its most concentrated: that is, as nearly as possible without normative reference to the straight world. Among the ghetto works I most liked were Andrew Holleran's *Dancer from the Dance;* Ethan Mordden's three volumes of short stories on gay life in Manhattan in the late seventies and eighties; and, most recent and one of the best, the English author Neil Bartlett's beautiful *Ready to Catch Him Should He Fall.*

The proto-ghetto books differed from ghetto ones mainly because their characters lacked a gay community, and sometimes even the name "gay" for who and what they were. As a result, these novels and stories emphasized individual courage rather than a group identity. They nevertheless belonged with ghetto literature, rather than with either closeted or assimilative fiction, sharing with ghetto fiction an astonishing, sometimes arrogant disregard for the surrounding straight world. Some of the works I put in the proto-ghetto category were Tennessee Williams's early and amazingly unabashed short stories ("Hard Candy," "Desire and the Black Masseur," "Two on a Party," and others); Christopher Isherwood's masterpiece *A Single Man;* and James Purdy's novels of rapturous violence *Eustace Chisholm and the Works* and *Narrow Rooms.*

Ghetto literature was preceded by, and in some ways formed against, something I called "closet" literature: fiction, that is, that saw homosexuality as something defining indeed, but horrifyingly so. One wants to say that this was literature too remote from a modern gay man's experience to be relevant. But such a judgment would not be quite true, for in a sense the closet can never die. So long as homosexuality continues to be defined (as, in an obvious sense, it must) as a *sexual* identity, books about it will be both exciting and threatening. That was the source of closet literature's truth and power. James Baldwin's *Giovanni's Room,* the closet novel *par excellence,* was a reminder of where we had come from, and where most of us, at some point in our gay lives, had been: alone, fearful, disgraced, excited. It was faithful, in some horrible way, to the experience of sexual need and shame. Gloomy and unfair as much of it was, closet fiction had the great virtue of taking sex seriously. It did not whimsify it, nor denature it of moral meaning.

Both ghetto and closet literature were followed historically by different kinds of gay fiction. The two main branches of this new literature I called "assimilative" (or "homosexual") and "transgressive" (or "queer").

Assimilative gay literature began to be a possibility in the wake of Stonewall and the settling-in of gay liberation. Its writers included some of the best-known gay writers in America, such as the late Robert Ferro, David Leavitt, Stephen McCauley, Christopher Bram, Michael Cunningham, and others. This literature broke away from the ghetto tradition by placing its gay characters either outside the ghetto or in a hostile relation to it. But the books were also outside of the symbolic, literary ghetto: nothing but their inclusion of a gay character would have made one think these were gay books. Assimilative stories were deliberately integrative and frequently concerned a gay character's coming to terms with his family, living with straight friends (often women), or finding a lover and settling down in a monogamous relationship. A surprising number of them were about raising children.

Assimilative literature could be thought of as fiction about gay men for straight readers. It showed gay life within the implicit or explicit context of mainstream life, and tacitly appealed to mainstream values — especially those of the family, or of monogamous love. It was not the same thing as closet literature, for it claimed the right of gay people to exist — provided they resembled straight ones. These books, while well written, were rarely brilliant or witty. (Stylistic brilliance of the Wildean sort was perhaps too identifiably "gay.") Their strength lay rather in an appeal to a common humanity: "We're all looking for love" or "We're all mystified by our parents." These novels *were* about people who "just happened to be gay." Some assimilative titles would have been Gore Vidal's brave early novel *The City and the Pillar* (though not his more radical *Myra Breckinridge*); David Leavitt's *Equal Affections* and *The Lost Language of Cranes;* Stephen McCauley's *The Object of My Affection;* and Michael Cunningham's beautiful *A Home at the End of the World.* Perhaps the most popular of all gay books (among both gay and straight readers) would fall into this category: Armistead Maupin's *Tales of the City* series.

The transgressive, or "queer," writers were quite different, at least on the surface, from the assimilators. And they too numbered some respected, if less-known writers, many from the West Coast: Dennis Cooper, Robert Glück, Kevin Killian, Paul Russell, the late Sam Dallessandro. Their stories were frequently ones of horror, dissociation, or emotional numbness. They were often shocking in their presentation of extreme psychological states and extreme sexual acts, such as mutilation and murder. "Transgressors" were like assimilators, however, in disdaining the ghetto, though for a different reason: what they loathed was its bourgeois complacency, indeed its rather vulgar success. The queer writer was queer first; gay second. *Queer* in this context did not primarily mean "homosexual," but "estranged" or "marginal." Queer writing was fascinated with sex, but contradictory about it. On the one hand, because it saw homosexuality as "transgressive," it could present gay characters as heroes of the sexual margin. On the other, "transgression" could take so many forms — including cross-dressing, bisexuality, radical or reactionary politics, or mere *anomie* — that it became hard to keep the homosexuality as such separated from the general transgressiveness that was praised.

The queer writer *par excellence* was Dennis Cooper, whose brilliant novels *Try, Closer,* and *Frisk* exemplified the frightening coolness and unemotionality of radical narrative. In *Frisk,* for example, one of the characters asks another to shit in the toilet and not flush. He adds: "I'm not being abject . . . It's not, 'Ooh, shit, piss, how wicked,' or anything. It's, like I said, information."[2] Queer writing was often pornographic or parodic of pornography, and brilliantly captured the dissociation of sexual obsession. Its other great insight was that, just as "love" could be put in ironic quotation marks, so could something as seemingly objective as "sex." Nearly all the sex scenes in Cooper were fascinating — the right, fetishistic word — *because* they were mechanical. In no case did they call forth irrelevant words like *abject.* It was not sex that formed the basis of these novels' queerness, but rather a sort of vacuum which sex tried vainly to fill. "Queer" titles included Killian's *Shy,* Glück's *Elements of a Coffee Service* and *Jack the Modernist,* Paul Russell's *The Salt Point* and *The Boys of Life,* and Sam Dallessandro's collection of stories *The Zombie Pit.*

Neither the assimilationists nor the queers were attempting quite what the earlier gay authors had attempted: namely, to create a literature of gay *identity,* of heroism and separateness. Nor did they seem to proceed from a sense of joy (even privilege) in being gay. None of them found the world to be well lost for love. The assimilative books, while completely unabject and "pro-gay," nevertheless continued a narrative of *acceptance* by the straight world that was present in earlier works like Gordon Merrick's saccharine *The Lord Won't Mind.* The transgressive titles repudiated the straight world (construed as something much larger than the mere mass of heterosexuals), but in that repudiation continued its power, and assigned homosexuality a position only on the margins of society — powerless, undignified, desperate. In both assimilative and transgressive texts, homosexuality lost all particularity of social reference; the gay characters didn't act or talk "gay." Whether insiders or outsiders, they were virtually indistinguishable from straight ones.

Was this a step forward? Many thought it was. I disagreed. It seemed (and still seems) to me that there is a tremendous, if unacknowledged, pressure on gay writers to tone down the sexuality of their characters and their story, to make them more "universal." But I do not think that a literature, or a life, that blurs the outlines of our identity can fully represent us either to ourselves or to the straight world. Nor do I think that fiction (or, as yet, a free homosexuality) can do without "identity" altogether, even were such a denatured representation (or life) desirable. In the case of literature, at least, Flannery O'Connor was right: "when the life that actually surrounds us is totally ignored, when our patterns of speech are absolutely overlooked, then something is out of kilter. . . . An idiom characterizes a society, and when you ignore the idiom, you are very likely ignoring the whole social fabric that could make a meaningful character. You can't cut characters off from their society and say much about them as individuals. You can't say anything meaningful about the mystery of a personality unless you put that personality in a believable and significant social context."[3]

The ghetto and pre-ghetto writers, by contrast, *did* insist on a gay particularity and were thus as necessary as the actual ghettoes many of us inhabited. Both fictional and urban neighborhoods stood for an identifiably gay life, and were thus living refutations of the belief that gay people didn't really exist, or were not really different. Both institutions, ghetto and ghetto literature, made a radical and complex claim: that gay life *was* different from straight life in some important ways; and that the differences wouldn't soon go away. Ghetto writers had posed, if not solved, the peculiar difficulties and triumphs of gay life by insisting on three things. The first and most important was that sexuality was central; to make it peripheral or adventitious risked erasing the characters' homosexuality altogether. Second was an insistence on the characters' slight, but important, separateness from the world (a separateness that is always evoked for me by E. M. Forster's famous description of the proto-ghetto Cavafy: "a Greek gentleman in a straw hat, standing absolutely motionless at a slight angle to the universe.")[4] Third, they insisted on joy, even arrogance, in that separateness, rather than shame, guilt, or boredom. The sexual and social particularities of their characters might be social disabilities, but were nevertheless personal advantages.

What I was calling "ghetto fiction" was gay not incidentally, then, but essentially. It was not enough that it simply take place *in* the ghetto; it had, as it were, to be written *for* the ghetto. It was not intended primarily for a nongay audience: like life in the actual ghetto, it took homosexuality for granted, and did not explain it. It was not enough for there to be one or two gay characters swimming in a welter of straight ones, even if the gay characters were "good" and the straight ones "bad." The purpose of ghetto literature was not to award points for sensitivity. The gay protagonist would see himself in only incidental relationship to the straight world: George in Isherwood's *A Single Man,* for instance, lives in a perfectly "straight" neighborhood and has a perfectly "straight" job teaching at a local college. But he holds himself indefinably aloof from both. Even his best friend Charlotte knows him less well than he knows her. These books saw heterosexuality and the life of the family as interesting, perhaps, but essentially irrelevant. (This *lack of relevance* struck me as one of the infallible signs of "gay fiction.") And they described, or envisioned, a homosexuality that was separate, unself-pitying, even cocky.

While I still think that my five "houses" have some descriptive value, as a taxonomy they leave something to be desired. My map of gay fiction was incomplete, and thus inconclusive. (I would now make a place for a "house" of

AIDS fiction, for instance.) Nor do I particularly like my own invented terminology, especially of "ghetto" and "proto-ghetto": terms that are both too limited and too negative to convey what I meant. Though the five categories indicate stubborn differences in how we represent homosexuality in fiction, I now think that what I was talking about all along was a far more basic polarity: between the literature of gay assimilation, on the one hand, and that of gay identity on the other.

The literature of assimilation includes much more than my original "assimilative" house (represented by authors such as David Leavitt, Michael Cunningham, Stephen McCauley, and Christopher Bram). Indeed, it includes some writers one might have thought diametrically different: Dale Peck, Dennis Cooper, Paul Russell et al. What the two houses have in common (as I hinted even in my original essay) are an indifference to the gayness of the story and characters and a tendency to see them as part of some larger trend or group. Robert Ferro and David Leavitt, for example, want to place gay sons in relationship to their birth families. Dennis Cooper and Sam Dallessandro want to relate their characters to a surrounding world of anomic punks and pedophiles, who may or may not be specifically gay. Whether transgressive or assimilative, then, many writers of the past fifteen years seem to have moved decisively away not just from the actual ghetto in which Andrew Holleran and Ethan Mordden set their stories, but also from the metaphorical ghetto of gay particularity. Similarly, the three categories of closet, proto-ghetto, and ghetto fiction came to seem one larger category predicated upon gay identity. For all their differences, the characters in Tennessee Williams's short stories, James Baldwin's *Giovanni's Room,* James Purdy's *Eustace Chisholm,* and Ethan Mordden's "tales of gay Manhattan" all see themselves as *essentially* gay, see their homosexuality as telling an important truth about them.

Looked at this way, my attempt takes shape as yet one more argument in the long American debate over assimilation. As I write this introduction, for instance, three important statements — by an American Jew, an African American, and an American homosexual — have been recently published. Alan Dershowitz in *The Vanishing American Jew* (1997) worries that Jews have become too Americanized. Randall Kennedy, in a provocative essay in the May 1997 *Atlantic Monthly,* "My Race Problem — And Ours," takes exactly the opposite view: American blacks *must* assimilate to the larger American culture, or at least not take bogus refuge in myths of racial identity. Daniel Harris, finally, in *The Rise and Fall of Gay Culture* (1997), sees in the undoubted success of the post-Stonewall gay movement a troubling forgetfulness of, and contempt toward, the traditions of camp and effeminacy which made gay culture a genuine criticism of mainstream culture. My contribution to the debate is to apply some of these arguments to gay *literature,* specifically.[5]

But assimilation and identity in literature are slightly different from what they are in sociology or politics. I myself failed to see this clearly enough in my original "Five Houses" article, in which I differentiated "houses" based primarily on the kind of story they told: that is, was the gay character in the closet or out of it? living in the Village or the suburbs? alone or with a lover? In my intemperance, I made it seem that David Leavitt's worst flaw as a novelist lay in his unforgivable plot choice: how dare he situate his characters in the bosom of their families! This was a stupid mistake because it seemed to imply that only certain kinds of stories could be told—a dogma which, *mutatis mutandis,* a homophobe like Jesse Helms would be happy to believe too. I repudiate it now.

The assimilation I am now thinking of is of course partly a matter of plot—for it is impossible to divide style from story, especially in realistic fiction and especially in an outlaw fiction like our own—but it is also a question of audience and of artistic ambition and success. "For whom is this book written?" becomes a question one wants to ask. For other gay men? For already-sympathetic straight readers? For your mother? Your lover? Your tricks? And if a book seems written primarily for a cross-over audience—say, the straight white middle-class female audience which forms by far the largest segment of the book-buying public in America—how much has the author compromised on certain gay particularities (sex, for instance, or campy humor) in order not to offend?

As for the second question—artistic ambition and success—this is of course a matter of taste and argument. But here too assimilation plays a part. Most novels, whether gay or straight, popular or highbrow, radical or conservative, are assimilative in the sense that they *flatter* their readers, assuring them that they are in the right, morally or politically or aesthetically. The best works, on the other hand, are too complex to be reduced to any one meaning, even one the author himself or herself may personally embrace. Indeed, such books *resist* simple readings and are thus partly unassimilable. The pleasure we take in the greatest works always has an admixture of pain to it—something unpalatable, impenetrable, hostile, immoral, difficult. I have no idea how many of the books I have chosen for my canon of gay fiction are "great" or even "very good." My claim is more modest: that within the field of gay writing, these are the works that are most "resistant" and thus offer the most strenuous pleasures to an attentive reader.

And in my present view, Leavitt's flaw has nothing to do with his situation of the gay man in his family nor with his sexual prissiness. "The Term Paper Artist," one of the three novellas in his new book *Arkansas* (1997), emphasizes neither. And yet the story is (to my mind) obscene—not because of sex, but because of Leavitt's ingratiating smarminess. How he pats himself on the back for feeling bad that Ben got caught for turning in a term paper Leavitt wrote for him! And how warmly he later absolves himself by making Ben gay after all — maybe it was all for the best! "Obscene" may seem too strong, but I find myself averting my eyes from these scenes of self-approbation quite as much as a different reader might avert his eyes from Dennis Cooper's scenes of sexual violence. What makes me squirm is the smugness in which the author seems to be forcing the reader to collude. And in this respect "The Term Paper Artist" seems no different from *The Lost Language of Cranes*. The hero is still that lovable David Leavitt, the earnest A-student in life.[6]

Leavitt's is what I would call an *artistic* assimilation, related to but separable from the social assimilation of a character. By contrast, it is "resistance" which is the artistic equivalent of the "ghetto" of my original essay, whether or not the story actually takes place there or indeed has anything to do with the narrative of post-Stonewall life. Tennessee Williams, James Baldwin, Christopher Isherwood, and James Purdy are, in this sense, "ghetto" writers: neither they nor their characters can be easily absorbed, digested, changed. In any case, the question of artistic ambition and success is not irrelevant. It is in the light of the best works that we best understand the others, and we must ask how much an author has dared as well as how much he has succeeded.

I realize, of course, that in some sense what I am calling "resistance" is excellence, and that such excellence can and does occur, no matter what the story, assimilative or scrappy. (And failure, needless to say, occurs on both sides of the fence as well.) But I think that the excellence of much gay literature *is* related to its multiple resistances to easy assimilation, and further, that it is hardly surprising that a novel that unthinkingly accepts the virtue of political assimilation runs the risk of being not only less gay, but less good.

Indeed, the astonishing success of both gay liberation and gay literature in our own day has had paradoxical results. Before Stonewall, one thing gay fiction had *going* for it was that it was "obscene" (in the usual, sexual sense): virtually any story that talked honestly about gay men would seem edgy and dangerous. Nowadays, by contrast, gay life is perfectly representable and can even be brought home to meet Mom. This new acceptability, while delightful in real life, has mixed benefits for literature. One danger for a member of our minority is simply that of being swallowed up; a second is the danger of being turned into a tame freak, like a court dwarf. The gay novelist, in order to be read, published, and praised, runs the risk of succumbing to these dangers. He succumbs whenever he agrees a) not to talk too much about sex, and b) not to make his gay characters attractive, demanding, successful, or self-confident. It is astonishing how many gay stories — including some of the most rebarbatively "transgressive" — are still about waifs. Sexlessness and weakness are still the gay man's passport to acceptability.

Christopher Isherwood saw these two alternatives with utter clarity as early as 1964, in his greatest novel, *A Single Man.* Its main character is a late-middle-aged Englishman transplanted to southern California, where he teaches English at a third-rate state college. He is "single" because his lover Jim has died a year before in a car accident. Neither Isherwood nor George italicizes the fact that George is gay. Even so, George is perfectly aware that the rest of the world does, and in a memorable scene (as he sits on the toilet), George contemplates his prototypically straight neighbors the Strunks, so terrified of the monstrous in any form: What would they make of *him?*

Mr. Strunk, George supposes, tries to nail him down with a word. *Queer,* he doubtless growls. But, since this is after all the year 1962, even he may be expected to add, I don't give a damn what he does just as long as he stays away from me. Even psychologists disagree as to the conclusions which may be reached about the Mr. Strunks of this world, on the basis of such a remark. The fact remains that Mr. Strunk himself, to judge from a photograph of him taken in football uniform at college, used to be what many would call a living doll.

But Mrs. Strunk, George feels sure, takes leave to differ gently from her husband; for she is trained in the new tolerance, the technique of annihilation by blandness. Out comes her psychology book—bell and candle are no longer necessary. Reading from it in sweet singsong she proceeds to exorcise the un-speakable out of George. No reason for disgust, she intones, no cause for condemnation. Nothing here that is willfully vicious. All is due to heredity, early environment (Shame on those possessive mothers, those sex-segregated British schools!), arrested development at puberty, and-or glands. Here we have a misfit, debarred forever from the best things of life, to be pitied, not blamed. . . . So let us be understanding, shall we, and remember that, after all, there *were* the Greeks (though that was a bit different, because they were pagans rather than neurotics). Let us even go so far as to say that this kind of relationship can sometimes be almost beautiful—particularly if one of the parties is already dead, or, better yet, both.[7]

Although much has changed in the nearly thirty-five years since Isherwood wrote his masterpiece, the two principal enemy attitudes toward homosexuality endure: namely, the forbiddance to touch—"I don't give a damn what he does just as long as he stays away from me"—and pitying contempt, or what Isherwood calls "annihilation by blandness." The Strunks aren't even very *good* "enemies." Both are (by their lights) broad-minded and tolerant. Both would claim they are making allowances for people like George. (Indeed, Mrs. Strunk actually invites George to dinner, though she rescinds the invitation when the alternative date he suggests is one on which some of their other—i.e., straight—friends will be there.) But it is the Strunks' very friendliness that is dangerous to a gay man; for if he accepts it, he agrees to take his life on the Strunks' terms, to be sexless and pitiable. George won't sign such a contract, and neither should we. "Your exorcism has failed, dear Mrs. Strunk, says George, squatting on the toilet and peeping forth from his lair to watch her emptying the dustbag of her vacuum cleaner into the trash can. The unspeakable is still here — right in your very midst" (*A Single Man*, 29).

Mr. and Mrs. Strunk are the two most influential critics of gay fiction. Nor are they invariably heterosexual. Leavitt, one of the writers who has most successfully removed the sting of "pornography" from gay fiction, has deplored earlier gay novelists' attention to desire. This is, to him, the "dreariest aspect of gay experience." He vows not to make their mistake, to avoid "the traditional gay male distractions."[8] And indeed, in his own books, sex rarely appears, or else it makes him squirm with embarrassment. (For instance, he imagines his hero Philip in *The Lost Language of Cranes* going to peep shows in Greenwich Village not to be turned on, but to have a good cry.) But there are other ways of deglamorizing desire. Radical, sexually explicit authors like Dennis Cooper have taken a strangely parallel path by hinting that our erotic lives are meaningless: "Oh who cares about this anymore," he writes of a character's first sexual memories. At best, sex is merely *interesting*: "I'm not being abject. . . . It's, like I said, information" (*Frisk*, 69).

But in my view, George was right: gay men *are* "unspeakable" — strange, dangerous, revelatory — and the challenge to the gay writer is knowing how to incorporate the "unspeakable" into art, to make it beautiful. He must not make it beautiful by ignoring or trivializing, but by using it, finding a form for it. This challenge is analogous to the one Milan Kundera describes when he writes of Stravinsky's *Rite of Spring*: "Until Stravinsky, music was never able to give barbaric rites a grand form. We could not imagine them musically. Which means: we could not imagine the *beauty* of the barbaric. Without its beauty, the barbaric would remain incomprehensible. (I stress this: to know any phenomenon deeply requires understanding its beauty, actual or potential.) Saying that a bloody rite does possess some beauty — there's the scandal, unbearable, unacceptable."[9] So too, to say that male homosexual desire, that complicated, barbaric drive toward another man, is beautiful — that is a scandal. How much easier it is to reduce that story to one of "acceptance" on the one hand (how can we call that nice Philip "unspeakable"?), or one of mere sex on the other ("It's, like I said, information"). And to write beautifully about such monsters is also a scandal. Indeed the beauty of artistic form (according to Kundera) is what makes knowledge possible. What is necessary, as George saw, is to insist that the monstrous be acknowledged, not wished away or exaggerated.

The difficulty of writing gay literature lies in knowing how to refuse these too-easy narratives, to tell one's story without selling out to the Strunks. Another way to put this would be to say that the best, and most dangerous, gay literature refuses to turn gay men into victims. The modern American faggot is not content to be innocent, cute, or helpless. Unlike ancient Greek *eromenos,* Native American *berdache,* or Neapolitan *feminiello,* he does not confine himself to the passive role either in life or in bed: he wants it all.[10] The writers I most honor in this book are those who have made the greatest claims for homosexuality, imagining it not as a disability but a gift, not as a jail but a club one might wish (at least retrospectively) to join. Like Edmund White, an uneasy clubmember, I have "caught myself imagining that gays might someday constitute a community rather than a diagnosis."[11] That such an image of homosexuality is quite new, a by-product of postwar American confidence, leads me to conceive of the period covered by my book as the age of gay identity: the age, that is, of gayness conceived as an identity. Before the war, gays were merely a "diagnosis," and after the growth of gay rights, they are coming to seem a mere option.

My own life, which is nearly coterminous with this period, has confirmed what some of these earlier writers such as Isherwood once guessed, and perhaps a personal anecdote will explain why.

In 1994 I was invited to come back to my alma mater, Kenyon College, to give a talk on gay literature, a talk from which this book ultimately derives. The invitation had its ironic side. After all, being gay had almost gotten me disinvited twenty-eight years before when, as a freshman, I came across a small box on my medical questionnaire that asked whether I had "homosexual tendencies," and foolishly checked "Yes." I'm not sure, even now, why I did it — Bravery? Provocation? Shame? In any case, for this act of stupid honesty I was swiftly labeled a problem student and assigned to the dean of the college for academic advising and moral surveillance. The dean (a former swimming coach known universally as "the Toad") took a very stern line with me. He made me promise I wouldn't "act on" these tendencies while I was at Kenyon and left the strong impression that if I did I could expect not to be there for long.

Nowadays, I look back at that scenario with amazement. Did good colleges actually believe they had the perfect right to investigate their students' sex lives? Was it so obvious to doctors that homosexuality was a medical condition like whooping cough or tuberculosis? The answer to both questions is "Yes." More heartening is the answer to a third: Did I really so cavalierly admit to being gay? The answer to this, too, is "Yes." And if so, my willingness to check the "homosexual" box in 1966 can stand as a seamark of changing attitudes to homosexuality. For even if my bravery was 90 percent bravado, I must have sensed, as early as 1966, that I could get away with it. Three years before Stonewall and only a month after a psychiatrist had told me he "had nothing against homosexuality, it's just a piss-poor way to lead your life" — even then, I was making a guess that being gay had a future.

I, too, have been proved right. This book is a tribute to that future, so hard to imagine in earlier decades and so precarious in our own; a praise of the stories we gay men have written for each other (and for anyone else who was interested in them), encouragement and advice for people following a sexual hunch.

My life has been utterly molded by that hunch, and I realize now that I was extremely lucky to have begun following it when I did. The student rebellions of the late sixties, the drugs and music, the shift in expectations of masculinity and femininity allowed a gay man to ride a wave of huge liberation. This wave carried us farther inland than all the sensible argumentation and courageous White House picketing of early gay groups such as the Mattachine Society. To have been even a bit older would have meant shouldering an almost intolerable weight of shame and guilt, a burden that we see so clearly in Edmund White's autobiographical novels *A Boy's Own Story* and *The Beautiful Room Is Empty*. To have been just a little younger would have meant carrying an almost equally heavy weight of respectability or nihilism, as we can see in David Leavitt's novels of assimilation to family life or Dennis Cooper's of boredom and abuse.

I suppose what I'm saying is what Wordsworth said of his own youth during the French Revolution: "Bliss was it in that dawn to be alive, But to be young was very heaven." Because I was young in that Stonewall dawn, I grew up with a hopefulness about my sexual identity, a willingness to trust it, that seems rarer in men who came out much earlier or later. As a result, I am impatient with gay men and gay stories that seem *ungrateful;* which find either doom or success too easily, or in which gay life is simply another So What, as boring and empty as any other.

I have also never forgotten the Toad's unfairly coerced (and subsequently ignored) promise not to "act on" my homosexual desires. This, I knew even in 1966, was an unacceptable compromise. For me, a homosexual life *has* to be acted on, or it doesn't count. In literature, too, I most love writers who "act on it" by writing books which are sexy, witty, dandyish, arrogant, or obsessed — in other words, gay through and through.

A word about how I have laid out my canonizing survey of gay fiction.

Because it is so personal a book, a sort of gay *biographia literaria,* I have mostly followed my own reading history and the history of gay publication: I begin with a novel that was both *my* first gay book and one of the first masterpieces of gay fiction, James Baldwin's *Giovanni's Room* (1956). The works with which I wished to compare it were products of the same period: Tennessee Williams's gay short stories, published mostly between 1948 and 1954. More problematic are some of my later chapters — for instance, the ones comparing James Purdy and Dennis Cooper, or Christopher Isherwood and David Leavitt. Here I can plead neither autobiography nor coevality. The reason they are together is that they illuminated certain permanent arguments in gay fiction: in the first case an argument about sex, violence, and pornography; in the second an argument about what "just happening to be gay" might look like and mean.

Even with these anomalies, I have followed the broad historical arc of gay fiction since World War II, but have been egotistical enough to see in literary history my own roughly simultaneous history writ large. Thus Part One runs from the first intimations of homosexual identity with its attendant guilts and shames (James Baldwin and Tennessee Williams) to the aggressions of gay dandyism (Gore Vidal and Boyd McDonald) to a specifically sexual violence that seems a recurrent theme in male fantasy, and certainly in gay male fiction (Dennis Cooper and James Purdy). Part Two, a single chapter, is about the brief licenses of the gay ghetto, using two books (by Larry Kramer and Andrew Holleran) that appeared in the same miraculous year, 1978. Part Three is about the different accommodations gay men have made to the larger world of their families and straight friends: its first chapter is about two authors (David Leavitt and Christopher Isherwood) who have invented characters who "just happen to be gay"; the second concerns two others (Michael Cunningham and Ethan Mordden) who have imagined gay "families." Part Four is on AIDS and its destruction of both the gay ghetto and other former assimilations (John Weir, Samuel R. Delany, Christopher Davis, Dale Peck). Part Five is about two writers (Neil Bartlett and Edmund White) whose work looks back at the fifty years of modern gay fiction and life and, in different ways, sums it up.

I have deliberately chosen not to end the book with AIDS, even though AIDS literature is without doubt gay fiction's boom industry. One reason is that, even rhetorically, I didn't want this grim disease to have the last word. But also, the age of AIDS fiction may itself be coming to an end, just as the age of ghetto fiction has — both because of new drug treatments and because the disease is simply no longer a gay preserve. "AIDS fiction" can be, and is, written by anyone about anyone. To that extent, it begins to slip out of the purview of this book, just as coming-out stories begin to seem mere variations on what a well-read Edmund White character calls "another unhappy American childhood."[12]

My canon is not a mere list of good books or, despite its hubristic confidence, a prescription to authors of how or what they should write. It is rather an argument about how to be gay — how to lead a good life as a gay man. I realize, in fact, as I come to the end of this project, how tangled that question is, how little we know how to talk about sex, how strange it still is to lead a gay life. Indeed, I hope straight readers, too, will recognize in these questions some of their own. For as it was women and slaves who were the experts on liberty in ancient Athens (as Orlando Patterson argues in *Freedom*), so it is the sexually constrained who can give us the deepest understanding of sexual liberty.[13]

But the book is not only about sex. Dandyism, too, is one of the great gay traditions and has been equally useful in undermining what one might call the cult of dullness — a cult whose priesthood includes psychotherapists, professors, and even gay novelists. If I seem to exaggerate the importance of sex, friendship, violence, and wit in this book, it is because all these have been for me ways out of dullness. If I dislike, feel oppressed by, some of the authors I discuss, it is because they seem to have allowed themselves to be assimilated to that deadly ideology. I have sometimes wanted to say to them what Auden mentally said to Thomas Hardy. Citing Hardy's epitaph for himself — "I never cared for life, life cared for me. / And hence I owe it some fidelity" — Auden campily snorted: "I never cared . . . *Never?* Now, Mr. Hardy, really!"[14]

[PART ONE]

SHAME, IMPUDENCE, AND ECSTASY

Chapter One

FROM THE CLOSET TO THE THEATER (VIA THE ELECTRIC CHAIR)

JAMES BALDWIN'S *GIOVANNI'S ROOM*

Giovanni's Room was the first gay book I ever read, and I remember vividly with what terror I checked it out of the Carnegie Library in Pittsburgh (concealed with ostentatious casualness in a stack of other books), with what transport I read passages like Jacques' speech to the narrator David ("Love him. . . . Do you think anything else under heaven matters?") and with what unspeakable desire I read David's sentence, as he is being pulled down onto Giovanni's bed, "With everything in me screaming *No!* yet the sum of me sighed *Yes.*"[1]

Like most readers, I took from *Giovanni's Room* what I needed from it and what I understood. What I needed was a coming-out story. I needed to hear that men did sleep together, that there was a world of such men, including places they met, and that one man could love another. I needed to see in print a vindication of the sexual desire that I then felt so intensely myself. Pornography was not the answer, though I was eager to see it. (For many men of my generation, pornography was one of the few signs that gay people even existed.) What was most necessary was a thoughtful channeling of all those erotic riots into something lucid and powerful. I needed not to feel, but to understand, these riots. *Giovanni's Room* was such a channel.

But I understood the book only in part. I absorbed something of the atmosphere of guilty pleasure from the bar scenes. I remember with great clarity David's friend Jacques picking up the redheaded boy in Mme. Clothilde's bar. Giovanni's famous "room" I remember in that metaverbal way one often remembers great poems or music: its atmosphere, its "feel" were very strong, though I couldn't have described the place or how Baldwin had made it so strangely stifling: I'm not even sure I recognized that it *was* stifling, for to me it was liberty itself. I remember something, but very little, about David's girlfriend Hella: she didn't fit into my daydreams any more than into David's. I understood less, because I needed less, the whole melodrama of Giovanni's murder of the bar owner Guillaume, his sentencing to the guillotine, and David's monologues of remorse.

What I saw imperfectly if at all was the moral harshness of the book: for example, Giovanni's bitter, truthful cry, "You love your purity. You love your mirror" (186). I forgot until an adult rereading that the story concerns the corruption of an "innocent" heterosexual boy by urban vice, and that Giovanni's heterosexual credentials were impeccable until the death of his infant son, which sent him in despair to Paris. I completely forgot Baldwin's assumption of the foregone rightness of heterosexuality which is exemplified in David's motherly landlady in the South of France who advises David to "get married and have babies" (92) and to "make a little prayer from time to time" (96).

Rereading books that meant a lot to us in youth is always an experience of chagrin as well as rediscovery. In the case of *Giovanni's Room* it was something else too: an adult realization that a) the book was a good deal more complicated than I had thought, and b) the complication was not always lucid; it was as confused as it was complex. In addition, it became clear that, whatever I could take from it now, it would *not* be the defiant pleasure of coming out, comfort at the possibility of sex and/or affection, insight into a gay life. The terrible, uncharitable, self-lacerating clarity with which Baldwin willed himself to see gay life has either dated or was always simply so personal, so Baldwinian, that its usefulness to another gay man was limited. And if the book was not about coming out, was not an encouragement to come out, what then was it?

In some ways a more interesting, and in others a more chaotic, book. And yet *chaotic* seems the wrong word for a novel whose prose style drips such honey, and whose morality lays so heavy a hand on it. The narrative of shame and guilt and at least occasional triumph that I remembered from my adolescence is in fact a far more muted narrative of betrayal, confusion, self-deception, and despair.

And yet is there *no* connection between the book I first read in 1966 and the book I now have before me nearly thirty years later? Is Baldwin not at all interested in the possibilities of a shame-free life as a gay man, or of love between men, or (more problematically) of a life lived without reference to women? Can we, in other words, still use *Giovanni's Room?* If so, how and with what reservations, if any? What is its place in the living mainstream of gay fiction?

Giovanni's Room tells in a series of flashbacks the story of a young white American, David, who has lived several years in Paris, where he has fallen into (or perhaps pretended to "fall into") *le milieu* — the gay world. Pretended to fall into because, despite his fascination with *le milieu,* he is engaged to an American woman, Hella, whom he has met in Paris. She has taken off to Spain to sort out her feelings for David. But though she is absent for most of the book, her return has all the catastrophic power of a Racinian king come back to exact vengeance.

David's entrée to the gay world is a Belgian-American businessman named Jacques, for whom David has a genial contempt, whom he sponges off when he needs money. Jacques, and the other gay members of his world, are all (according to David) hovering like sexual vultures around him, eager either to get into his pants or at least to know that some other man is. One night when David is particularly hard up, Jacques invites him to dinner. Afterward they go to Jacques' favorite gay bar, run by his morally sleazy, if socially aristocratic, friend Guillaume. There is a new bartender there named Giovanni — as his name suggests, a native of Italy, who has been working for Guillaume three weeks. Under the fascinated gaze of Jacques and Guillaume, David makes friends with Giovanni, deluding himself at first that they are "just friends." But Giovanni has apparently already fallen in love (or in need) with David. Together, he, David, Jacques, and Guillaume go to an early-morning café after the bar closes, where Jacques picks up a redheaded boy, and Giovanni cements his friendship with David. Too "tired" to go back to his own flat, David allows himself to be talked into going back home with Giovanni. There, in Giovanni's small *chambre de bonne,* they make love.

But all is not well in this room. Skipping over an unspecified length of time after the successful seduction of David, Baldwin reveals that their relationship is no longer a happy one. (Was it ever?) David is now "horrified" by Giovanni's room, which seems to him a subaqueous atmosphere in which one could drown, a place in which he is losing his manhood. Worse, Giovanni has revealed the full extent of his own desperate need to be "saved" from this room, from the shame of homosexuality, from a general sense of failure. David loses interest in, or becomes frightened of, Giovanni and begins to break off their affair, stranding Giovanni in his solitude and shame.

But the homosexuality Giovanni represents to David will not go away. He catches himself staring longingly at a sailor who, seeing David's glance, looks back at him with contempt. To convince himself that he is not really gay, David has a brief drunken sexual affair with an American named Sue which predictably proves nothing. When his official girlfriend Hella returns from Spain, he embraces her feverishly, and even decides it's time to break up with Giovanni, marry Hella and go home to America.

But he still imagines that he can somehow combine friendship (with its sexual overtones) with Giovanni and "love" for Hella. Hella dislikes Giovanni ("a sordid little gangster") and can't understand why David is spending time with him, why David feels responsible for him. David and Giovanni finally break up for good, and Giovanni falls into a kind of despair. Guillaume has fired him; so he becomes a prostitute. Eventually, desperate for money, he goes back to Guillaume to beg for his bartending job back. Guillaume invites him to his apartment — presumably to seal the deal with sex — and Giovanni kills him.

News of the murder is widespread. To escape the horror, David and Hella go to the South of France. Hella is still mystified as to why David is so upset — Guillaume after all was just "a disgusting old fairy" and she never liked Giovanni. Hella finally realizes that David is or was in love with Giovanni, or at least that he desires Giovanni in a way he does not desire her. She confirms her suspicion by catching David at a gay bar in Marseilles. In an angry fight she breaks off their relationship and leaves France for America. David is left behind, and the novel ends where it began, with David standing at the window of "this great house in the south of France as night falls," looking out but also looking at his reflection in the window. Giovanni will be executed in the morning for Guillaume's murder, Hella has fled him and Europe, his life is in ruins and yet he must pick up some of the pieces and go on. He too will go home, with a weight of guilt on him that is perhaps inexpiable: "I must believe, I must believe, that the heavy grace of God, which has brought me to this place, is all that can carry me out of it" (223–24).

Giovanni's Room is not a difficult book in any obvious way. Its language, while extremely beautiful, is not "original" as Joyce's is, for instance; its subject matter, while shocking to its first audience, is hardly pornographic and is in any case not shocking now; its ideology, to use an inappropriate word, is largely biblical — the book ends in a sort of Pauline rapture of despair. Its literary tradition, should one look for such a thing, is pure American, or at least Jamesian: for the book essentially follows a young man to a misunderstandable and possibly corrupt Paris and shows what awful things happen to him there. It is not even "difficult" (for whites) by being a "black" novel, at least not on the surface. David, its protagonist, is "blond" and therefore presumably "one of us."

At the same time, *Giovanni's Room* is deeply ambiguous — about the nature of its subject, about its protagonist, about the purpose for telling the tale — and consequently very difficult indeed, perhaps more so than Baldwin knew. Which young man is the Jamesian ingenu, for instance, David or Giovanni? Indeed, who *is* David? This question turns out to be hard to answer, and the answer one gives turns out to depend on what kind of book we think he's the protagonist *of*. If, for instance, we read *Giovanni's Room* as I did when I was fifteen — that is, as a glorified coming-out story — then David is primarily a gay man, and his "story" is about leaving the closet. There is some truth to this version of the events of the novel, and yet how much this formula leaves out: David's abandonment of Giovanni, Giovanni's murder of Guillaume, Hella's flight back to America, and David's own far-from-upbeat conclusions about his homosexuality and that of everyone around him. Not only are these events not quite covered under the rubric "coming-out story," they seem to belong to another kind of novel altogether.

Is David's a cautionary tale? Is the point of the book in fact precisely opposite to what I had seen in it when I was fifteen: is it in effect a "going-in" novel rather than a coming-out novel, one that shows the terrible mistake of homosexuality? This too is unsatisfactory, despite Baldwin's highly unflattering picture of Guillaume's bar and its habitués, one of whom (Jacques) gives what amounts to a magnificent rhetorical justification of homosexuality, indeed of all illicit sex, in his speech about not making your five minutes "dirty." Even Giovanni, who often seems ambivalent about homosexuality, taxes David with *inventing* a guilt about it that he doesn't really need: "You love your purity. You love your mirror."

Is homosexuality, then, not the point of the novel at all? Is the guilt David feels necessarily for his unorthodox erotic life, or is it not for his abandonment and betrayal of Giovanni, of Sue, of Hella, of Jacques — of everyone around him? In that case, who is David? What kind of abandoner? Does he abandon insofar as he is a man (Hella's opinion), an American (Giovanni's), or a homosexual (his own)? And why, then, does he abandon and betray? Do we understand the answer to that question any better than we understand what decision he has reached about his sexual life?

All three stories are plausible, even forced upon us. They inhabit one another like Russian dolls; only from moment to moment their relative position and size change, so that we are unsure what the "shell" story is, and what the kernel. The "crime" that David worries endlessly about is now homosexuality, now concealment of homosexuality, now cowardice. His "fears" — of which he is preternaturally full — include fear of his homosexuality, fear of sex with anyone, fear of Giovanni, fear of Jacques, fear of Hella. Even nostalgia for America frightens him at one point: "I had never realized such a sentiment in myself before, and it frightened me."

Indeed the constants of this story are not any of its plausible topics — Europe versus America, homosexuality versus heterosexuality, male versus female, natural versus unnatural — but the various shadings of anxiety, doubt, and guilt. But there seems no clear *cause* for them, or rather such a plenitude of causes that the reader is left in a state of anxiety scarcely less painful than David's own. Every attempt we make to grasp the story turns out to be inadequate: we have reached, not bedrock, but a new shifting sand.

To take only one example: if, as the construction of Part One seems to suggest, the story is primarily one of David's acknowledging and accepting his homosexuality — "With everything inside me screaming *No!* yet the sum of me sighed *Yes*" — we would know where we are with David: he would either live up to his homosexuality or not. One way or another, we would be able to triangulate Baldwin's, and our own position, from such a story. This happens, for example, in a beautiful earlier novel, Fritz Peters's *Finistère,* also about an American in France. In that novel it is quite clear that Matthew's suicide is caused by the *unjust* hatred of homosexuality, the *unjust* hypocrisy of those around him. We wholeheartedly pity Matthew as we never do David.[2] But in *Giovanni's Room,* no sooner has Baldwin led climactically up to the sex scene, than he immediately withdraws the promise of even carnal happiness by flashing forward to the gloomier and guiltier David awaiting Giovanni's execution in the south of France. The moment of bliss isn't even transient, it is false. Like Jehovah, what Baldwin gives, he also takes away.

In this book, unlike works of his that either don't discuss homosexuality or make it peripheral, Baldwin's gifts seem to fight each other: his absolute clarity of moral vision becomes, in this book, a tantalizing confusion. His fidelity to fact — to what is outside one in the world — disappears into a haze of beautiful language and moral speculation. (Is it an accident that the novel takes place in France, that home of *moralistes?*) His characters also escape him, seeming to speak out of no particularized historic experience. (His choice to make his main character white is a token of the slight unreality of Baldwin's character-drawing in this novel.) Even the moral speculation seems uncharacteristically airy and ungrounded: what is it speculation *about* — homosexuality, dishonesty, American-ness? Something about his subject, something probably but not only about homosexuality, seems to have so disequilibrized him that the novel seems not a revelation but a dazzling concealment, a triumph, and a failure, of rhetoric.

In this respect *Giovanni's Room* reminds me of nothing so much as *Hamlet.* Like that play, it is dazzlingly overwritten, so much so that it is often impossible to see what is being described beneath the unbelievable luxuriance of style. Sometimes in *Giovanni's Room,* as in *Hamlet,* I wonder if there is not less there than meets the eye, or find myself resenting what Camille Paglia has called *Hamlet*'s "hostile virtuosity of language."[3] As in *Hamlet,* some of the most important events are not seen but described, and thus become part of the problem, not the solution: for example, David's "decision" to abandon Giovanni when Hella comes back, or his decision to abandon Hella and go to the gay bar in the South of France. Just as in the play scene in *Hamlet,* the reader can only infer the motives of the characters, and the inferring may say more about the reader than about the characters. In any case, there is silence precisely where we should like more information. Both works, finally, share a kind of moral hypersensitivity, and indeed their unity is largely created by a mood of apprehensiveness: "Who's there?"

The teasing difficulty of the novel can be seen in the perplexing ramifications of its central symbol: What exactly is Giovanni's room meant to represent, and why is it so menacing? And questions about the room lead us back to questions about the main characters: Who or what is Giovanni? Who or what is David?

One's first guess is that Giovanni's *chambre de bonne* in an unfashionable suburb of Paris functions as a simple cipher for homosexuality. It is, after all, to this room that David goes the morning after he first meets Giovanni, where "with everything in me screaming *No!* yet the sum of me sighed *Yes.*" It is where he lives with and attempts to love Giovanni. It is what he feels he must abandon when Hella returns from Spain.

But although homosexuality is one of the meanings of Giovanni's room, it is not the only one. Giovanni, for instance, is *already ashamed of* his room, even before David comes there. We learn this when the foursome of Jacques, Guillaume, Giovanni, and David have left Guillaume's bar and are on their way to a café to have breakfast. Jacques and Guillaume talk snottily about Giovanni's apartment, Jacques because he has been passed over in favor of the young handsome David, and Guillaume because he is an evil aristocratic queen. " 'He lives in a dreadful street, near *Nation*,' said Guillaume, 'among all the dreadful bourgeoisie and their piglike children.' 'You failed to catch the children at the right age,' said Jacques. 'They go through a period, all too brief, *hélas!* when a pig is perhaps the *only* animal they do not call to mind' (63). And, again to Giovanni: 'In a hotel?' 'No,' said Giovanni, and for the first time he seemed slightly uncomfortable. 'I live in a maid's room' " (63). The neighborhood is later described fairly neutrally: "The street he lived on was wide, respectable rather than elegant, and massive with fairly recent apartment buildings; the street ended in a small park. His room was in the back, on the ground floor of the last building on this street. We passed the vestibule and the elevator into a short, dark corridor which led to his room. The room was small, I only made out the outlines of clutter and disorder, there was the smell of the alcohol he burned in his stove" (86).

The source of Giovanni's discomfort in the taxicab cannot be (yet) homosexuality, for nothing has happened there yet. We have no indication that Giovanni is anything more than situationally homosexual, playing along to get his *carte d'identité* from Guillaume. Even if he *is* gay we have no reason to think that his room has anything to do with it. (He's not using it, as far as we know, for sex with men.) If anything he's uncomfortable because it's small and distant. His shame, in other words, is a purely social one at being comparatively poor, at being a foreigner, at being vulnerable.

And yet, how quickly the room takes on an almost separate existence, becomes almost a third character! Three passages in particular capture its death-in-life: "I remember that life in that room seemed to be occurring beneath the sea. Time flowed past indifferently above us; hours and days had no meaning. In the beginning, our life together held a joy and amazement which was newborn every day. Beneath the joy, of course, was anguish and beneath the amazement was fear; but they did not work themselves to the beginning until our high beginning was aloes on our tongues" (99). And again, at the beginning of Part Two, Chapter 3:

> I scarcely know how to describe that room. It became, in a way, every room I had ever been in and every room I find myself in hereafter will remind me of Giovanni's room. I did not really stay there very long — we met before the spring began and I left there during the summer — but it still seems to me that I spent a lifetime there. Life in that room seemed to be occurring underwater, as I say, and it is certain that I underwent a sea change there. To begin with, the room was not large enough for two. It looked out on a small courtyard. "Looked out" means only that the room had two windows, against which the courtyard malevolently pressed, encroaching day by day, as though it had confused itself with a jungle. We, or rather Giovanni kept the windows closed most of the time. . . . To insure privacy, Giovanni had obscured the window panes with a heavy, white cleaning polish. . . . Giovanni had said something in the taxi about his room being very dirty. "I'm sure it is," I had said lightly, and turned away from him, looking out of the window. Then we had both been silent. When I woke up in his room, I remembered that there had been something strained and painful in the quality of that silence, which had been broken when Giovanni said, with a shy, bitter smile: "I must find some poetic figure." (112–14)

The room is a place of disorder:

> Before and beside me and all over the room, towering like a wall, were boxes of cardboard and leather, some tied with string, some locked, some bursting, and out of the topmost box before me spilled down sheets of violin music. . . . The table was loaded with yellowing newspapers and empty bottles and it held a single brown and wrinkled potato in which even the sprouting eyes were rotten. Red wine had been spilled on the floor; it had been allowed to dry and it made the air in the room sweet and heavy. But it was not the room's disorder which was frightening; it was the fact that when one began searching for the key to this disorder, one realized that it was not to be found in any of the usual places. For this was not a matter of habit or circumstance or temperament; it was a matter of punishment and grief. I do not know how I knew this, but I knew it at once; perhaps I knew it because I wanted to live. And I stared at the room with the same, nervous, calculating extension of the intelligence and of all one's forces which occurs when gauging a mortal and unavoidable danger. . . . I understood why Giovanni had wanted me and had brought me to his

last retreat. I was to destroy this room and give to Giovanni a new and better life. This life could only be my own, which, in order to transform Giovanni's, must first become a part of Giovanni's room. (114–16)

How difficult all this is, how beautiful, and how disingenuous! And all three qualities are products of the same thing: a determination that this room shall mean everything without being anything. (It is "every room I had ever been in" — as if *rooms themselves* were somehow dangerous.) To this end a luxurious prose style and a moral voice of great solemnity are wheeled into place: not a single ironic thought, not a smile, is allowed to crack this face. The passages are a brilliant example of the power of a forbidden object: the sexual act that is supposedly at the very heart of this room's "disorder" is never described. And yet, obviously, every detail is carefully, not to say compulsively, marshaled to "mean something": even the wallpaper figures a couple "hemmed in by roses." Even the light in the ceiling is an image of a "diseased sex."

The sheer rhetorical virtuosity works in contradictory ways: both to build up and to undermine the sense of menace David and Baldwin feel in the presence of this room. That is, the details of decay, the melancholy cadences, the barely repressed hysteria all do create an unforgettable impression of stagnation and despair. At the same time, not only does the room not provide David with the "key" to its disorder, neither does the description of it give the reader such a key. The description is so hyperbolic, so needlessly horrific, that the sophisticated reader is not sure how to take it. Is the disorder to be sought in the things themselves, or rather in the beholder's panicky view of them? Is David like the governess in James's *Turn of the Screw?* Something, plainly, is going on, but is he imagining it or seeing it? And in any case, what is it that is happening there?

Giovanni's despair and David's terror have to be taken on faith, for there is almost no objective correlative action to justify the extreme rhetorical fever of these pages. As T. S. Eliot said of *Hamlet:* the emotions are "in excess of the facts as they appear."[4] And the harder Baldwin works to make us feel the menace of this room, the more confused the explanation becomes. Take for example the end of the last passage: "Under this blunted arrow — the light bulb on the ceiling — this smashed flower of light lay the terrors which encompassed Giovanni's soul. I understood why Giovanni had wanted me and had brought me to his last retreat. I was to destroy this room and give to Giovanni a new and better life. This life could only be my own, which, in order to transform Giovanni's, must first become a part of Giovanni's room" (116).

Unless we are simply hypnotized by Baldwin's cadences, we are puzzled to know what this passage is saying. I am not even thinking of the egregious gothicisms of the "blunted arrow" and "the smashed flower of light," but of the explanation given for why Giovanni "had brought me to his last retreat." (Why "last," for instance, except that it sounds good, and rhetorically ups the stakes?) "I was to destroy this room and give to Giovanni a new and better life." But what does it mean for David to "destroy this room?" What is wrong with Giovanni's old life? Why *must* it be destroyed? (Mere housecleaning, apparently, won't do the trick: "But I am not a housewife — men never can be housewives" [116]). Even if we can imagine that the room needed destroying — or at least, cleaning — what exactly was the sequence of thoughts in Giovanni's mind? How did Giovanni know at first sight that David would be the one to shatter this diseased illusion? Love at first sight is improbable enough; need-to-save at first sight is so improbable as to be weird.

"This [sc. "new and better"] life could only be my own, which, in order to transform Giovanni's, must first become a part of Giovanni's room." David's explanation, like much soteriology, seems to border on the ineffable. How exactly is David to give Giovanni a better life? Not just by loving Giovanni — that would be too simple — but by becoming a "part of Giovanni's *room*" (emphasis mine). But this suggests that the saving requires David's life to become as disorderly as Giovanni's. And how would that help either of them?

Even as this wildly overblown explanation is being given, there is a kind of grimly funny dissonance between it and the grave language it is being given in, as though everything David was saying were lucid, indeed self-evident. Similarly "transparent" is the opening of Part Two, which states with complete seriousness, "In the beginning, our life together held a joy and amazement which was newborn every day. Beneath the joy, of course, was anguish and beneath the amazement was fear; but they did not work themselves to the beginning until our high beginning was aloes on our tongues. By then anguish and fear had become the surface on which we slipped and slid, losing balance, dignity, and pride" (99).

"Beneath the joy, *of course,* was anguish . . ." Like the menace of the room, this "of course" has to be taken on faith, for we have no particular reason for thinking that anguish always underlies joy, or fear amazement. (Indeed, even the homophobic assumptions of the mid-fifties make a *little* room for joy: Jacques, for instance, does in a famous speech to David in Part One.) Once again, metaphors run away with meaning as Baldwin/David tries to nail this "anguish" down: "Giovanni's face, which I had memorized so many mornings, noons, and nights, hardened before my eyes, began to give in secret places, began to crack. The light in the eyes became a glitter; the wide and beautiful brow began to suggest the skull beneath. The sensual lips turned inward, busy with the sorrow overflowing from his heart" (99). Lips turned inward indeed — it sounds like a bad acid trip! And the longer David works at convincing us that something terrible was happening to Giovanni, the less I understand what that terrible thing was: "It became a stranger's face — or it made me so guilty to look on him that I wished it were a stranger's face. Not all my memorizing had prepared me for the metamorphosis which my memorizing had helped to bring about" (99–100).

I do not quote these passages simply to mock them. A serious subject requires serious, sometimes allegorical, treatment. But Baldwin seems in passages like this to be offering the horror without explaining it. He obviously wants us to understand something, but may not be able to tell us just what it is we are to understand: it may be too horrific to contemplate directly. For the horror of Giovanni's room really goes beyond even the most rabid homophobe's "anguish and fear." (The "key" to the disorder, remember, is not to be found in any of the usual places: including, perhaps, gay self-hatred.) So while the room horrifies David because of the sexually perverse acts that take place there, gay sex is only part of his fear of it. (If it were the totality, then why would a love affair with David mean escape from his room for Giovanni?) What the other components of his fear and anguish might be takes us from Giovanni's room to Giovanni himself, and from Giovanni to David. (It is thus that the central symbol of the book evaporates before our eyes, needing to be explained by more and more things that we first think *it* will explain.)

Giovanni, then, is himself the room: this place of confinement, poverty, disorder, and "diseased sex." But he means far more — and far worse — to David. It is not his sloppiness that frightens the American, but his neediness. He is a second Joey (David's first male sex-partner, whose story is included as far as I can see for just this foreshadowing purpose). And Joey scared David by being too soft, too empty, too fillable ("The black opening of a cavern in which I would be tortured till madness came, in which I would lose my manhood" [15]). "Manhood" to David means not sexual potency but responsibility of any kind. It is Joey's need that drives David away.

But need in *any* form disgusts and frightens David. It is not confined to gay men for instance (if Giovanni is one). For example, not only is Joey threatening, but so is David's mother, about whom he has nightmares: "blind with worms, her hair as dry as metal and brittle as a twig, straining to press me against her body; that body so putrescent, so sickening soft, that it opened, as I clawed and cried, into a breach so enormous as to swallow me alive" (17). So far, so Freudian: he is frightened of women, of the vagina dentata, of being swallowed. Perhaps, one could argue, that that is why he is frightened of gay men, because they are, after all, a sort of woman — though without the convenient "cavern" in which to lose one's manhood. The theory will not explain why David is also disgusted by his father, an impeccably heterosexual figure (he is having affairs with women during David's adolescence). "Now that he was trying to find out something about me, I was in full flight from him" (25). After a car accident David is with his father in the hospital and starts crying. His father "stroked my forehead with that absurd handkerchief as though it possessed some healing charm. . . . He was almost weeping himself. 'There's nothing wrong, is there? I haven't done anything wrong, have I?' And all the time he was stroking my face with that handkerchief, smothering me" (29).

This fear of smothering is David's defining characteristic, and it is what he is afraid of in Giovanni. But, as we have seen, the smothering is only remotely a sexual characteristic, whether of straight women or gay men, whether of lovers or relatives or friends. It is so huge a fear that anyone can evoke it. It is this fear that seems to me the most interesting, if weirdest, thing in David, and neediness the most surprising characteristic of Giovanni.

At first glance, neediness doesn't seem to be Giovanni's besetting sin. Quite the reverse: he seems cocky, casual, charming. His first conversation with David at Guillaume's bar is full of urbanity: " 'You are an American?' he asked at last. 'Yes,' I said. 'From New York.' 'Ah! I am told that New York is very beautiful. Is it more beautiful than Paris?' 'Oh, no,' I said, '*no* city is more beautiful than Paris —' 'It seems the very suggestion that one *could* be is enough to make you very angry,' grinned Giovanni. 'Forgive me. I was not trying to be heretical' " (46). Again, when Giovanni is telling the story of his meeting with disgusting old Guillaume, he does so with seeming *disinvoltura:* "C'était un film du far west, avec Gary Cooper." David, however, sees — or thinks he sees — "terror" and a "terrible desire to please" in Giovanni (81–82). Thus, despite Giovanni's airy conversation about the necessary, unpleasant steps by which he got his *carte d'identité* (i.e., by letting Guillaume fondle him), we are meant to believe, with David, that Giovanni is terrified of displeasing Guillaume. Perhaps: it is certainly plausible that Giovanni should wish to please in order to eat. But why a "*terrible* desire to please"? The style is so bantering, so Parisian, that one can easily forget that Giovanni is really a poor boy from southern Italy, one who seems to believe that the "old ways are best," as when he says " 'these absurd women running around today, full of ideas and nonsense, and thinking themselves equal to men — *quelle rigolade!* — they need to be beaten half to death so that they can find out who rules the world' " (105–6).

The two Giovannis, the sophisticate and the peasant, confuse the reader. They do not add up to one whole Giovanni; they are merely contradictory. The contradiction has a particular effect on the gay reader trying to make sense of him. For Giovanni has one charm for a gay man if he is a "Parisian," quite another if he is a "peasant." The charm of the first is sophistication and elegance, of the second (according to gay folklore) virility. Giovanni is "good for business" at Guillaume's bar because of the latter, one would imagine. But which kind of man is David falling in love with?

This would seem an important question to answer, and yet David seems unaware of it — or unable to solve it. Here, as in so many crucial corners of the novel, where knowledge of a character's thoughts and feelings might come in handy, we do not know what David is attracted to. Giovanni is, to be sure, good-looking — "insolent and dark and leonine" (39) — but David has so successfully resisted other good-looking men in the recent past (he had been entangled with a sailor, but he was "drunk") that that reason seems insufficient. He sees that Giovanni is in some sense "on an auction block," though he stands there "with arrogance" (40). He might pity or admire Giovanni, then, but this is not followed up. And the seedbed of David's *grande passion* is strangely unexamined: when Jacques maliciously suggests that David offer Giovanni a drink, "I felt, somehow, elated." And when Giovanni accepts — "I drink no alcohol while I work, but I will take a Coca-Cola" — "I realized that I was quite happy to be talking with him." For a character usually quite unafraid of self-examination (provided it's gloomy enough), to be "somehow elated" and "happy" seems stingy (43–45).

And what is Giovanni offering David? What does he represent to David? That too is unanswerable, though Baldwin seems to imply that the answer is self-evident.

Let us say, for instance, that Giovanni is primarily the "peasant," the virile Italian in a world of Parisian epicenes. Then his attraction for David becomes the attraction of the masculine. Further, because David professes himself so turned off by the screaming queens, it is an attraction *between* masculines, a kind of friendship. They team up, so to speak, *against* the trivial, disgusting world of Jacques and Guillaume. They are allies.

But, as we have seen, this is not how Giovanni sees it — he wants someone to "save" him. Far from being a reliably virile stud, Giovanni turns into quite the reverse: a shrewish, hysterical wife. This is seen in the great confrontation between him and David after David has left him for Hella: " 'You know I cannot be alone. I have told you. What is the matter? Can we never have a life together?' He began to cry again. I watched the hot tears roll from the corners of his eyes onto the dirty pillow. 'If you cannot love me, I will die' " (182). At the same time, he is like the jealous husband whose wife has cheated on him: "You are evil, you know, and sometimes when you smiled at me, I hated you. I wanted to strike you. I wanted to make you bleed" (181). Sometimes, he is like a betrayed straight man: "I have never known anyone like you before. I was never like this before you came. Listen. In Italy I had a woman and she was very good to me. She loved me, she loved *me,* and she took care of me and she was always there when I came in from work . . . I was young then and did not know the things I learned later or the terrible things you have taught me. . . . I thought all men were like me — I thought I was like all other men . . ." (182–83).

Then there is yet another Giovanni, neither woman, man, nor friend, but "European," "Italian." In a passage that might have come out of Menotti's melodrama *The Saint of Bleecker Street* (composed two years before in 1954), he declaims: "I wanted to stay there forever and eat much spaghetti and drink much wine and make many babies and grow fat. You would not have liked me if I had stayed. I can see you, many years from now, coming through our village in the ugly, fat, American motor car you will surely have by then and looking at me and looking at all of us and tasting our wine and shitting on us with those empty smiles Americans wear everywhere and which you wear all the time . . ." (183).

Giovanni's love of David is a huge jumble of emotions — or perhaps simply attitudes, impersonations of emotions — some of them conventionally "male," some "female," some admirable, some petty. We react to some of what he says with pity, to some with laughter, to some with astonished assent, as when he tells David, "You do not love anyone. . . . You love your purity, you love your mirror — you are just like a little virgin, you walk around with your hands in front of you as though you had some precious metal, gold, silver, rubies, maybe *diamonds* down there between your legs! You will never give it to anybody, you will never let anybody *touch* it — man *or* woman. You want to be *clean.* You think you came here covered with soap and you think you will go out covered with soap — and you do not want to *stink,* not even for five minutes, in the meantime" (186–87). Indeed, Giovanni is such a mixture of self-knowledge and ignorance that we do not know where to place either him or David. Sometimes he seems to be advocating a return to the strictest village morality, as when he wishes he had never left Italy and his beaten, grateful wife. At others, he voices exactly the opposite opinion, the opinion of an urbanite and sophisticate, as when he tells David that "we have not committed any crime" (107). At yet others, he seems to be saying homosexuality may indeed be a "crime," but that the crime is as unavoidable as "stinking," and that the opposite of the crime, innocence, is just the illusion of coming into the world "covered with soap."

Is this characterization, then, deliberately complex or is it merely confused? This would not matter if it were not for Baldwin's wanting to make Giovanni (at least sometimes) his own spokesman, to allow Giovanni to speak the truth to David, and thus to the reader. So much of what Giovanni says rings true in this way, seeming to break the novel's proscenium and guide us to a correct view of homosexuality and of David himself, that we are then shocked and puzzled by retreats back into the proscenium — by Giovanni's lachrymose self-pity on the one hand, or his unbelievable earlier Parisian suavity. Baldwin can't decide whether Giovanni is to be a full character, or a commentator.

And this brings us to David. For one reason we can't decide if Giovanni is a character or a commentator is that we are never sure who is the main character in the book. In one sense it must be David: he simply talks the most, and it is his story for the most part. On the other hand, David is the oddest of narrators precisely because he is, though windy, quite incapable of seeing himself, or at least seeing his sexuality, honestly. There is a fatal deadness or hollow at his center — or so at least Giovanni and Hella both hint in some of the most passionate and memorable scenes of the novel. The hollowness is certainly not lack of self-consciousness, for David is nothing if not aware of how he feels and (usually) what he thinks. It is not that there is no searchlight turned upon him, but that it so thoroughly avoids looking in certain places. This is what Giovanni means, I think, when he says, "You love your purity, you love your mirror." David does not want to see certain contradictions in himself.

But what are those contradictions? It would be so much easier if we could simply write them all off to the "contradiction" of having to live straight while being gay or to the very fact of homosexual desire itself. David himself would probably prefer it if his unorthodox sexual life were the "problem" of his character. But as we have seen, David's fears, and therefore presumably his unconscious loves, go far beyond that. It is dependence, need, attachment of any kind that so unnerve him that he can't look at them. If the "key" of Giovanni's room is unknown, how much more unknown is David's! For unlike Giovanni, David has the habit of self-reflection — indeed it is a *bad* habit! — and still he doesn't know what he feels, or he is at the mercy of torrents of feeling.

Giovanni and Hella and Jacques, indeed all the people David has used and thrown away, are all, arguably, saying something quite different from what David would say himself. Despite the homophobia that pervades all of their thinking, each of them is telling him his homosexuality isn't the problem: he would like to think that it is, because thinking so gets him off the hook: he could be suffering from a "neurosis," for example. He could be a "sinner." He could be "doomed to be a wanderer" (perhaps David's own favorite). But his real problem is that he's cold and loveless, that he's in love with his innocence ("your mirror").

Now we can see why Baldwin has made David a white man, not black. For though David resembles Baldwin in being gay and American — and even in being squeamish about both — he is unlike Baldwin in hewing to the dream of innocence, which is the necessary fantasy of white Americans. And now we can see why, though he talks a lot, he has nothing to say — indeed talks so much *because* he has nothing to say. The talk covers up an ignorance, even from himself.

It is this combination — a deeply paradoxical one — that makes the ending of the book unusually confusing. For by every convention of narrative — especially that by which we grant the teller of any story the privilege of understanding it — David ought to be telling the truth here, ought to be summing up what we have just read. Because he is far from stupid, what he says is not only beautiful but plausible. But here, as so often before in this troubling novel, we can feel the evocation of a depth that is not really there, a merely rhetorical "boom" like that of the Marabar Caves in *A Passage to India*, a muddle, not a mystery. But perhaps we can understand why the boom is so dead, so deadening, why the sounding of the depths proves so unsatisfying. For it may be that the very gestures toward understanding are themselves a deflection of understanding, an unconscious desire to be told a lie.

Here is the end of the novel. Simultaneously looking at himself reflected in the windows of his rented house, and imagining Giovanni's last hours, David makes a sort of resolution: "I long to crack that mirror and be free. I look at my sex, my troubling sex, and wonder how it can be redeemed, how I can save it from the knife. The journey to the grave is already begun, the journey to corruption is, always, already, half over. Yet, the key to my salvation, which cannot save my body, is hidden in my flesh. . . . I move at last from the mirror and begin to cover that nakedness which I must hold sacred, though it be never so vile, which must be scoured perpetually with the salt of my life. I must believe, I must believe, that the heavy grace of God, which has brought me to this place, is all that can carry me out of it" (223–24).

The language is biblical: "grave," "corruption," "salvation," "flesh," "grace." And we realize, if we hadn't before, that the novel is a deeply Pauline meditation on the flesh, the "members" which Paul so longed to unite under one Head. Baldwin is, however, not a believer, and we need not take him at face value in this sudden seeming profession of faith. Nonetheless, the feeling of not only this passage, but the whole book, is that there *is* a "flesh" that is separate from, perhaps inimical to, the spirit. What does it mean that David must "crack the mirror" in order to be "free"? The metaphor is troubling if only because the American neo-Freudianism of the fifties would surely have read this mirror as an admission of the homosexual's deep-dyed narcissism.[5] Is Baldwin then saying that the homosexual is trapped less by the fetid squalor of Giovanni's room than by the dangerous glittering restless world of self-absorption? The conclusion seems drearily probable. And the citation from Paul that precedes David's resolution would seem to nail it down: "When I was a child I spake as a child, I understood as a child, I thought as a child: but when I became a man, I put away childish things." What David now "knows" is that he must grow up: what is homosexuality, after all, but a failure to mature? What Baldwin might be saying, then, is that he and David must renounce this "troubling sex" if they are to "save it from the knife."

And yet, he makes an unexpected swerve from this probable narcissistic interpretation when he writes, "the key to my salvation, which cannot save my body, is hidden in my flesh" (223). A dark saying; what can it mean? The salvation cannot save his body, but only perhaps his spirit. But what does it mean for his soul to be saved? That answer is "hidden in my flesh." He must do something contradictory: both "cover that nakedness" which the "mirror" so pitilessly reveals and at the same time "hold it sacred." The nakedness itself is "vile" and must be "scoured perpetually with the salt of my life" — the salt, presumably, of tears, the salt of which Lot's wife was composed and which is the very sign of barrenness and therefore of homosexuality. Some duty seems imposed on him now, some cleansing must be undertaken.

But cleansing of what? What does it mean to hold the body sacred? There are two possibilities, neither entirely satisfactory. One is that in scouring the flesh that has so betrayed and soiled him, David will to some extent expiate the guilt of his homosexuality. Scouring would presumably involve a painful renunciation of homosexual pleasures and an attempt to return to God an again-untarnished flesh. The other possibility is more intriguing, certainly to a modern gay reader: namely, that David's salvation may be precisely an erotic one, that the key that is "hidden in his flesh" may be homosexual desire itself. To hold it sacred may mean to allow it expression with less of the judgment and self-laceration we have seen in his story so far. What must be "scoured" may be not the sexual desire itself, but the insane suspicion of pleasure which has ruined not only his own life, but that of Giovanni and Hella as well. It may be a brave hope, an act of faith indeed, to go on with his life still unconvinced that his flesh is anything but "vile" and *yet* to hold it sacred.

How are we to choose between these two options? The book's ending does not exactly help. It ends with David, having completed his meditation and memory, leaving the house in the South of France, leaving his past, leaving Giovanni, and setting out on a journey of his own. Indeed, we are encouraged to think that this journey, unlike the merely touristic one that took him to France in the first place, will be his first real journey "as a man." (He has put away childish things, after all.) Everything suggests a new beginning: the time is morning, the door is locked behind him. He sees men and women waiting for the bus and notices that "they are very vivid" (224) (a vividness we have to take on faith, as usual, since David seldom describes but rather interprets what he sees). The idea seems to be that they are *there* in some important way they weren't before; perhaps, even, that the world exists for David. (Is this "cracking the mirror" of narcissism?) Naturally, Baldwin has been careful to put both men and women in his final tableau, as if to say, "This combination of male and female is precisely what makes for a real, not illusory, world."

But David is still gloomy, and his gloom does not comport with the manful shouldering of his new burden: "The morning weighs on my shoulders with the dreadful weight of hope, and I take the blue envelope which Jacques has sent me [announcing Giovanni's execution] and tear it slowly into many pieces, watching them dance in the wind, watching the wind carry them away" (224). Is this meant to signal the end of his morbid past? of his perversion? of his self-absorption? "Yet, as I turn and begin walking toward the waiting people" — the world he hopes to join, or the jury of his peers always finding him guilty? — "the wind blows some of them back on me." The image is a troubling, perhaps a chaotic one. The movielike ending, so neat and visual, of the pieces of Jacques' letter is a cliché, but we must try to do it justice. What does it mean for these pieces of paper to be blown back on David? That the past is inescapable, perhaps; that though he can lock the door, he cannot so easily leave Giovanni behind. It is important, perhaps, that it is the despised Jacques whose words literally come back to haunt him, for it was Jacques who gave the great, the only, vindication of homosexuality in this book when he earnestly told David to "love him. . . . Do you think anything else under heaven really matters?" (77). In this sense, what comes back to him may be *good* advice rather than past sins. Jacques, the gesture may say, was *right*.

But in a more obvious way, the image is one of simple confusion, of torn and unspellable communication, a sybil's meaningless prophecy. The picture is one of distraction, bits of uninterpretable stuff coming at one like hornets. David is perhaps blinded by these bits of paper; whether they signify something good or bad is irrelevant. Is this, then, what it means to "find the key," to "find salvation in the flesh"? If so, is the key accepting or repudiating one's homosexuality? Is it allowing oneself to be partially blinded or distracted by the past? Is it merely going doggedly on? Is the tearing of the letter a liberation from the past or a commitment to it? What is the "dreadful hope" which he now shoulders?

I would like to think that Baldwin, having so pitilessly exposed David's self-absorption — some of the best passages of dialogue are precisely the ones between David and Giovanni or David and Hella, where they rightly accuse him of a self-serving "purity" — is now dissolving that fatally seductive egotism, drying it up, throwing it to the winds. I would like to find in this ending a change of narrative from one of paralytic shame to one of burdensome but manageable guilt. Perhaps David will now do something (perhaps write this "confession"?) that will forever change the lives of people like himself and Giovanni, and in that way "save" Giovanni. This change might involve showing homosexual love as a possibility, rather than as the mere contradiction in terms which both Pauline theology and neo-Freudianism would make it. I would like to think, finally, that the ending suggests that we can proceed with our lives even in the face of a dreary and encumbering past, and that the stain of our past can be accepted and even prove the "key to our salvation." I want to think that the answer to David's life is repudiation not of his homosexuality, but of the lovelessness he inflicted both on Giovanni and himself.

But then I pull myself up: How likely is it that Baldwin would write a story of gay liberation, even in such muted harmonies? How likely is it that any of his contemporaries would have read the story that way even if he had written it that way? Are the ambiguities of Baldwin's prose meant to direct the close reader to an unsuspected, ungloomy meaning? (If so, he would be a very close reader indeed.) Is David to be seen as a gay man, or *seen through* as a liar, a self-deceiver, a hard-hearted narcissist? Is Baldwin in this novel really so different from David? Is he really so in control of his highly flammable material that he can write my self-enacting parable of ignorance?

My guess is that Baldwin, raised to be a fundamentalist preacher from his youth, probably *was* just as horrified by homosexuality as David or Giovanni or Guillaume. He seems a sort of Protestant version of one of the Catholic novelists with whom he was contemporary, Mauriac or Graham Greene, about whom Auden once wittily wrote: "There is a certain kind of Catholic novelist who would rewrite the fall of Eve like this: 'And when the woman saw that the tree was poisonous and that it was hideous to look at, she took of the fruit thereof and did eat. We are not born quite so corrupt as that."[6] But in Baldwin's world we *are* born as corrupt as that and, worse, lack even the putative bliss of paradise to compensate the enormous sacrifices of life on earth. I do not think that it was possible for him — as it was for a few more fortunate contemporary writers like Tennessee Williams or Fritz Peters — to make a surgically precise division between his homosexual self and his writing self. I do not think that this kind of "control" over his writing was even necessarily interesting to him: does the preacher have "control" over his sermons? At the same time, he was the subtlest and most profound of American moralists, and as well, a born outsider. His blackness made him an exile in his own country; his homosexuality exiled him from even the black community. He cannot have failed to connect the two exiles.

Is *Giovanni's Room,* then, a pro-gay or an anti-gay novel? Neither. The most we can say for it as an apology for homosexuality is negative: that it enacts for us, if we read it with extreme care, the very process of self-blinding, love of a false "purity," love even of "sin," that is common to both white racism and gay self-loathing. It does not praise the closet; neither does it raze the closet. The closet, Baldwin seems to be saying, is wherever the mind goes to be *unaware of itself,* wherever it goes to be artificially "innocent." Giovanni's room is not a closet in this sense, for Giovanni, far more than David, is aware of the self-deceptions of "innocence."

But David's narrative of Giovanni's room — that is a different case. With each beautiful, sober, ruminative sentence David convicts himself of false innocence, and locks himself in a closet far worse than any Giovanni could create.

TENNESSEE WILLIAMS'S GAY SHORT STORIES

Although *Giovanni's Room* was my first gay book, I (like most gay men of my generation) had no idea until much later that it had predecessors: John Horne

Burns's *The Gallery* (1947), Gore Vidal's *The City and the Pillar* (1948), and Fritz Peters's *Finistère* (1951). Least of all did I know of the rich treasure of gay fiction to be found in Tennessee Williams's long-uncollected short stories. It was not until 1985, when New Directions published *The Collected Stories of Tennessee Williams*—complete with a bibliography, an autobiographical essay by Williams, and a generous appreciation by Gore Vidal—that it became possible to see not only Williams but gay literature in a new light.

The vista had been obscured by the last years of Williams's life and career, his long descent into alcoholism and addiction, his many theatrical failures, his depressions, his incoherent appearances on college campuses. With the publication of his stories, however, many of which had been written in the period of his greatest achievement—the forties and fifties—it became possible to reassess Williams. This was perhaps especially true of the half-dozen gay-themed stories in the collection, stories which made the hints of homosexuality in the more famous plays suddenly richer and more explicit. (The stories I am calling "gay" are: "Desire and the Black Masseur," "Hard Candy," "The Killer Chicken and the Closet Queen," "The Mysteries of the Joy Rio," "The Night of the Iguana," "One Arm," and "Two on a Party." (Several others, including "The Mattress by the Tomato Patch," "Three Players of a Summer Game," and "The Yellow Bird," might be considered gay around the edges because their female protagonists force us to pay attention to that gayest of subjects, male sexiness.) Indeed these stories are not only his best stories, but among his best works. Honest, amused, unhysterical, and beautiful, they form, it seems to me now, one of the central pillars of modern gay fiction.

Nearly all of Williams's gay stories antedated *Giovanni's Room* (1956). All but the last ("The Killer Chicken and the Closet Queen," 1978) were published in two collections: *One Arm* (1948) and *Hard Candy* (1954). It may come as a surprise to the unprepared reader, therefore, that they are more, not less liberated (and liberating) than Baldwin's murky masterpiece. They are witty, romantic, light, comic. They are compositions of the surface, not because they are "superficial," but because they see and love what can be perceived with the senses. They are sensuous works as Baldwin's novel is not. It is perhaps no accident that not only their subject, but their effect on the reader, is diffusedly erotic, or that they communicate that heightened interest in life which sexual desire creates. Baldwin's Calvinist self-examination, so horrified as to be presented in the form of a confession, seems designed by contrast to desensualize not only homosexuality but everything else. How few *actions* one remembers from this great novel—and by contrast, how many *speeches!*

Williams was perhaps not capable of Baldwin's kind of self-examination, or was perhaps simply uninterested in it. He certainly avoids it in his fiction—or makes fun of it. In one of his last stories, a hilarious farce called "The Killer

Chicken and the Closet Queen," he transposes all the anguish of *Giovanni's Room* into the major key: the beautiful, seductive, and completely amoral chicken queen not only causes the closet queen to "corrupt a minor" (himself), but to lose his job, deceive his mother in order to inherit her money, and — it is strongly hinted — contemplate killing her. Guilt is so little a part of this story (except as an object of mockery) that it is simply called "tragic sickness" — a sickness that can be cured by a little self-interest and the right drugs.[7]

Unlike Baldwin, Williams is on our side, on his own side. His is not a narrative of tragic, but of comic, self-division — though his comedy, like Chekhov's, is never far from pathos. It is always clear in a Williams story that the gay character is, if not absolutely right, right in respect to everyone else. Mr. Krupper, the old ugly man who visits the Joy Rio theater for sex in "Hard Candy," is morally and emotionally superior to his dull, hard-hearted, unimaginative family. Anthony Burns, the pale, practically invisible white man who needs punishment by his black masseur, thereby achieves completion in his life. Billy and his friend Claire in "Two on a Party" are superior to the "straight" world — what Gore Vidal calls the world of the "squares."[8] By taking seriously what the straight world would treat as ridiculous — Mr. Krupper's lust, the need of Anthony Burns for atonement, the real, if limited "love" of fag and fag hag in "Two on a Party" — Williams strikes a blow for the small, the unimportant, the gay, the female, the unedifying, the alcoholic. (Frank O'Connor thinks this attention to marginal characters the peculiar gift of the short story as a medium: if so, Williams shows himself in this respect, too, a natural short story writer.)[9] By ridiculing what the "squares" take seriously — family and children, female moral nobility, religious virtue, the sublimity of "love" — he subverts our notions of seriousness itself.

Williams's gay stories could be said to justify the desires of gay men, and yet *justify* is exactly the wrong word. *Qui s'excuse s'accuse.* And Williams's great conceptual advance in writing about gay men lies precisely in a refusal to justify homosexuality. Indeed, the most astonishing thing about these stories, even today, is their lack of special pleading. And while they are not, obviously, pornographic — or even graphic — neither are they in the least apologetic. Or rather, as we shall see, Williams so plays the *game* of apology that he whisks the reader right by the Cerberus of homophobia. And throughout, he seems to assume (unlike most other gay writers of his own, or of any later period) that these moral outcasts — a one-armed male hustler, a fag and his hag, an old man looking for sex in a movie theater — are worthy of being taken seriously.

This handful of stories is more significant than their small number would suggest. Not only are they true to the experience of gay desire, they often create that experience in the reader (straight or gay), and thus, while never seeming to raise a political voice, strike the most unmistakable of blows for what would later become gay liberation. For they make desire for a man so palpable, so funny, so pathetic, and so recognizable that one faces the choice as a reader either not to read them at all, or to follow where they lead. This challenge to the straight world marks the enormous difference of Williams's short stories from *Giovanni's Room,* where the author seems to be apologizing, in both the theological and social sense. Homosexuality in Baldwin is so fraught with contradiction and danger that writing about it is always defensive. In Williams, by contrast, one is never given an acceptable alternative to "liking" the gay character. If one dislikes him, one is equated with characters in the story who also dislike him—characters who are invariably prudes, rednecks, pathetic losers. Williams, no less conflicted as a man than Baldwin, nonetheless as an artist poses homosexuality in such a way that one is caught liking it.

Thus, though Williams is, like Baldwin, indirect in his presentation of gay sex (there are no dirty words); though few of his characters are, by Stonewall standards, out; though Williams himself was only intermittently honest about his homosexuality—nonetheless his writing is anything but closety. Baldwin, as we saw, was paralyzed by the question of homosexuality to the point of incoherence. Williams is far less frightened of it and far clearer (and funnier) in talking about it. Indeed, the measure of Williams's accomplishment is precisely his ability to find homosexual desire funny as well as touching. Such a comic vision would have been quite beyond Baldwin, and was even—until *Myra Breckinridge*—beyond Gore Vidal. While there are, of course, elements of self-doubt in both his characters and the narrator of these gay stories, there is also (and more significantly) triumph over self-doubt, and a calm assertion of the rightness of gay desire.

Tennessee Williams apparently told Gore Vidal, "I cannot write any sort of story unless there is at least one character in it for whom I feel physical desire." Perhaps this is why Williams falls into a class of gay writers I would call "carnal." His characters have bodies, his narrators and the other characters in the story are intensely aware of those bodies. Even a minor character like the marvelously venal movie usher George in "The Mysteries of the Joy Rio" (a first version of "Hard Candy") gives off an unmistakable whiff of male rut as he impatiently waits in his "tight faded uniform" for his sluttish girlfriend Gladys. And as Vidal points out in his appreciation of Williams in the *Collected Stories,* "When Tennessee wrote *A Streetcar Named Desire,* he inadvertently smashed one of our society's most powerful taboos. He showed the male not only as sexually attractive in the flesh but as an object for something never entirely acknowledged, the lust of women. . . . the male as sex object is still at our culture's center stage."[10]

Less obvious perhaps is how many of the stories feature *wounded* men, men who have been betrayed by their bodies. (Brick in *Cat on a Hot Tin Roof,* and in its predecessor, "Three Players of a Summer Game," has broken his leg running hurdles at the high school track.) Of these the most troubling is Oliver, the murderous "hero" of "One Arm," who lost his right arm in a car accident and with it "the center of his being." Oliver had been a champion boxer before his accident. After it, he is completely unsuited to the middle-class world: all he was good for was fighting. He soon realizes that the beauty of his face is marketable, and he becomes a hustler. He exchanges, in other words, the aggressive right arm for the passively beautiful face; he chooses — or permits himself — to become an object, something to be consumed. Picked up by a rich man to make a blue movie, and humiliated by his having to do it, Oliver kills him, flees, is caught and sentenced to the electric chair. The action of the story is the story of his last days.

Among other things the story asks what constitutes male desirability. We are never allowed to turn our attention from this question, or from Oliver's body. It is, among other things, one of the sexiest stories I can remember, not only because Oliver is sexy but also because Williams is, in his slightly sadistic *forcing* of our eyes in that direction. The fact that Oliver has suffered such a cruel demotion by the loss of his arm paradoxically makes us all the more aware of his body, makes his carnal charisma all the more magnetic. One feels toward him (as presumably the man he kills did) both maternal and vicious: here is this strong man whom I can comfort, whom I can possess. It is about the rape, the homosexualizing of a straight man — a "rape" which is eagerly colluded in by writer and reader alike.

That is the exciting, the pornographic side of this story, the side that gives the sense of power, and of violation. But there is another story here, sadder and more troubling. This story concerns Oliver's gradual thick realization that for him this worship from other men *is* love, all the love he's ever going to give or get. "Those rainbows of the flesh," the erotic illusions he has inspired among so many men, turn out to be as much love as he has. The final heartbreaking, dazzling symbol of this is that when he finally is executed, he clutches the letters written to him between his legs when the electricity is turned on. They are, sexual desire is, the self — not the heart or the mind, but the cock. What an idea!

And in his transformation from thug to punk he manages to accept his beauty — as straight men so often cannot — and to realize he is that humiliating, glorious thing: an object of lust. He has unusual authority because he speaks as both a straight and a gay man, because he dwells between the two worlds, or in both. And what he says, haltingly, is of importance to those of us who are more entirely gay. At the very end of his life, the day before his execution, a closety Lutheran minister comes to "console" him, for very mixed reasons indeed. Oliver decides to give himself to the minister as a final offering, a final return of affection or lust that he was never able to give before to any of the men to whom he meant so much. He makes the minister give him a back-rub. The minister, suddenly aware of Oliver's desires (and his own), pulls back:

> "No!"
> "Don't be a fool. There's a door at the end of the hall. It makes a noise when anybody comes in it."
> The minister retreated.
> The boy reached out and caught him by the wrist.
> "You see that pile of letters on the shelf? They're bills from people I owe. Not money, but feelings. For three whole years I went all over the country stirring up feelings without feeling nothing myself. Now that's all changed and I have feelings, too. I am lonely and bottled up the same as you are. I know your type. Everything is artistic or else it's religious, but that's all a bunch of bullshit and I don't buy it. All that you need's to be given a push on the head!" (187)

This speech, in all its glorious inarticulateness, is one of the great defenses of gay liberation, all the more powerful in coming unwanted, unplanned from a man who probably doesn't think of himself as gay but has recognized that he is enmeshed in gay men's desire, that their lust for him has consequences, that he "owes" them something. This recognition is like the falling of a huge Bastille of male imperviousness, a realignment of sexual meanings. There is no difference between him and the Lutheran minister: but ironically it is the mostly-straight Oliver, not the certainly gay clergyman, who sees and honors lust. What a magnificent indictment is his contemptuous raging accusation: "I know your type. Everything is artistic or else it's religious, but that's all a bunch of bullshit and I don't buy it." In enunciating this sudden insight, Oliver frees not only himself but the modern gay reader as well. How many of us, still, retreat to art or religion to excuse or justify our queer desires! How few of us can admit we are over our heads in sexual, affectional debt! How hard it is, even now, to see that all these evasions of desire are "a bunch of bullshit."

What is a "push on the head"? A threat, of course, a return to the violence by which Oliver made his living as a boxer and later as a murderer. But it also means to push the minister down to his knees and make him give Oliver a blow job. Finally, it is what St. Paul calls a *metanoia,* a conversion, a change of mind. The minister, so locked in his unspeakable fantasies of a golden panther licking and penetrating him, can't see what's in front of his eyes. He needs, and Oliver knows it, to "change his mind."

Pitiable, dense, violent, mesmerizing Oliver is the furthest realization of homosexuality in Williams's fiction, and yet he is nothing like the conventional idea of a gay man. He may not *be* a gay man. And yet he represents in hyperbolic form the threat of homosexuality: he is a beautiful man, a dangerous man, a violent man, and—while uneducated—a man who finally sees what the educated minister misses entirely: that we have debts to pay to Eros, that the male body must also pay those debts, because that body has also incurred them. Consequently for Oliver to confess his willingness to pay back is a revolutionary thing—the straight man confesses his weakness, of which the wounded body is a symbol—his radical guilt. A guilt thought payable heretofore only by the weak, by women, children, and homosexuals, is payable by everyone. And not to acknowledge your erotic debt is a "bunch of bullshit."

"One Arm" is a good example of a profoundly gay story—or a story with profoundly gay consequences—which is nonetheless indirect about the main character's sexuality. It is certainly not a propagandistic piece either pro or con homosexuality. Nonetheless, its attention to the male body—its beauty, its fragility—is deeply queer; much queerer in fact than most subsequent fiction about gay men. Indeed, to some extent, it is the willingness to focus the reader's attention on male desirability which marks the gay enterprise in fiction; mere presentation of characters who "happen to be gay" but have no bodies (as is the case with much recent gay fiction) is easy in comparison: a reader of *The Lost Language of Cranes* or *A Home at the End of the World*, for instance, is rarely forced to confront the possibility of lusting after a man.

This indirectness of Williams has been impugned as mere cowardice. And Williams himself, long adroit at getting out of tight spots, frequently "justified" his artful dodging: "I do not deal with the didactic, ever."[11] As with most artists, this is both true and false. He mainly doesn't want to be *pinned down*. This goes beyond an attitude toward his own homosexuality to an attitude toward his work. Nonetheless, I believe that in his best stories, there is an identifiable and radical gay attitude, something better than mere propaganda or role-modeling. There is a powerful subversive voice that both honors gay desire and mocks those who would censure or smash it. And all this is done with the calmest, most smiling ease, so that the reader may not be aware at first what he has had done to him.

Among those who seem unaware of Williams's stylistic rapier are, ironically, certain gay critics who want to like Williams—after all, he is one of our success stories—but who can't help regretting the indirection and self-doubt of his fiction. They wish Williams had been either a different kind of man, or a different kind of writer. They would like it if he had come as far out in 1954, the peak of McCarthyism, as they did in 1984, fifteen years after Stonewall. They would prefer him to have written stories not of "losers" like "One Arm" or "Desire and the Black Masseur," but of dull, sober "winners" like *The Lost Language of Cranes.*

One such critic, John M. Clum, a professor of drama and English at Duke, puts the case in " 'Something Cloudy, Something Clear': Homophobic Discourse in Tennessee Williams" in the Winter 1989 number of the *South Atlantic Quarterly,* "Displacing Homophobia." This earnest article clears up a few false leads more or less deliberately sown by Williams, but otherwise darkens counsel by holding Williams to anachronistic standards of "liberation," by neglecting to distinguish between his life and his work, and by reading the work with a kind of grim solemnity that utterly falsifies it.[12]

Though Clum is right, for instance, that "Williams's theoretical separation of his homosexuality from his work is in conflict with his many assertions of the highly personal nature of his work," this commonsensical judgment bears less fruit than it might: "in conflict with" and "highly personal nature of his work" are both weasel-phrases that mean less than they seem to. Clum is right, too, to dispute the wishful claim of some pro-gay critics[13] that Williams's treatment of homosexuality becomes more "liberated" as his career goes on. Change, indeed, that treatment has undergone, but not, Clum rightly argues, for the better. In particular, Williams's defensive claim that "I do not deal with the didactic, ever" is, Clum shows, simply untrue, especially at the end of Williams's career—a phase which saw the incoherent, but certainly overtly gay *Memoirs,* the chaotic novel *Moise and the Age of Reason,* and several failed plays. *Small Craft Warnings* and *Vieux Carré* are indeed nothing if not "didactic." (His very last play, on the other hand, *Something Cloudy, Something Clear,* is an austere, undidactic meditation on the necessity of using others, and the inescapable guilt such using incurs.)

But while Williams's numerous denials of having written a gay play ("I don't find it necessary," he disingenuously and haughtily put it) do suggest a "split personality" in the man, they do not prove that this split personality necessarily affected, let alone warped, Williams the artist. In fact, the greatest weakness of Clum's article is precisely the failure to distinguish between the two. The essay ends, for instance, with a sad head-shake over one of Williams's minor poems, "Intimations," which begins wryly: "I do not think that I ought to appear in public / below the shoulders." Clum, however, is not amused: "While the poem is about mortality, it also suggests Williams's sense of separation from his own physicality and sexuality as well as his confusion of private and public selves. In 'Intimations' only the mind is public: the body, of which only the belly and loins are specifically mentioned—appetite and sexuality—are private and already 'swathed in bandages' to cover their disease. This is a regrettably fitting self-image for Williams the homosexual and for the homosexuality he depicted throughout his career."[14]

There are obvious problems with adducing "Intimations" as evidence of Williams's attitude to homosexuality—and they are problems that pervade Clum's article. First of all, it isn't a very good poem; and while failed works of art may tell us something about the artist, they are powerless to explain successful works of art — which are of course the very ones we want to understand.[15] Second, is it really as odd as Clum pretends that an old man should detest his decaying body, or that the mind, not it, should be "public"? Think of "Sailing to Byzantium"! Finally and typically, he is simply deaf to the poem's tone: the first line is some kind of rueful joke, not a solemn pronouncement. As a result the tone of "regret" Clum adopts in his conclusion makes him sound like a prissy bureaucrat dealing with an office irregularity.

This attitude of pursed disapproval vitiates Clum's reading of the two important works he discusses in the first half of his essay, the short story "Hard Candy" and the play *Cat on a Hot Tin Roof.* He is particularly self-righteous when he calls *Cat on a Hot Tin Roof* "the most vivid dramatic embodiment of Williams's mixed signals regarding homosexuality and his obsession with public exposure."[16] He has overstated his case. The "mixed signals" Clum deprecates were *necessary* in 1955; every gay person in the country was "obsessed" with "public exposure." (Do we say Larry Kramer's play *The Normal Heart* is "obsessed" with AIDS?) Public exposure — which Clum tosses off as if it were a minor inconvenience — meant you could be sent to jail, lose your job, be committed to a mental hospital. Isn't Clum coming perilously close to blaming Williams for his bizarre failure to live the life of a tenured gay academic in 1989?

Cat on a Hot Tin Roof can take care of itself. "Hard Candy," however, suffers badly and undeservedly from Clum's dogged but tone-deaf reading of it. And since it is one of Williams's best stories, and since academic manhandling of delicate texts is so common, I would like to defend it. In so doing I mean also to defend the half-dozen other explicitly gay stories which are easily demeaned by well-intentioned, but tone-deaf readings. Indeed, the tone *is* the story, from the earliest ("Mysteries of the Joy Rio," begun in 1941 and published in 1948) to the latest ("The Killer Chicken and the Closet Queen," published in 1978, that *annus mirabilis* of gay fiction). As Williams himself irritatedly told Gore Vidal, who had tried to spruce up one of his stories: "What you have done is remove my *style,* which is all that I have."[17]

"Hard Candy," the principal story of a collection published in 1954, tells the story of "a seventy-year-old retired merchant named Mr. Krupper, a man of gross and unattractive appearance and with no close family connections.

> He had been the owner of a small sweetshop, which he had sold out years before to a distant and much younger cousin. . . . But Mr. Krupper had not altogether relinquished his hold on the shop and this was a matter of grave dissatisfaction to the distant cousin and his wife and their twelve-year-old daughter whom Mr. Krupper, with an old man's interminable affection for a worn-out joke, still invariably addressed and referred to as "The Complete

Little Citizen of the World," a title invented for her by the cousin himself when she was a child of five and when her trend to obesity was not so serious a matter as it now appeared. (335)

From the very beginning of "Hard Candy," we are in the presence of a particular kind of voice, a storyteller's voice. Like all good storytellers, Williams is both serious and amused. His is a voice that knows it is being heard, knows it has an audience. (Baldwin's first-person narrator is talking only to himself: hence, perhaps, the sublime monotony of his voice.) His choice of how to begin, what facts to emphasize, what words to use are all part of a secret shared openly with the listener. There is bound to be, the listener knows, a certain exaggeration in what Williams says, but it is an exaggeration we both see through and accept, like children who both believe and disbelieve that Jack's beanstalk climbed all the way to heaven. Hence, for instance, the decision to make Mr. Krupper not just homely, but "gross and unattractive": we recognize in these hyperbolic words an exaggeration meant for our delight. Williams is playing that oldest storyteller's game: pretending to be disgusted or shocked or sorrowful over something that delights him just as much as it does us.

Whether we "like" or "dislike" Mr. Krupper is quite irrelevant: he is the "hero" of this story. Furthermore, it is already apparent that he is more interesting in his grotesqueness than the respectable cousins with their fat little daughter. Mr. Krupper is now so old and repulsive that his sensible dull family don't even wonder how he spends his day, except to be annoyed that he regularly grabs a pocketful of hard candies before going out. Did they bother to look, they would see that for most of the morning Mr. Krupper does nothing more peculiar than sit on a park bench — but of course they *don't* bother. Like all the sensible older children of fairy tales — though they are chronologically younger, they seem older — they ignore romance even when it is right under their eyes. And Mr. Krupper, despite being "gross and unattractive," is indeed romantic — at least in the sense that he has a secret, an inside as well as an outside. The story Williams is about to tell concerns that secret, which will lead us and Mr. Krupper to his own last day.

The art, as in all of Williams, lies in the delays, in the indirections, in the style. Take the following passage, which Professor Clum deals with very harshly: "In the course of this story, and very soon now, it will be necessary to make some disclosures about Mr. Krupper of a nature too coarse to be dealt with very directly in a work of such brevity." We recognize the same voice that pretended to be so scandalized by Mr. Krupper's "grossness." We lean in: "The grossly naturalistic details of a life [that word *gross* again!] . . . are softened and qualified by it, but when you attempt to set those details down in a tale, some measure of obscurity or indirection is called for to provide the same, or even approximate, softening effects that existence in time gives to those gross elements in the life itself" (337).

This passage is deeply, but obviously, deceptive. Williams teases us by withholding what these "disclosures" must be; but once again the listener comprehends perfectly the reason for the teasing, the timing, the sense of being *toyed with*. "When I say," he continues, "that there was a certain mystery in the life of Mr. Krupper" (and doesn't he linger slightly on the word *mystery?*), "I am beginning to approach those things in the only way possible without a head-on violence that would disgust and destroy and which would actually falsify the story" (337).

Clum, predictably, scents self-loathing and homophobia in this curlicuing paragraph—qualities that were hardly avoidable in 1954 by any gay writer. What he fatally misses, or dismisses, is the tone that mocks and undercuts the very censoriousness of the words. Williams the narrator enacts the role of a prude: indeed, it is one of his greatest, and most common disguises, just as "Monsieur Remorse" is one of Falstaff's. Part of the ineffable comedy of this story is precisely the combination of a prudish schoolmarm's voice and a quite different, amoral voice which is defiantly interested in all sorts of unrespectable things: sex, violence, drunkenness, madness. Notice the artfulness with which Williams teases out the following sentences, deferring the moment of dirty truth we know must come: "But our old man, Mr. Krupper, is a bird of a different feather, and it is now time, in fact is probably already past time, to follow him further than the public square into which he turned when the cousins no longer could watch him. It is necessary to advance the hour of the day, to skip past the morning and the early afternoon, spent in the public square and the streets of that vicinity, and it is necessary to follow Mr. Krupper by streetcar into another section of the city" (339). Williams could not torment us more delightfully than with this artificially prolonged sentence. How wittily Williams makes it clear, without saying a word, that if Mr. Krupper is not like the "nice old men, the sweet old men and the clean old men of the world," why then he must be . . . a *dirty* old man! Notice, finally, that we follow this story with bated breath because we both know and do not know how it must end. "And now Mr. Krupper has arrived within a block of where he is actually going and which is the place where the mysteries of his nature are to be made unpleasantly manifest to us." "Unpleasantly"! To say so is to free himself from the responsibility of taking any further moral line on Mr. Krupper's still-to-be-revealed obloquy. Yet Mr. Krupper has apparently gone nowhere more "mysterious" than a dingy movie palace in a bad part of town: "And if we followed Mr. Krupper only as far as the door of that cinema, nothing of an esoteric nature would be noticeable unless"—he goes on, elaborately deadpan—"you thought it peculiar that he should go three times a week to a program changed only on Mondays" (340).

With the impudence of the true storyteller, Williams now tears off the mask of polite interest, and summons our every voyeuristic impulse: "But naturally we are not going to follow him only that far, we are going to follow him past the ticket window and into the interior of the theater." In this brazen transition, the gloves come off and he turns on the reader as if to say: "You pretend to be satisfied with leaving dear old Mr. Krupper at the cinema's door. But you are avid for scandal." Consequently, "*we* are going to follow him . . . into the interior of the theater" [italics mine]. The "we" grabs us by the neck and marches us right into that dirty theater, and we go, squirming in pleasure; for we are no better than the storyteller or than Mr. Krupper himself. At this moment comes a completely convincing change of tone:

> And right away, as soon as we have made that entrance, a premonition of something out of the ordinary is forced upon us. For the Joy Rio is not, by any means, an ordinary theater. It is the ghost of a once elegant house where plays and operas were performed long ago. . . . Actually it is only when the lights are brought on, for a brief interval between shows or at their conclusion, that the place is distinguishable from any other cheap movie house. And then it is only distinguishable by looking upwards. Looking upwards you see that it contains not only the usual orchestra and balcony sections but two tiers of boxes extending in horseshoe design from one side of the proscenium to the other, but the faded gilt, the terribly abused red damask of these upper reaches of the Joy Rio never bloom into sufficient light to make a strong impression from the downstairs. You have to follow Mr. Krupper up the great marble staircase that still rises beyond the balcony level before you really begin to explore the physical mysteries of the place. And that, of course, is what we are going to do. (340–41)

Strangely enough, after so much burlesque of the grand manner, so much play-acting of shock and mystery, we are in the presence of the real thing. Why is this? Partly because, even while laughing at this desire, we have half *wanted* to find mystery at the end of this journey. Partly because the scene now is hushed and dark. Partly because we are in that utterly mysterious place, an empty theater. Indeed, despite all the joking, we are about to see a "mystery." Sex is in our nostrils. Mr. Krupper climbs to the upper balcony, long closed off, and therefore perfect for his purpose, which is to seduce any young man who ventures up there, using the "hard candy" in his pocket as an icebreaker. These are the "mysteries of the Joy Rio" (to use Williams's title of an earlier version of the story). And on this particular day, the last of his life, Mr. Krupper is to succeed beyond his wildest dreams.

The description of his success — so equivocal, so limited — is as complexly funny as the rest of the story. Is it homophobic, as Professor Clum thinks? Only if one reads and doesn't hear, only if one listens with a tin ear. Here is Mr. Krupper's entrance into the box and his half-terrified, half-joyful discovery that it is already occupied: "At first Mr. Krupper thinks this nearly invisible companion may be a certain Italian youth of his acquaintance who sometimes shares the box with him for a few minutes, at rare intervals, five or six weeks apart. . . . The slight odor that made him think it might be, an odor made up of sweat and tobacco and the prodigality of certain youthful glands, is not at all unfamiliar to the old man's nose" (342). "Sometimes shares the box with him"! The harsher truth behind this polite fiction nevertheless leaves the fiction intact. If anything, it intensifies the fundamental truth that this is indeed a "sharing," or that each man must partly think so. The contrast between the actual Mr. Krupper or the actual "Italian youth of his acquaintance" and the characters of each man's fantasy is both funny and devastating. And from now on, Williams allows similar multiple ironies to pile up. He both enters Mr. Krupper's breathless, fearful adoration and hovers just outside it: the complex effect is breathtaking in its comedy and pity.

For the youth is *not* Bruno, it appears. To find out who it is, Mr. Krupper "strikes the match and leans a little bit forward. And then his heart, aged seventy and already strained from the recent exertion of the stairs, undergoes an alarming spasm, for never in this secret life of his, never in thirty years' attendance of matinees at the Joy Rio, has old Mr. Krupper discovered beside him, even now within contact, inspiring the dark with its warm animal fragrance, any dark youth of remotely equivalent beauty" (343). Once again, the baroque langue, with its grandiloquently repeated periods, is parodic; but can we say it is false? In a gesture fraught with contradiction, with self-respect and abjectness, desperation and hope, Mr. Krupper nudges the sleeping youth and offers him — oh inadequate! — a hard candy, followed by eight quarters which "descend softly, with a slight tinkle, and Mr. Krupper knows that the contract is sealed between them" (345).

This passage causes Professor Clum a few bad moments. He discovers in it something called "the pederasty/hunger nexus," which must of course be extracted like a bad tooth.[18] "Pederasty" is a particularly low blow. Mr. Krupper is not a lover of young boys at all. Nor is this "boy" young, or his delicious odors would scarcely reach "the old man's nose." This "contact" is, on the contrary, the most delicate of transactions, one in which any misstep will lead to unpleasant consequences: violence or disgust on the young man's part, loss of pride on Mr. Krupper's. What else *can* Mr. Krupper give this boy but food and money, and not much of either? He knows "that he is fat and ugly . . . he does not deceive himself at all about that." There is, further, "some danger that the youth will leave. . . . but the affirmative answer to the question Hungry? has already given some basis, not quite a pledge, of continuing association between them" (344). How delicately grim that phrase "continuing association" is, especially by comparison with what their "association" might be called by someone less charitable: a vice cop or a literary critic.

When the lights of the theater come on later that night, the body of Mr. Krupper is found kneeling, caught between two chairs in the upper balcony, "as if he had expired in an attitude of prayer" (345). Once again, the tone is everything: "expired" is slightly grandiose, and the "attitude of prayer" invites a complex disbelief. On the one hand, it is an unstated dirty joke: Mr. Krupper wasn't praying, he was *blowing* the kid. At the same time, the storyteller is daring us to say that this blow job was not prayer. The one response we are *not* encouraged to have is that of Professor Clum, who claims to discern a "harsh authorial judgment which places the narrator in a superior position to his central character and allies him with the 'average reader's' moral judgment."[19] To the contrary: "harsh judgment" is left to Mr. Krupper's poor dull cousins and their ever-fatter daughter, who exclaims with triumph: "*Just think, Papa, the old man choked to death on our hard candy!*"

Williams's art, in all his best stories and plays, is one of tone. It is possible to crush them into a readily portable box — homophobia, dysfunctional family, and so on — but the actual stories are far more flexible, and therefore paradoxically far tougher than that carrying-case. Unlike the nervous stage direction in *Cat* on which Clum earlier hangs so much "internalized homophobia," the self-amused narration of "Hard Candy" does *not* tell us what Williams thinks, let alone what the reader should. This "not-telling" *is* the story, in many ways, and Williams — not Mr. Krupper — is the story's main character.

Is any kind of "not-telling" (Williams's "obscurity and indirection") by definition homophobic? Only by a narrow definition of that tendentious word. It is true, of course, that Williams is not writing propaganda: only Gore Vidal, among his contemporaries, was. (And *The City and the Pillar,* though personally and politically brave, is a journeyman's novel.) It is also true that his style is not "grossly naturalistic" — but then, Williams's pretend shock at this "grossness" is obviously exaggerated. In my opinion, Williams is not only not "homophobic," but is honest in ways that might shock John Clum, or any critic eager to find only reassuring stories of gay life. He is honest about our overwhelming need for beauty, a need which forces (and justifies) paying for it. He is honest about the terrible depredations of old age and about the loneliness of the unmarried (and therefore especially the gay). He is grimly and wittily honest about the tyranny of the nuclear family and its self-protective meanness.

But he is more than honest. While "Hard Candy" may not be an uplifting picture of gay old age (today, I suppose, we would just pack Mr. Krupper off to a meeting of Seniors Acting in a Gay Environment), it is far from droopily pathetic. For despite the irony that cloaks Williams's description of Mr. Krupper's sexual "mystery," his actions *are* brave, just as in *Così fan tutte* Fiordiligi's protestations of being unmovable as a rock are both sincere and self-deluded.

To pursue beauty with almost no chance of reward, to remember what one desires in the face of incredulity or scorn, *is* heroic. Gay liberation is built on nothing else.

This is why it is disingenuous, to say the least, for Clum to reprove Williams for not having "allow[ed] space for alternatives to Mr. Krupper's Joy Rio meetings." Where, pray, would Williams have found such a space during the "first half of this century," in the provincial American towns where "homosexual encounters" were and are necessarily "furtive"? It is not Williams who has forbidden Mr. Krupper access to such space, it is the world. And even here I must disagree with Clum's moralistic formulas. What incenses him is that Mr. Krupper's encounter is not only furtive (which is true), but "impersonal," a mere "appeasement of hunger" (which is false). Mr. Krupper's blow job *is* an act of worship as the narrator, comically but not untruthfully, says. But Clum is quite deaf to the tone of Williams's lines: lines which in their delicacy, wit, and understatement tell a completely different story from the doctrinaire cautionary tale of "split personality" Clum predictably finds.[20] It is the voice of Williams's comic prude caught looking through the keyhole that makes "Hard Candy" "grotesque and touching" in ways Clum doesn't hear.

Nor is Williams "homophobic" when he tells the story of Mr. Krupper's final visit to the Joy Rio theater. The homophobia is mostly in Clum's own mind, showing itself in his superior, dismissive tone and in his trivializing of Williams's poker-faced defense of Mr. Krupper's cautiousness as "a little treatise on mystery." It is also present in his reproof of Mr. Krupper for pursuing "beautiful (of course) young men." What is the meaning of this sarcastic "of course"? That Clum himself would never do anything so "grossly naturalistic"? That he pities Mr. Krupper for chasing the *merely* beautiful? It is in offhand comments like this that Clum shows his true colors: the green of envy and the gray of high-minded academic puritanism.[21]

What most bothers Professor Clum is the very thing that constitutes Williams's greatest achievement: the way he takes seriously someone unimportant, in this case an old, ugly, sexually successful troll. And as we shall see throughout this survey of gay fiction, what most annoys homophobic readers, whether gay or straight, is precisely success. Pathos, freakishness, infantility — all these are more palatable than even the tiniest victory. And Mr. Krupper *is* victorious. He did not "choke to death on our hard candy," as the Complete Little Citizen of the World crows; did not, that is, die of the emotional inanition which accompanies her family's corporal bloat. He choked on a different hard candy altogether: surfeited, even satisfied.

Is Williams the storyteller "in the closet"? Not in any way that still counts. His stories, far from seeming dated or embarrassing (except to the ideological), are on the contrary visible signs of his gayness. They are also, like Mr. Krupper, "heroic, determined"; indeed more so than *Giovanni's Room,* published two years after "Hard Candy," a novel which despite its comparative openness about the topic of homosexuality, despite not seeming to evade it with the word *mystery,* is finally far more homophobic, far less able to tell us anything *about* homosexuality than Williams's half-dozen funny, tragic, elegant vignettes.

The characteristic most typical of Williams, and typical by its absence in Baldwin, is wit. Baldwin's book is almost humorless, as nightmares and obsessions tend to be. By contrast, Williams writes *about* nightmares and obsessions, and his tone is light. We see this even in his most fantastic, potentially least lively stories "Two on a Party" (about the half-generous, half-needy relationship of a fag and fag hag) and "Desire and the Black Masseur" (Williams's most fantastic story, in which a bland, almost invisible white man goes to a huge black masseur to be pummeled into expiation, sexual release, and death). Williams's wit is far more than jokes, or even than a command of farce plotting, deflated expectations, and grandiose language. It comes closer to being a kind of vision, a doubleness of sight which both sees through pretenses and imbues them with beauty. This doubleness is, like "imagination," a developable faculty of the mind: one could say that Mr. Krupper's cousins suffer from its lack, what Blake called "single vision and Newton's sleep."[22] So does a literal-minded reader like Professor Clum, who mistakes doubleness for "duplicity."

But Williams's doubleness has nothing to do with lying. Indeed, he is a great hater of the social lie, the "mendacity" Big Daddy smells in his house, the "bunch of bullshit" Oliver smells in the Lutheran minister. Williams's great strength as a writer may in fact lie in his resistance to any didacticism — theological, political, or psychological. He has no *ideas,* even the "idea" that imagination, say, is better than literalism. (Miss Jeelkes, the heroine of the story "The Night of the Iguana," is imaginative — and a vulture.) The best consequence of Williams's doubleness is a tough skepticism which is nonetheless hesitant to tear off people's social masks, even in a supposedly good cause. Rather, his stories invite — indeed, compel — us to oscillate rapidly between different judgments of the same person or the same act. His art is frank, candid, childlike, and greedy. It also has a saving streak of vulgarity which will always make it vulnerable to high-minded dismay.[23]

But Williams was quite right that his best works were not "didactic." It is small-minded criticism which earns that adjective.

Chapter Two

SEXUAL DANDYISM AND
THE LEGACY OF OSCAR WILDE

One of the few things that was readily conceded, even in the dark ages of the forties and fifties, is that we gay men certainly did have a sense of humor. (Most despised social groups are found to possess this interesting, mildly enviable commodity.) And certainly in my own coming to gay consciousness, laughter played nearly as important a role as sex. I still remember an unusually precocious gay friend asking me in eleventh grade whether I knew what "camp" meant. I tried, like the dumbest ox of a heterosexual, to guess: all to no avail. But how could I have known? It was the suburbs, it was 1965. (How did *he* know?) But like M. Jourdain who discovers he's been speaking "prose" all this time, I eventually realized years later that I'd been speaking camp: not in the sense of doing bad Bette Davis routines — I was, and am, allergic to drag — but in the sense of exaggerating in a certain self-conscious way, and of responding in a certain way to such exaggerations.

An essential element of camp is shamelessness or (to give it its Latinate equivalent) impudence. Camp in this sense has been a weapon. Shame, after all, was what had bound most gay men in the tightest, keeping us earnest, fearful, and abject. We needed to learn that there was another way of regarding the painful emotions of humiliating need — emotions especially connected with sex, but also with effeminacy, intelligence, sentimentality, and envy. For me, camp was not a series of jokes so much as a search for signs of freedom from crippling shame. I was listening, head cocked, for echoes of a more ironic universe than the one I had been raised in.

Thus, though one often thinks of camp as being silly, flighty, effeminate, this is not the whole story. The only way out of the prisons into which gay men were thrown by American middle-class culture — especially in its religious and psychiatric forms — was by shamelessly declaring that those prisons simply didn't exist, that one's presence in them was an illusion or an act. We gay men have been forced by oppressive circumstances to imagine the categories of sexual desire and affection differently, for if we didn't, we simply accepted rules of behavior by which we were invariably found wanting. In *The Picture of Dorian Gray* Oscar Wilde gives a trenchant one-sentence encapsulation: "To become the spectator of one's own life is to escape the suffering of life."[1]

If shame provided both Tennessee Williams and James Baldwin with their greatest themes, shamelessness has been no less fruitful for other gay authors and no less necessary for other gay men. It is the precondition for honesty about sex and a useful corrective to romancers of the Williams variety and to moralists of the Baldwin variety. It forms a large part of whatever it is we mean by the "gay sensibility." It is one of the continuing legacies of Oscar Wilde, and one of the gifts gay men of all sorts — not only intellectuals and artists — have bequeathed to the larger world. It has been a necessary component of a self-respecting gay man's life, a mental attitude, even a virtue.

When such impudence is incorporated into a work of art (as in *The Importance of Being Earnest,* for example), it gives us the unsettling pleasure of watching characters who seem to be watching themselves, who are both playwright and critic simultaneously. Algernon (like Wilde himself) regards his life as a series of theatrical gestures, to be judged on their momentary flair rather than on any inner consistency. ("Now produce your explanation, and pray make it improbable," he admonishes Jack Worthing in Act 1).[2] In fact, Wilde's comedy gives the audience the uneasy feeling that the actors are more alive, self-aware, and clever than it is: whose performance is being watched, judged, and found wanting, ours or theirs? The greatest modern example of this Wildean inversion of power is Gore Vidal's Myra Breckinridge, dandy and dominatrix. In Myra, we hear again Wilde's impudent, indeed arrogant voice, only now enabled to speak openly of the sexual matters it formerly had to hint at.

But impudence of this sort is not limited to art, and indeed finds some of its greatest expressions in forms not explicitly fictional. Like camp, which is both a kind of expression and a way of responding to expression, shamelessness is a kind of response, whether to a book, a dreadful movie, or a story told by a friend. In this sense, shamelessness and camp are prototypically critical acts; indeed, they are criticism conceived as a way of life and an art. One of the greatest modern examples of this gay dandyism, Boyd McDonald, was not a novelist at all, but a compiler of data for what he unironically called a sexual history of our time. Nevertheless, he so perfectly exemplifies the attitude I am trying to capture that he joins my pantheon of great gay writers, just as Samuel Johnson joins Harold Bloom's *Western Canon* as the indispensable, indeed "canonical," critic.[3] Boyd McDonald was for me one of the keys to a grown-up, unashamed gay life, one who not only disentangled me from my own hypocritical knots, but showed me the hypocrisies in the world's mendacity about sex. Homosexuality was, for McDonald, less "a very natural thing" (the title of a sweet pro-gay movie from 1973) than a private club to which certain obsessed, lucky people had the good fortune to be elected. He also showed me ways in which an adult gay man could think about, talk about, and have sex: ways that were unashamed and unabject, but at the same time too witty and self-aware ever to be boringly "normal."

GORE VIDAL'S *MYRA BRECKINRIDGE*

When Camille Paglia's *Sexual Personae* was detonated in 1990, *New York* magazine was one of the first to notice the mushroom cloud. In a punchy cover story[4] it invited various people to talk about Paglia's provocation, among them Gore Vidal. Vidal's reaction was unusually clever and unusually shameless: Paglia, he said, "sounds like Myra Breckinridge on a roll. . . . I have no higher praise." Vidal's choice of his most famous creation, Myra Breckinridge, transsexual and dominatrix, was an inspired one: not only is the comparison perceptive, but it is gloriously egotistical, in precisely Myra's way.

One might say that Vidal had virtually invented Camille Paglia. Such an invention would only have delighted Paglia herself, as confirming her Wildean belief in the power of literature to anticipate mere life. Like Paglia, Myra is a monstrously self-pleased, opinionated, arrogant, sexually anomalous self-creation: "I am Myra Breckinridge whom no man will ever possess. Clad only in garter belt and one dress shield, I held off the entire elite of the Trobriand Islanders, a race who possess no words for 'why' or 'because.' "[5] Note Myra's contempt for Margaret Mead's Trobriand Islanders, a contempt that anticipates Paglia's infamous assertion: "If civilization had been left in female hands, we would still be living in grass huts."[6] Both of these androgynes implicitly and contemptuously ask: Who wants to live in a place without *rules*? Both invert sexual roles; Myra of course literally, by undergoing a sex change from male to female, Paglia by seeing herself as a proponent of "drag-queen feminism"[7] or as a gay man trapped in a lesbian's body. Both are seeking not accommodation or harmony, but power and revenge. Their revenge is acted out in books (*Myra Breckinridge* is written in the form of notes Myra makes toward the "literary masterpiece" she modestly claims to be writing). In addition, Myra and Paglia are masters of a style Paglia would call (following Nietzsche) "Apollonian." This style, orderly but "not necessarily just, kind, or beautiful," can be heard not only in Paglia's epigrams — "Promiscuity in men may cheapen love but sharpen thought" (*Sexual Personae*, 27) — but in Myra's: "It is hate alone which inspires us to action and makes for civilization. Look at Juvenal, Pope, Billy Wilder" (*Myra Breckinridge*, 27). Do Myra and Paglia actually *believe* what they are saying? A question not to be asked. What matters is the manner: imperious, confident, exacting and exact. Its bark is worse than its bite, of course: but what a bark!

This manner is an old strand in gay male culture, and exists to even the score between the clever but endangered gay man and his thuggish straight enemies. It even has its real-life embodiment in the altercation that led to Wilde's imprisonment for sodomy. When the Marquis of Queensberry, father to Wilde's boyfriend, Lord Alfred Douglas, got word of their affair, he left a letter for Wilde at his club insultingly addressed to "Oscar Wilde posing as a Somdomite [*sic*]." Wilde, with the insane arrogance of the gay dandy, foolishly decided to sue Queensberry for libel, a suit he must have known he would lose.[8] Often, dandyism is mistaken for its cousins, the merely snobbish superiority of the social climber, the disdain of the intellectual, or the foppishness of the worldling. But what makes Wilde still a heroic figure for many gay men, and what has kept his brand of dandyism alive in art, is not snobbery but aggressiveness: he is not merely passively superior, he is on the attack. His art is fueled, as Myra says "civilization" is, by hatred.

One crucial context into which the dandyish voice has spread is sex, about which the late-Victorian Wilde could only speak in code. In a sense, sex is the logical target of dandyism, for the application of the language of shamelessness to such a shame-ridden subject as sex is necessary. (It is also hard to do, since most people are more unnerved by sex-talk than by sex itself.) And one of Vidal's greatest achievements in *Myra Breckinridge* is the pornographic scene in which Myra rapes the young stud Rusty with a strap-on dildo: a scene that is "gay" precisely in its combination of voyeuristic heat and laughter. Indeed, Vidal shows how close both are to each other: the link is self-consciousness, which makes sex perverse, but also makes it ironic. Myra is not simply raping Rusty, but quite consciously acting "rape" out, like a scene from *Enema Nurse* or any other one-handed novel. This self-consciousness is style, is dandyism. To treat the most bodily, least spiritual things as aesthetic *gestures* is the essence of it.

The plot of *Myra Breckinridge* is simply and devastating. Myra is the new identity of Myron Breckinridge, an unhappy gay man who has undergone surgery to change his sex. Myron was a pretentious aesthete and cinema fanatic, and so is his new incarnation Myra. As the novel opens, she has arrived in Los Angeles, where she intends both to pay homage to the great films of the forties and (less sentimentally) to blackmail her uncle Buck Loner, "the Singin' Shootin' Cowboy." What Myra wants is a share of Buck Loner's enormous wealth, wealth founded on his entirely bogus "Academy of Drama and Modeling." The property on which the Academy is situated, Myra will remind Uncle Buck, was left jointly to Buck and his sister, Myra/Myron's mother, Gertrude. Gertrude being dead, it now belongs as much to Myron (or rather to Myra, who is masquerading as Myron's widow) as to Buck. Buck Loner is dumb and mean. He certainly has no intention of letting even so fine an example of "feminine pulchritude" (i.e., Myra) get her hands on his money. But as a delaying tactic (while he investigates Myra's claim to part of the property), he offers her a job at the Academy teaching "Empathy" and "Posture." "Oh," she writes, "we are a pair of jolly rogues! He means to cheat me out of my inheritance while I intend to take him for every cent he's got, as well as make him fall madly in love just so, at the crucial moment, I can kick his fat ass in, fulfilling the new pattern to which I am now irrevocably committed. Or as Diotima said to Hyperion, in Hölderlin's novel, 'It was no man that you wanted, believe me; you wanted a world.' I too want a world and mean to have it" (18).

The world she means to have is one in which "the feminine principle" "regain[s] once more that primacy she lost at the time of the Bronze Age when the cock-worshipping Dorians enslaved the West, impiously replacing *the* Goddess with a god. Happily his days are nearly over; the phallus cracks; the uterus opens; and I am at last ready to begin my mission which is to re-create the sexes and thus save the human race from certain extinction" (6). Underneath this grandiose claim to be redressing an ancient injustice and saving the world is a smaller, funnier, and nastier desire: namely, to take revenge (on Myron's behalf) for all the indignities visited upon him during his years on earth as a homosexual. Men like Buck Loner, sleazy and exploitative, must be punished for what they did to Myron.

Myra is a terrible intellectual snob, and her experience dealing with the terminally thought-free Californian students at the Buck Loner Academy is shot through with refreshing contempt. Among Myra's first students in "Posture," for instance, are a sincere young man called Rusty and his girlfriend Mary-Ann: "He is tall with a great deal of sand-colored curly hair and sideburns; he has pale blue eyes with long black lashes and a curving mouth on the order of the late Richard Cromwell, so satisfyingly tortured in *Lives of a Bengal Lancer*. From a certain unevenly rounded thickness at the crotch of his blue jeans, it is safe to assume that he is marvelously hung. Unfortunately he is hot for an extremely pretty girl with long straight blonde hair (dyed), beautiful legs and breasts, reminiscent of Lupe Velez. She is mentally retarded. When I asked her to rise she did not recognize the word 'rise' and so I had to ask her 'to get up' which she did understand" (27). Myra's distaste for such plebeian phrases as "get up" betrays her queenly, male origins.

Myra's plan to wreak vengeance on the male sex takes an interesting (and fateful) turn when, instead of seducing Buck Loner, she begins to seduce Rusty.

Seduce is perhaps the wrong word. What she does is rape him — both literally (with a strap-on dildo, while pretending to give him a physical) and emotionally (by treating him like a "boy"). Eventually, she will seduce Mary-Ann and thus put Rusty permanently out of the erotic loop by making him (and all men) sexually irrelevant. This scheme will make Myra Breckinridge not so much Woman Triumphant, "whom no man will ever possess," as Faggot Triumphant, whom no man will ever humiliate. The gradual predatory attack on Rusty is one of the hottest such scenes in any novel, gay or straight. But, like *The Story of O*, Myra's prose is as elegant as it is pornographic: "Now in the person of Rusty, I was able, as Woman Triumphant, to destroy the adored destroyer" (150). (It sounds like *Britannicus!*) Just as Myra is dandyishly committed to truth, no matter how cruel ("No truth should ever be withheld. Without precise notation and interpretation there is only chaos" [37]), so Vidal is committed to presenting the scene with virtually no moral indignation — hence its combination of sexual heat, linguistic elegance, and wit. If we laugh, it is with a red face. *I* certainly remember reading it with caught breath and a knot in my Jockeys.

After the rape, Rusty disappears from the Buck Loner Academy and Mary-Ann is worried. It turns out that, humiliated by Myra's rape, he has fled to Letitia Van Allen, a sexually voracious Hollywood agent, who is delighted to have the services of "the best Grade A stud I have ever had" (167). Indeed, Rusty's excellence in bed takes a sadistic turn, to Letitia's delight: Letitia likes to be beaten up, and Rusty, smarting from Myra's unmanning rape, is just the man to do it. Strangely, as Myra's second, ultimate triumph of seducing Mary-Ann becomes more and more possible — she brings Mary-Ann "accidentally" to Letitia's beach house, where Mary-Ann of course sees Rusty and divines his purpose — Myra becomes not more but less domineering. "Never in my life," she sighs sentimentally, "have I felt so entirely warm and contented" as when comforting Mary-Ann by taking her in her arms (173). No longer do we hear the arrogant voice of the virago (and the faggot), but instead that of the sensitive woman: "I must have Mary-Ann but only if she wants me" (175). The old Myra would never have spoken like that.

Ultimately, indeed, Myra's experiment in androgyny fails in two ways. She loses interest in avenging Myron by torturing men like Buck and Rusty: the rape seems to have satisfied her every wish in that direction. More materially, she is run down by a car and awakes to find herself in the hospital, deprived of her sustaining hormone shots. "Was it an accident, or was it . . . who? Rusty? Buck? I am suddenly filled with suspicion. Two weeks ago I was almost run over in front of Larue's. A coincidence? Well, if either of those sons-of-bitches did this to me I will have his God-damned head or my name is not Myron Breckin-ridge!" (203). The change of name from Myra to Myron (which Myra herself does not seem to have noticed) signals the apex of the novel. For "Myra" is now turning back, unwillingly, into Myron; and in one of the funniest short chapters in world literature, discovers the fact. Chapter 41 runs, in its entirety: "Where are my breasts? *Where are my breasts?*" (210).

The novel ends in a state of deceptive harmony: something akin to what Myra has earlier decried as the "Tahitianization" of intellect and style in California. Through whatever malign influence, her hormone shots *were* stopped; but instead of returning to the sexual predations of the homosexual "Myron," she becomes a parody of bland heterosexual womanhood, full of bemused, forgiving shakes of the head over her own former arrogance: "What an extraordinary document!" she coos. "I have spent all morning reading this notebook [sc., the text we ourselves have read, aka *Myra Breckinridge*] and I can hardly believe that I was ever the person who wrote those demented pages." Three years have apparently passed between chapters 41 and 42; and Myra (now Myron, though still ball-less) has actually married Mary-Ann, with whom s/he lives contentedly in the San Fernando Valley. But just listen to her prose: she has *become* Mary-Ann, it seems: "The house is modern with every convenience and I have just built an outdoor barbecue pit which is much admired by the neighbors, many of whom are personalities in show business or otherwise work in some capacity or another in the Industry. Ours is a friendly community, with many fine people to share interests with" (211). Myra/on and Mary-Ann have become Christian Scientists because "we tend to believe that what happens in this life is for the best." Rusty, by contrast, has become the "Number Four Box Office Star in the World," and also, "I'm sorry to learn, a complete homosexual, for which I feel a certain degree of responsibility and guilt" (212). Her analyst and dentist, Dr. Rudolph Montag, has himself gone Californian, and devotes himself to eating ice cream. And as s/he looks back over the tale of Myra Breckinridge, Myra/on clucks his/her tongue: "it is a proven fact that happiness, like the proverbial bluebird, is to be found in your own backyard if you just know where to look" (213).

Myra, who is fascinated by what she calls the "uterine mysteries," remains nonetheless completely alienated from them. She is nowhere more of a "man" than when, ball-less, she rapes Rusty or less literally screws Buck Loner out of half his property. And, in a brilliant irony, she is nowhere more "feminine" than when she becomes "Myron" once again — only a bland sexless Myron, assimilated to the California suburbs s/he formerly abhorred: "Ours is a friendly community, with many fine people to share interests with." Heterosexuality, it would appear, is as devastating to your prose as to your wits.

If, as Liam Hudson and Bernadine Jacot have claimed in *The Way Men Think,* "men's tendency [is] to conceive of people as though they were inanimate, and of inanimate objects as though they were people," then Myra/Myron is the most masculine creature imaginable.[9] Not only is she capable of raping

Rusty without a single twinge of what the "entirely emotional" Dr. Montag calls "male empathy" (164–65), she can even (as we find out in a casual aside) undergo her own sex-change operation *fully conscious;* thus treating her/ his own body as an "inanimate object": this is the very acme of male self-realization, ironically perfected in the act of emasculation. Maleness is, in Myra Breckinridge, not refuted or destroyed (as she piously claims to wish) but trans-figured from literal to symbolic possession of a phallus. Her willfulness and aggression, her hostility to any kind of weakness or vagueness, her embrace of power for its own sake and love of aesthetic over moral beauty are all acts of the same "thrusting" will that dominates Rusty and hopes to "shatter" (but cannot) the "uterine mysteries" (189–90).

Myra's claim to be wreaking vengeance not for personal pleasure, but for the future of the human race, is thus to be taken with a large grain of salt. (She is at her most amusing when acting the role of farsighted intellectual, just as Falstaff is most subversive when he plays "Monsieur Remorse.") She undertakes the reformation of Buck Loner because she enjoys it, just as she rapes the handsome dumb Rusty because she enjoys it, even though the dildo she uses on him can convey no literal sensations to her. It is the idea of sex that she likes. So, too, with her proud, reasonable defense of bisexualism as the path of the future. Though officially committed to the belief in the parity of the sexes and sexual orientations, in fact she rather dislikes women: "I am jealous of all women though I do not need to be" (37). Nor, except for arid liberal theorizing, does she much like lesbians (whom she refers to dismissively as "les girls").

Another name for this thrusting will is (in both senses of the word) *discrimination.* Myra, like Vidal, Camille Paglia, Boyd McDonald, Diana Vreeland, and other gay and metagay writers, is a committed worshiper of discrimination, even if that means hurting people's feelings or ridiculing pious social fictions of equality. As Paglia herself has seen, late-romantic dandyism is completely different from early-romantic democracy: "High Romantic politics were populist and democratic, but Late Romantic ones are reactionary. Dandyism is 'a new kind of aristocracy,' a 'haughty and exclusive' sect resisting 'the rising tide of democracy, which invades and levels everything.' "[10] The dandy, the aesthete, the faggot are all rightly mistrusted by good liberals because their alienation is radical enough to push them into the reactionary camp. Even in the least haughty, most genuinely democratic of these writers, such as Boyd McDonald, there is nonetheless a strong whiff of elitism. Though he lived the last years of his life in an SRO hotel, he didn't go to Harvard for nothing: he always uses "hards on" for the plural of "hard on." The effect is both funny and unnerving.

It has always seemed to me obvious that in Myra Breckinridge Vidal has not only created his greatest gay men (though Myra is, strictly speaking, neither male nor gay), but also struck his fiercest blow for gay liberation. It is here, rather than in the politically courageous but artistically timid *The City and the*

Pillar (1949), that he makes his most characteristically arrogant moves. (The earlier novel wants you to like it. *Myra Breckinridge,* hostile and virtuosic, doesn't care.) It is here that the gay reader, or the interested straight one, can find a continuation of the Wildean dandyism that subordinates everything — morality, knowledge, even pleasure — to the demands of beauty and power.

It thus occupies a special place among gay novels. Not only is it good in itself, so to speak, but it makes a new and dramatic move in the discourse of gay fiction: it allows the queen, Myra, to dominate the discussion. By doing so, Vidal is able to state the worldview of the sexual outsider with brutal and contemptuous clarity. This is not a book that pleads for anything, let alone understanding, forgiveness, fairness, or the mere redress of grievances. It is a book on the attack. Like its main character, it asks nothing from the straight world, and instead pronounces judgment on it.

The judgment is conveyed not only in what Myra says but how she says it. Her characteristic voice — ruthlessly judicious and at the same time extravagantly untrue — praises the films of Pandro S. Berman in ridiculously grandiose language: "MGM without Pandro S. Berman is like the American flag without its stars" (31). It is the expression of a gay fantasy of total control: Can you stop me? Can you say I'm *wrong*? This dream of control goes far beyond sex (Letitia Van Allen's taste for getting beat up is bumptiously "normal" by comparison) to a quasi-Nietzschean transvaluation of values.

One value that has been transvalued is "decency" — that hypocritical regard we all show to "the opinions of mankind." "Decency" is a quality we can neither do with nor do without. Indeed, one is never sure if it's a virtue or a vice. If the former, then its opposite might be the vice of indecency or obscenity; if the latter, its opposite might be candor. Perhaps its most shocking antonym is shamelessness, or better, a refusal to be shamed. This last is Myra's virtue/vice par excellence. The refusal to be shamed lies at the heart of gay culture. Homosexuals and aesthetes have perfected this unnerving candor, which simply doesn't bother to lie. *The Importance of Being Earnest,* for example, is funny in just the opposite way of most comedies: not because the characters are dissembling their motives, but because they are revealing them so shamelessly. When Algernon asks Cecily if he may look at her diary, she quickly covers it up, while blushfully saying the most unblushing lines: "Oh no. You see, it is simply a very young girl's record of her own thoughts and impressions, and consequently meant for publication."[11] Myra, too, is shameless in various ways. One is the affectation of total objectivity which is her secret dream of omnipotence; another is her unashamed elitism. She thus attempts to outdo the *nouveau roman* by describing a stain on the wall of her motel room: "The mark on the wall is two feet three inches wide and four feet eight and a fraction inches high. Already I have failed to be completely accurate. I must write 'fraction' because I can't read the little numbers on the ruler without my glasses which I never wear" (8).

Again, "More than ever am I convinced that the only useful form left to literature in the post-Gutenberg age is the memoir: the absolute truth, copied precisely from life, preferably at the moment it is happening . . ." (17). That neither
Myra nor anybody else *can* tell "the absolute truth, copied precisely from life"
does not undermine the radicalness of her impudent attempt, for the intention
to tell "the absolute truth," unvarnished by kindness or sentiment, is itself
shameless. It is not an innocent shamelessness, but precisely an experienced one,
defying the viewer to look back, as it were.

We see Myra's shamelessness not only in this highly self-conscious affectation
of objectivity but in the unfiltered arrogance and elitism that are her natural
mode of thinking. She is arrogant, of course, in obvious and discomforting
ways, as in her anti-Semitism and racism. She refers to one of the few black
teachers at the Buck Loner Academy, a "recent convert to the Bahai religion," by
various uncomplimentary nicknames: Bahai, Black Beauty, Mother Africa,
Darkness at Noon. Her colleague Miss Cluff is "lean and profoundly Lesbian"
(70). Dr. Montag, Myra/Myron's friend and analyst, "was a nonconformist; he
chose to be a dentist, that last resort of the rabbi *manqué*" (75). Or: "Intellectually, Dr. Montag is aware of the variety of normal human sexual response but,
emotionally, no dentist from the Grand Concourse of the Bronx can ever accept
the idea that a woman could or should find quite as much pleasure with her own
sex as she does with men" (86). In a last disdainful gesture, Vidal moves Dr.
Montag to L.A., where, at the end of the book, he gives way to his greedy
appetite for ice cream.

This is the bitchiness of the aesthete, dandy, and faggot. It is intended not
so much to damage blacks, lesbians, or Jews as the mild-mannered "decent"
reader's sentimental assumptions about them. It attacks the usual American
expectation that one will soft-pedal one's harsher opinions of others, being
particularly careful not to hurt their feelings. Myra, the dandy (and ex-gay
man), has no sympathy with this view. She argues with the Bahai convert who
actually *believes* in the "Buck Loner philosophy" of making his untalented
students feel good about themselves. He tries unsuccessfully to persuade Myra
" 'It is necessary to have love for all things, particularly those young people
entrusted to our care.' " Myra is having none of it: " 'Love,' I said, 'ought never
to exclude truth.' 'But love does not wound.' . . . He continued for some time in
this vein," she adds frigidly (70).

Myra's deeper arrogance lies in her mastery of aesthetic detail, especially of
film; but more important, in her implicit judgment that any opinion *not* so
detailed is simply worthless. Her diaries are full of observations like "Rusty's
voice was deep and warm and he gave me a level gaze reminiscent of James
Craig in the fourth reel of *Marriage Is a Private Affair*" (117). Notice that the
reference must be not only preternaturally clear (the "fourth reel") but arcane
(*Marriage Is a Private Affair*). The queenly note is struck, as usual, by an

inversion, in this case of the usual valuation of such things as "detail" and "obscurity." In a culture that worships the big gesture, the sloppy emotional release, the vague idea of depth (a culture, Myra darkly suspects, of television watchers), it is revolutionary to be interested in the small exact detail, the "insignificant," the merely outward. This inversion is one of the oldest and most potent queenly/homosexual weapons. (Cf. Algernon's "I hate people who are not serious about meals. It is so shallow of them.") It will be heard again in Boyd McDonald's maniacal attention to the butts of forgotten movie stars; in Paglia's impudent claim in *Sexual Personae* that *Auntie Mame* is the greatest American novel of the mid-century;[12] and in Diana Vreeland's most vivid memory of the Occupation of Paris in World War II: finding cold tea in a flask she thought contained brandy.[13]

The essence of Myra's intellectual/aesthetic attitude is a kind of excessive obsessional clarity, which is funny but not entirely dismissable. (We are, after all, officially committed to the virtue of clear thought and feeling, even though most of the time we have no intention of living by such counsels of perfection.) Her enemy throughout is the *blurry*: speaking, resignedly, of her students at the Buck Loner Academy, she says, "Traditional human speech seems to have passed them by, but then one must never forget that they are the first creations of that television culture which began in the early Fifties. Their formative years were spent watching pale gray figures (no blacks, no whites — significant detail) move upon a twenty-one-inch screen" (26–27). She dislikes the pot she smokes at her student Clem's party: it gives her a hangover and renders the others "passive." She dislikes whimsy, a blurry form of wit that melts distinctions in a warm bath of good humor: "They wear buttons which, among other things, accuse the Governor of California of being a Lesbian, the President of being God, and Frodo (a character in a fairy tale by Tolkien) of actually existing. This is all a bit fey for my taste" (50). Buck Loner "represents all that I detest in the post-Forties culture: a permissive slovenliness of mind and art" (44). California, where the novel takes place, is itself the symbol of all forms of blur: "of course Clem is Jewish but he has been entirely absorbed by California, that great sponge into which all things are drawn and promptly homogenized, including Judaism" (89).

Thus, although she "share[s] the normal human response to whatever is attractive physically in either sex" (86), Myra for most of the book relishes the sex roles she intends to shatter (otherwise what would there be to shatter?). And the book is not (despite Myra's official commendations of bisexuality) a plea for reason in sexual affairs, but a rationalization of power: women's power, gay men's power. Her very body is a battlefield where masculinity and femininity perpetually wage war, a warfare made even more explicit in *Myron,* the sequel to *Myra Breckinridge,* where Myra and Myron duke it out over which one is "real" and which one belongs in permanent exile on the set of *Siren of Babylon*

(1949). There is nothing soothing about Myra's views, except when she is re-transformed into Myron at the end and begins to write *Reader's Digest* prose.

This is the power of the book for gay men, as well; for it gives us in Myra a champion, someone almost ridiculously clearheaded about the sleazy evasions of culturally imposed heterosexuality (perhaps best symbolized by the constantly horny, terminally stupid Buck Loner). Although Myra is not, in any simple way, the "hero" of this book — there is much that is ridiculous about her, as even "Myron" knows at the end — the others are simply worse. Buck is a sleazebag who never had much talent to begin with, and now exploits the talentlessness of others. Rusty, after his rape, becomes a violent misogynist, breaking (to her delight) most of Letitia Van Allen's bones. Mary-Ann seems (until Myra starts falling in love with her) "mentally retarded" precisely because she is "nice." The straight swingers like Clem, who organize the orgy Myra attends, are "physically unimpressive males forced to rely upon personality and money to get girls to bed" (88). Note the dandyish contempt for anything nonphysical (such as "personality and money"). A big or small dick *is* the truth about a man: the book *is* the cover. Wilde himself could not have done better.

By refusing to concede moral primacy to such blurry emotions as "Empathy" (her ironic teaching assignment at the Academy), Myra can see what others cannot. But *all* sexual outsiders (especially gay men) see what Myra sees. The novel liberates by daring to show heterosexuality from the outside, as one possible construction of the world among many others — not, as the dominant society would prefer, as the only possible construction. To reduce, however unfairly, heterosexuality to the instance of Buck Loner is to see it clearly and direly indeed. As we shall see, this inversion is one of the jokes Boyd McDonald repeatedly makes as well.

Indeed, to see the straight characters Buck Loner, Rusty Godowski, Mary-Ann Pringle, and Dr. Montag as "ridiculous" is far more liberating than to see them as "dangerous." Vidal's great achievement is to realize that seeing "objectively" entails precisely the forbidden fruit of seeing people *as objects,* which Myra at times seems to think the condition for the possibility of any knowledge. Myra, we may recall, saw even herself (or rather himself) as such an object when she remained conscious "during all stages of my [sex-change] transformation." In this way, the weapon of objectivity is turned first against herself (as it is for all gay people), but then, triumphantly, against the enemy.

BOYD MCDONALD'S *STRAIGHT TO HELL*

The editor of *Straight to Hell,* an obscure man named Boyd McDonald (1925–1993), was, by all usual standards, a failure. An alcoholic and perhaps, in today's jargon, a "sex addict" as well, he is remembered (in true dandy fashion) only by his work: a chronicle of gay sex in the years that followed World War II. He would seem at first glance utterly removed from the category "dandy," someone utterly indifferent to outward appearances and thus an unlikely successor to fops like Beau Brummell; someone uninterested in being bad or "damned," and thus an unlikely descendant of Byron or Baudelaire. He was also one of the first to show me how, in true Wildean fashion, one could use the categories of sexuality that oppress gay people by inverting them, turning them against the oppressor.

He is also the only writer of nonfiction I have included in this book. But though he was not himself a "creative writer" — whatever that means — he was an influence on some who were, including Gore Vidal and William Burroughs, who apparently read his revolutionary sex magazine *Straight to Hell* with eagerness and admiration.[14] His name is unfamiliar even to many gay men, but he is and was a hero of mine, one of the first writers I came across who talked about being gay the way my friends and I did. Indeed, he came to *seem* a friend; and for this reason, I have found it nearly impossible to refer to him here as "McDonald." He was always, to me, "Boyd." Anything more formal would be almost false to his no-nonsense, unpretentious voice.

Straight to Hell, variously subtitled *The New York Review of Cocksucking, Archives of the American Academy of Homosexual Research,* and *The Manhattan Review of Unnatural Acts,* was a periodical magazine published from the early seventies through the mid-eighties. (It continues to be published by a different editor.) Its main subject — words are inadequate to say just *how* "main" — was sex between men, as reported in explicit letters from hundreds of correspondents throughout the country, and in commentaries and reviews by Boyd himself on the same subject. *Straight to Hell* not only put the sex back in homosexuality but back in everything. Boyd McDonald was constitutionally unable to see the world through other than sex-colored glasses — not the glasses of the pornographer or the preacher, but of the historical researcher meticulously gathering "facts." McDonald was ideally suited to such a view, being profoundly unjudgmental. His unjudgmentalism — or amorality, as it sometimes seems — permeated everything he wrote about, from blow jobs to Hollywood movies to current politics. He looked at sex with interest, enthusiasm, heat — but never with solemnity. His was the clear-eyed, unsentimental view of the urban homosexual, and it is a permanent achievement even now, more than twenty years after the magazine's foundation. He was in many ways the Myra Breckinridge of sex: obsessed, dandified, cruel, and funny. *Straight to Hell* is shamelessness taken to the next power.

Straight to Hell was founded when McDonald stopped drinking and started receiving a welfare check to cover his unemployment. He turned the money over into printing up letters he'd solicited in the gay press about foreskin fetishism, then an interest of his. (He liked to say that *Straight to Hell* was the only gay sex magazine funded by a grant from the U.S. government.) From the prepuce, he turned his attention to the whole man, and his newsletters began to include true stories from correspondents with all sorts of sexual interests, not just that particular one. *STH* grew within ten years from the smallest of small magazines, with a circulation of a few hundred, to a magazine known to many gay men of the seventies, with a paid circulation at its peak of ten thousand. Subsequent collections in book form — *Meat, Cream, Smut,* and so on — regularly sold as many as fifty thousand copies. At the time of his death in 1993, there were no fewer than thirteen titles in this series, the most recent being *Raunch, Lewd,* and *Scum.*[15]

STH was a formative influence on me and, I suspect, on a generation of gay men who came of age in the seventies, after the Stonewall riots and the antiwar movement. We were different from earlier generations of gay men partly because we were simply more numerous — we were part of the baby boom — but also because we were far more self-confident, even arrogant. We demanded sexually explicit literature and got it; but we wanted that literature to be proud, not ashamed. That was harder to come by. *STH* answered the need for unashamed discussion of sex and in so doing helped create the modern gay man. It singlehandedly transferred erotic discourse from the realm of shame and fantasy to that of shamelessness and truth. After *STH,* with its hundreds of letters from ordinary gay men reporting thousands of unrepented homosexual acts, ordinary pornography's appeal to furtive pleasure and unreal fantasy seemed tame. Mere pornography was to *STH* what fantasizing about your neighbor's sex life was to watching him go at it through a carelessly uncurtained window. No matter what your neighbor looked like (within reason), he was hotter in actuality than the hottest image you could mentally make of him.

But *STH* also transformed gay sensibility, and did so in a way strikingly like Vidal's in *Myra Breckinridge.* The poet Thom Gunn, who was an early fan of the magazine, said he was far more influenced by "the wit and style" of *Straight to Hell* than by the "tiresome campiness" of the early-twentieth-century novelist Ronald Firbank, often held up as an avatar of "gay sensibility." Gunn's comments indicate a fissure in gay history, as does *STH* itself: the fissure between a homosexuality defined not by its sex acts but by the sublimations of them, such as opera and ballet,[16] and a homosexuality that was primarily sexual: a gay man was a man who sucked cock. *STH* in fact somewhat bridged the fissure because McDonald's writing style and deadpan humor *were* camp in some way. What was uncamp (or at least "untiresome") was his combination of this style with the subject matter of actual, down-and-dirty sex, of wit with lust. Most writing about sex, then and now, tended to be either naughty or sentimental. *STH* was neither, but rather openly, dazzlingly obsessed.

I don't remember when I first became aware of *STH,* though I know I had a subscription to it as early as 1974. At the time I was teaching at a small college, which, though only thirty miles from Washington or Baltimore, seemed utterly stranded and straight. McDonald's magazines were one of my lifelines to — not the gay world, but the world of gay men, the world of gay sex. Far more than any political organization, *STH* inspired and informed me about what was going on. Reading these "dispatches" from the sexual front — the wartime terminology is somehow appropriate — I realized that men were having sex with each other everywhere all the time, and was thus encouraged to go and do likewise. As I hoped, and as *STH* documented, no Sears men's room was safe, no movie theater, no train station, no college gym. The prospects were dazzling because they were real. One of my favorite letters from *STH* says it best:

> One night in Odessa, Texas, where the air is the consistency of evaporated Vaseline, and smells like it, I saw two guys on line in an almost empty Taco Bell. They were 25–28, very well built, nicely dressed cowboy fashion, hats and boots, great shirts, nice asses. It wasn't until they sat down — they were the only other ones in the place to sit down — that I saw they were madly in love. They stared into one another's eyes, played kneesies, one had a definite hard on, couldn't see the other's groin, and they could hardly keep their hands off one another. They left in a welldiggers' truck. It's everywhere. (No. 47 [1980], 19)

What you got when you opened your *STH* envelope was a small — 8″ x 5″ — "chapbook," suitable for one-handed reading. It was always very elegant in appearance, printed on high-quality paper in a professional layout, with crisp typeface and clearly reproduced dirty photos. Frequently McDonald added bizarrely Victorian curlicues around the covers, or the coat of arms of the house of Windsor: an *hommage* to the queenliness he otherwise disdained. There were almost never any typos, and indeed, Boyd gleefully quoted errors from less scrupulously edited journals like *The New York Times,* which he referred to as his "principal competitor." The look and feel of the magazine were as clean as the subject matter was dirty.

STH was thus in marked contrast to such superficially similar enterprises as today's fanzines. McDonald's "chapbooks" were witty in combining elitist style and democratic content; indeed the very word *chapbook* is pure Boyd, being both archaic and up-to-date. ("Chapbooks" are cheap books, small collections of popular ballads, poems, and stories.) By contrast, the look of many 'zines is ostentatiously casual, even slovenly; an effect of collage is often attempted, with individual cutout letters scattered all over the page, like a poison pen letter in an Agatha Christie novel. Sometimes the lineation is deliberately off: as if the 'zine had been typed rather than word-processed. Often printed on bad paper, 'zines make an overt visual claim to having been just "thrown together." They are a protest against too much forethought, though to my mind they protest too much.

Boyd's magazine was exactly the reverse, and for interesting reasons. Where the average 'zine is meant to look wrong, *STH* was meant to look right. The 'zine subverts, or hopes to, the very notion of what a "right" look for a magazine would be; Boyd ostentatiously played by the rules, and thus inverted the usual meaning of style and substance by dignifying low sex with high cultural accoutrements. *STH* was meant to criticize and even compete with the straight press, to beat it at its own game. The 'zine, by its deliberately unprofessional look, disdains the mainstream press and opts out of competition altogether. It is interesting, in this connection, that *Christopher Street* magazine, founded about five years after *STH,* also attempted a direct comparison with the straight press, in its case with *The New Yorker,* which it obviously and deliberately resembled in its first years.[17]

What was in *STH* fell into two categories: the larger part was letters and questionnaires written by correspondents about their sexual pasts and presents. They were short or long, well or badly written, a turn-on, a turn-off. Some of the correspondents were plainly educated, some almost illiterate. The style ranged from the witty to the plodding to the frankly salacious; the stories from the well-constructed to the off-the-cuff to the incoherent or inconclusive. Boyd always claimed to have altered nothing about these letters, except by shortening them for publication. Some people have charged that he wrote them all himself, as is the practice in "Letters" columns in commercial sex mags such as *Forum* or *Variations.* But there is nothing less like the overwritten, solemn erotic letters from "Mrs. L.H. of San Diego" about how bondage saved her marriage than the letters we find in *Straight to Hell.* Whether they are well or badly written, tell a hot or merely a weird story, the *STH* letters are always unpredictable, not written to any rule, and almost never obviously "uplifting." Many of them are stories of, if not outright failure, at least less than ideal success: many of them end, for instance, with something like "We arranged to meet the next week, but he didn't show up" or "I have always regretted not going back." If this is pornography, it's incompetent. Furthermore, the variety of styles is so great that if Boyd did write them all, his achievement is equal to Balzac's, and *STH* the greatest novel of the twentieth century. Even I do not think Boyd McDonald capable of that kind of genius.

The rest of the magazine was by Boyd and consisted of book reviews and political commentary. Every now and then he would throw in a brief fictional piece of his own, such as the Myra Breckinridge–like "The Man in the Nylon Jock Strap," but his gifts were really not fictional.[18] His unmistakable prose style got in the way of his characters' conversation, all of which tended to sound like his own (another reason I do not believe he wrote the letters he published).

But his laconic captions to photographs of political figures were inspired. One of my favorites showed Bert Lance, Jimmy Carter's indicted treasury secretary, holding his infant grandson and beaming heterosexual innocence at the camera. Boyd's three-word caption summed up the sleaziness of the man and of the media: "Grandfather Exploits Baby" (no. 38 [1978], 17).

Another regular section of the magazine was composed of news-clippings from the straight press, which does print astonishing things, if you keep your eyes open. These stories often appeared under the German title "*Nachrichten aus der Straight-welt,*" news from the straight world, and were adorned by an engraving of the two-headed eagle of the Austro-Hungarian empire. (If this is camp, it is so in a way far beyond the casual dish of girlfriends in the bar.) Besides politicians, Boyd's favorite news items concerned sports figures who seem to be considered interesting no matter what they do. A typical entry runs: "Howdy, sports lovers. Doug Williams of the Tampa Bay Buccaneers vomited at 12:30 P.M. September 11, according to the *New York Daily News,* whose large staff of jock-sniffers (sports reporters) adores male athletes in sickness and in health" (no. 48 [1980], 14). This not only satirizes the triviality of the daily press, but impugns the heterosexuality of its reporters ("jock-sniffers").

Perhaps the best way to give an idea of what it was like to open up one of these eagerly expected envelopes is to describe what appears in the first ten pages of a random issue, number 45.[19] The cover shows a beautiful boy from the rear, his balls hanging tantalizingly between his thighs. To his right, in italic script, is the title *Archives of the American Academy of Homosexual Research,* one of Boyd's many poker-faced names for *STH;* above it, elegantly reproduced, is an engraving of a caryatid. To the left of the boy is another engraving of a Renaissance pediment, below which is a holiday subscription offer: "This Christmas/Hanukkah give *STH* to someone you love; next Christmas/Hanukkah you may not love him enough to."

As you open Issue 45, you see on the left the masthead of the publication. "THE MANHATTAN REVIEW," it reads, in capital letters: "Archives of the American Academy of Homosexual Research." In addition to the mailing address is a description of the magazine: "A magazine for the lower and upper classes: always coarse, never vulgar. Vulgarity is for the R.M.C. (Rising Middle Class)." The masthead concludes with a quote from Gertrude Stein which Boyd particularly liked: "What a day is today! — that is to say,/What a day was the day before yesterday." The significance of its inclusion was always (to me) mystifying, though I liked the quote. Knowing Boyd, it would be hard to say, however, whether this was included as an unequivocal enthusiasm for Stein, or a mockery of her dizzy prose.

The first article is an interview with a middle-aged man who had had a fifteen-year affair with one of his employees, a handsome younger married man. Boyd calls it, in his parody of tabloid style, "Rhapsody in Green," an allusion to the fact that the straight man was kept, and thus essentially a prostitute. (So much for heterosexual identity!) The interview is remarkable for several things. One is its truthfulness, rather than fantasy: the interviewee often doesn't give Boyd what he is plainly angling for. For instance, one of Boyd's creeds was that sex was the main pleasure in life. The interviewee refuses to parrot this line: "I am made happy by love, money, intellectual interests, entertainment, work and sex, with a question mark over the sex" (5). The second remarkable thing is simply the interviewee's own intelligence and perception about himself, qualities that are not usually associated with sex writing. "What was [the younger man's] character?" Boyd asks. The interviewee answers: "He was neither nice nor predatory. Confident. Limited. Energetic. Very tough, though not necessarily physically. He was fraught with weaknesses, mostly emotionally. Limited is a better word. He prized security. He was occasionally warm, more often friendly, but never more, and often less" (4). This is a marvelously exact, ungrandstanding description of the straight men in our lives. Another is even more dazzling: "Indifference came easily to him," a sentence any novelist would be proud to have written.

The next six pages can be described more quickly, beginning with two letters from Boston ("Bostonian, 29, Cruises in Cop Drag" and "Horny, Can't Study" — the latter asking wistfully "Anyone out there from MIT? Write Dave, Box 290, 118 Mass Ave. Boston"). The title of another long interview gives an adequate idea of its subject: "Sucks 15 Youths in Woods." A third ("Priest Meets Sir Winston, Picks Up M.P.") is an astonishing tale about cruising a "handsome blonde M.P." in the House of Commons *while meeting Winston Churchill*. (Was this "made up?" I doubt it. Gay life *is* such improbable contradictions.) The tenth page concludes with a clip from the *Berkeley Barb:* "There is an unofficial race on between *Hustler* and *Playgirl* as to which will show the first completely erect male penis." Boyd comments witheringly: "Even I know that there is no such thing as a female penis. Things have reached a pretty pass when homosexual editors have to correct their 'straight' brethren on the subject of women," and titles the story "A Golden Treasury of American Authors." (Notice that, as in *Myra Breckinridge,* even the counterculture is a fit target, primarily because of its contempt for precision.)

If there is a theme to Boyd's writing, and to the *STH* series itself, it is that (as he put it) "In the long run, the only thing that has any real class, or real dignity, or respectability or responsibility is the shameless truth" (no. 48 [1980], 2). This is not only the voice, but the very assertion of Myra herself. Unlike pornographic magazines, however, *STH* did not sacrifice truth to shamelessness — did not, that is, incite its writers to greater and more lurid displays of "shamelessness." It was the true story, not the hot one, that Boyd was after; or rather, as he said, a true story was by its very nature hot, hotter than any fiction. His maga-zines went beyond shamelessness to something for which we have no word: "unashamedness" will have to do. Boyd always instructed future correspon-dents to write only what actually happened, not to spruce anything up. There was nothing to be ashamed of in a story that ended badly or inconclusively. You didn't need to claim that sex was better than it was for your story to be absorb-ing. No truth was too small to tell, just as no cock was too small to be sucked.

As a lover of facts about sex, Boyd was necessarily a hater of respectability, which tends to blur such facts. (In another resemblance to *Myra,* the tendency to blur, whether through inattention, dishonesty, or sentimentality, is the en-emy.) He particularly loathed what he saw as the mainstreaming of homosex-uality symbolized by "gay weddings." He felt that most so-called gay leaders — publishers, politicos, spokespeople — were cowards. "The gay press has to be sexless because they are public. And in order to be publicly gay they have to be closet homosexuals. . . . My books are all about their private lives. It has nothing to do with gay liberation, gay rights, gays in the military, civil rights, fundrais-ing, political candidates, and all that stuff. If you're going to be a lobbyist or lawyer running a fundraising campaign, you cannot be sexual." To him, in fact, there was "no such thing as an open homosexual. There are people who are openly gay, which is something else again. Gay is abstract. Homosexuality is very specific, like in my books."[20]

Homosexuality was for McDonald an obsession, as he often said. The word is notable, and points to the ongoing truth and radicality of his work. It is not even obsessiveness itself that is so radical, for if so we are all radical. Rather, it is *not concealing* one's obsession. (Note, again, the resemblance to Wilde's com-pletely candid characters in *Earnest.*) He wanted to return to sex its raw, un-pretty power. He never, for example, speaks of sex as "fun" or "playful," as was the manner of such seventies classics as Silverstein and White's *Joy of Gay Sex.* One almost feels sex was for him a sort of job (only an interesting one): a duty, a privilege, an election. While he was never solemn about sex — never a preacher like D. H. Lawrence, for instance — he was fundamentally serious about it. This utterly differentiated him from those middle-class gays who want to be just like straight people, with their own weddings and commitment ceremonies, their own Absolut Vodka ads in the *Advocate,* their own congressmen and bishops. But it also would differentiate him from modern "queers" with their bland, whimsical embrace of free-floating undefined desire, now expressing itself as drag, now as bisexuality, now as "playing" at gender or S and M. What he would find missing from both pictures of homosexuality, I think, is precisely what he found missing from Randy Shilts's *Conduct Unbecoming:* "This book by Randy Shilts about gays in the military, *Conduct Unbecoming,* is written in what I would call a US-Department-of-Agriculture *Crop Bulletin* style, or an

Associated Press style. It's absolutely without feeling, passion, heat, lust, or specifics about sex. . . . It's like, 'A soldier had homosexual sex with a sailor' — that's as much as they're going to tell you about it. . . . My books tell what the soldier and the sailor *do.*"[21] Despite Myra's lip service to bisexuality, her rapt pornographic description of Rusty's rape is exactly in the Boyd McDonald manner: he would not have had to ask *her* for a more explicit description of Rusty's underwear, as he did many of his inattentive correspondents.

Boyd himself always called *STH* a work of research and spoke, quite unironically, of its importance to future historians. *STH,* he claimed, told the story of what people were actually doing sexually in the "Golden Age of Cocksucking (1940–1980)." His scrupulous adherence to the truth, refusal to tart up the stories with pornographic prettiness (such as eight-inch dicks, etc.), and witty commentary on both the letters and news from the world make these magazines indeed a work of permanent interest: a possession for the ages, as Thucydides said of his own exact history.

Like Myra, McDonald claims not to have the interest in his sexual fantasy that so many of his readers had: "Just the facts, ma'am" would seem to be their motto. In a brilliant response to one of his correspondents, he writes:

> No, I don't jack off to S.T.H. letters. I am apparently one of the few men who doesn't. I do beat my meat relentlessly, and sometimes have to get off a bus to stop the bratty thing from demanding attention, but my enslavement to reality is so total that my S.T.H. work does not give me hard ons, or should I say, hards on. . . . I publish these letters because they are true, they are news, they are history, they are important evidence on an important subject and I'm interested in fact, not fiction — in what did happen, not what could have happened. Somebody has to counteract all the chicken-shit that's published. All too often — in reading and in life — we look for sex and only find love; all too often we want a nice piece of meat or a nice hot suck hole and only find a wonderful human being.[22]

This remarkable piece of prose shows McDonald at his best and most characteristic. What I notice is its combination of elitism and populism. That is, he's interested in these letters because they are true, not because they are glamorous or pornographic or literary, or come from important people. He is even antiintellectual in his contempt for "chicken-shit" publications, by which he certainly means magazines like *Christopher Street,* newspapers like *The Advocate,* and high- or middle-brow novels by the then-burgeoning Violet Quill writers. At the same time, he is picky about the proper plural of *hard on:* is it "hard ons" (surely the people's choice); or is it "hards on" (the preference of Ivy Leaguers like himself and other people who actually say *shat* for the past tense of *shit*)?

His amusing description of having to get off the bus in order to take care of his "bratty" penis is similarly high-toned, as is his "enslavement to reality." In all this, he sounds like a gay S. J. Perelman, simultaneously using and making fun of the trashy conventions of B-movies and pulp fiction.

It is extremely hard to do justice to sex in words or to do justice to oneself as an intermittently sexually obsessed human being. Sexual desire simply corrodes the social mask we all wear. Boyd's greatest contribution, besides the accumulation of a huge amount of sexual data, was the creation of a language in which to talk about sex. What was that language? One can indicate it inadequately but accurately by saying what it didn't do: namely, titter, snicker, or sneer. He was completely uninterested in the naughtiness of sex or in the nervous deflection of that naughtiness into smirks and giggles. What Gunn called the "tiresome campiness" of old-fashioned gay sensibility comes in part from the notion that talking about sex is deliciously wicked. And if what you're after is the sense of being bad, then you can positively increase that sense by burying your talk about sex under more and more layers of double-entendre and irony — as in Firbank, whose novels are relentlessly sexual, but so convoluted as to appear written in code.[23] The wickedness purveys not only the delights of shame, but the headier addictions of superiority and spite: of being one of the few who can crack the code, so to speak.

While I think more highly of Firbank than Gunn did or Boyd would have, I agree with them that there was a need, in the seventies, for a new language of gay sex, one that would acknowledge the fact that we were suddenly and unprecedentedly free to have sex — and to talk about it. Shame, for the first time since 1920s Germany, was optional, not required. Boyd manages to take from Firbank his refreshing, amoral arrogance while leaving behind the shame that created it. He manages to take from pornography its obsessiveness while leaving behind its strong tendencies toward sentimentality or convention. His style of talking about sex — or allowing other people to — was not therefore *merely* honest or *merely* witty; it was both. (So, too, in *Myra* our heroine is never, even in the orgy scene at Clem's, unconscious: she describes Clem's penis with unflattering irony as "the tiny treasure.") The letters were put in a context of ironic headlines, political commentary, and questionnaires that brought Boyd's own voice and attitude into the picture. The magazines are more than their letters.

To give an idea of what that "more" is, I'd like to quote one of Boyd's funniest self-written articles. Entitled "New Hope for Ageing SM Freaks," it is about — or at least begins by being about — the 1980 shooting of diet-book author Herman Tarnower by his mistress, Jean Harris.[24]

"He hit me," Mrs. Jean Streuven Harris, 56-year-old headmistress of a girls' school, told the cops; "he hit me a lot." He was her lover, Dr. Herman Tarnower, creator of the best-selling "Scarsdale Diet," a typical heterosexual who, even at age 69, was able to get what heterosexuals call "a pieceass" whenever he wanted one to slap around. "He slept with every woman he could," Mrs. Harris reported — meaning, presumably, every time he could get his antique dick hard, since the bundle he made off his diet book and his medical practice meant that money was no hindrance. Mrs. Harris, her lips swollen from the medic's blows, came to the attention of police after she whipped out her rod (for she is apparently an armed Right Winger) and with four bullets put the calorie-counting cardiologist on the ultimate diet, death. (No. 47 [1980], 4)

Besides being a flawless parody of a forties hardboiled detective story (once again, thoroughly in Perelman's manner), this comment is funny because it takes the cultural narrative about "typical homosexuals" and inverts it. Thus, Dr. Tarnower was "a typical heterosexual . . . able to get what heterosexuals call 'a pieceass' whenever he wanted one to slap around." Even the victim is not spared: she is "apparently an armed Right Winger," for in Boyd's world, as in Wilde's and Vidal's, there *are* no innocent victims. By talking about "typical heterosexuals" McDonald inverts the balance of power, making heterosexuals, not homosexuals, seem the odd, distinct class. McDonald thus does in his way what Foucault and Myra Breckinridge were doing at the same time: calling into question the very existence of such classes as heterosexual and homosexual.

Calling into question, but not finally denying, however. Boyd was not an intellectual and would not have followed the current arguments about the origins of the concept of "homosexuality," though he is aware that before Stonewall it was possible for a straight man to have sex with another man without applying the label "homosexual" to himself. (This is why the forties, fifties, and sixties were, for him, "The Golden Age of American Cocksucking" — a phrase that calls out for a coffee-table book.) But he seems ultimately an inverter, rather than a subverter, of the sexual paradigms: that is, he wants homosexuality to continue as a category, the better to trip up and confound and embarrass heterosexuals who think they have everything figured out. He writes characteristically: "my fondness for exhibitionists does not mean that I'd like to live in a nudist colony. On the contrary, there could be no indecent exposure in a nudist colony. The fact that we live in a clothed society makes exhibitionists rare and valiant. In the same way, the fact that we live in a sex-negative society makes active homosexuals valiant. There would be no thrill in homosexuality if the church and state did not supply aphrodisiacs by attacking it."[25]

Boyd was fundamentally an anarchist and a guerrilla fighter, not a revolutionary, if by "revolutionary" we mean one dedicated to the overthrow of the present system. He was neither for nor against the present system; he had scorn for liberal and conservative alike. Boyd thought that one was finally alone in the world and that there was a limit to what the government, or even gay liberation, could do for or against one. He might have agreed with Samuel Johnson, who had a vein of the same bloody-mindedness: "How small, of all that human hearts endure, / That part which laws or kings can cause or cure!"[26]

In my view, Boyd McDonald himself was a valiant figure in gay history. Not only did he encourage a generation — my generation — of gay men to have all the sex it wanted and to tell the truth about it; but he posed sex as the ineradicably weird thing it is, quite irreducible to any ideology, whether of the right or of the left. It will never be polite, never become a mere lifestyle or choice, according to McDonald. All we can do with it is tell the truth about it, and get as much as we possibly can. Why should we have lots of sex? Because (as he puts it in a rare sincere moment) sex simply makes us nicer people: "The prudes pretend that they are the ones who are decent, and the ones in the toilets are indecent, but it's just the other way around. Prudes are mean, and they have a huge deficit in their lives. . . . Some of the most disreputable people are actually much more valuable to society than the respectable people."[27] We will see this view again in Samuel Delany's *The Mad Man*.

He died as he had lived, alone. His body was found in the single room at the Riverside Hotel that he had inhabited for years. He was an odd, obsessed, contradictory man — an unhappy one by many standards, though not, perhaps, by his own. If, as he believed, there are some people to whom homosexuality has a lot to offer, who can profit by their estrangement from the world and its numbing pieties, Boyd McDonald was one of homosexuality's luckiest legatees. He offers us hope, not by vague uplifting sermons but by his mere survival, his refusal to join any club. He was as stubborn and ineradicable as homosexuality itself.

Chapter Three

IMMODESTY AND IMMOLATION

There is a thread of obscenity that runs, red and glistening, through the web of gay literature. We have seen it in Tennessee Williams, Gore Vidal, and Boyd McDonald — even though in none of these cases is the intention or result "pornographic." What we have found in these authors, rather, is what one might call a voyeuristic impulse that invites the complicit reader to construe these scenes sexually. Part of the excitement of reading Williams's short stories, *Myra Breckinridge,* or *Straight to Hell* is that of seeing what one shouldn't see.

This obscenity is hardly surprising, given the fact that homosexuality itself has been one of the things that must be performed offstage (the root meaning of *obscene*). To be homosexual is to be literally unrepresentable. As we have seen, Boyd McDonald was a rigorous subscriber to the view that even today homosexuality (as opposed to "gayness") was private and not presentable, presumably because it was a totally *sexual* identity. Indeed, the only surprise is how quickly a wholesomely prurient interest in the sex lives of fictional characters has been cast off by some newer gay writers, such as David Leavitt, Stephen McCauley, Michael Cunningham, and others. One can understandably desire to tell a story about men who "just happen to be gay" and whose sex life, therefore, is as ordinary and as off-bounds as that of straight characters in "good" novels. But there is a kind of wishful thinking going on among these gay writers and their critical supporters. We are meant to believe that being homosexual carries no weight of social stigma or psychic warfare; that "no one cares" what you do in bed; that gay literature must "get beyond" an "obsession" with sexuality if it is to "mature."[1]

These priggish, plausible notions need challenging; and all have been challenged by a series of gay writers who have kept their eyes fixed in the most honest, voyeuristic way on sex, on what it means for men to have sex with other men. They have refused (unlike the "chicken-shit" gay authors Boyd McDonald had such scorn for) to "translate" homosexuality into either the sublimated language of high culture (as Edmund White has done) or the "mature" (non-sex-obsessed) middle-brow fictions of David Leavitt and his followers. Their books capture the unsafeness of sex, and thus do justice to it.

Further, they arguably do justice not just to sexual passion "in general" (what a profanation of *those* highly specific joys!) but to a peculiarly male experience of sex; one, that is, which includes and enjoys objectification of the body (one's own or someone else's), domination, promiscuity, perversion, and fetishism. Indeed, these writers might be said to explore the "gayest" topic of all: what it means for one man to desire another. Is this eros "the same, only different" by comparison with straight desire? Or (as we might suspect) are the very different sexual assumptions of males and females geometrically exaggerated when it is two men who are erotically involved?

Among the writers who have investigated these questions, and who have kept sex on the front burner of their fiction, are two novelists from widely different gay "generations" and with far different attitudes toward the sex they so vividly present: James Purdy and Dennis Cooper. Purdy is the older. Born in 1927 (and thus a rough contemporary of Boyd McDonald), he came of artistic age in the early fifties (his first novel *63: Dream Palace* was published in 1956, the same year that *Giovanni's Room* saw the light of day). Despite a long and productive career over the next forty years, he remains an outcast and an anomaly. A living voice of the fifties, he brings into later times the ineradicable scars of self-loathing, scars his characters transmute into stigmata of transcendence. For a scar, as many of Purdy's most extreme characters realize, is something to rejoice over, not regret. The tragic liberation his gay characters occasionally achieve, achieves a great deal for us too, precisely because they have labored against such odds, because their victories must be bought at so high a price. Their greatest enemy — gay desire itself — lies within them, and their victory is the Pyrrhic one of submission to that enemy. The most perfect example of this baroque paradox is Daniel Haws in *Eustace Chisholm and the Works* (1968), who atones for having rejected Amos Ratcliffe's love by offering himself as a sacrifice to the sadistic Captain Stadgers. As the language of even my brief description suggests, Purdy's vision of eros is a fundamentally religious, even mystical one.

Dennis Cooper is a postwar baby boomer, with all the invulnerability and entitlement that identity suggests. Born in 1953, he published his first book, a collection of poems called *Tiger Beat,* in 1978, the year that also saw Purdy's *Narrow Rooms,* Larry Kramer's *Faggots,* Edmund White's *Nocturnes for the King of Naples,* and Andrew Holleran's *Dancer from the Dance.* Despite the coincidence of dates (and subject matters), he is in some ways Purdy's exact opposite. Where Purdy finds transcendent value in love and self-abnegation, Cooper denies transcendence to either. His world is a world not of depth but of surfaces, and of these he is an absolute master. Even his "surface" is a new one. It is not the Wildean surface of camp wit, nor — despite some resemblances — even the surface of Bret Easton Ellis's *American Psycho* (1991), with its ridiculous density of social reference. Cooper's is, so to speak, a psychic surface, or rather, psyche *as* surface. The destructive fantasy of Cooper's characters is made genuinely shocking and dangerous by its bored casualness. If everything is difficult in a Purdy novel — made so by social restrictions, by family tyrannies, but most of all by one's own resistance — nothing is difficult in one by Cooper. In the latter, there are no strictures against any act, except in the mind. And even the minds of his characters are puzzled to locate the precise source of the resistance; his books are memoirs by men who aren't sure they have anything to remember.

A third author, Samuel Delany, might be brought in by contrast here, though I will be discussing him later on, in the context of AIDS fiction. Born in 1942, Delany straddles the generations represented by Purdy on the one hand and Cooper on the other. He is neither as "deep" as Purdy nor as designedly "shallow" as Cooper. Although the most overtly pornographic of these writers — there are far more sexual acts per square inch of his erotic novels — he seems paradoxically the least sexually obsessed, the sexually happiest. Even the most violent and disturbing of his erotic works (the long-suppressed *Hogg,* published in 1973 and reissued in 1994) is trying to work out a solution to the tyrannies of sex, tyrannies which drive Hogg and his group of violent enforcers to rape teenage girls, pummel whores almost to death, or pierce their own penises with dirty safety pins. How, Delany seems to be asking, can we retain the energies of sex without being destroyed by them, or without destroying others in the process? Delany's books are shocking precisely because they are serious but not solemn. His kind of seriousness, however, seems very different from either Purdy's or Cooper's, being neither tragic nor nihilistic.

With pornography, we touch necessarily on the question of masculinity (both because it is overwhelmingly *men* who enjoy pornography and because pornography italicizes maleness and femaleness). With masculinity we touch on questions of how the male constructs the sexual world — constructions that lead directly to a taste for erotic fetishization such as pornography provides. Is there such a thing as the male erotic mind, for instance? And if there is, what do we make of it? Is it biologically hardwired, a pure social construction, or a mixture of both? These subjects are all huge and much debated in our own time. But while I am both a philosophical and biological layman in these matters, I will lay my own hand on the table.

I assume for the purposes of this chapter that there *is* a "male" way of looking at the world, and especially of conceiving sex; a way that is abstract and fetishistic, capable of dissociating love from lust, of concentrating obsessively on a certain activity or body part, of keeping kindness sealed off from desire. That maleness of conception is both a glory and a burden, and its tendency to abstraction, perversion, and fetishization is at once its greatest achievement and greatest temptation. The two authors with whom I will be concerned give diametrically opposite readings of it — Cooper turning his stories of sexual violence into abstract aesthetic objects themselves, and Purdy refusing to do so, but instead risking artistic pollutions and annihilations like those his characters undergo in their flesh. The origin of what I am calling "masculinity" is unimportant for my reading of Cooper and Purdy. (Of course it has a large component of social construction to it; but perhaps also a component that is biological.) Rather, what counts is their implicit description of maleness, a description I find also in sexological studies and in my own observation.

In an era that fears generalizations, perhaps especially about the two sexes (or genders), my assumptions may seem dangerously retrograde. I am emboldened to make them — as heuristic tools for understanding these fictions — by what one might call the more extreme examples of sexual differentiation. It is men, and not women, who are a) fascinated by pornography, b) sexually promiscuous, and c) sexually criminal. Women do not, by and large, buy pornography or collect it; do not generally seek out multiple sex partners; and are almost never sexual predators, abusers, murderers. Pornography, promiscuity, and perversion seem to be a male preserve.[2]

It would be odd if male homosexuality, the erotic relationship between two men, did not reproduce these vices and indeed geometrically increase them: the lust of one man for another man does not double, but squares itself, so to speak. It would be odd, too, if gay literature — the literature by, for, and about gay men — did not have a significantly "pornographic" impulse. Indeed, according to many, homosexuality is itself a perversion: a deliberate, conscious, and perverse thwarting of a natural heterosexual impulse. (It is the idea that gay men choose male partners *against even their own desires* which constitutes the judgment of the Catholic Church against the "sin" of homosexuality.)[3] In our own time, the AIDS epidemic has raised anew the dilemma of promiscuity. Gay men in the sexual free-for-all which was the seventies not only had more sex than they had in earlier, closeted days, but *much* more, with many more partners, and performing many more kinds of sexual acts, including quite advanced ones such as piss-drinking and fist-fucking. I myself enjoyed both activities; but I cannot deny that they were and are extreme, even "perverted." Like Camille Paglia, that strange advocate for male homosexuality, I think that it is the right and even the duty of intelligent beings to question, undermine, and disregard the "natural" and the "easy," finding in "pleasure" a subtext of pain or degradation.[4] But then, I too am male.

Dennis Cooper, the author of eight books of fiction and poetry on mostly sexual topics, provides a useful case study. His brilliant and unnerving fiction strikes me as interestingly "masculine" not only in its voyeuristic obsessions but even in the way he deflects those obsessions, making boy-love, mutilation, and murder simultaneously erotically hot and aesthetically cool: both an obsession and an irony. Indeed the deflection becomes itself the story of some of his most characteristic fiction, such as *Frisk,* the novel I am going to examine. A story about getting literally under various boys' skin, it is also a tease: seeming to offer the reader an analogous exploration of "Dennis's" interior, but finally dodging away when our eager hand reaches out to touch him.

Dennis Cooper is an intellectual's pornographer. (Samuel Delany, by contrast, is a pornographer's intellectual, and James Purdy is not a pornographer and doesn't write for intellectuals at all, but for "the soul," as he told a *Penthouse* interviewer in 1974.)[5] The obscenity in Cooper is ironized, italicized, made into a cold abstraction. As if to compensate for the sterility of the flirtation, the promised, fantasized acts have become far more violent and perverse than is customary in ordinary pornography. But throughout, the real thrill (at least for me) is the ruthless narrative control Cooper exercises over the reader and even over himself: the thrill isn't so much in the acts described as in the conscious fetishizing of those acts: a double fetishization, as it were. The kick one gets is in watching him watch himself get hard. Like other flirts, Cooper both entices and repels. His style is a splendid accomplishment, as virtuosic in its way as Edmund White's or Dale Peck's, and much funnier. At the same time, he so refuses any pleasure to the reader that he himself does not mete out that I rarely close his books without feeling vaguely cheated, *had.*

What I find most alluring and yet chilling is precisely Cooper's weird version of masculinity, a masculinity based not on the usual culturally acknowledged trappings — love of sports, possession of muscles, the usual kinds of thuggishness — but on a way of thinking that I myself possess and ambivalently revel in. It is a maleness that is, as I will suggest, closely connected to fantasies of dominion, violence, purity, and control. All of these are recognizable components of much pornography — including straight or gay bondage scenarios — but in Cooper's hands they become fantasias on masculinity itself, masculinity conceived of as, in Henry James's phrase about Gilbert Osmond, "an ecstasy of self-control."[6]

I have been helped in seeing this element of Cooper by several books. Camille Paglia's *Sexual Personae* is the best known, and the most reviled. While Paglia is an intemperate writer, given to hyperbole and sensationalism, she has explained what I only suspected: namely, that gay men are not the *opposite* of heterosexual men, but their logical continuation. Masculinity, to Paglia, is a flight from the mother (in her view not only a man's actual mother, but "mother nature" as well). The male homosexual is merely flying farther and faster: hence her rather romantic picture of the great ages of Western art as essentially gay achievements: "Athens became great not despite but because of its misogyny. Male homosexuality played a similar catalytic role in Renaissance Florence and Elizabethan London. At such moments, male bonding enjoys an amorous intensity of self-assurance, a transient conviction of victory over mothers and nature. For 2,500 years, western culture has fed itself on the enormous achievements of homosexual hybris, small bands of men attaining visionary heights in a few concentrated years of exaltation and defiance."[7] Male eros is to her inseparable from male fear, on the one hand, and male achievement on the other. It is the origin alike of pornography and of art.

What Paglia puts rhapsodically, others have put with more nuance. The French feminist philosopher Elisabeth Badinter, for example, in *XY: On Masculine Identity* (1992, English translation 1995), describes masculinity as a difficult *achievement:* "From the XY chromosome to the sense of male identity, which marks the culmination of a man's development, the road is long and rife with pitfalls. A little longer and a little more difficult than the road to female identity, contrary to what was believed for so long." She sees that male identity is a "protestation" and therefore an unconscious acknowledgment of fear. "This protestation is primarily addressed to the mother. It consists of three propositions: I am not her. I am not like her. I am against her."[8] Unlike Paglia, Badinter tends to see homosexuality as a stage on the way to heterosexuality, rather than as an extension of heterosexuality to further, more symbolic control over nature (by means of artworks and technology, for instance).

Liam Hudson and Bernadine Jacot, in their elegant book *The Way Men Think,* a study of "the imaginative lives of men," combine Paglia's and Badinter's perceptions in an interesting analysis of why "masculine" men (even today) are drawn to certain fields of intellectual labor: science and technology, for instance. They hypothesize something they call the male "wound": that is, the necessary dissociation the male infant must make from his mother, a dissociation impossible to, unneeded by, the female infant. "This first step, the one that the little boy takes in order to free himself from his symbiotic connection to his mother, Greenson refers to as *dis-identification.* The subsequent step, independent of the first, and which enables him positively to identify with his father, Greenson calls *counter-identification.* The first establishes the boy's separateness; the second, his maleness. *It is these two developmental processes in combination which we call the male wound*" [italics in original].[9]

Hudson and Jacot see both costs and benefits in the male wound. The costs are "personal insensitivity" and "misogyny"; the benefits — ambivalent ones — are "the idea of agency . . . to act on the world in the light of [one's] own needs and intentions," "the wound as a constantly replenishing source of psychic energy," and finally, "the notion of abstract passions." In the last case, they are particularly interested in high-achieving males such as Sir Isaac Newton, for whom the intellectual passions of his life were "the more enduringly gratifying the more completely divorced from human relationship they are." But forming the dark side of the same capacity for abstraction are the "male vices" of sexual crime, "intimate violence" (hurting or killing of "loved" partners), promiscuity, and an addiction to the perverse. Students of gay male life as well as literature will recognize them in this description.

Most interestingly to me, Hudson and Jacot list several "diagnostic features" of the "passionate abstraction" they saw in Newton, features which are strikingly applicable to Cooper's fetishistic heroes: "a preoccupation with *control* — usually symbolic, but sometimes literal; the use of apparently abstract and technical ideas as a means of executing *primitively psychological* manoeuvres; a commitment to formal models, hobby-horses and *fixed ideas* pursued, sometimes, with a fervour that can seem scarcely sane; a preoccupation with *violence* — again, usually symbolic, but sometimes literal"; and finally, a love of ideological "purity" and fear of its opposite, "spillage."[10]

All these, it seems to me, are richly illustrated in Cooper's *Frisk* — and are (by contrast) interestingly absent from James Purdy's superficially similar *Narrow Rooms*. My point is not to identify Cooper as hypermasculine and Purdy as "feminine" or even "gay," but simply to name the quite different appeals each book is making: appeals that go to the heart of pornography, of gay men's relationship to violence and desire, and perhaps also of the possibilities of gay fiction.

DENNIS COOPER'S *FRISK*

In *Frisk* (1991), Dennis Cooper has placed a knowing distance between the "real" Dennis Cooper who lives in Los Angeles and writes books, and *Frisk*'s main character, who lives in Los Angeles and writes books and whose name happens to be Dennis. As the latter might say: Whatever. This fictional "Dennis" falls in love as a teenager with a beautiful boy he saw photographed in a snuff magazine (he and his best friend end up having sex with Henry several years later: the photo of mayhem was, it seems, posed). He gradually becomes drawn to punk (renaming himself Spit and hanging out at a bar called Flintstones) and sexual violence (he beats up his friend/trick Samson to see what it's like), starts hiring porn stars (like the luscious Pierre) whom he fantasizes killing. Eventually he ends up in Holland, where he claims to have murdered about a half-dozen men and boys. The centerpiece of *Frisk* is a long graphic letter from

"Dennis" to his best friend Julian and Julian's passive, cute younger brother Kevin, on whom "Dennis" has had a long crush: he wants them to join him in his windmill to kill some more boys.

Kevin and Julian come to Amsterdam — they've been living in Paris — to join him in his homicides or to rescue him from them. But luckily, there is nothing to join or rescue: when the moment of truth comes, Julian (ascending a Hitch-cockian staircase in the windmill to where the bodies are supposedly stashed) "smirked, pretend-hardened his eyes. 'Confess, asshole. . . . You're no John Wayne Gacy, correct?' I looked away for a second. 'Correct.' " And "Dennis," relieved to be rid of the burden of his fiction, confesses that he "couldn't and wouldn't kill anyone" and that "theorizing about it, wondering why, never helped at all. Writing it down was and still is exciting in a pornographic way. But I couldn't see how it would ever fit into anything as legitimate as a novel or whatever." The long letter he wrote Julian and Kevin was an attempt to get "some sort of objective analysis" or "the courage or amorality or whatever to actually kill somebody in league with them. You're the only ones who ever answered, though."[11]

The "real" Dennis Cooper — ironic quotes are mandatory here — doesn't write autobiography, then, despite the coincidence of names, places, fantasies: he writes about somebody like him doing these things. In so doing, he directs our attention to the *possibility* of such a story, the possibility that the author might be indeed a sex-murderer. This possibility is, needless to say, an arresting and novel one. The book, by so impudently identifying — or daring us *not* to identify — the author with its main character (a character who is either a mur-derer or a liar), calls our attention to its own fictionality, as if to say, "This is a novel." Furthermore, even in the novel, "Dennis's" story is about fictionality: he becomes turned on to violent death by looking at a photo of a "dead" boy: a boy who breaks the proscenium a few years later by actually appearing in Dennis and Julian's bedroom for sex. The photos were, of course, staged, not real.

The effect of Henry's resurrection from the dead, and of the novel as a whole, is like looking into a mirror on an acid trip. For if *this* fantasy, Henry the snuff model, can suddenly break through the proscenium, why not another? Thus, when "Dennis" goes to Holland and sends a long description of his sex-murders, we first take it seriously: the letter, with its beautiful squishy descrip-tions, is the equivalent of the photo the young Dennis had seen in "Gypsy Pete's" used-book store. (Are we, perhaps, like "Dennis" in Gypsy Pete's back room, jerking off while reading it? A rude question to ask, but one the book seems to demand.) But it, too, turns out to be staged. Dennis has actually killed no one, though he has intensely imagined doing so. When the confusion has been ex-plained, Dennis, Julian, and Kevin celebrate by using a new cute boy Julian has picked up at the railway station as a model for their own snuff photo, re-creating the "crater-like" wound Dennis had seen on the original model Henry's ass. The novel ends, as it began, with a screenplay: "Five. Close-up. The wound is actually a glop of paint, ink, makeup, tape, cotton, tissue, and papier-mâché sculpted to suggest the inside of a human body. It sits on the ass, crushed and deflated. In the central indentation there's a smaller notch maybe one-half-inch deep. It's a bit out of focus. Still, you can see the fingerprints of the person or persons who made it" (128).

The "fingerprints" are, of course, an artful reference to himself: to both "Dennis" and Dennis Cooper. Both have told a story about sex and violence; neither story was reliable (in the sense of being real); both stories might fall into the category of "fantasy." But "fantasy" is too severely psychological a word. What they fall into is precisely the category "fiction." The book is about writing a book, about "fictionality." Is anything we have read, is anything we have *ever* read (Cooper seems to ask), anything more than a "glop of paint" with "fingerprints" on it? And are the fingerprints not finally ours as well as the reader's, as well as, or even more than, the author's? This epistemological teaser is far closer to "what the book is about" than any of the acts described in it.

Despite its quasi-pornographic treatment of the subject, *Frisk* is really not about killing boys. Its events all take place in what Tennyson called "the palace of art," one of the houses to which gay fiction often gravitates, not because homosexuality is inherently ornamental, but because style diverts attention from any such dangerous sexual passion. One reads Cooper with the resentful admiration one accords an ingenious practical joke. If I were straight, or he were, I'd say Dennis Cooper was a *bullshitter* — meaning it in the usual male sense: grudging, but complimentary. Indeed, despite its deceptive appearance of mental vacuity, *Frisk* is a highbrow novel. It is about art, it is about itself. It is not surprising that Edmund White, an aesthete of an earlier generation, but one equally fascinated with the mirror of fiction, should have become one of Cooper's most enthusiastic admirers.

Because it is so relentlessly arty, *Frisk* is only superficially related to novels of sexual passion or abjectness such as James Purdy's *Narrow Rooms* or James Baldwin's *Giovanni's Room*. His freedom from the abject is paradoxically the source of the book's sexual heat and fictional menace. He even rejects the very word *abject* when he asks the hustler Pierre to shit in the toilet without flushing. Despite the plausibly raunchy subtext, Dennis is quick to explain his motives: " 'I'm not being abject. . . . It's not "Ooh, shit, piss, how wicked," or anything. It's, like I said, information' " (169). The cyberword "information" is "Dennis's" way of protecting himself from abjectness, from the power of anything other than information: especially from those tired old stage props, the "soul" and the "heart." Indeed, the novel is a redefinition, in comically literal terms, of interiority: "I enlarged the asshole with the Swiss army knife and worked one of my hands to the wrist inside. It was wild in there, like reaching into a stew that had started to cool" (106). It experiments with the fantasy that one might reduce oneself to a body, as when "Dennis" imagines seducing a Belgian boy on a plane: "if I could coerce that boy into one of the jet's little toilets with me, I'd turn psychotic, I'm sure . . . Actually it's more like my body would lose it, and I'd be observing the damage it does from a safe place inside" (47). But actually, of course, this fantasy could just as plausibly be called becoming "all mind," being a mere observer. For "Dennis" has entirely distant relations with bodies, whether his own or other men's: "Usually I don't notice my body. It's just there, working steadily." Indeed, he has a quite conventional ("male") disgust for the body: after he's killed and butchered an eleven-year-old boy — "we cut him apart for a few hours, and studied everything inside the body" — he thinks: "God, human bodies are such garbage bags" (106). The disgusted exclamation is as masculine (in Hudson and Jacot's sense) as the "studying" that preceded it.

Frisk is masterful in its psychology of male sexual need, showing its fantasy of touching pitch without being defiled. And although the bodies he dismembers are male, what they signify — the "unknowableness" of interiority — is female. By undoing the mysterious otherness of the body, Cooper's characters free themselves from interiority, from women, from mothers. (There are virtually no parents or women in his books.) By opening up the bodies of men, "Dennis" is undoing his own origins, making himself a self-creation. Why does one create this self? Not in order to have happiness, or perhaps even pleasure, both of which presuppose vulnerability. One is "Dennis," by contrast, in order *not to be controlled*. In Paglia's words, again, "Serial or sex murder, like fetishism, is a perversion of male intelligence. It is a criminal abstraction, masculine in its deranged egotism and orderliness. It is the asocial equivalent of philosophy, mathematics, and music."[12] The reason "Dennis" parts the anal lips to inhale the "reek" of his victims' bowels is not that he loves the smell of feces, nor even that he's a fetishist. He does not want to worship the shit that he coaxes out of the junkie as a true coprophile would — a few mouthfuls is all he really needs ("It tasted okay, kind of bland" [99]), then he impatiently wipes the rest on the floor. By contrast, in a video of coprophagia I once saw, the equivalent scene features a completely different kind of dialogue, in which the eater moans with pleasure, "This is where I want to be," and the feeder promises him "hours of glory and pleasure."[13] Needless to say, neither "I want" nor "glory and pleasure" forms any part of "Dennis's" vocabulary.

Indeed the absence of pleasure is one of the book's strongest flavors. Cooper is not putting a *desirable* male body on the stage: the boys he kills are rendered unattractive by their forced-feeding of drugs. Their cocks are never hard; their assholes are never clean; "Dennis" is never animated in their presence. It is

otherness itself he seeks — "I'm sure I've idealized brutality, murder, dismember-
ment, etc. But even slicked up, there's an unknowableness there that's so profound or whatever, especially when I combine it with sex" (78). His personal
pleasure is almost irrelevant to the exploration of bodies, to "information"-
seeking. Quite in the high-modernist tradition of Eliot, he sees the artist (himself) as having to "extinguish personality," not increase it. So, while Cooper's
novels are the very opposite of "abject," they are nevertheless self-abnegating.
His is the spirituality of a material world. He desires not experience but sensation. Hence the importance of drugs, for with them one can attain a simulacrum
of pure sensation.

The typical Cooper figure is either literally an adolescent or postadolescent
boy, or is such a boy's fantasy of independence: solitary, morally unrestricted,
sexually promiscuous, unemotional, and above all unindebted. Or in "Dennis's" own sassier language: "smart, cool, curious, horny, drugged." The very
style of this novel is appropriate to such a person — scrupulous and clean, as if
fiction itself were a purification rite proleptically warding off strong feeling by
means of words. It is a style that never breaks a sweat, Jeffrey Dahmer crossed
with Fred Astaire: "Part of me wanted to kill and dismember him . . . but most of
me gave him a towel" (38). By reducing the body to "information," Cooper
solves part of the problem of writing a genuinely horrific story in our time. His
style solves the rest, enabling him to tell his stories without lapsing into the
language of an outdated moralism — shock, horror, guilt, remorse, disgust. (Or
even joy: Sade's aristocrats exclaim with pleasure over the suffering of their
victims, and endlessly rationalize them. Cooper's heroes find, as "Dennis" tells
Julian, that talking about it doesn't help and doesn't delight.)

Here's an example of Cooper's style: "Dennis" is flying to New York to have
sex with — and, who knows, maybe kill — the porn star Pierre. On the plane, he
fantasizes killing a young "Belgian or Dutch" boy, "maybe twenty." "Dennis"
gets so excited thinking of him that he goes to the toilet to masturbate.

> I'm pretty sure if I tore some guy open I'd know him as well as anyone could,
> because I'd have what he consists of right there in my hands, mouth, wherever.
> Not that I know what I'd do with that stuff. Probably something insane . . .
> Spill the guts through my fingers like pirates supposedly did with doubloons or
> whatever. Except there'd be a smell, which I guess would be strong and hard to
> take. . . . I guess in a perfect world I'd eat and drink all that stuff and not just get
> nauseous. That's my dream. . . . If he were locked in this toilet with me, and if I
> had a knife, I guess, or claws would be better, I'd shut up that minuscule part of
> my brain that thinks murder is evil, whatever that means. I'd stand up, or try to
> stand up, then cut him to pieces. But since I don't have the boy or nerve or
> weapon, I just sit here scribbling, jerking off. (53–54)

What a splendid creation this deliberately flat, affectless voice is! Notice how it domesticates the *grand guignol* with unthreatening Americanisms like "I'm pretty sure" or "in my hands, mouth, wherever." Notice how movie culture — childhood recollections of Disneyesque "pirates" sifting doubloons through their fingers — makes the fantasy seem both endearing and cheesy, a fifties artifact. Notice that "Dennis" never loses his own sense of how ridiculous this looks, as when he starts imagining what he'd do if he had the kid in the toilet with him: "I'd stand up, or try to stand up . . ." Notice how he ingeniously improves his own script with a fine contempt for probability: "If I had a knife, I guess, or claws would be better . . ." Notice, finally, the deadpan wit of "That's my dream," which turns this scene of grotesque cannibalism into a teenage girl's reverie about the prom. The tone is neat, chic, casual — the very epitome of L.A. It leaves us alone, it doesn't ask us to *feel* anything.

In this respect, Cooper seems to form the end of a narrative on the crucial subject of sexual abjectness that begins with Baldwin and continues through Purdy and Samuel Delany. Baldwin shows in David an abjectness whose cause is never fully explained. (Is it his love of Giovanni, or the fact that he could love Giovanni as little as he did?) Cooper's characters are either beyond, or incapable of, the abject, which they tend to regard as a joke in bad taste. It is interesting that both writers are stylists — not incidentally but essentially. Not merely do they write well; their style dictates what they can and cannot say. With Baldwin and Cooper, style and subject go hand in hand, and indeed sometimes take over the subject altogether. (In Purdy, by contrast, one constantly feels a struggle with language.) Cooper's style is of course completely unlike Baldwin's. Where Baldwin self-consciously echoes the cadences and vocabulary of Shakespeare and the Bible, his sentences paying themselves out with Senecan gravity, Cooper sounds like no one but himself: that is, a late-twentieth-century American who has never had to worry about money. Just as there are no parents in any of Cooper's books, so there is no echo of earlier styles, whether "gay" or straight. Indeed, by confining his characters' emotions to those possible only in states of pharmaceutical numbness, he makes their beautifully meaningless language necessary and plausible. In it, what strikes one instantly is the absence of the reverberant boom of *meaning*.

Frisk is then a weird vision of freedom; in that sense, the very opposite of *Giovanni's Room*. The freedom turns out to be as great a burden, however, as Baldwin's absence of freedom. (How hard it must be to remember not to feel guilt when you murder an eleven-year-old boy!) Baldwin's David and Cooper's "Dennis" are identical in their wish to escape all constraints. But though Baldwin attacks David for desiring such heartless freedom and Cooper praises "Dennis" for achieving it, Baldwin's abjectness and Cooper's unabjectness are nevertheless cousins.

If we want accounts of sexual passion that take us to the other side of abjectness without landing us in shamelessness, we will find them in James Purdy. Purdy's vision is tragic and (in the widest sense) religious. Purdy takes seriously what Cooper phobically deflects: namely, the possibility of guilt. Unlike Baldwin, however, Purdy does not get so caught up in the emotion of guilt that he becomes enamored of it. He tells the story of a *release* from guilt, not a mere lyric celebration of it. Moreover it is a release devised neither by the clever defensive mind of Cooper's pretend-psychopaths, nor the grave morality of Baldwin's sexual scrupulists. Purdy's characters are delivered *through* and *by means of* desire. Sexual expiation is their way out; atonement, though not happiness, is their reward.

JAMES PURDY'S *NARROW ROOMS*

> O thinke me worth Thine anger; punish me . . .
> > John Donne, "Good-Friday, 1613. Riding Westward"

Though the configuration of actual characters repeatedly changes, there is only one story in *Narrow Rooms:* the expiation of the crime of love. And of the many pairs of haughty, tormented lovers — all of them male — the most important is Roy Sturtevant and Sidney De Lakes. It is Sidney's gradual acknowledgment and return of Roy's love toward which every event of this awkward, horrific, and sublime novel proceeds.

Purdy is a writer who does nothing by halves, and many good readers are put off by his excesses, emotionality, and rhetoric. Even the plot of *Narrow Rooms* is so improbable and so wildly obsessive, relentlessly repeating the same few themes, that one either gives in to it or throws the book across the room. Indeed, simply to tell the plot requires much more time and attention than with other books. More happens in five pages of *Narrow Rooms* than in entire chapters of David Leavitt. The following plot summary is long not because the novel is, but because so much is at stake in every plot turn. It is impossible to give a faithful impression of Purdy's fiction — the sense of doom and rapture resist a précis. But even a fairly plodding summation of this great erotic novel will show how widely different Purdy is from Baldwin on the one hand, or Dennis Cooper on the other; how his imagination boldly re-creates the love tragedy in gay terms. If we smile at his rhetorical slips — his odd fondness for calling West Virginia "The Mountain State" or Roy Sturtevant "the son of the renderer" — the smile may be a nervous deflection of Purdy's passion, an attempt to treat him ironically and keep him at a distance. But this is no more possible with him than with Wagner or Emily Brontë, nineteenth-century masters whom he resembles more than he does any contemporary.

Roy Sturtevant, vindictive, proud, violent, and excluded, has worshiped the handsome Sidney De Lakes since adolescence; a worship Sidney has repaid with contempt. While various attempts are made by Purdy and his characters to locate the source of the love-hatred (in Roy's poverty, in Sidney's slapping him publicly), it may antedate any of them. As the storyteller says: "Something was burning in his veins, having its origin perhaps from even before birth."[14] Roy himself confesses: "I don't have hold of him. He has hold of me. . . . The first time I played with my own cock it was while I looked at a snapshot of *him*. . . . He owes me his blood" (122–24). And even Sidney, who hates and fears Roy, finally recognizes that "He has been waiting for me all our lives; him, me, like two heavenly bodies in space that they have predicted will one day collide" (117).

After high school the tables turn, and Sidney falls from the brittle glory of being a football star to the nothingness of being a gas jockey. (Village opinion is that he wouldn't "amount to a hill of beans.") To punish Sidney and win him, Roy inaugurates a tormented, baroque scheme. He begins an affair with the beautiful doomed Brian McFee, bribing Brian with sex and drugs. When Brian is hooked on both, he commands him first to seduce, then to kill Sidney: they are always out hunting together, Brian will have the perfect excuse. At the same time, Roy sends Sidney an anonymous letter saying that Brian wants to kill him; and in a nightmarish scene the two boys, both of them in love with each other, hunt each other through the West Virginia hills until they meet up in the Bent Ridge Bar, where Sidney, terrified and confused, shoots Brian to death through the left eye. He is found guilty of manslaughter and sent to jail.

All this the reader is told much later. The novel proper begins with Sidney's early release from jail and Sidney's worshipful younger brother Vance asking the town doctor for advice about what to do with him now. Doc Ulric suggests that Sidney work as a male nurse for the fourth young man of the novel's doomed quaternity, Gareth Vaisey. (We later find out that the idea does not originate with the doctor but with Roy, who sees in Gareth yet another pawn he can sacrifice to get Sidney.) Vance is snobbishly horrified that any brother of his "is going to empty used chamberpots." Sidney, however, still guilty for his killing of Brian, thinks it fitting that he serve Gareth in the most menial ways. Service, indeed, is the lesson he has learned in prison: "Prison," he tells Vance, "had everything. They gave me many gifts" (39).

One of those gifts of service was sexual: Sidney was "used" in prison, as the weals on his chest and back tell even the priggish Vance. He does not yet know what to do with this "gift" — he is dimly aware of having to offer it finally to Roy — but serves Gareth Vaisey till then as body servant, nurse, and lover. When Gareth's haughty mother Irene catches the two in a ravenous act of mutual fellatio, Sidney is dismissed, leaving him at a loss for someone to serve. He turns, as Roy had planned all along, to Roy.

It is at this point in the novel — about a third of the way in — that Purdy himself signals a turn of the wheel. In a haunting, gnomic sentence, he addresses the reader directly: "*Behind this story so far is another story, as behind the girders of an ancient bridge is the skeleton of a child which superstition says keeps the bridge standing*" (58; italics Purdy's). That story is Roy's, to which Purdy now turns.

Roy, called with endless insistence "the renderer," has been pulling the strings of all the other characters—Sidney, Brian, Gareth, even Mrs. Vaisey and Dr. Ulric. Who is this "renderer"? When a prison psychiatrist asks Sidney the same question, he replies: "A renderer is what we country jakes call a man who collects carcasses and puts them in boiling water until they are rendered into lard which he makes into soap for people's hands. . . ." The psychiatrist interrupts: "I asked who he was, not what he does," but Sidney is unable or unwilling to answer that question: "Oh, you ask who? Well, I'll have to sleep on that question before I answer you" (66). Roy is both more and less than a "who."

As a "renderer," Roy is (like a hangman) obscurely polluted. He is also from the wrong side of town, though he ends up (like Heathcliff in *Wuthering Heights*) owning it. He is dark-complected so that some (like the snotty Gareth Vaisey) see him as an Indian or "nigger." At his best, he is handsome in a predatory way, looking to Brian McFee, for instance, like a "Leatherstocking." His body is lean and muscular—there is not an extra ounce of fat on his frame. These physical details are all significant because they locate Roy at the hypermasculine end of the sex axis, despite the fact that he is entirely homosexual. Purdy's story in fact imagines a homosexuality that is not less but more conventionally masculine than heterosexuality—and perhaps for that very reason more violent.

Roy is also, among other things, a sadist; and yet "sadist" trivializes Roy's (and Purdy's) identification of love with suffering, an identification more religious than pathological. The scene of Sidney's first return to Roy, for instance, crackles with erotic cruelty. "What did you do wrong this time?" are Roy's first words. With ecstatic inarticulateness. Sidney answers: "*She caught me touching Gareth*." Roy pushes his advantage further: "Supposin' I was to go to Mrs. Vaisey and get you took back. . . . What will I get out of it, Mr. De Lakes?" "All right, get Gareth back, and you can have me later on" (62). Everything Roy has said has placed Sidney in the wrong, reminding him in a way both cruel and truthful that he is not, and never has been, free. (As Sidney himself has said, "I sort of belong in jail" [157]). As he leaves to bully Mrs. Vaisey into taking Sidney back, Roy turns once more to him: "Just to make sure you don't light out, I will lock this door with a double lock. The sound ought to be familiar" (65). Sartre, I believe, said masochism was waiting in its pure form: Purdy would agree.

As Sidney awaits Roy's return, he remembers the dead Brian McFee. The whole Brian episode is the most touching in this book, for Brian was innocent as no one else in the story is. He was eager not only for sex and drugs, but for direction (from Roy) and love (from Sidney). When Roy forces him to seduce Sidney before killing him, Brian, hopelessly caught between them, writes Sidney a series of semiliterate letters confessing his love. The most heartbreaking of all is found on Brian's body at his death: "There will come the day when you will see I loved you best. . . . I have never wrote such a letter before, and I have the funny feeling somehow I won't never write another like it again maybe to anybody. . . . My idea of heaven is to be hunting with you in some beautiful park with mountains like here at home but where we won't need guns or prey but we will just walk together arm in arm in this good world and be by ourselves always together forever and a day" (92). Even the clichés ring true: it is signed with an X.

Paradoxically, it is the most feminized characters (like the momma's boy Gareth or the churchgoing Vance) who are most insistent on Sidney's being "masculine." In Vance's case, this masculinity means heterosexuality, and he is sickened by the suggestion (raised at Sidney's trial) that Brian and Sidney "had some deep and unwholesome friendship." In Gareth's it means insisting that Sidney kill Roy as a proof of his love for Gareth. But Sidney, who needs desperately to be "ruled" himself, cannot bring himself to do this. So when Roy succeeds in getting back Sidney's job with the Vaiseys, Gareth is coldly furious: "You shouldn't have come through him," says Gareth of Roy. Sidney says, "But I was drove out of your house by your Ma . . . What was I expected to do?" "Knock her down and stay . . . Kill the bitch and rule instead of her" (103).

The plot is now wound up, but not ready to go off yet: like *Tristan,* it combines a hypnotic languor with an overwhelming suspense. In a series of dreamlike episodes, Roy gets literally closer and closer to Sidney, haunting him like a hungry ghost. In one, Roy appears outside the Vaisey house on a winter's night, knowing that Sidney is inside sleeping with Gareth. Seeing him, Sidney goes out naked into the cold and falls at Roy's feet. Roy hoists him over his shoulders and deposits him back in Gareth's bed, saying contemptuously: "Unless I miss my guess, I'll be back for the both of you before too very long" (112). In a second, he appears at the Vaisey's intending (it seems) to evict them. Sidney interrupts them and makes yet another offer of himself: "I'll surrender to you, Roy . . . You can have me . . . instead of . . . them" (116).

It is after these surreal appearances that Sidney admits to himself for the first time what Roy has meant to him. This confession is (like so many passages in this novel) written with such incandescence that it seems to demand the extra intensity of music—Samuel Barber's, perhaps—to do it justice:

All those years, though I pretended I never saw him, I guess though I saw only him and knowed he was always present. . . . When he is happy, which ain't often, my heart beats better, but when he scowls and is mad, my heart is sluggish and beats thickly like now. . . . When he is quiet, I am at prayer. . . . Even when I surrender, if I do, and I know it is what I will have to do now, it won't be enough for him, or say I lay down my life for him and let him render me into fine perfumed soap for him to wash his hands with and maybe his rectum, it won't be enough. He will curse this soap for not being Jesus and his sunbeams. (117–18)

He makes a vow to himself: "*If I have wronged you, renderer, wronged you through the years as you are said to claim, then take something from me, but you must likewise pay me back also for what you have done to Brian and Gareth.* [Roy, in one of the many dreamlike sequences of this section of the novel, has raped Gareth on Brian McFee's grave.] *There must be restitution*" (136).

After so many psychologically, sexually, and physically violent acts, after so much longing and pride, something has changed about these two destined lovers: Sidney no longer hates Roy, and Roy (who has just seen the ghost of Brian McFee) is ready for the first time to confess his helplessness and guilt. " 'Listen then to how you egged me on.' He rose and took Sidney's face gently in his hand. 'Just by existing you did. Everytime you passed by me you threw off energy enough to make me want you forever. You commanded *me* by just your breathing . . . Like you do now.' " Both men are now searching for a way to be "free" of the guilt that links them, but Sidney is terrified that Roy wants him to be his murderer. "I can't kill you even for Gareth . . . I love him but not that much. . . . I will not kill you even to be free" (146). But Roy and Purdy have an alternative, sublime in its simplicity:

"Supposin' you were to nail me naked to the barn door all night, say, and then the next day at sunup you brought Brian McFee to see what you had done . . ."
"Brian is in his grave, you low son of a bitch."
"But he could be brought out of his grave." (147)

Roy is to expiate his relentless cruelty, Sidney his contemptuous pride by the ritual of nailing Roy to the barn door, then digging up Brian McFee's body to witness his suffering. This is Roy's final bargain, one in which he will suffer as much as Sidney. It is sealed not with a slap or a handshake but with a kiss:

"Kiss me, Sidney . . . if you want to be free."
"I'm kissin' you," Sidney said between his sobs. His face was wet from tears.
"Let me drink your tears. I ain't never drunk tears."
"Kill me, Roy, why don't you. I don't care. You can kill me, then render me, nobody will know."

"I don't want to kill you. Never wanted to. . . ."

He took out Sidney's penis and bent Sidney's own face over his penis, and said, "Cry on your own cock, Sidney. Go on, cry on it. Refresh your cock." (147)

"Du sublime au ridicule il n'y a qu'un pas" — and many readers will feel Purdy has long since taken that fatal step. It is probably too late, even in a plot summary, to make excuses for the novel. Nonetheless, clumsy as the conceit may seem, was there any other way to show not only Sidney's guilt, but the means of his liberation from it? Is it not precisely his erotic shame, his penis, which has both drawn him to, and kept him from, Roy for so long? And ignorance of it which has made him humiliate Roy in their youth, and kill Brian? And acknowledgment of it which now drives him simultaneously to punish and be punished by Roy? It is the breaking of his heart — his tears — allied with the strength and fatality of his desire — his cock — that permits his ultimate deliverance from Roy, and Roy's from him. Who is "commanding" whom in this sublime scene? At one and the same moment, each takes revenge on the other, each asks for punishment, and each overcomes his sexual shame. This is the loving pair that has been foreseen, as each has dimly perceived, from before their birth. "So the wheel had come full circle," Sidney thinks: "Roy would guide and keep him, he would not let him go wrong again, they would not part from one another ever after having only at last been united pursuant to so many devious detours and windings, as souls long separated from each other by the world's vicissitudes are said to enter paradise linked arm in arm" (152–53). This is either the work of a great writer, or that of a terrible one; there doesn't seem to be a middle ground.

Sidney does as he is "commanded": nails Roy to the barn door, then digs up Brian McFee's body and presents it to Roy at dawn. After this rite of crucifixion has been accomplished, the rite of erotic resurrection can follow: Sidney unnails Roy and carries him up to the bedroom, where they undergo something like a spiritual marriage, sealed with an act of fellatio (because the god is Eros, even a spiritual union must be physicalized). The enormous suffering of these men has finally softened their resistance to each other, permitting an ecstatic fusion like that in *Tristan und Isolde:* "There was no renderer, or son of a renderer, no scissors-grinder or cistern cleaner or tree surgeon or any of the other vocations attached to his enemy's name, and there never had been any Sidney De Lakes, a football star and gasoline station attendant, for he felt he was back thousands of years ago with this eternal lover or husband or sweetheart, whatever name, on whom he now poured out all his love" (173). (Cf. *"Nicht mehr Tristan. Nicht mehr Isolde."*) The novel, with its endless maddening erotic permutations, its repetitions and redundancies, its overdetermination and intensity, has in fact given the reader an *experience* of erotic eternity — so that Roy's dying question takes on unbearable power and pathos: "Why, why did it take you so long then?"

Ironically, what kills Roy is not his crucifixion, but the jealousy of Gareth who has, almost unnoticed, come along to watch the ritual: "What [Gareth] observed now both sickened and thrilled him, stirred in him his deepest yearnings and passion. The two men . . . kissed one another oblivious to any other time or place, thirstily, their longing for one another it was clear could never be appeased" (175). Unlike Irene Vaisey who, when she walked in on Gareth and Sidney "each holding the sex of the other in open, abandoned, furiously moving mouths . . . had just enough self-knowledge also to realize that it was her jealousy and envy which were making her so sick at this moment" (55–56), her son does not: "I'll give you just five seconds to tell me you love me the most, Sid, that you will leave that dirty motherfucker you're holding to your chest, and you come with me" (178). When Sidney refuses, Gareth shoots and kills them both. He gives his reason to a police officer as he himself lies dying in the hospital. "I couldn't be shut out again. I couldn't lose Sidney, you see. Yet that was happening right in front of my eyes, officer! Them shutting me out with their better love-making" (180).

I have called Purdy's fiction religious, and if this is true what is his god and what his theology? The god, as in courtly love, is love itself, a cruel deity who must be painfully served, and who takes no thought of human happiness. Hence the comparative absence of ordinary happiness, the lack of a happy ending, the absence of domestic pleasures (such as comfort or nurturance) — or indeed, of female characters. (Mrs. Vaisey is as stern and masculine as Volumnia in *Coriolanus*.) Hence, too, the overwhelming presence of wounded men in *Narrow Rooms* — and not just in the bloodbath of the ending. In Purdy's world we come into the world wounded, just as for the believing Calvinist we are born bearing the marks of original sin, and thereby an unpayable debt to God. In Purdy's religion of eros, we are indebted (as Sidney is) simply by breathing, by being beautiful, by making someone else desire us: as Roy despairingly tells Sidney, "Every time you passed by me, you threw off energy enough to make me want you forever" (146).

The novel begins and ends in wounding. When Vance visits Dr. Ulric to get his advice about what to do with Sidney now that he's been released from jail, he passes a young man in the waiting room who is "lavishly bandaged." He looks like someone Vance has noticed working on a road crew. The young man never reappears, but his woundedness and even the "lavishness" of the bandaging (the combination, then, of suffering and pleasure) certainly do. Shortly thereafter, Vance sees the weals and scars that mark Sidney's body: signs of a sexual suffering Vance does not want to acknowledge but Sidney refuses to conceal. Later, indeed, after seeing his nemesis Roy for the first time since his release, Sidney becomes "ecstatic," splashing the brown creek water on his chest "as if to draw attention now to the scars themselves" (12). Similarly, when he returns home from a day of force-feeding Gareth Vaisey, he holds up his hands to Vance for "show" (41); on them are the bite-marks left by Gareth's teeth.

But Sidney's are not the only wounds. Roy, the tyrant, is himself a map of scars. On the graduation day when Sidney slaps him publicly, Roy goes home and, with the razor his father used to kill himself (sublime overdetermination!), cuts a wedge of skin out of his own face where Sidney's third finger had struck him. Much later, when he begins his tormented affair with Brian McFee, Roy "put the scar of his self-inflicted wound directly over the boy's penis and felt it bob there again and again, that was all he seemed to want just then from the terrified, even slightly delirious McFee" (73). When he stands outside the Vaiseys' in the snow until Sidney comes out and kisses his feet, he punishes himself for having carried Sidney back to bed by slashing his arms, shoulders, and feet with a razor.

The novel ends, too, in wounds. As Irene Vaisey holds her son (for the first time, it seems), Gareth becomes a mask of blood: "The blood from Gareth's eyes ran now in little rivulets across all the features of his face, and against his lips and chin, one rivulet being joined by another, that by still another, until his entire handsome face was nothing but rivulets of blood." The scene is a Protestant *pietà,* but (consistently with Purdy's male-only vision) a *pietà* from which the mother is perversely excluded. For in a final daring and arrogant swerve, mother love itself is subordinated to the homicidal male love that has killed the son she now holds in her hands. It is to *that* love that her own is compared, not the other way around, and the effect is like a blow: "It was then that Irene Vaisey lay her head down upon his face, kissing him again and again, and holding him to her more tenderly than Sidney had ever held her son, as tenderly perhaps as the renderer's son had finally returned Sidney's love and late embraces" (185). Her love *perhaps* equals the love of Sidney and Roy, which has brought such destruction to her son and her.

Besides being a sign of ontological obligation, wounds here send a powerful sexual message. The wound shows that one is both tough and soft, that one has been penetrated and that one has resisted the penetration. The scar is the site of this contradiction; a sign of weakness felt, acknowledged, and displayed—and thus turned, paradoxically, into strength. *Virescit vulnere virtus:* manhood does indeed flourish in such a wound.

Paradoxically, in Purdy's surreally all-male, all-gay world, "manhood" implies homosexuality.[15] Thus Sidney is simultaneously ashamed and proud of his prison wounds precisely because they signify sexual submission to another man.

He won't hide the weals that mark his body from his "use" in prison. Just so, he refuses to apologize to Mrs. Vaisey for having sex with her son: "I *won't* share your and Vance's views on it [i.e., homosexuality]" (57). Nor will he pretend to Vance that he's not really gay: "Oh, I am, I am. . . . It's *not* over and done with" (41). If a paradox may be permitted, a scar is shameful but nothing to be ashamed of, like the prison that "had everything" and "gave me many gifts" (39).

By contrast, it is being ashamed of shame that distinguishes (and marks as inferior) Vance and Gareth. Vance feels that Sidney is too good to "empty used bedpans." Sidney disagrees, knowing that a life of service is right for him: "I sort of belong in jail" (157). Gareth has contempt for Sidney's painful, slow journey toward Roy and his own homosexuality, calling Sidney a "coy little faggot." While there's some truth to that, that is not the whole truth. For Sidney achieves the peace that forever escapes Gareth, who is reduced to the ignominy of merely dying in his mother's arms. He never understands the beautiful language of shame.

Purdy is essentially rewriting the myths of courtly love, the elaborate rituals of deference and deferred desire, of service and suffering. He is rewriting them to suit a homosexual subject, a homosexual love. In courtly love, the chief obstacle is the difference of sexes, which courtly love distorts and exaggerates for erotic and aesthetic purposes. The chief symbol of victory is deflowering. Neither the obstacle nor its reward is obviously applicable to gay life. Take the obstacle. Marriage not being an option and the partners being of the same sex, it would at first seem that there would be no obstacle to happiness *except* the social restrictions placed on homosexuals. Purdy, interestingly, does not dwell on these social restrictions at all. *Narrow Rooms* takes place almost entirely without reference to the social world we live in and which most "realistic" novels anatomize. Hence perhaps his coy references to West Virginia not by name but as "The Mountain State." And what a place this small-town West Virginia turns out to be — a place where every young man in town is ruggedly handsome, sexually available, and gay! No: this world is not meant to remind us of our own. Purdy's world is, rather, the romantic landscape of *Wuthering Heights,* his West Virginia a place sufficiently remote and unknown to permit him to tell an inner story of passion among men. And as for the reward: Purdy knows, as do his readers, that gay men fuck first and love later. Neither Sidney nor Roy is unfamiliar with the other's body: "Do you know how many times I've had him in the woods, the cornfield, back of the gym?" Roy contemptuously asks Brian McFee (77). Sexual pleasure is easy for gay men: harder is the higher eroticism of intimacy, sacrifice, and perversion. Happiness is not achieved by a single person in this book. Neither is it sought.

When he finally "reports in" to Roy — the military phrase is touching and desperate — Sidney is acknowledging a fundamental relation between them that he would never have acknowledged before: a relation of love, desire, and service. He has not gotten rid of but eroticized his shame, and in that sense overcome it. Or perhaps not "overcome," but sublimated it, taken it to a higher turn of the erotic spiral. There is another obstacle besides shame, however. This obstacle is that a gay man is sexually attracted to men, that is to something masculine; but that yielding to homosexual desire (on either side) can make both partners seem unmasculine, even feminine. Thus there is an interesting farcical or tragic instability in gay desire: the moment of sexual success is also a moment of potential failure, that is, loss of desire. (Much gay humor is built on just this paradox: "Get *her!*") In his elaborate fetishistic plot, Purdy has contrived an erotic machine to keep Roy and Sidney essentially masculine — that is impervious — until the moment when neither is impervious and yet both are dominators, when Sidney nails Roy, by Roy's "command," to the barn door. Their tenderness is thus made hot, still dangerous, still exciting: thus the tears Roy sheds when Sidney pulls the nails *out* of his body are "hotter than blood" (172). Love hurts far more than pain.

The obstacles in this male courtly love quest are then internal, not external — no "forms" need to be observed, for they are all already outsiders — and the sexual reward is made coterminous with suffering. Mere happiness, mere pleasure is not the goal. That is why there are so many false pairs before we reach the true one (Roy and Sidney). The reader, like Sidney, must be led through the partial or inadequate loves — the merely "natural" ones — before he can settle on the complete one. Why are the false ones false? Because one or the other of the partners is insufficiently masculine, which means (in this book) tormented and angry. Brian is beautiful, for instance, but a boy. He is *too* willing to love Roy, *too* willing again to transfer that love to Sidney. He is easily manipulated. He exists to get stoned, fucked, hurt, used, and killed. Gareth, by contrast, is less easily won. But he is a male Turandot, an ice princess, haughty and spiteful. He turns into a nagging wife. He is therefore not desirable.

It is notable that though Sidney finally acknowledges a deep, indeed unpayably deep obligation to Roy, and though Roy finally agrees to make "restitution" for the death of Brian McFee, neither of them uses the other sexually: that is, penetrates the other's ass. (They perform the more brotherly rite of fellatio.) The sexual subjection and feminization implied in passive anal intercourse is transferred instead to the symbolic realm. Sidney "reports in," thus acknowledging that Roy is his commanding officer ("I ain't never been commanded so before," he explains to the envious horny Gareth [159]). Roy, for his part, submits to penetration not by Sidney's cock but by the nails that punish him. Both have submitted, both have dominated; both are on top and on bottom. The erotic charge has been preserved, though at the price of suffering and death.

The effect of this erotic machine, like that of heterosexual courtly love stories, is precisely to make love more precious and more unnatural. In both cases, the love test is a sign that the man has something to learn. In this gay romance, because both lovers are men, both have something to learn. Indeed, given the taboos against homosexuality, the sick shames and guilts that we all grow up with, this love-testing is an arguably crucial part of growing up as a gay man. Coming out, on this deepest level, is not simple, and cannot be accomplished (at least according to Purdy) by mere choice. It costs something, it is not without pain. A great deal of hatred and self-hatred needs to be consumed before one is capable of this kind of love. The violence that seems so ingrained in males is not, in Purdy's view, to be written off, wished away, or sentimentalized. Rather, it is to be *used,* ritually and aesthetically, to purify and make possible the difficult painful love between men. We will see this same ritualizing of violence in *Ready to Catch Him Should He Fall.*

Homosexuality in Purdy is essentially a form of ecstatic shame—a shame which his characters transform into a richer pleasure, and a transcendent love. The blood that makes them blush is the same blood that flows so freely from their veins. Is he saying therefore that gay men ought to stay in, or go back into, the closet? No: if only because his fiction seems unusually unsuited to any purely social or political morality. It is his lack of interest in such morality that makes him say he is not a "gay novelist," though he is not in the closet about being gay himself. Does he then imply that homosexuality, by being inherently shameful, is to be deprecated or avoided in oneself? No, again. Indeed, it is because of its difficulties that it is to be acknowledged and embraced. Like many gay men of his generation (and even of later ones) he sees homosexuality as an outlaw eroticism, and the outlaw life is by definition not easy. In this respect he is not entirely different from his rough age-mate Boyd McDonald, though, unlike McDonald, Purdy draws tragic conclusions from that outlawry, not comic ones.

It *is* true, I think, that Purdy does not see homosexuality as a culture. (In this, too, he is like Boyd McDonald, with his scorn for the "secondary sexual characteristics of homosexuality: ballet and opera.") For that reason, it is not to Purdy something to be fought for, modified, or defended. Homosexuality is a fate, not a culture or a choice. But even more radically (as we have seen), love itself, in Purdy, is such a fate. We have no choice over whom we fall in love with, or who falls in love with us; and yet—as *Narrow Rooms* argues—we are bound to these unchosen lovers as surely as if we had signed a contract in blood.

If this is a fair description of Purdy's fiction (or at least the erotic and gay portion of it), then why should anyone read it? Isn't it the dreariest kind of self-loathing made into a narrative? Why should we put up with pages of semi-coherent purple passages, all-too-transparently personal sexual fantasies, interchangeable characters, unvaryingly heightened emotional states, unbelievably contrived plots? For the same reason we want to hear *Tristan und Isolde* or read *Wuthering Heights:* for an experience of passion, which is, of course, literally "suffering." Purdy sees, as do Wagner and Brontë, that love is unthinkable without such suffering, that such suffering may even conceivably be its highest expression. Purdy is — of all gay novelists — the only one who has ventured into this very specialized realm and gotten out alive. Indeed, I would go further. Purdy not only appropriates the narratives of tragic passion for gay men, but shows that in an important sense, gay men *own* that narrative: that we can extend and develop that narrative precisely because the element of shame (not just guilt) is there to be exploited and overcome. For only when an obstacle is placed in the way of love — the incest taboo, the elaborate rituals of courtly love, homosexual shame — does it become precious and desirable. In this respect *Narrow Rooms* and *Eustace Chisolm and the Works* continue and expand the classic (heterosexual) love stories of the West: the *Hippolytus,* the *Romance of the Rose, Anna Karenina.*

If this all sounds simply ridiculous, there is no way to argue the point. To like Purdy, you have to have a certain taste for paradox, sadomasochism, and possibly religion. But then, these tastes *are* often found together, as Novalis noted two hundred years ago in the *Psychological Fragments:* "It is strange that the association of desire, religion and cruelty should not have immediately attracted men's attention to the intimate relationship which exists between them, and to the tendency which they have in common."[16] Nowhere else in contemporary gay American fiction do I find anything like this tragic view of love; nowhere else do I see exemplified so clearly (if hyperbolically) the necessary unity of worship and hatred, domination and self-sacrifice, violence and desire. Nowhere, in particular, do I see the peculiar dangers and difficulties of gay male passion so completely acknowledged and made beautiful. It struck me as I was writing this book how one of the great genres of mainstream literature — the tragic love story — has surprisingly few exemplars in gay fiction. The great exception is James Purdy.

[PART TWO]

GHETTO FREEDOMS,
GHETTO FOLLIES

Chapter Four

THE LIFE OF DESIRE IN 1978

The year was 1978, nine years into the so-called Stonewall revolution. Homosexuality had come out of the closet with a vengeance. Not only was the fact of it suddenly acknowledged by the straight world (Gay Pride parades were now a regular event in every major city in America), but it had begun changing from a personal (though of course humiliating) disability into a group identity: a "community" if you were being polite, a "ghetto" if you were not. This all happened very quickly. It was as if after so many years of repression, the oppressors themselves — the church, the psychiatric establishment, the police — had simply lost interest. Perhaps it was no longer much fun to attack gay people now that there was an actual gay press to report police injustices, congressional bigotry, and gay-bashings. Even the American Psychiatric Association resigned itself, under pressure from a few courageous members, to depathologizing same-sex love: homosexuality was deleted from its list of mental disorders in 1974, the greatest mass cure in history as some gay wit put it; to be replaced in due time by "ego-dystonic homosexuality": the disease of feeling *bad* about being gay. Oh, for a pen to do justice to *that* irony![1]

I had moved in that year from Maryland, to Boston, and was suddenly free as never before to make homosexuality a part of my life — a major part, as it happened, but one I hoped to integrate with others, such as my career and family. By comparison with Annapolis, and even Washington, D.C., Boston seemed a gay man's paradise. You had more choice than the one bar in Annapolis that went discreetly gay every other Thursday after 10 P.M. And even in Washington, I'd noticed that people who lived on Capitol Hill (a gay neighborhood) often avoided the bars there: they didn't want to mix work and play — or risk their GS ratings by being seen by their nongay neighbors. Boston seemed different, perhaps because of its large student population, which was freer to experiment than congressional aides or closeted midshipmen. The point of living in Boston's new gay ghetto, the South End, was precisely *to be seen*. You didn't have to separate the part of you that sought sex from the part that went to work, made friends, or loafed. On the street, every day of the week, going down for a quart of milk or coming home from work, over coffee or a magazine rack, I saw versions of myself, or myself as I secretly hoped to be: gay men who were seemingly well adjusted and happy, not in the least the monsters of my parents' imagination (or my own). As Samuel Delany writes in *The Mad Man*, a memoir (among other things) of the sex clubs of the same period, "It was only through a few years of doing what I was doing and looking at the people I was doing it with, many of whom seemed no less happy than anyone else, that I began to ask that most empowering of questions: Could all these people around me be both crazy and damned?"[2]

There were flies in the KY, of course, such as failed *chanteuse* Anita Bryant's nearly successful anti-gay campaign in 1977. Gay rights were (and of course still are) unrecognized by many states. Less obvious — they were hard to see — were the lingering sequelae of the self-mistrust, even self-hatred, to which so many gay men had become accustomed. It did not occur to me then — or not often anyway — that the enthusiastic fornicating that characterized my friends' lives could be anything but desirable; though in moments of sexual truce I found myself wondering uneasily just how much further I intended to go. (Plenty, as it turned out.) But if I did sometimes doubt, I took courage from my own resilient desires and the ghetto's ethic of cheerful hedonism. And if I needed an intellectual justification (but surely I didn't?), I had Boston's own radical journal *Fag Rag* to assure me that "indiscriminate promiscuity" was itself "an act of revolution."[3] Why, sex was practically a *duty!* So, despite multiple infections which only a few years before would have depressed and disgusted me, I repeatedly bathed in the warm current of sex that lapped around the newly bricked sidewalks of the South End, not knowing a treacherous riptide was just offshore. The important thing, at least in my memory, was the simple overwhelming fact of freedom. And while I was confused and a bit scared about how to be gay (how *was* I to integrate so many contradictory desires into my life?), I guessed as I had in my first year at college that being gay had a future, and that the future was happening then and there.

Two books have captured that year, one haloing it (despite the author's own satiric intentions) in a golden light of regret and romance, as if it had already begun to vanish; the other snapping it in a harsh unflattering flash. The first, Andrew Holleran's *Dancer from the Dance*, seemed to me then the best gay novel I had ever read, the closest to my experience and the most penetrating in its analysis of same-sex desire. It still does. The other, Larry Kramer's *Faggots*, I detested. But while I cannot say I have enjoyed *Faggots* much, then or since, I see more clearly now what it is, and have begun to accord it a grudging respect. It is hard, after all, to argue with Kramer's prescient fear that gay men were "fucking themselves to death," when AIDS was waiting not three years down the road to confirm it. But I cannot like this book for that reason alone: a novel is not a prediction.

These two books continue to offer a sharp and illuminating contrast between two visions of gay freedom, visions which are still alive. *Faggots* (as its nasty little title suggests) aims to deflate and disenchant the illusions gay men have about themselves. *Dancer*, as *its* title suggests, has tolerance and even love for those illusions. Yeats's line, "How can we know the dancer from the dance?" is a question with no answer. The word *faggots* is an answer with no question. Both novels display the follies of the new gay ghetto; but where Kramer sees only stupidity and self-destruction, Holleran sees a quixotic experiment one would hesitate to call a failure.

LARRY KRAMER'S *FAGGOTS*

Last year over a dinner of Korean hot-pot, my friend Kevin illuminated *Faggots* and *Dancer from the Dance* for me. I had been complaining of the former — that it was overheated, self-absorbed, nagging: all the usual complaints, made not only by me but by many other critics[4] — and contrasting it irritably with what I saw as the subtlety and finesse of the latter. Kevin said he couldn't see the difference. They were both good comedies; what more was I looking for? Style! Probability! Pathos! I began, when he interrupted me to say: "*I* like *Faggots* because I'm a neurotic Jew; *you* like *Dancer* because you're a neurotic Catholic."

I stopped in my tracks. Despite Kevin's rather cavalier collapsing of sects (I was not a Catholic), he was right. What I'd been complaining about — the improbability of the plot, the (to me) peculiar inhibitions of the characters — was less a topic than a convention, a language Kramer was speaking. The endless jokes about therapy and excrement struck Kevin as funny because they seemed the preoccupations of a "neurotic Jew." Once one simply granted that Kramer was writing a gay *Portnoy's Complaint,* much fell into place. One of the things that fell into place was the genre of *Faggots.* It's a cross between the sitcom, the talking-cure, and the practical joke (more on the last in a moment). Kramer, like his hero Fred, was a screenwriter, with the script of Ken Russell's *Women in Love* to his credit. And some of the longer scenes, in which many different characters converge on the same spot — the Toilet Bowl, for instance — cry out for screen treatment. In these scenes, the dialogue has the tightness of a good script, full of double-takes and other hints to the viewer of what the character's really thinking, what he's trying not to say, etc. You don't notice this at first because the rest of the novel is written as an interior monologue, in the deaf, logorrheic voice of the long-term analysand or the "life of the party." These passages are so bullying that many readers — I, certainly — want to get away from them.

The combination makes the novel too long to *watch* — and watching is, I think, what Kramer the scriptwriter had in mind. *Faggots* would make a great two-hour movie — it sometimes reminds one of *The Ritz* — it makes a ponderous four hundred-page book, especially one that claims to be a *jeu d'esprit*. Where a film or TV show would ruthlessly cut all the connecting stuff — information about Fred's parents, endless plays on words, and so forth — a "psychological novel" seems to demand it. But the connective material is neither interesting in itself nor (by novelistic standards) particularly well done. Stream of consciousness is not the same thing as stream of unspoken thoughts. (The great masters of the style, like Joyce, aren't really representing "thoughts" at all, but mental things for which there is no name.) Kramer merely encourages his characters to free-associate — useful on the couch, less so on the page — and the result feels calculated and self-consciously "spontaneous." By contrast, when he stops monologuizing and writes sitcom scenes, when the characters become the two-dimensional stage figures they secretly long to be, he is objective, terse, and funny.

The problem is that we can't just skip over the gassy, fifty-minute-hour parts. Kramer is a narrative control-freak, and won't let us go until he's told every last joke. And the reason for *that* is that underneath the lava flow of words is a solemn moral, just as underneath neurotic Fred is a warm, wonderful human being. We are not to be spared a single drop of that human warmth. Nor are we ever to be allowed out of Kramer's sight long enough to form our own opinions about the gay ghetto, or love, or sex, or parents, or the body, or art. He's always there like some monstrous nurse, force-feeding us the laughs till we give in and say we "got it." To be *forced* to laugh is a mixed blessing that quickly becomes a mixed curse. So while Kramer's opinions are often sharp and memorably expressed, they're also in a strange way humorless. After a very short while, I find myself cursing good jokes as well as bad, especially those that all-too-transparently mask some moral point or other. When the characters are allowed to speak, they are funny; when they are forced by Kramer to "stand for" something they are not.

But as I thought about what Kevin had said, it occurred to me that he was righter than even he realized. The "Jewishness" of *Faggots,* for example, is not incidental but deliberate and important. The clash of two minority identities is what makes Fred Lemish (and his creator) who he is. Indeed the novel's first page explicitly connects the two when in newscaster's deadpan it enumerates the number of "faggots" in New York City: "There are now more faggots in the New York City area than Jews. There are now more faggots in the entire United States than all the yids and kikes put together. (This is subsidiary data, not overtly relevant, but ipso facto nevertheless.)"[5]

When he tells us "this is subsidiary data, not overtly relevant," we ought to disbelieve him. Subsidiary to whom? Not to Fred and not to Kramer himself. What if there really *were* "more faggots in the New York City area than Jews"? What would it say about New York if the dominant minority were not serious, diligent, intelligent Jews, but anti-intellectual and hedonistic faggots? Or to put it in terms of this novel, what if New York were characterized by Billy Boner and Randy Dildough (whose names speak for themselves) rather than Abe Bronstein, the self-made straight millionaire who wants to leave his mark by financing the first respectable gay film?

The comparison between these new and old minorities is continued a paragraph later: "The straight and narrow, so beloved of our founding fathers and all fathers thereafter, is now obviously and irrevocably bent. What is God trying to tell us . . . ? . . . Is there indeed a God who would understand such as: 'Baby, I want you to piss all over me!'" (17). This question plainly expects the answer No, as Latin grammars used to say. And Kramer, together with his hero Fred, is clearly on the side of the God of his fathers, even when (as here) he finds himself at the Everard Baths. This is a big problem, because he is also, at least theoretically, on the side of Fred and all the other "bent" sons. *Faggots* is a drama of paternal repression and filial disobedience. Or to put it another way, it is a battle between Fred's "Jewishness" and his "queerness."

This psychomachia is projected onto the gay world as a whole. Its inhabitants can be identified as either "faggots" or "Jews." (Most, alas, are "faggots.") By "faggot" Kramer means anyone who evades responsibility; by "Jew" he means anyone who accepts it. There are a few gentile faggots who are mature (i.e., unhappy) enough to be honorary Jews, especially Fred's best friends, Anthony Montano and "Gatsby." Anthony Montano is forty or so, has a demanding job to which he is "married," engages in sex only with reluctance, and thinks gay men incapable of love. Despite being an Italian-American Catholic, he sounds exactly like Fred and even says "Oi": "*Oi, what am I doing here doing these things?*, Assholes are un-Godly, used for shit, not miraculous channels for the birthing of babies like the ladies have . . ." (195). Gatsby is a Northern European version of Anthony: "Tall, Blond, Handsome, Fred's Trinity" (20), a perpetual chaser of men who turn out to be disappointments. He, like Fred, is writing a novel about modern gay life which Gatsby calls "an exercise in self-loathing." (Gatsby, by the way, seems to be a portrait of Andrew Holleran.) Similarly, the word *faggot* can extend to certain nongay people such as "New York's leading fag hag," Adriana la Chaise, who displays her faggot credentials by slumming at louche bars like The Pits and thus wasting her "brains, her abilities, and her energies."

Straight men, to the small extent that they appear in this novel, never evade responsibility, though they are given to swatting their gay sons. In any case their gay sons are terrified of them, and believe that they now chase dick in a belated search for daddy's love. And while gay women also don't cut much of a figure here, it is curious that in the sexual free-for-all of the last scene on Fire Island, Abe's wife Ephra is successfully seduced by Nancellen Richtofen, and that this seduction seems to be the *only* one in the book that promises happiness—or even sexual relief. (Otherwise, the sole appetite that is regularly gratified is hunger: Fred sublimates his frustrated longing for Dinky Adams in an orgy of chocolate-eating.) The interesting characters—really the *only* characters—are those who are both "Jewish" and "faggots": men like Anthony, Fred, and Boo Boo Bronstein, Abe's erring son. In them the clash of the two cultures is particularly evident, or at least noisy.

Unfortunately, the collision turns out to have somewhat predictable consequences: "gay" culture is a lightweight in this match, and its pan flies up and kicks the beam when counterpoised with the "unending powerlessness in Jewish history," as Abe puts it to himself. If being a faggot means "all we do is fuck," in the words of Jack Humpstone (aka, Laverne), and if faggot culture has enshrined fucking as the central act of a gay man's life, then our hero Fred *really isn't gay.* For though he does his share of fornicating, it is with the rectitudinous purpose of finding a boyfriend who "reads books, loves his work, and me, too, of course, and who doesn't take drugs, and isn't on unemployment" (22). While this desire is promptly mocked by Anthony Montano, Fred never gives up on it.

The novel asks a question, and the plot is a lab experiment to answer it. Is there a gay equivalent to the straight, middle-class dream of security and modest success? Is the gay man perhaps even *freer* than his straight friends? Can he, should he, jettison middle-class aspirations entirely (as radical journals like *Fag Rag* then advised)? Does gay culture offer something worse than, equal to, or better than the bourgeois dream? Or does it in fact destroy happiness, security, and even life? In this light, Fred's journey into "This Faggot World" becomes an attempt to find out whether his desires can be met in the gay ghetto, and whether they are the right desires at all.

The answer given by the book is not only unequivocal, but essentially assumed from the start.

Question A: Can the desire for faithful love be satisfied in the gay world? Answer: No.

Question B: Is the desire to be "married" the right one? Answer: Yes. Constricting as middle-class culture is—symbolized best in Ephra Bronstein's antiseptically untouched apartment, whose bathroom even her ex-husband is not allowed to use — it is nonetheless the best, perhaps the only game in town. Certainly the alternatives — being pissed on by a total stranger at the baths, for instance — are not immediately appealing. Furthermore, it turns out that indeed there aren't very many faggots who are looking for love as Fred is. If they have jobs, they are either martyrs to them like Anthony or use them to exert unjust (usually sexual) power over others. They don't read books, even though many have been to good colleges. If they are rich they use their money for drugs and hustlers and parties, not for the good of the gay community. If they are under- or unemployed (like Fred's friends Mikie and little Bilbo), they use their welfare checks for drugs and tricks and parties. "Faggots" are men who can barely take care of themselves, let alone anyone else. Indeed, they don't seem men at all, but boys — charming, fickle, dirty. If we forgive them it is only because they are moral children who can scarcely be held accountable for their actions.

So the culture clash is unavoidable on the one hand — "gay" and "Jewish" really can't coexist, one must dominate the other — and yields a foregone conclusion on the other: it's better to be Jewish than gay. Fred's journey is the proof. One particularly clear proof-text comes at the end of it, when Fred is having an argument with the feckless Dinky Adams. Dinky is trying to persuade Fred that they're better off as "just friends." Fred sees at once that this is an Evasion of Responsibility, and sings a big moral tune in indignant response: "no relationship in the world could survive the shit we lay on it. It tells me we're not looking at the reasons why we're doing the things we're doing. It tells me we've got a lot of work to do. A lot of looking to do. It tells me that, if those happy couples are there, they better come out of the woodwork fast and show themselves pronto so we can have a few examples for unbelieving heathens like you that it's possible" (337). A stirring sentiment with lots of trumpets and drums. But notice the language Fred uses. Dinky, that avatar of ghetto culture, is an "unbeliever," a "heathen" — a gentile in fact, a worshiper of idols and false gods. That makes Fred a Jew not just in the ethnic or religious sense, but in the cultural one: a believer in faithfulness, that greatest of Jewish virtues. Dinky, the representative gay, is also (and damningly) the representative goy. Gay culture is finally pagan, and thus incompatible with fidelity.

This might be a serious moral debate but for the fact that all of the weight is on Fred's side and none on Dinky's. Dinky (as his ridiculous, unmanning nickname suggests) is not even grown-up in his pleasures. He embodies not so much hedonism as impulsiveness. He can offer no counterargument to Fred either by word or deed. The entire "heathen" world represented by ancient Greece (that continual reference point for gay culture) is reduced to its worst argument, Dinky, while the entire Judaic world is summed up in its best, Fred. The possibility that there might be a hedonism more subtle and pleasurable than Dinky's never crosses Kramer's mind; nor the possibility that Fred might be pursuing self-righteousness rather than love. The further possibility that the dichotomy might be false, that one could live by different rules from either Fred's or Dinky's, or that the heathen and Judaic ethical worlds might encounter one another less aridly than they do here, barely exists.

But am I not just taking all this too seriously? Certainly my friend Kevin thought so. After all, it's a comedy, not a philosophy text. But I don't think this is the best way to defend the exaggerations of the novel. For despite its obviously over-the-top style it *is* making an important point and asking us to agree with it. That point is simply that gay men are destroying themselves and each other by not realizing love is more important than sex. I wouldn't mind the improbabilities of the set pieces (for instance, the "burial-alive" of Boo Boo Bronstein on Fire Island) if they weren't so plainly meant also to be taken seriously and symbolically. At one moment we're laughing heartlessly (these are the good moments); at the next, we're laughing with a heart all too obviously full. In fact, Kramer *wants* us to be caught between the rock of finding his novel "just a farce" and the hard place of finding it a coruscating exposé of gay life. Either way he wins. The jokes always have a design on us.

Even the most obvious feature of this novel, Kramer's manic prose, which loops around every which way, strikes me as less interesting than it appears. The sentences want to be taken in contradictory ways: as improvised, Whitmanian effusions, but also as deep home-truths. The *Chicago Tribune,* responding to the Whitman voice, called *Faggots* a "Vesuvian explosion about gay life." But its reviewer simply bought what Kramer was selling — the image of himself as a destructive, magnificent force of nature. We're meant to look at this mad improbable proliferation of characters, situations, and motives in awe: laughing but shaking our heads in respectful amazement. But this is not a fact but a pose — and a self-serving one at that.

Faggots is really not so much a good or bad *book* as an ingenious *trap.* And if you start writing about it as if it were merely a book, you fall into that trap. It begins with an insult — "There are 2,556,596 faggots in the New York City area" — and dares you to return it. If you do return it (by complaining that the word *faggots* isn't funny, to take an unimaginative example) you quickly brand yourself someone who has missed the point, who has no sense of humor, or who is himself a "faggot" (i.e., dumb and defensive). *Faggots* is the tar baby of gay fiction: touch it, try to get underneath its surface, and you're caught.

Why should we be surprised by this? You don't write a book called *Faggots* and expect people to thank you for it. And in a weird way, Kramer is quite indifferent to whether you like or dislike him. So for instance if you simply laugh at the antics of these "faggots" and pay no attention to the fairly obvious homophobia underneath them, that's fine with him. If you do pay attention to the homophobia, that's fine too, though for a different reason: he expects you to dislike it, indeed he's set up the whole book in order that you dislike it. So when you come along and obligingly object to some gratuitous slur or other, you're merely complying with his directives.

Kramer is playing a very old game which I remember from childhood. It's called "I don't care if you like me." If you play this game, you are always a winner. Either the other little boys will say, Oh but we *do* like you, and you'll have friends (on your own terms); or you'll be proved right. (You also get to prove them wrong: how stupid they are!) It's heads I win, tails you lose. That's why criticism of this book — which has been plentiful — misses the point. You can say anything you like about it, that it's long-winded, improbable, self-righteous, hyperbolic, and all you've done is describe it. You might as well complain that a sonnet is artificial or fourteen lines long. Long-windedness, improbability, self-righteousness, hyperbole are its means as well as its ends. And all Kramer needs to say in response is, "Yes, you're right. So?"

One of the many ways Kramer seems not gay, in fact, is that he is a sort of practical joker. (As I remember it, we sissies were the ones the straight boys always wanted to play practical jokes *on*.) He has the practical joker's sadistic mentality, too: the concealment of hostility under humor, the desire to look good by making someone else look bad, and most of all the drive to make something, anything, happen. The practical joking goes on at all levels of this novel. Buckets of water are of course set up for most of the "faggots" (e.g., handsome desirable Lance Heather turns out to have *no dick!*). But they are also provided for the reader, and the mechanism is simplicity itself. The trip wire is our dislike — and what could be easier to engage? Why not make every gay character unhappy or repulsive, for instance? That will do the trick! At our first mental reservation, the bucket starts tilting. "What's the matter, no sense of humor?" A second provokes a seeming olive branch ("Hey, seriously . . . the gay community really does have a lot of shit to work through"). A third jerks it back ("But you guys *still* got no dicks!") then says, hands raised in innocent amazement, "Hey I was just kidding!"

The practical joke is a perfect machine. It never fails because the practical joker is always in the right. It is the automatic refuge of the clever unloved child. Even when one wants to pay *Faggots* the compliment of taking it seriously, it will take its revenge. I too am aware of positioning myself under the bucket of water.

Get ready to laugh.

The nearly four hundred pages of *Faggots* cover only three days, from the end of the gay winter "season" in New York on Friday to the beginning of the summer season at The Pines on Sunday. During this period, at least a half-dozen bars or sex clubs open, including the infamous Toilet Bowl, dozens of encounters take place among people destined to meet each other again many times, and Abe Bronstein's "faggot" son Richie stages his own self-kidnapping, which ends in a mock-burial alive on Fire Island. The novel is so crowded with characters and schemes that one sometimes loses track of the main one: Fred Lemish, about to turn forty and finally find happiness as a "Homosexual Man," pursues and loses the handsome, evanescent Dinky Adams. In so doing, he pursues and finds (as he often portentously reminds us) Himself. (I noticed while writing this chapter that "F. Lemish" was an anagram of "himself." An accident? *You* be the judge!) By facing any illusions he might have had about "This Faggot World," he finally realizes that these selfish desperate men—let's be honest: faggots—wouldn't recognize True Love if it sat down before them with big brown eyes, years of therapy, and a degree from Harvard.

Over many previous years, Fred has tried to shape himself into the person he thinks he ought to be: he now has a "hairy chest, wide shoulders, at last a thirty-inch waist." He has come to terms (so he thinks) with his homosexuality and his ambivalent love for his parents, mean Lester and do-gooding Algonqua. He is the author of the screenplay for a modestly successful cult film, *Lest We Sleep Alone,* and wants to write another about gay life in the modern world. But time is running out. Here is his pep talk to himself: "this was the last chance. Harden up now, slim down now, grab your man now—because, over forty, it wasn't going to be easy to accomplish any of these things . . . Fred was—in short—your average, standard, New York faggot obsessive kvetch" (27–28).

Fred's love life has been problematic. His adored Feffer, for instance, "a Wisconsin Phi Bete," had been "wonderful until Fred unfortunately discovered he wanted to tie Fred up and beat him." Plainly not husband material. Right now, Fred is working on the equally untrustworthy Dinky Adams: "tall, dark, bright, gorgeous, with honors from Georgetown." (All of Kramer's characters tend to come with educational pedigrees, the better to scold them for failing to live up to their promise.) Soon enough, the charm's wound up:

> Fred had, at thirty-nine, hoped love would come by forty.
> He had only four days to go.
> Forty years old!
> And beloved Dinky would soon be coming back!
> And beloved Abe would produce Fred's screenplay!
> And Life would at last be in order! Love and work co-joined! (30)

A coming-of-age story, then, mixed with elements of the *Bildungsroman,* the picaresque novel, and the quest. The plot is ingenious, bringing together a vast number of characters in several huge (and repetitive) set pieces: "the last city orgy of the spring season" at Garfield Toye's CPW penthouse, the opening night of the Toilet Bowl, symbol of the ghetto's disgusting decadence, and a sequence of parties on Fire Island. In Kramer's fictional economy, more is more and once is never enough. And as we soon learn, any character we meet once we meet again, less because he or she is personally *necessary* than because the world Kramer is describing is a ghetto, insular and inbred, and he wants to make sure we know. *Everyone* is related by ambition, boredom, and lust. Within a few pages, we've met Fred's two best friends, "Gatsby," "who had received this name at Princeton because he was from St. Paul, Minnesota, and wanted to be a writer" (20) and Anthony Montano, "who was married to his position as Vice-President and Creative Director, in charge of the Winston Man, at Heiserdiener-Thalberg-Slough" (22). The three are virtually the only members of the gay world Kramer has any use for. Their attitudes toward "love," however, are widely different. Fred is looking for it with eager hope, Gatsby with resigned despair — the novel he's working on, "an exercise in self-loathing," asks "how can two guys who don't like themselves ever let anyone else like themselves?" (20–21). Anthony disbelieves entirely in love between men, advising Fred instead to get a dog: "Dogs are faggot children" (22).

These three are the (comparatively) still point of the turning faggot world, though Fred is certainly less still than either Anthony or Gatsby. From these three, as from some insanely hypertextual Web site (though this of course is chronologically absurd), the reader can double-click his way to Irving Slough, Anthony's employer, an aging leather queen whose ad in the *Avocado* (the *Advocate,* get it?) has been answered by Dinky, who once had a six-year affair with Jack Humpstone (aka, Laverne), who — with his "sisters" Patty and Maxine — owns Balalaika, situated above the Toilet Bowl, at whose opening the Winston Man (Winnie Heinz), desperate at the prospect of middle age and completely out of his mind on angel dust, leaps to his death, to be quickly replaced by succulent Timmy Purvis, just off the bus from Mount Rainier, Maryland, as the most desirable model in the Hans Zoroaster agency (Hans Zoroaster being Irving Slough's faithful but neglected lover — remember Irving Slough?); while in an adjacent back room Boo Boo Bronstein (to his horror) stumbles upon his prodigiously endowed nephew Wyatt, whom he persuades to deliver a fake ransom note to (of all people) Boo Boo's kindly father Abe Bronstein, the cake millionaire, who is touring the Toilet Bowl at the suggestion of Fred Lemish, our hero, whose screenplay on "This Faggot World" Abe hopes to produce with the help of Randy Dildough, that handsome if closeted executive who, as a youth, honed his taste for sadism on toothsome Robbie Swindon, who therefore grew up to be a faggot and have meaningless sex later that weekend with Fred Lemish (who nonetheless wonders whether this is "Mr. Quite Possibly Great Love Number III?") but of course runs off afterward, leaving Fred with no option but to bid a final farewell to Fire Island and the Ice Palace, where he sees many sad reminders of the empty life that late he led: the Divine Bella (a talentless gossip columnist), his former boyfriend Frigger, Little Bilbo the ex–concert pianist (what a waste of talent!), Mikie, Josie, Dom Dom, Anthony, Gatsby, Sprinkle, and finally Dinky himself—faithless, small-souled, sluttish Dinky, such good sex though, who drags our hero back to his house for yet another tantalizing fuck and Fred follows, yes he does, despite knowing better, and they're having sex and Dinky is reaching for "the Lemish cock" when suddenly the Lemish soul rears up and cries, "You are Unwanted, I reject you through and through," and with this declaration relives all the beatings, emotional and corporal, which have caused him so much suffering, and "the beatings turn into . . . tears" which are themselves transformed into anger and, yes, Shit!, as Fred takes a deeply symbolic crap on Dinky's beautiful garden, thus signaling to the reader and himself that his journey is Now At An End.

Oh, it's so mad it just makes your *head* spin!

I have of course exaggerated Kramer's breathless style, but his novel does make several odd assumptions. One is historically peculiar: namely, that gay men in 1978 were terrified of coming out and still playing games of concealment that would make sense only in an episode of "The Dick Van Dyke Show." Boo Boo Bronstein, for instance, evolves a rather baroque plan to get his hands on a million dollars: he will get himself kidnapped and Abe will ransom him. But both the goal and the means of its execution seem imprecise. Why exactly does he need the million dollars? It has something to do with not thinking he can ever attract a man without it. The second part of the scheme is equally bizarre: that this will be how Abe finds out Richie is *gay*. To find it funny I would have to believe, for instance, that the character has no choice but to form this ridiculously convoluted plot. But what were the obstacles in the mid-seventies to someone like Richie, a young man who would have come of sexual age at the very moment of Stonewall, attended Yale when the first gay student organizations were starting, and moved back to New York at a time when it was as easy to pick up a sexual partner as a quart of milk? What would he have needed the money for in an age that opened the sexual gates to anyone presentable? Would his first gay sexual partner actually have been an unattractive "portly, gentile professor"? And would he really have been so sexually naive as to wonder *why he got an erection?* ("How did it turn into such a straight and hard flagpole without my even knowing it?" he asks himself with nauseating whimsy [58].) Would a rich young man in the rebellious and sexually overheated seventies really have feared to answer an ad in the distant *Avocado*, or truly believed he *had* to marry that "spaghetti heiress, Marci Tisch" (61)? Kramer, I think, betrays his own age (he was born in 1935) in constructing Boo Boo's sex life. The year seems to be 1963, not 1978.

A second odd assumption concerns the humor itself. Kramer seems to believe that improbability and overintricacy are sufficient jokes, as if the novel were a fictional Rube Goldberg machine. But this is precisely where Kramer (to my mind) plays it safe by playing it sloppy. What makes Goldberg's inventions funny is the sober madness that lies behind them; nothing could be less like Kramer's impersonation of a Vesuvian force of nature. Goldberg invites us to wonder at the sort of mind that could contrive an enormously complicated but perfectly logical device for, say, lighting a cigarette. But we never sense how the minds we meet in *Faggots* work, why they choose the bizarre, even unpleasurable things they do. The purpose is to trivialize those minds, not revel in them. Again, Goldberg's "solutions" are precise and elegant. When you see the final result (a lit cigarette), you think for an instant that this was the only reasonable way to achieve it. Kramer's contrivances are sloppy and impressionistic by comparison. He has his characters do "funny things" rather than be funny; we're meant to find it all deliciously "wacky."

Besides being sloppy, Kramer's manic jokiness does a serious injustice to an important part of gay experience (at least mine): namely, that sex was fun, and sometimes ecstatic. But one of the oddest assumptions of this highly sexed novel is that no one actually likes sex very much. Kramer's gay characters (from Fred to Hans Zoroaster, Irving Slough, Randy Dildough, Lance Heather, the Winston Man, Timmy Purvis, and Garfield Toye) are all just naughty boys, and their sexual transgressions seem mere moral tics. I can imagine that the spectacle of sexual voracity might *be* funny, but it would not *feel* funny. The lech is deeply serious about his mania. But Kramer's faggots (though lust-driven to a man) never take their lust seriously. When we first meet Irving Slough, for example, he is piercing his lover's nipple. At first, the point seems to be: How decadent! (This was after all only 1978, and nipple-piercing was as yet rare. I still remember my very trendiest friend saying of his own nipple-ring, with thrilling indifference: "I *always* wanted to have it done.") But the really shocking point is that neither Irving nor Hans is even paying attention. Getting pierced is about as interesting for them as buying a new shirt. That, of course, is "the joke." But the joke short-circuits whatever power lurks in sadomasochism, a power which might, if acknowledged, have accounted for these characters. As a result of Kramer's going for an easy and automatic irony — Why, Martha, I believe these sick people actually *enjoy* being hurt — Hans and Irving are left with no coherent motive for their otherwise relentless pursuit of sex.

Again, when Boo Boo Bronstein has sex for the first time, we are told that he is overwhelmed by "the guilt, ah yes, The Guilt!" (60) — a phrase whose capital letters and comic exclamation mark signal winkingly that we all know what *that's* like. But we actually don't. One of the most difficult, most absorbing things about becoming gay in the seventies was just this: the exploration of "guilt." How much was real and how much was Memorex? How much could be accepted without turning into a self-hating faggot? How much could be thrown away without becoming a monster? How much was negotiable? In this novel, guilt is simply assumed. It is on the one hand a sign of election: for many of the "faggots" are simply incapable of it. On the other, it is supposedly "funny," a mechanical neurotic scraping open of unhealed wounds. It's good for you but rather disgusting — like taking a shit.

Indeed, this comparison is not adventitious, for *Faggots* constantly (if jokily) directs our attention to Fred's habits of evacuation and indeed uses for its epigraph a quote from Evelyn Waugh: ". . . the ancients located the deeper emotions in the bowels." We are accordingly shown Fred taking a dump in Ireland, at his "Henry James abode" on Washington Square, and finally on Dinky Adams's garden on Fire Island. And since anal eroticism plays such a central part in gay sexuality (a Canadian judge once marvelously said that leaving anal intercourse out of gay sex would be like leaving Mozart out of music), Fred's ambivalence to his butt can stand for his ambivalence to homosexuality itself.

Unfortunately, Kramer can't go further than seeing the most obvious contradictions between being a "nice person" like Fred and doing a "dirty" thing like (for example) getting a rectal douche from Dinky. The Whole Subject consternates him so much that he starts sounding like a coy eight-year-old: "As Dinky had squeezed it in, Fred realized, horror of horrors, that he was getting turned on. He liked this Dinky! He liked that he was having his first douche with someone he liked. He liked that he was evidently likeable enough for Dinky to get such a nice big hard-on over him. He liked it all. Yes, he did" (31–32). This grown-up baby-talk continues as he takes his first tentative steps into rimming: "And in he stuck his tongue into Dinky's asshole. He just did it. It tasted good. It tasted very good. It was smooth and clean . . ." (33). But despite *chattering* about how much he likes it, the tone makes it obvious that he's just nervous.

This is why *Faggots* fails (for me) as satire. For even satire rests on a certain mystery. Its characters can be ridiculously obsessed, but we have to believe that their obsession makes sense, that it is worth devoting one's life to. It's perfectly possible, for instance, to use shit to convey the compelling madness of some vice without automatically trivializing the vice. In the following passage from the *Dunciad*, Pope not only mocks but creates a dialogue for two antiquarians so obsessed with collecting Greek coins that they are more than willing to acquire (or sell) them "used," with no care for their immediate provenance:

> "True, he had wit, to make their value rise;
> From foolish Greeks to steal them, was as wise;
> More glorious yet, from barb'rous hands to keep,
> When Sallee Rovers chas'd him on the deep.

Then taught by Hermes, and divinely bold,
Down his own throat he risqu'd the Grecian Gold,
Receiv'd each Demi-God, with pious care,
Deep in his Entrails — I rever'd them there,
I bought them, shrouded in that living shrine,
And, at their second birth, they issue mine."
  "Witness great Ammon! By whose horns I swore,
(Reply'd soft Annius) this our paunch before
Still bears them, faithful; and that thus I eat,
Is to refund the Medals with the meat.
To prove me, Goddess! clear of all design,
Bid me with Pollio sup, as well as dine;
There all the Learn'd shall at the labour stand,
And Douglas lend his soft, obstetric hand."

                                            (*Dunciad* IV, 375–94)[6]

Am I wrong to hear in these grave periods a kind of deranged majesty as well as
an obscene joke? Indeed, isn't Pope's attention to the coins' second nativity in
itself an act of worship? (Douglas's "soft obstetric hand" is beautiful as well as
disgusting.) And if so, isn't the "joke" deeply unstable, uniting the supposed
satirist to his supposed target? By contrast, I find it hard to believe Kramer has
identified himself with any of the obsessions in *Faggots*. He has simply presented them as self-evident absurdities.

  Indeed, Kramer's book is less a satire than a denigration; and it denigrates by
trivializing. Even the characters' names are trivial: diminutives like Mikie, feminine nicknames like "Tante" or Laverne, humiliating childhood names like Boo
Boo, vaguely sexual names like Dinky or overtly sexual names like Randy Dildough. Their purpose is to make gay men seem not so much dangerous as silly.
This is really a far more damning attitude than out-and-out hatred or disgust,
both of which suppose the thing hated has a certain power. Indeed one of the
ongoing insults of this book is the way its targets prove themselves unworthy
even of being shot down. They're so ridiculous they virtually self-destruct.

  Take Winnie Heinz the Winston Man, for instance. He's from a rich Main
Line family — and a good thing, too, for he's far too lazy to work. Second, he's
stupid. When a teacher at his prep school tells him he's going to be a "fairy,"
he doesn't know what that means (the Hill School must not have been doing
its job) and has to ask Sammy Rosen, who is predictably poor but bright, and
also has a crush on Winnie. Third, he's monstrously (and improbably) self-
possessed. When Sammy asks him what he'll do after college, Winnie simply
gazes at himself in a mirror and says, "I think I'm very handsome. Don't
you? . . . I guess that means I have to be a famous model" (85). Fourth, he's not

only a narcissist but an anti-Semite. When Winnie and Sammy have sex, "holding on to each other's dickies . . . as if each were rather hungry from some already precocious deprivation now being at last fulfilled," Winnie "even return[s Sammy's] kisses . . . not worrying that the lips, too, were Jewish" (87). Even his penis is trivialized as a "dickie" shooting its "little load."

It's hard to know what's most vile about Winnie Heinz, isn't it? And Winnie Heinz is in many ways the very embodiment of the gay ghetto. You do the math.

Why, given such a presentation of the "facts" of gay life, would anyone be gay? The answer, I think, is that no one would. Being gay is a crippling deformity to nearly everyone in this book. Perhaps, if one is as decent and intelligent as Fred (with a good education and stiff moral backbone, courtesy of the do-gooding Algonqua), one can reach the point of separating oneself from the madding crowd of other "faggots," and declare that one plays by one's own rules, not those of any "ghetto." Such a person can conceivably reach the point of declaring that he is "not gay, not a fairy, not a fruit, not queer, not a faggot. I'm a Homosexual Man. I'm Me" (381). But absent Algonqua, the average gay man in Kramer's ghetto is doomed to failure — and a mingy, embarrassing failure at that: death by self-caricature. Here are a few of the *idées reçues* that we are meant to grin and bear, the pathetic options for gay life:

1. leather men: never truly masculine, always "pussycats"
2. gay ghetto boys: substitute sex for love
3. middle-class gays: secretly corrupt
4. older gays: predatory
5. younger gays: stupid

Kramer is aware, of course, that these are clichés, and is embarrassed enough to perpetuate them under cover of jokes, but not enough to question them further.

In the following passage, for instance, the unflattering definition of a *faggot* is swathed in yards of cute rhetoric and the ponderous humor of a very long sentence:

The strange bedfellows [i.e., Balalaika, a dance bar, and The Pits, a sex club housed in the same building] were to get along just fine, even after The Pits became a wee bit too notorious for the quality of its stage show, all those outré extensions of the anatomy's natural abilities, all played in various forms of repertoire, thus causing overflow crowds of uptown slummers, visiting firemen, and other assorted pleasure seekers, including New York's leading fag hag, Adriana la Chaise, disguised as a man, who, while a faggot to the extent that she evades the responsibilities that her brains, her abilities, and her energies, in a more enlightened age, would have channeled, via adult commitments,

via more positive injections, into a needful society, was, nevertheless, by cli-
toral choice, straight, though it was her habit to enjoy slouching in dark corners, wearing military attire, sailor's suits or soldier's, and watch the boys do
things to each other, and enjoy fainting when the beauties on the stage wilted to
the floor, only to be watered by huge blacks wearing hip-length Goodyear
waders and furry guardsman's toppers and tipping wax from large Rigaud
candles that sizzled neath their stream, her distinguished presence, albeit in
mufti, being naturally noteworthy enough to enter the Divine Bella's twice-
weekly column in *Women's Wear,* so that Billy Boner, who owned The Pits,
then imposed strict membership and attire and inspection requirements, which
only made business even better, both downstairs and up. (39–40)

There's so much going on in this pretend-dizzy sentence that the actually
offensive definition of a *faggot* passes almost unobserved — or as unobserved
as Kramer's heavy-handed irony can make it. A faggot, it turns out — and
nothing in the book contradicts it — is simply someone who wastes his god-
given "brains," "abilities," and "energies" by failing to pursue "adult commitments." This definition underpins the moral of the book four hundred pages
later: "I say I know what I want and I ain't gettin' it. I say I'm settling for too
fucking little. . . . I say I'm not going to find love here. And even if I could, how
could it survive and grow? I say it's time to move on" (371–72). Another way to
put it would be to say that a "faggot" to Kramer is a contradiction in terms: a
man who's really a "girl," who perversely seeks pain rather than pleasure,
whose sexual appetite is so weak as to require "blacks" in "waders" to stimulate
it. Homosexuality is not a real thing in Kramer's book, but a false echo of
heterosexuality.

Once one has noticed it, this complacent construction of homosexuality as a
shadow sexuality, almost a fetish or paraphilia, affects everything Kramer has to
say about gay life. As a community, the gay ghetto is a shadow of the straight
world. It eagerly copies that world by trying to create its own equivalents of love
and marriage. In this attempt it utterly fails. Without exception every gay couple
in this book is a) unfaithful or b) unhappy. The implicit message is that faggots
cannot live faithfully or happily with each other. All that sex and drugs can do is
divert them from the painful self-contradictions of male-male desire, a desire
which is shown time and again to be the merest psychic compensation for a
distant father (Fred's Lester) and a close-binding-intimate mother (Fred's Algonqua). The dismal categories — already clichés — of fifties psychiatry are thus
dutifully reproduced. We would have to agree with these clichés if we are to find
Kramer's satire pointed.

And not just pointed — "brave," "prophetic," "honest." For throughout,
Kramer plays the role of the one honest man who will tell the truth, all others

(even kind Gatsby and guilty Anthony Montano) being finally too cowardly. He is the moral doctor administering an unpleasant but curative purge, the kind-but-stern father giving a much-needed spanking. Even if this were true, one would resent the way the choice was forced upon us, the way every fight is decided far in advance, like studio wrestling. In this light, it is appropriate that the novel ends in a literal wrestling match between Abe and his son Boo Boo on the sands of Fire Island—half Abraham-and-Isaac, half Oedipus complex, and in its more-is-more prose, all Kramer: Abe "pins him under his girth of years of living and food and knowledge. And the son knees back in protest and suffocation and not quite so experienced heft. And together they toss and they turn, like some biblical nightmare brought up to date. . . . Hitting and elbowing and kneeing and scratching and off sides and on sides and slugging it out and who's got the penis, who's got the testicles, where is the rectum, where is the scrotum, who is the Master, who is the Slave, which one the Top Man, which one the Bottom, who the Dominant, who the Submissive, who the S and who the M, and which one's got the BALLS!?" (364–65). While Abe is gently mocked throughout much of *Faggots,* isn't this punishment just what venal Boo Boo needs? And isn't Kramer himself really an Abe, and the whole gay community really a son that needs to be spanked? Isn't this what all us silly boys have been waiting for all along—hand-to-hand combat with a real man? a Pop to pop us?

A wit once said of a book that it was both new and good. "Unfortunately, the parts that are good are not new, and the parts that are new are not good." The same can be said of *Faggots.* The parts that are good are not particularly gay, and the parts that are gay are not particularly good. The good parts include quasi-Jewish jokes like the scene when Ephra interrupts Abe's frantic pacing after he's received Richie's fake kidnapping note: "How do you know I am not sleeping?" asks Abe; to which Ephra responds with tragic *froideur:* "An ex-wife knows" (280); or the scene at the Toilet Bowl, where Richie (Boo Boo) realizes his nephew Wyatt is coming on to him ("I think I'm having an anxiety attack." "What's an anxiety attack?" . . . "Feeling your nephew's cock is an anxiety attack" [238]). Another sort of successful comic turn in *Faggots* involves a character speaking rationally in a completely irrational situation. The first scene of the book, where Fred is at the baths trying to act Dionysian, is such a scene. So is the scene in which Abe, on his tour of the gay underworld dressed in his jaunty De Pinna seersucker, tries to strike up a conversation with a clone in a University of Miami baseball shirt: "What did you study there, if I may ask?" (235). (What a great *Christopher Street* cartoon!) One of my favorites is the scene where Fred stumbles upon his first great love Feffer, strung up and being whipped by Lance Heather and Leather Louie: " 'Hi, Lemmy.' Feffer focuses his eyes, looks down, and smiles kindly. 'I tried to call you but you weren't home. I didn't want to talk to your machine' " (267).

And the parts that are "gay" — well, which parts *are* they? To be sure, 99 percent of the characters are homosexual. But the important characters, Fred especially, seem indifferent to or unaware of any of the traditions of gay culture, such as camp, aestheticism, and amorality. And as for the gay culture that was being invented all around him, a culture of promiscuity, Fred finds it unreal and hence not even speciously attractive. He is never seriously tempted by the mirages of desire. Nor is he ever comfortable being part of a community that was then revisiting questions of sexual ethics: What if serial monogamy, or even polygamy, were the best way to organize a gay life? What if promiscuity were something other than a deficiency? What if we lived our lives not for duty but pleasure?

These questions are occasionally raised, but not allowed to resonate. For to explore them further would be to raise the possibility that desire was not merely ridiculous (as this book pretends) but perverse, funny, or tragic; that the highest flights of altruism are often joined to the deepest degradation. This conjunction is what Camille Paglia saw more clearly than Kramer: "The first medical reports on the disease killing male homosexuals indicated men most at risk were those with a thousand partners over their lifetime. Incredulity. Who could such people be? Why, it turned out, everyone one knew. Serious, kind, literate men, not bums or thugs. What an abyss divides the sexes! Let us abandon the pretense of sexual sameness and admit the terrible duality of gender."[7]

Whether one agrees with Paglia about "the terrible duality of gender," she has accurately described the terrible duality of Eros, who is both beautiful boy and terrible god. At the opposite extreme, Fred Lemish enunciates a rationalist approach not only to sex but to all desires when he says impatiently, "Everyone knows what they want. They just won't examine their behavior closely enough and see what it means" (191). Fred of course is a character in a book, and not simply Kramer himself. But it's what Kramer believes. His certainty that we need to "examine our behavior" to "see what it means" is the source of his impatience and political activism. But what if this were not true? What if we had only an approximate and occasional knowledge of what we wanted? What if it were impossible to disentangle clear motive from obscure, and thus to "see what it means"? Or alternatively, what if our fantasies were not just delusions, but ambiguous visions? What if our eros were a platonic signpost and not just a humiliating cul-de-sac? To these questions, *Faggots* has nothing to reply. Even the destruction that Kramer sees with such uncanny clarity as early as 1978 — "We're fucking ourselves to death" — is conceived without grandeur.

It is these same questions, raised in a different, more wondering voice, which form the subject of Fred's friend Gatsby's "exercise in self-loathing," *Dancer from the Dance.*

ANDREW HOLLERAN'S *DANCER FROM THE DANCE*

Dancer from the Dance tells exactly the same story as *Faggots*. Indeed, the resemblance is so close as to be eerie.

Both have set pieces in which various characters we will meet again converge on a certain place: the Twelfth Floor for Holleran, Capriccio or the Toilet Bowl for Kramer. Both novels see the emerging gay ghetto through jaundiced eyes. Both main characters have *left* the gay world by the end of the novel, Malone by literally swimming away from it (and perhaps drowning), Fred Lemish by realizing it can't satisfy his deepest desires. Both novels make comedy out of the sheer preposterous variety of gay men in the seventies: leather queens, twinkies, naïfs, hustlers, and so on. Both novels take note of the astonishing drug use and sexual promiscuity of the gay ghetto, and both hint more than once that gay men are, in Kramer's words, "fucking themselves to death." Both the main characters are about forty when the novel ends. Both end on Fire Island. Finally, both can be thought of as "innocents abroad" novels. Both feature a main character who is in, but not quite of, the gay world.

The resemblances are sometimes even more exact. Both use lists (of people, places, clothes) as a recurring stylistic device. Both novels feature a mad queen on roller skates. (She was in fact based on a real person, Rollerina, whom I recall whizzing up Fifth Avenue in her fairy-godmother's outfit during Gay Pride Marches in the early eighties.) *Faggots* mentions the "Winston Man" and *Dancer* the "Marlboro Man." In both, the main character reflects that "we have the ultimate in freedom and we're abusing it" (Kramer) and that "We're completely free and that's the horror"[8] (Holleran). In both, an older gay man "explains" the odd fact of being ignored by a younger one by imagining that the youth is simply afraid. In *Faggots*, Hans "asked one of his rhetorical questions: 'Do you think that boys all over the world are wondering if somewhere out there there is a group of intelligent, like-minded individuals, devoting ourselves to stimulating pursuits, and if they could only find us, we would be the perfect future . . . ?'" (*Faggots*, 78). And in *Dancer,* more crisply, "an older, gray-haired man" says to his friend, "an even older fellow": "'I find him so beautiful . . . like a Kabuki, that long neck, those heavy-lidded eyes. He never looks at me, do you think because he's afraid?'" (*Dancer,* 46). In both there are descriptions of the strangeness of dancing at a disco: Boo Boo Bronstein dances alone, "eyes closed of course," and can thus "pretend they were all, every one of them, his dancing partners!" (*Faggots*, 165). Holleran's novelist-narrator reflects that there are moments on the dance-floor "In the midst of all the lights, and music, the bodies, the dancing, the drugs, you are stiller than still within, and though you go through the motions of dancing you are thinking a thousand disparate things" (*Dancer,* 132). In both there is an allusion to the fire at the Everard Baths.

They are different in every other respect.

Faggots is manically overplotted (and that is the point). *Dancer* is languorously underplotted (and that *may* be the point). *Faggots* is satiric in intention and sarcastic in style. *Dancer* is ironic in intention, and lyrical in style. *Faggots* is mocking, *Dancer* sentimental. *Faggots* is moralistic, *Dancer* dreamy. Fred Lemish thinks he is ugly; Malone knows he is handsome. Fred wants a lover, Malone wants . . . well, *all* lovers. Fred has a résumé, Malone keeps a diary.

But the hugest, most obvious difference is one of tone and attitude. Kramer has no doubts about what he sees in the gay ghetto — he hates it — but Holleran *does*. *Faggots,* as its name suggests, is intended as a slap in the face, a wake-up call, a cold shower, to the gay community. As long as somebody gets the point and changes his life for the better (getting out or changing his life), it has succeeded. *Dancer* has no such intention, or rather, its intentions are multiple and even contradictory. Indeed, the two letter-writers whose scabrous ruminations frame the novel raise this question themselves. Is Malone's story tragic or just ridiculous? Is he a good man tragically caught in a bad world, or a silly deluded "circuit queen"? While Malone, like Fred, musters the courage to leave the circuit, his decision is hardly moral, but rather prudential. He realizes that he is simply too old to keep on, that the beautiful boy he watched playing soccer in Central Park, and whom once he would have had to pursue or at least "memorialize" in conversation with friends, is young enough to be his son. The world of desire he has inhabited and embodied is suddenly one from which he is excluded, and the only way to minimize the pain of that loss is to leave it before it leaves him.

A further distinction can be made by comparing it with a book that seems even closer in style and atmosphere. *Dancer*'s model (as Kramer rightly saw) is *The Great Gatsby*. But here too there are illuminating differences. Holleran is far more lyrical than Fitzgerald, and verges on the sentimental. (Fitzgerald is seldom sentimental, though his main character is.) His topic, however, is Fitzgerald's: the fragility, and terrible disappointment, of beauty. Like Gatsby, Malone hoards in his memory a gallery of "enchanted objects" — beautiful men like the young soccer player, men who represent whole possibilities of life.[9] His story, like Gatsby's, is about the gradual disenchantment of those objects. But where Gatsby's "count of enchanted objects" can be "diminished by one" when he finally gets Daisy, Malone's is ever increasing. He is compared to the man who drinks sea-water: one taste only makes him thirst for more. Gatsby's tragedy is to discover that there is a price to be paid for getting what you want: hope. (What does it mean to *hope* for something you now possess?) Malone's is to discover that hope never dies at all. Fitzgerald is finally more of a satirist than Holleran. Where Holleran sees "illusive" (not "false") beauty in Malone's story, Fitzgerald finds mere secrets: the "real" history of Gatsby (aka Jay Gatz), the "real" selfishness under Daisy's beauty. Nick Carraway is finally soured on the whole cult of Gatsby because it is based on lies, but Holleran's analogous witness is less certain. Yes, Malone has deceived himself and others; yes, he loses everything as a result. But has he not perhaps "lived for other things" as Sutherland puts it at the end?

The most interesting revision of *Gatsby* that Holleran performs is to my mind a specifically *gay* one. Holleran sees that the source of sadness in our life is that we have, not too little, but too much freedom. I call this a gay insight not because I think it limited to gay people, but because the seventies ghetto was an actualized case of that excessive freedom. In that brief period — astoundingly, heartbreakingly brief in retrospect — gay men had an almost unlimited liberty. And the freedom had not just a licentious but an ecstatic quality: *anything seemed possible.*[10] In this sense, the ghetto Malone entered was a kind of *a fortiori* argument about freedom. It could form a perfect fictional crucible: what if we took a character, Malone, with virtually nothing to stop him, and put him in a time and place where he could seemingly sail all the way home? What would a human being do in a state of near-zero "drag" on his freedom and will?

It is a literary experiment that has been only occasionally performed in the past, most relevantly by Shakespeare in *Antony and Cleopatra,* another tragicomedy of love. Shakespeare's hero too throws away everything — reputation, power, family, life — on a "gypsy's lust." At the same time, the play makes us believe, if only for a moment, that this act of prodigality is "the nobleness of life," and indeed that *not* to squander would be a mistake. Enobarbus is sardonic but not wrong when he tells Antony, who wishes he had never met Cleopatra, "O, sir, you had then left unseen a wonderful piece of work, which not to have been blessed withal would have discredited your travel." Antony's greatness — and the peculiar greatness of this tragedy — shows itself not in what he keeps, but what he can afford to lose: "His delights / Were dolphin-like; they showed his back above / The element they lived in. In his livery / Walked crowns and crownets; realms and islands were / As plates dropped from his pocket."[11] In *Dancer* Malone (whose first name, interestingly, is Anthony) is another man who has everything and throws it away on "the cheapest things in life: beauty, glamour . . ." Like Shakespeare's Antony, Holleran's destroys himself with a kind of drawn-out grandeur that is as exhilarating as it is depressing. And like Shakespeare's play, the great power of this book — a power out of all proportion to its lyric style — rests on its willingness to understand why Malone would do such a thing.

If to Kramer, the liberties of the gay ghetto were mere license, to Holleran they are simultaneously a temptation and a vision of possibility. The erotic charge of New York may be a "drug," but if so, we are all addicts. That is why, for instance, the novel is not an "exposé" of sexual obsession, even though such a diagnosis might be plausible in Malone's case. For Holleran, sexual pursuit is *itself* the shadow of a yet more intoxicating freedom. This is why in a passage notable for its ingenuity as well as its helplessness, he changes his mind three times as to what the book is "really about," ending up finally with "the city," New York, as the only adequate symbol of some huge hunger of the heart.

> Furthermore he saw as he sat there that what he truly was in love with — or any of us, for that matter — was not Rafael, or Jesus, or the man we had been watching on the dance floor for four years now, but our own senses, the animal bliss of being alive. He had come to adore, true climber on the ladder of love, not only Rafael but all the Rafaels in this street — and that what he loved, finally, was only the city. And that if we had no human lover at the moment, we had instead the color of that indigo that precipitates like an extraordinary dye on late-summer evenings at the end of city streets; the breeze bathing his face and shoulders; the sweet comfort of the sweat, drying on his chest; the merengue coming through a window, the fragrant heat, the warm, redolent, perfumed evening; the little moon hanging in the band of light blue sky high above the indigo, floating in a silvery blaze high above the island, the rooftops. He sat there long after everyone else had gone inside, finally brought to rest, a witness of the summer moon. (176–77)

Malone's is not, admittedly, a choice that leads to happiness, but then happiness may not be his goal: "as the city began to cool at last, sitting in the camaraderie of queens, he sat thinking that at least he had stripped his life down to that one single thing — love — and this was where love had led him, this was where he was, as his father had been led to Ceylon in search of oil" (176).[12]

A profound ambivalence toward his main character and his world distinguishes Holleran also from Kramer. One of the default jokes in *Faggots,* as we saw, was that the gay world was a ghetto in the worst sense: insular, provincial, self-referential. This perception is exactly the same reached by Malone, who, at one of the many low points of his life, sighs, "Oh God, is it really time to move to San Francisco?" (158). The difference between the two is that Kramer's assertion is assumed while Holleran's is discovered. Kramer takes the boundaries of the ghetto as a predictable (if "sad") fact; Holleran, by following Malone from his straight unhappy youth into the ambiguous pleasures of the ghetto, makes the reader keenly aware of its freedoms, and only later of its tragic limits.

The result is that we have some conception of the *beauty* of the gay ghetto, and therefore of why Malone stays in it so long. Even Holleran's marvelous lists (of people, parties, events) are the exact opposite of Kramer's. Holleran's seem to open out onto infinity as if they could go on forever; Kramer's to be a set of constricting, frightening funhouse mirrors. Kramer poses gay life as an absurdity — How could anyone think they were enjoying what is so plainly unenjoyable? — Holleran as a mystery that cannot be resolved, but can be deepened.

The protagonist of *Dancer* is a young man called only "Malone." His childhood is not the stuff of gay horror stories or even of "serious" psychological novels ("Another unhappy American childhood," says a catty Edmund White character of such solemnly conventional books).[13] It contains no etiology of homosexuality. Indeed, Holleran seems to insist on the "normality" of Malone's childhood in that regard. His homosexuality is not to be accounted for by anything: it is a given, a mystery. If anything, Malone's childhood hints at the etiology of the romantic. Raised by loving parents in Ceylon during what Holleran calls "the Golden Age of the American corporation," he is himself a golden boy, with all the charisma that phrase implies, but none of the hardness of heart: his eyes are always "full of emotion." He is nothing like a superficially similar character in *Faggots,* the Winston Man.

As a boy, his nature is strangely plastic: "he was always dreaming." When the boy Malone goes to the movies to see Errol Flynn in a pirate movie, for instance, and comes out afterward, "there were the cocoa palms, the lapis lazuli waters of the film itself" (61). What would have been "romance" for other children back in America is for Malone the most actual fact. His dreams can and do come true. It is this belief of his, entangled with Catholic religiosity, that also marks his "career in love."

After an irreproachable youth and young manhood, during which he attains every social success but lives as if behind a wall of glass; after prep school, Yale, a stint in Stockholm, a law degree, a responsible job, Malone falls unexpectedly and miserably in love. The object of his love is an oblivious eighteen-year-old named Michael Floria, a gardener at the huge house in the Washington suburbs where Malone has been living. Until now, he has had no inkling of his true desires, knowing only that when he went out on dates with women, he felt "the ache of too many smiles with too little feeling." But when he learns that Michael is about to leave for college, "it was then he felt his own wounds. It was very definite, as if he had been stabbed." His legs start trembling even as he shakes Michael's hand and wishes him "the very best of luck" (71).

"That night," writes Holleran, "he got up out of bed and put on his maroon polo shirt, which everyone said he looked so handsome in, and went downstairs and drove off in his car, where he did not know." He ends up in Dupont Circle, where he "got out under the green trees and met a man and went into the park and blew him" (73). This long-delayed sexual and emotional awakening horrifies Malone at first: when he gets home he washes out his mouth with soap and writes luridly self-condemning passages in his journal. ("IF THE EYE OFFENDS THEE, PLUCK IT OUT," he storms, quoting Jesus [76].) He throws himself desperately into his work as a corporate lawyer. But "the great fault in his character was slipping after all these years." And one night, "high in a fluorescent cell" above Wall Street, where he is working on a "promissory note for the Republic of Zaire" — what precision of reference! — he is saved by a Puerto Rican messenger boy, who comes into his office with "a batch of Telexes from his boss in London." Malone looks up at him: "how could he know that his desires, his loneliness, were written on his face as clear as characters on a printed page?" The messenger kisses him, and "it was the kiss of Life. . . . Malone sat there with an expression on his face such as the Blessed Virgin wears in paintings of the Annunciation" (76–77).

The religious allusion is funny but not casual, for this has been indeed Malone's conversion. All the pieces of his life that had been broken and separate come together like the dry bones in *Ezekiel*. Malone becomes "gay" and with the confidence of the convert leaves Washington, quits his job, and moves to Sheridan Square, the heart of the new gay ghetto. There, in the final ravishing lines of the third chapter, he sits on his stoop "like a monk who comes finally to the shrine of Santiago de Compostela — devoted not to Christ, in whom he no longer believed, but love" (78).

The rest of the novel concerns various events that flow from his conversion. There are only three of them. The first is his meeting with his first and only boyfriend, Frankie, who inaugurates the long stream of Mediterraneans the blond Malone will love. Malone first spots him emerging from a subway tunnel, his eyes "so still, and calm, and grave, it was as if a medieval age lived in them" (80). He knows he should do something — this is why he moved to New York — but what? He then spots Frankie twice more, and the third time is lucky. In a comically exact scene, he runs into "Mr. Oliveiri" at the Ninth Avenue VD Clinic. There they finally talk and within a page or two have become lovers, moving into an abandoned factory building in a deserted part of town; where, "perched like arboreal creatures," they survey the New Jersey city Frankie has left for Malone — the home of Frankie's wife and child. Mostly they do nothing but make love and watch the "snow-white" ocean liners sail slowly out to sea; and Malone feels whole for the first time, rejoined to his childhood in the tropics, separated forever from the "sterile years of his wasted youth." Holding Frankie in his arms late at night, "he felt as if they were on some high promontory above the world, as solitary as shepherds on a crag in a canvas of Brueghel — all alone in the blue, windy, gentle world" (85).

This idyllic life is fatally interrupted by another idyll, just as Malone's dream of the tropics in Errol Flynn's movies was interrupted by the real tropics. In his love for Frankie, his regression to a kind of sexualized childhood, he has seemingly never noticed gay New York before. But when Malone goes out one hot afternoon to buy fruit he passes a man "as beautiful, as strangely moving" (89) as Frankie and without a word goes up to his apartment to have sex with him. This he does every day afterward. He has discovered, with a mixture of horror and delight, that the city is full of Frankies, full of "love."

Life with Frankie now comes to seem irritating and dull. Frankie is no longer the ideal lover, but a prosaic "husband" who comes home grouchy from work, wears glasses to "look intellectual," smokes pot, watches TV, and has a bad temper. "For such a handsome boy," the narrator later writes, "his soul was a dead weight" (119). Malone now begins his descent on that slipperiest ladder, What If: "What if Frankie was a trap?" And it is his journal—symbol to him of the rich life of imagination—which gives him away. Coming home one day from yet another afternoon of love with a stranger, he discovers Frankie silent and enraged. He has left work early and read Malone's artless journal entries describing his sexual encounters. Frankie, who has given up everything for Malone, who is "a Latin, a Catholic," has no intention of allowing his "wife" infidelities. He beats Malone up. Malone runs away, finding himself eventually in the Village. There, huddled in a doorway holding his broken rib, he sees emerging from the Magic, Fantasy, and Dreams Ball a bewigged figure, Sutherland, dressed as an eighteenth-century countess. " 'Help me,' said Malone. 'My dear,' said Sutherland after taking one look at his terrified face, 'the house of Guiche shall never refuse the protection of its manor to the poorest of its subjects,' and he assisted Malone into a cab pulled up at the curb" (92).

This rescue is the second event in Malone's gay career. For in Sutherland, Holleran has given Malone a dandyish Sancho Panza, both guide and foil. It is the brittle, funny, unsentimental Sutherland who eventually introduces Malone to the gay world: he takes him dancing, and (as the title of the novel suggests) that activity becomes the central metaphor for the whole book. For "dancing" one could read "desiring." And much of the rest of the novel-within-the-novel is nothing but vignettes of the life of desire, whether on the dance floor of various discos, in the men's room of Grand Central Station, on the streets of the Lower East Side, or at Sutherland's Madison Avenue apartment, from which he hangs out the window dressed as an Italian peasant woman telling the passersby (in Italian) to come up and suck his twat, or stands by a grand piano in a "black Norell" singing (apparently for himself alone), "This time we almost made the pieces fit, didn't we?" (119).

I say "nothing but vignettes," and it is true. And yet I feel about these vignettes (some of them as brief as a clause, others a dozen pages long) as Randall Jarrell felt about one of Whitman's poems: "It is only a list—but what a list!"[14] Has anyone, including Holleran's great model Fitzgerald, ever conveyed the feeling of desire better than Holleran in these vignettes? Desire, not sex—for Holleran almost never follows Malone into the bedroom. Holleran is the master of that state of mind in which one finds *everything* erotic: not merely the beautiful faces, but the streets themselves, the "heartbreaking indigo" of the horizon at the end of the street, the bliss of being on the dance floor at 4 A.M. or of wringing out your T-shirt in the gutter afterward, your "bones light as a bird's," and so full of joy you had to scream; the sight of Sutherland picking pubic hairs out of his teeth after a day in the men's room and stammering in bliss: "Oh my dear, there is no other time, no other time at all, but now, when the city is overripe, like a fruit about to drop in your lap, and all the young stockbrokers' underwear is damp!" (195). Perhaps the most erotic is the soft darkness, so fraught with hope, of "those two symmetrical parks on Second Avenue between Fifteenth and Seventeenth streets" (135) where, on two occasions, the narrator overhears Malone's sad conversations with Sutherland about the death of his dreams.

The third event of Malone's life comes at some unnamed point in the midst of this dancing life. (Time has become by now as irrelevant to the reader as to Malone — ecstatically irrelevant, so to speak.) Sutherland has decided, for reasons of prudence, that he must have money and decides to sell Malone: "People wanted Malone the way they wanted vases from China, *étagères*, Coromandel screens" (174). Malone has by now attained a sort of acme of felicity/misery in that he simply drifts without volition: his desire has been so refined as to seem desireless. He consequently goes along with Sutherland's scheme of not just making him a hustler but marrying him off to a rich man, a plan which takes final shape in the person of John Schaeffer, an intensely shy young millionaire who has just graduated from Princeton and discovered he's gay. He is to be Sutherland's mark, the proposed "husband" for Malone. The sale ends in the sublimely venal "Pink and Green Party" Sutherland throws for John's and Malone's "elopement" at Fire Island. It is after this party that Malone, disgusted with the life he has been leading, ends it — or at any rate leaves it. He is last seen swimming away from Fire Island toward the innocent white fences of Sayville for which he had always longed. He is never seen again.

But that is not quite all.

I have retold the story of *Dancer* as if it were simple, straightforward, and consecutive. In fact it is not. Malone's life and death appear within an embedded novel (*Wild Swans*). Surrounding it on either side are letters between the author of *Wild Swans*, a fellow dancer who misses Malone and has written it as a sort of homage to him, and a friend who has moved to "the Deep South" in order to get away from the "circuit." These letters are also part of the book's "plot," though it's easy to ignore them at first. They serve many functions, of which the most useful is to make forever unaskable questions that would, if asked, destroy the book: Why doesn't Malone ever fall in love again? How does he pay the rent? How does Sutherland manage to take all that speed and maintain not only his health but his wits? *It's just a novel* would be the shrugging answer to these unimaginative questions. Further, it is a novel *within* a novel, and thus scarcely to be held to the strictest standards of probability.

(But I find I must interrupt myself to deal with the objection that it is "implausible." How implausible *is* it? I have certainly known many gay men who lived all but entirely for love, men whose careers were put permanently on hold, or relegated to mere daytime drudgery; men who may indeed have drawn a paycheck, but who (like Malone) came to life only at night or on hot afternoons with strangers. We *do* know how Malone manages to feed himself after he quits being a lawyer. The food he survives on — "love" — is as cheap but as priceless as the consecrated Host.)

The letters also serve to initiate a rich pattern of duality: head and heart, Southerner and New Yorker, a career in "law and business" and one in "love." Throughout, it is doubleness that rules. The two letter-writers, for instance, themselves exemplify the two parts of Malone's life: the dutiful domesticity of his youth, the erotic searches of his manhood. So close is the resemblance that it is as though the two writers between them have divided up the life of the now-vanished Malone: the southern one now lives with "Ramon," one of the Hispanic men Malone has constantly fallen in love with in New York, while the other (like Malone at the grim end of his career in love) has begun hustling. It is as though *The Great Gatsby* had not ended with the death of Myrtle and Gatsby, and had strongly hinted that Nick Carraway *was* Gatsby writing his own story. The dyad finds another, completer representation in Malone and Sutherland themselves. While the story is primarily about Malone, Holleran has saved himself from too close an identification with his charismatic hero by inventing Sutherland. Sutherland's wit and unsentimental hardness keep Malone and Holleran honest. They give the reader a stand-in, someone to tell Malone to grow up or to start hooking: "Get yourself a good price, Gigi" (145). Malone, for his part, is a useful corrective to Sutherland. Witty as Sutherland is, a book about him would be dreadful. Like all actors, Sutherland needs the boundary of lights and a curtain, for the aesthetic finish of his life would crack under too much surveillance. (Sutherland himself tells Malone, who has been maundering on about wanting to move away from New York with Sutherland: "Not for a moment. . . . I exist only in New York, take me off this island and I evaporate. . . . Imagine having dinner each night, alone, the two of us. I'm amusing, I'm full of life, I'm a creature of the city. Transplant me and I'd die in your very hands" [144].) Sutherland is enchanting as an alternative argument about the good life, but can't — and luckily isn't forced to — exemplify that life.

Finally, the letters allow a close reader to find two separate endings in it. After the Pink and Green Party, while Malone swims away to his death, Sutherland supposedly overdoses on a handful of pills. The "novel" *Wild Swans* ends, in fact, with Sutherland's funeral at Frank E. Campbell's. But even this egregiously melodramatic ending is doubtful. For one thing, it's not clear that Malone *is* dead. (He has been sighted in Singapore and Sydney.) While the southern writer finally stops this infinite regress of fantasy about Malone with a sensible un-flattering "He was in the end a circuit queen" (249), the doubt has been sown. And sown more than casually. For although it may be impossible to determine whether Malone is dead, it appears from some of the first letters that Suther-land, at any rate, is not. We read on page 12, for instance: "Flamingo had a White Party last night — two muscle numbers came in DIAPERS, Bob wore a sequined Halston top, the Baron Ambert was there, and two Egyptian women who were running around with Sutherland and who asked me if I thought they should paint their cunts!" But if Sutherland can come back to life, why not Malone? And if Malone can come back to life, what are the consequences for the novel?

Dancer is a novel that opens out into another novel, with unsettling, magical results, just as Corneille's *L'illusion comique* reframes its pastoral drama by showing the actors backstage afterward, their costumes half-off, dividing the evening's take. Furthermore, because the letter-writers themselves so strongly recall the two contradictory wishes of Malone — for domesticity, on the one hand, and "some adventurous ideal of homosexuality" on the other — we have to entertain the idea, if only momentarily, that one of them may actually *be* Malone. This possibility serves to make him not a moral "lesson," like Gatsby, but a romantic legend like the Dutchman in Wagner's opera who appears first as a painting on the wall of Senta's house, then walks right through her door.

It is no mere metafictional possibility that makes Malone "important" to us, as well as to the New York letter-writer. Like him, we "want to know where he ended up; it's important, because he was somehow the one who seemed above it all, and what he is doing now that it's over . . . fascinates me" (246). The question he has raised by *being* Malone, the bomb whose explosion he has both touched off and contained, is important.

The question is simply this: "Can one waste a life?" One can pose the chal-lenge in other ways: Should Malone have stuck it out as a lawyer, thus fulfilling his family's dreams for his success? Or should he (as he did) have broken with that life in order to become something he barely knew how to be: a post-Stonewall gay man with unlimited freedom? Is the good life being a family man or a hooker? living in Sayville or the Pines? When Malone comes home to his apartment one morning after a night of sex, he passes all the young men in business suits going in the opposite direction, to work. He hides behind a pillar to avoid being recognized by someone he used to know — or rather, by someone he used to *be*. The question, for us and for him: Ought he to be ashamed? Has he anything to hide? "Can one waste a life," the narrator asks; "Especially now?"

The word "waste" rings out memorably even earlier, at the very beginning of the book. In chapter 1, the narrator is going out to Fire Island to collect Malone's things after his mysterious death. As he goes, he remembers Malone once saying, "I am not spending next summer here. I'll go out west, I'll lie in a tent in Africa, I'll do anything but waste another summer on the Island.' 'Waste?' said Sutherland, turning his head slightly as if he had heard a bird chirp behind him in the bushes. 'Who can waste a summer on the Island? Why, it's the only antidote to death we have'" (26). This is Sutherland's first appearance in the novel proper, but he is there entirely and at once in the single word ironically repeated: "Waste?" This mocking word embodies the dandy's implicit challenge to Malone's high-minded romanticism. But it is not a question that easily goes away. Can a life be wasted? "In that narrower, human sense, of course it can [be wasted]. Malone worried that he had wasted his; and many felt he had" (33). But what does the narrator think? Does he agree with those many? He answers his own question and in so doing disrupts any easy solution. The people who think Malone has wasted his life turn out to be *snobs*: "smug people who had bought their own houses out here and arrived by seaplane with their Vuitton" (34), as he says with devastating economy. But what equivocation! We had seemed to be going in one direction — to a sad shake of our head over Malone's "wasted" life — only to find ourselves uncomfortably likened to the sort of smug bourgeois who would shake *his* head over it.

So despite his confident "Of course it can," the narrator can't quite shed his doubts, and makes a second attempt to decide whether Malone has wasted his life: "He wanted to be liked, and so he ran away to New York — away from his own family — and he vanished on Manhattan, which is a lot easier than vanishing in the jungles of Sumatra. And what did he do? Instead of becoming the success they expected him to be, instead of becoming a corporate lawyer, he went after, like hounds to the fox, the cheapest things in life: beauty, glamour . . . all the reasons this beach had once thrilled us to death. But the parties, the drugs, the T-shirts, the music were as capable of giving him his happiness as this sea I sat beside now was of stinging beneath the whips that Xerxes had his servants turn on the waves for swallowing up his ships" (34).

Observe the complex combination of voices in this perfectly timed paragraph. The assertion that it's easier to vanish in Sumatra than Manhattan is both funny and disturbing, turning Manhattan into a perilous romantic island and Malone into a nineteenth-century British explorer gone native. The fact that the T-shirts, drugs, music, and parties "once thrilled us to death," on the other hand, is silly and up-to-date; but by mentioning "us" implicates the narrator in the ridiculous excess it mocks. As for the final comparison to Xerxes, with its magnificent rhythm and stately sequence of interlocking clauses — *it* sounds like Cicero; which makes Malone's lust seem as kingly, if as irrational, as the Persian tyrant's rage. The passage is thus as full of wonderment as of mockery;

full of unexpected moves that make it impossible for us to reduce it to any one moral point of view. Its purpose is neither to glorify nor to trivialize Malone's choice, and it certainly doesn't answer the question. In it, in the whole novel, "the little is made great, and the great little," as Hazlitt said of *The Rape of the Lock*. "You hardly know whether to laugh or weep."[15]

So can one waste a life? No: only smug people would think so. And yet, "Of course one can."

In posing the question "Can one waste a life?" *Dancer* is doing something that may not be apparent at first. Although it contains the single best description of coming out in gay fiction, it puts that story in a larger, more ambitious context: that of staying out. "Staying out" means keeping one's eyes open to the contradictions, comic and pathetic, that now seem an unavoidable part of one's new life. "Staying out" means being willing to ask what constitutes the (or at least *a*) good life. Because the book covers a surprisingly long (though unspecific) period of time — five to eight years — it gives its protagonist, narrator, and author ample time for second thoughts about their new career in "love." When Holleran's narrator imitates Malone and starts hustling, for instance, he shows up at a hotel room only to realize he already knows his client: "*WE KNEW EACH OTHER AT CHOATE!*" (16–17) he writes gleefully to his more subdued friend in "The Deep South." The line is funny, but can one really reconcile "*CHOATE*" (respectability, education, friends, youth) with being a male prostitute? And is it necessarily *guilt* that asks this question? You don't need to have gone as far as the narrator (or Malone) to have felt its power. Many gay men must have wondered, as I did in those days: Can it really be *me* in this public park at 3:25 A.M.? And what exactly do I feel about being here? Heroic? Foolhardy? Scared? Remorseful?

To ask such a question is to be Holleranian, because to be gay is, for him, an essentially divided mentality. Indeed, he quotes the Bible to that effect: "The Bible says, a man divided is unstable in all ways" (63). Not only his hero, but Holleran himself has been this "unstable" man — an early escapee from the ghetto and at the same time its most profound chronicler, the best-known of post-Stonewall writers and yet a pseudonymous one. He has felt, has *absorbed*, the shock of living a life nothing had prepared him for. This has placed him, uniquely I think, in a position to reflect the full spectrum of hope and fear that Stonewall made possible. As a *gay* author, he is the one whose mind is most interestingly not-made-up. Not for him the good-hearted but slightly unthinking conviction of a writer like Armistead Maupin that being gay is absolutely OK, that it is merely another form of love; nor the radical gay liberationist's millenary confidence in a nonpatriarchal future; nor even Ethan Mordden's half-serious assertion that gay culture is not merely equal, but superior to straight ("gringo") culture. But neither does Holleran subscribe to Larry Kramer's fanatic hatred of the ghetto's hedonism, for he sees his hero pursuing however foolishly "some adventurous ideal of homosexuality" which may "leave him flat" but is certainly not contemptible. Nor finally does Holleran claim the sort of freedom from definition and interference that his rough contemporary Edmund White seeks, a freedom which sometimes seems bought at the price of joy.

The ghetto life that Holleran takes as his subject means not only the beginnings of visible gay life in New York, but the growth of gay consciousness — a consciousness which Holleran sees to conflict *necessarily* with family, religion, education, career. (He is famous for not having come out to his parents. Unlike the archetypal New York waiter who claims to be "working on a novel," our best novelist apparently told his parents he worked as a waiter.) Nor is the conflict one to be soothed away by ingenious placations or compromises. Holleran's Catholicism, to take the most obvious example, runs deep: so deep that membership in Dignity, the gay Catholic group, would hardly solve the problem for him. In an amusing essay in Brian Bouldrey's anthology *Wrestling with the Angel,* he describes walking by a church where a Dignity mass is going on: "I felt sorry for the men inside, sympathetic to their attempt, and superior to what seemed to me their naïveté. Don't even try, I thought, as I walked past, on the way from the gym to the baths (my new church), you're just kidding yourselves. There can be no commerce between, no conflation of, these two things. Fellatio has nothing to do with Holy Communion. Better to frankly admit that you have changed gods, and are now worshipping Priapus, not Christ."[16] But membership in the decent, dull Human Rights Campaign wouldn't resolve his conflict either. Indeed, legal reform has even less to do with one's true allegiance ("love") than Christianity.

Holleran's religion (whether Christian or gay) is maximalist and intransigent: he wants to believe *the whole thing*—otherwise, what's the point? So when Malone comes out, he "knows" that this action means an abrupt break with his past: "My only hope," he writes melodramatically in his diary, "is with those men circling the fountain. They are my fate and if I wish to have Life, it must be with *them*. What is most remarkable, I have no choice. I who have never been constrained by poverty, disease, accident, am now constrained by this. God's joke. His little joke" (75). And indeed *Dancer* can be thought of as a novel of faith — or rather, of the impossible contradictions of faith.

Dancer is the first, and perhaps the best, gay novel to take as its subject the consequences of conversion to this erotic "faith." It is about what it means not just to "be gay," but to live a gay life, here construed as a life of *desire*. These are consequences about which (I believe) everyone feels somewhat ambivalent; so does Holleran. *Dancer* refuses the narrative of the closet (homosexuality as irremediable moral wound) without embracing the narrative of liberation (homosexuality as necessary next step in the Revolution). It sees the ridiculous and venal things gay men do to each other as clearly as Larry Kramer's *Faggots* does, but sees them sympathetically and from within. Kramer, by contrast, is always standing like some ravenous wolf outside the party. And unlike Edmund White's waiflike sissies, honeycombed with self-dislike, Malone has a gift for joy and thus a chance for happiness.

This deep awareness of contradictory faiths is why *Dancer,* though brilliantly funny, is also touching. Its comedy resides in the constantly veering attitude the reader finds himself obliged to take toward Malone's ten-year search for what he calls "love" and most of us would call something less polite. For example, much as we relish Malone's melancholy, we are never allowed to take it unironically. His quite sincere longing to raise a family, for instance, is unsentimentally deflated by Sutherland: "children require a womb, and a womb is connected to a vagina, and the thought of cooze makes you vomit. Such a small detail" (142). At the same time, his melancholy is never merely ridiculous. When he first begins to realize he's gay, and sheds "hot tears" over Michael Floria, a "perfectly oblivious senior going off to Beloit College on the swimming team," the narrator points out: "A sensible man would have laughed at Malone; would have called him melodramatic, sentimental; would have told him to get on with life, and stop thinking he had been cast into outer darkness — nonsense!" He's right; but in a characteristic correction he adds: "But Malone was not this sensible man. Some live more for love than others. And he experienced a death that night, as he lay upstairs in the widow's house, on that vast floor of empty rooms in whose hallway outside his own the odor of cold cream, the sound of a television program being watched downstairs, hovered" (72). So though Holleran mocks Malone's reduction to "helplessness and hot tears," he equally mocks the "sensible man" who so bluffly calls it "nonsense!" (Who wants to sound like *that?*) And the final phrase is just as ironic. Malone, we are told, "experienced a death that night." The phrasing is deliberately stagey; and yet, what is it if not a "a death" to discover yourself — for all you know, forever — isolated in a huge house with an old woman slathered in cold cream? This is death in one of its most grotesque forms — the smiling one — and Malone might as well be dying. No wonder Malone lies there, "staring at the ceiling like the effigy on an Etruscan tomb." The comparison is comically grandiose but not false. How else would the dutiful, well-educated Malone, who leafs through picture books of French cathedrals on Connecticut Avenue, who thinks the rich sensual life is always somewhere else — how else would such a Jamesian person conceive of his grief?

Malone's emotions are always bigger than his circumstances warrant. But as in *Così fan tutte* (another work about the intoxicating, illusory shimmer of freedom), the fact that the feelings are exaggerated does not mean they are false. Fiordiligi, too, believes everything she's heard about love: her music constantly alludes to the baroque operas in which the princesses of Greek fatality and Roman duty play out their tragic roles. She, too, "lives more for love than others," more even than her sister Dorabella. But I do not laugh when she swoops a despairing twelfth down to a chest C-sharp in *"Per pietà . . ."* Nor do I laugh when Malone lies on his bed like a dead Etruscan prince.

After all, Malone *is* a "prince," if of an American kind. Given enormous wealth in the form of looks, education, diligence, hope, popularity, and a good job, Malone proceeds to turn his back on all of it, preferring the yet more exquisite promissory note of "love." In so doing, he performs an act of squandering possible only to a prince. But an Antony who is not magnificent is merely squalid. A Malone who is not ecstatic is merely debauched. And Holleran's novel presents in a most complex and truthful way what it is like to have almost infinite freedom; to feel regret over one's use of it, and yet to resist giving it up.

And rightly to resist! Destructive as the dancing world is in this novel, far worse is the world of one's family, of straight friends, of the cold-cream widow in her vast Bethesda house, the miserable pretend-dates Malone used to have with women. The novel has nothing good to say about the "straight" world, though Malone deludes himself that he would like to live in it — in Sayville, in Ohio, or in the small airport on the Florida Keys. And if the gay men on the circuit are indeed "prisoners," as Holleran suggests at one point, what a jail! After a night of dancing "they would walk up Broadway together, exhausted, ecstatic, their bones light as a bird's, a flotilla of doomed queens on their way to the Everard Baths because they could not come down from the joy and happiness. They looked, these young men gazing up toward the sky with T-shirts hanging from their belts, like athletes coming from a game, like youths coming home from school, their dark eyes glowing with light, their faces radiant, and no one passing them could have gathered the reason for this happy band" (40).

Nor is Malone's choice over yet, though the world he inhabited is dead. How much better is any of us at combining a gay life with a family life or a career? The choice goes far beyond homosexuality: it is a choice for pleasure, illusion, romance, possibility — for a diary rather than a résumé, to use Sutherland's witty distinction. It is a choice more people arguably need to make, though its results are, as Holleran shows, desperately disappointing. It is an experiment in pleasure that has martyrs. Malone is one, as are many of his (and my) generation. The fact of Malone's homosexuality is important — that is, the novel could not be transposed into heterosexual terms — because gay men in the seventies were among the freest people in the country, at least if they were white, handsome, and willing. The social experiment that Stonewall evolved into in the seventies was more than legal or political rights; it wasn't about getting the vote. It was an experiment in hedonism. To that extent, *Dancer from the Dance* seems to me simply accurate as a reflection of what we thought we could have. It is more than accurate in its profound imagination of the consequences of that experiment: consequences which Holleran sees, three years before the AIDS epidemic, to be tragic.

Dancer from the Dance is thus the most contradictory of coming-out novels. It eschews those staples of Stonewall fiction the evil homophobe and the healthy homosexual. No one forbids Malone to pursue his ambiguous career in love. ("We're completely free, and that's the horror," he says at one point.) The warfare is internal: within the gay community (the marchers at Gay Pride on the one hand versus the circuit queens on the other), and within oneself (the part of Malone that still loves his family and "loathes" being gay versus the part that is radiant with exhilaration and capable of bliss). Coming out, here, is about one's proper relation with "the cheapest things in life" — "beauty, glamour" — exactly the sort of thing you don't learn at Harvard. Holleran, a Harvardian and reader of Santayana, would perhaps agree that it is the error of an un-civilized man to treat pleasure harshly; it must be smiled, not frowned, away. But to learn this lesson is impossibly hard. (Santayana, that old closet-case, certainly never learned it).[17] For the old forbiddances were partly right: a life lived stupidly for pleasure soon becomes not only dull but coarsening. On the other hand, as gay men have good reason to know, a life suspicious of pleasure is equally fatal, turning one into a perpetual male virgin like poor John Schaeffer, locked into romantic dreams of his squash-playing straight friends, Tom Es-terhazy and Bunny Molyneux.

By one reading, therefore, *Dancer from the Dance* is a cautionary tale: don't do what Malone did. Even the "novelist" letter-writer finally agrees that Mal-one's life was horrifying as well as enviable. But it is also, and far more inter-estingly, a tale of triumph. When Holleran writes that in Malone's first blissful weeks with Frankie "the false years of dutiful behavior fell away" (87) one wants to shout Yes in agreement. (I remember those years, and they *were* false.) The great third chapter of *Dancer,* which tells the story of Malone's youth, remains the finest apology for coming out in our literature; the remaining chap-ters are the finest imagination of the cost of coming out. But even at the end of the novel, when so much in Malone's life is gloomy, there comes a moment when his face lights up at the sight of all these handsome men dancing: "It was his joy that there were men who loved other men" (230). For all the sadness, for all the *tendency* to sadness of this novel, it strikes me as fundamentally joyful.

Perhaps this is why, when I first read *Dancer* in the early months of 1979, Malone's story seemed to offer a clue to my own. The ten years that had elapsed since Malone's move to the ghetto in 1969 had of course been decisive ones. (He might not have recognized the sheer proliferation of gay life since the Stonewall Riots — an event neither he nor his creator refers to any more than Jane Austen to the rise of Napoleon.) And yet, though I was one beneficiary of a flowing tide of public sentiment and involved in political action (as he was not), I was almost as puzzled as Malone to know what kind of world I had strayed into, what being gay would mean for me.

In that now-distant winter I was more than puzzled, I was sick — yet *another* venereal disease! I could thus entirely identify with the main character of *Dancer,* who met the first love of his life at the Ninth Avenue VD Clinic. Indeed, the scene at the Tufts Skin Clinic, a place to which I was (unfortunately) no stranger, could have come straight out of Holleran. Three kinds of people patronized it: black female prostitutes, white gay men, and a handful of terrified suburban couples in for a premarital Wasserman. As the couples clutched each other for safety, the brazen hookers smoked and the gay men cruised. Cruised? At a VD clinic? All I can say is that there was a spirit of soldierly camaraderie in those pre-AIDS days, a whole repertoire of wry shrugs and impatience to get back to the front. Under my own pose of wartime toughness lurked, even then, a sort of thrilled terror: Where would it all end? But even as I asked myself this dispiriting question, I was calculating the exact number of days that would have to elapse before the Flagyl took effect and I could call the sullen, adjacent blond whose phone number now rested optimistically in my right jeans pocket.

It was as I recuperated from my parasites that I began reading this book about someone like me — not just in "the physical riots of the soul" (Holleranese for VD), but in a scared hopefulness toward gay life, the life I was leading but finding hard to understand and sometimes to like. It was a life, as Holleran said many years later in a talk at Harvard, that nothing in my upbringing could possibly have prepared me for. (Even though I was out to my parents, as Malone was not, I could hardly have brought myself to talk about *amoebas* with them, let alone how I got them.) But if I was terrified and depressed, I was also exalted. And it was exaltation that *Dancer* got absolutely right and what made it for me and my friends *the* gay book, the one that most adequately captured not just the miseries, but the splendors of us courtesans.

[PART THREE]

FOUR DEGREES OF ASSIMILATION

Chapter Five

VIRTUALLY NORMAL,
AND VICE-VERSA

In his Introduction to *The Penguin Book of Gay Short Stories* (1994), David Leavitt tells us, with a becoming show of modesty, how he came to write his first novel, *The Lost Language of Cranes*. In writing it, Leavitt wanted to undo the "damage" done to young gay men by previous works: the semipornography of Gordon Merrick's *The Lord Won't Mind*, the "tendency to romanticize rejection" of *Dancer from the Dance*, and the sexual fixation of even a serious (i.e., family) novel, Robert Ferro's *The Family of Max Desir*. His objection to all three was really the same: namely, that they glamorized sex and beauty, and that this glamour might lead impressionable and unironic readers to imagine that there was no hope for them in the real world: "Was sex between men, I wondered, the exclusive property of the beautiful, the muscular, the superhuman?" Having frightened himself with this erotic bogey, he reminds himself that sex and beauty, "the dreariest aspects of gay life," need not be the subject of gay fiction after all; *he*, at any rate, will eschew such dead ends and show gay people in the round. "For contrary to popular opinion, most gay men *do* want more from their lives than a few decades spent panting after unattainable perfection." In fact, it was "in direct response to the dearth of decent gay literature that characterized my adolescence [that] I started my own first novel, *The Lost Language of Cranes*."[1]

Everyone who has read much gay fiction or much criticism of gay fiction over the past twenty years will recognize Leavitt's plea, even though his reasons for making it are a bit disingenuous. (Ambitious to make his mark, he must discredit his predecessors.) But though his point is somewhat crude, and though it is unclear that the inexperienced reader's is the taste writers ought to consult, we know what he means. Surely there is a "gay story" that can place the gay person in relation to other parts of his life besides sex: to the relation with his family, for instance, or to his career, or to politics. Indeed, much of the fiction of the past fifteen years (coinciding roughly with the AIDS epidemic and the death of clone culture) has expanded gay subjects in precisely the way Leavitt has desiderated. Besides Leavitt's own novels (one of which takes the unusual subject of a family in which not only the son but the father is coming out), there have been, for example, Michael Cunningham's beautiful and melancholy *A Home at the End of the World* (in which three Generation X-ers halfheartedly form a "model" family consisting of a straight man, a straight woman, a gay man, and a baby), Stephen McCauley's *The Object of My Affection* (in which a gay man and a straight woman go through parallel pangs of disprized love), and a surprising number of stories about raising children (for example, Jonathan Strong's *Elsewhere*). There have been stories in which the sexuality of the main characters has been largely irrelevant to the story being told: one of infidelity, or boredom in the relationship. There have been "genre" books — ranging from gay cookbooks to murder mysteries — in which the homosexuality of the participants has been purely nominal, which could in fact serve Leavitt's purposes of showing that a gay life can extend anywhere and that we can gradually rewrite all the genres of literature, substituting a pair of men or women for the usual couples, with a gay man for the hero, a straight man for the villain, and so on.

All this is harmless enough, and arguably even helpful both to Leavitt's putative younger gay reader and to the culture at large. But its helpfulness is strictly superficial: at best a sort of homosexual trickle-down effect. It is admirable to write stories about a gay secret agent (as John Preston did in the Alex Kane novels),[2] thus implying that gay men might be action heroes quite as well as straight ones; but much of what is done in this line is wishful thinking only. Of course gay men can be secret agents, truck drivers, or detectives; but how many do you really know? The pleasure of these stories is that they allow the reader to daydream, to imagine that the man shooting the bad guys — and thus exemplarily masculine — is also "one of us." These books accomplish less than their promoters might claim, however. The appropriation in most cases has been too easy, treating the sexuality of the characters as if it were a mere component, an ingredient one could switch at will without changing anything "important." But such an approach is superficial and dishonest — as much so as the Benetton ads that tokenistically juxtapose four white children and a fifth black one, as if the statistical occurrence of blackness in America as a whole were customarily reproduced in actual small groups. While the intention may be good, the advertisement is not much more than a fantasy of a world in which black and white would meet and interact as equals.

Furthermore, although I sympathize with Leavitt's desire for new kinds of gay stories, I don't think that Leavitt himself has yet written them. In his anxiety to keep his gay characters "normal," he has made them dull. He hasn't queered the suburbs, as he would like, but rather suburbanized the queers. The best things in his stories and novels are in fact the least gay: for instance, the thorny relations between mother and son, the comic rivalry of siblings, or a young man's awkward eagerness to please. None of these is a particularly gay subject, and they seem (in Leavitt's hands so far) small successes — emotionally constrained and intellectually safe. His cautious naturalism accurately reproduces the neuroses and minor pleasures of middle-class people. Is it surprising that his first published story saw the light of day in *The New Yorker?*[3]

But at what cost has the naturalism been achieved? What has Leavitt paid to "tell something like the truth" about his gay life? One cost is that of surprise, the quality in imaginative fiction that pulls aside the veil of habit and convention. Although Leavitt's plot in *The Lost Language of Cranes* is a "new" one in the sense that it is not only gay but about a gay father coming out to his gay son, the element of surprise seems merely superficial — a mechanical rearrangement of possibilities like the latest episode of "E.R." or "Chicago Hope." Once one accepts the homosexuality of the father and son, the novel goes down as easily as Cream of Wheat, with predictable crises predictably resolved. The emotional, intellectual, and aesthetic frames of reference are nothing we don't share ourselves, nothing new. Only the mother and wife Rose upsets our expectations by her rage at the twin betrayals of her son and husband, by her refusal to forgive them. This refusal is the best thing in the novel, because it is the most surprising and the least palatable.

But one of the fictionally useful things about sex and beauty — "the dreariest aspects of gay life," according to Leavitt — is that they *are* surprising, still untamed enough to shake us out of our complacent moral and aesthetic judgments. So while I applaud Leavitt's attempt to tell a story about gay men in which sex doesn't play the leading part, reading him makes me realize how lucky, in retrospect, earlier gay writers were. With no models to go on, with no hope of describing a healthy gay relationship or a gay man with "an integral role in the unfolding family drama" (Leavitt's phrase), while writing stories that were caught between the genres of confession, case history, and pornography, these writers were sometimes capable of seeing through the social lie. Tennessee Williams was right to follow Mr. Krupper to the Joy Rio theater; or rather, he had the ability to see past its doors. As he puts it profoundly in "Hard Candy," "To notice something you would have to be looking for something." The extreme marginality of early gay writers may have destroyed them personally, but it sharpened their vision. They were indeed "looking for something." They were half-finding, half-creating what they "saw."

Leavitt in that respect is luckier as a gay man, less lucky as a gay writer. He comes, one might say, belatedly — after Stonewall, after disco madness and sex on the piers, after AIDS. Those stories have been told, the boundaries laid out. There is far less need for Williams's kind of apprehensiveness, that forward-feeling sensitivity that made him look under the surface of small-town life in "Hard Candy." Not only can Leavitt's father and son go freely to *their* dirty movie theater, they can have phone sex, affairs, or even true love. Their spasms of shame and self-reproach seem endearingly old-fashioned rather than revelatory. (Indeed, in the son, they seem self-indulgent and unreal.) His choice of a gay man's relationship with his family and (straight) friends is his attempt to break out of conventional gay subjects. But so far I find comparatively little that is unconventional in his treatment of it. In *The Lost Language of Cranes,* for instance, all the power of the novel is concentrated in the mother. The father is a cardboard figure of angst, the son of puppyish good intentions and vulnerability. The gay characters, in other words, are the least interesting. The same is true of *Equal Affections.* Told from the perspective of a gay man "married" to a lover, it is really about other people, especially his dying mother, who is the only character capable of surprising us (as when it turns out that, though Jewish, she has gone to see a Catholic priest before her death).

I would not complain so about Leavitt were it not for the fact that his perfectly adequate, if unheartstopping gay fiction is often taken to be the best there is. This irritates me for two reasons. One is that Leavitt himself has so shamelessly courted such classic status. His explanation of how he came to write *The Lost Language of Cranes* (that is, as a "direct response to the dearth of decent gay literature") is an embarrassingly obvious example. More recently, his celebrated spat with Stephen Spender (over whether he plagiarized Spender's 1951 memoir *World within World* in his own, now-suppressed *While England Sleeps*) has permitted him—especially since Spender's death—to assume a roomy mantle of injured merit and misunderstood artistic seriousness.[4] His recent novella *The Term Paper Artist* reveals him at his most immodest. Appearing in the story as "David Leavitt," an important writer who has retired to his parents' house in Los Angeles to lick his wounds after a plagiarism scandal, he consoles himself by contriving an ideal situation in which to award himself the praise the world has so piggishly withheld: he will write brilliant term papers for dumb UCLA students and in return get to blow them. But one suspects that the reward the non-fictional Leavitt receives is less sexual than literary, that his real pleasure comes from imagining the fulsome praise that might accompany the fictional Leavitt's A papers, and writing dialogue for his fictional counterpart that pats both of them on the back. In the following scrap of conversation, for example, "David" expostulates to a prospective client who wants a paper on Henry James: "I'm a famous writer. I have a novel under contract with Viking Penguin. You know, Viking Penguin, that gigantic publisher, the same one that published *Daisy Miller?*"[5]

The second reason I feel impelled to object to the near-instant elevation of Leavitt to classical rank is that the writing itself, while workmanlike, is so thick and clunky — as full of stylistic clichés as of moral ones. The conclusion of the introduction to *The Penguin Book of Gay Short Stories* is a case in point. A story about a fund-raiser he helped organize "during the frightening days when the American right wing . . . was attempting to use the National Endowment for the Arts as a weapon in its never-ending battle against sexual self-expression,"[6] it ends with a self-serving description of a minor piece of agitprop in which a young man and young woman who "identified themselves as 'a fag' and 'a dyke' " walked onto the stage and asked everyone in the audience who was gay to stand up. "Nervously, about a quarter of us did so." (Nervously? At a Harvey Gantt rally?) After a brief sermonette about the Danes' wearing of yellow stars during World War Two in solidarity with the Jews, the "dyke" asks again, "Would all of you in the audience who are gay stand up?" Naturally, most of the now-cowed audience does: "as for the others, they remained in their seats, eyes grim and steadfast, clutching their armrests as if for dear life." The smugness of the political judgment is exceeded only by the banality of the prose: "frightening days," "a weapon in its never-ending battle against sexual self-expression," "eyes grim and steadfast." Even more constipated is the prim moral which he claims for his anthology: "One hopes a reader [of *The Penguin Book of Gay Short Stories*] will reach the last page having learned a few things, chief among them just how much of a mistake it is to draw conclusions about other people's lives." This moral grandstanding and overstuffed writing go together and are as connate in Leavitt's fiction as his essays, as I will show in my discussion of *The Lost Language of Cranes,* the novel that saved gay literature from itself.

Why, then, has he been taken for a great writer, indeed pushed into the role? My guess is that his novels have answered a felt need for gay fiction that wasn't too gay, gay fiction that your mother could read without turning a hair. One can congratulate oneself on liking this handsome, talented gay man. And indeed it *is* easy to like Leavitt: he is decent and intelligent and has sensible political opinions. (So does Samuel Delany, but try finding a review of his extraordinary and dirty novel *The Mad Man* in any major journal or newspaper!) The ambiguous example of Leavitt's success suggests in turn that the mainstreaming of gay stories is harder to accomplish than one might have thought. There is a tendency for the family story, for instance, to take over the gay person's story, even when it is the gay person who is telling it, as though there were a fictional imbalance of power corresponding to the social imbalance in the real world. (We will see this usurping phenomenon again in Michael Cunningham's novel *A Home at the End of the World*.) The gay story must still, even now, fight to make itself heard among the thousands of easier, more automatic stories of "the unfolding family drama."

Perhaps this is why Robert Ferro felt it necessary to have the main character in *The Family of Max Desir* cruised by a counter-boy on the way to selecting a gravestone for his mother, a scene that elicits Leavitt's disapprobation.[7] Even if the scene is a bit contrived, Leavitt was wrong to imply that it simply exploits sex or that the novelist is improperly sexually obsessed. Gay life, gay fiction may *need* this "obsession" as a way to stay self-aware. Sex need not be the only focal point of such a self-awareness, though, given the usual definition of a gay person, sexual choice seems a logical differentia. Ethan Mordden, for instance, concentrates on what membership in an urban gay "community" might mean, while Neil Bartlett tries to find a continuity in gay life from the late nineteenth century to our own day. But some kind of definition is essential. Otherwise, at least practically speaking, our little island of same-sex stories will be simply swallowed up by the much larger, more familiar heterosexual sea.

In this chapter, I would like to examine two books that seem to shed light on just this issue of the proper degree of separateness, and at the same time, of the possibilities of harmony between the gay minority and the rest of the nongay world. They are separated by many years, the earlier, Christopher Isherwood's *A Single Man* having appeared in 1964, the later, Leavitt's *The Lost Language of Cranes,* in 1986. And yet they are alike in several ways, most generally in a plainness of style, a lack of special pleading (or appeal to special, i.e., gay, audiences), an absence of ghetto focus, a desire to situate their gay characters in the midst of the whole world, not just their own tortured psyches or a small circle of "sympathetic" friends. Both offer visions of moderate happiness. Both might fairly be called books about someone who "just happens to be gay."

But the differences are as great as the similarities. Isherwood's book, despite its early date (or because of it), preserves the sense of radical edge about homosexuality, the sense of not fitting in, that I think still needs preserving; yet does so without inflicting any melodramatic suffering or freakishness on its main character. Isherwood's George is a comparatively happy man whose singularity does not come from any excess of misery. He has been happily and successfully "married" to another gay man, Jim, and their marriage has ended not because of any incapacity for intimacy (such as psychiatrists regularly claim to find in homosexuals) but because Jim had been killed in car accident the year before. At the same time, George is a loner, not because he is gay, but because he is fifty-eight and an expatriate. His solitude suits him, and yet has its drawbacks. He is lonely, for one thing, and growing old; desperate to find a new Jim and, though spunky in his cheerfulness, not at all sure he will. Time is against George, not only as it is against all of us, but obviously, unmistakably. His day (which constitutes the action of the novel) is a series of skirmishes with time; and even if George "wins" in some equivocal sense, even if we are rooting for him (as we are), we are also aware that the battle is ultimately a losing one; that even when successful, George's "singleness" demands formality, distance, un-intimacy —

all products of the time he does not have. Love itself, far from being self-regulating, is so unstable and so painful that couples cannot survive, as George says, without frequent fights and separations.

A Single Man dares to situate the gay man, in other words, not in the hyper-romantic Tennessee Williams–land of hysteria and loneliness, but in a larger prosaic world where, nevertheless, terrible things can also happen. Nothing, including love, is given us in Isherwood's world; it too must be fought for, compromised over, treated unsentimentally. His main character is a warrior, if an unlikely one, neither a romance demigod on the one hand nor a sentimental naïf on the other — exactly, in other words, the sort of protagonist Leavitt desired to see in a gay novel. It is strange, then, that he never mentions Isherwood in the Introduction to *The Penguin Book of Gay Short Stories.*

Leavitt's book, while written overtly to counteract what he saw as a mistaken focus on rejection and desire, finds harmony within character, family, and society — but finds it, in my view, too automatically. His novel does not face the worst dissonances — contradictory impulses, dangerous desires — within oneself or within society. Reading *The Lost Language of Cranes,* one would never guess — despite an occasional reference — that AIDS was ravaging an entire gay generation, that black lesbians were in any way different from white gay men, that love of anonymous sex could coincide with love of another human being, or that discovering your father was gay might be incestuously terrifying. The book achieves its repose largely, though not entirely, at the expense of honesty and wit; and nervously ignores people's actual differences, the stubborn resistances of oneself to happiness, the tragic historical situation in which one lives. The author of this comfortable, soothing, wistful book seems older than his twenty-five years.

By contrast, *A Single Man,* though written by a man in his late fifties, seems young and cantankerous. It is full of contradictions, disharmonies, self-deceptions, and fights — all so honestly and humorously presented that they make their own kind of harmony, one that does not automatically evade dissonance. One finishes it thinking not only that one knows, in a remarkably complete way, what it is to be this "single man," but also what "singleness" is. It is a book that offers not premature union and forgiveness, but insight into the permanently radical condition of homosexuality. And unlike Leavitt's earnest decent novel, there is not a cliché in it.

DAVID LEAVITT'S *THE LOST LANGUAGE OF CRANES*

The Lost Language of Cranes (1986) was, by Leavitt's own account, his riposte to Andrew Holleran's *Dancer from the Dance.* It is interesting, in this regard, that Leavitt's stand-in in the novel, Philip Benjamin, is a copy editor of romance novels: bodice-rippers that he treats as fundamentally ridiculous. Philip's disdain echoes Leavitt's own judgment on other kinds of gay novels — not only romances like Holleran's, but fantasies like *The Family of Max Desir* or *Sturm und Drang* horror stories like James Purdy's *Narrow Rooms*. Perhaps another way to put it would be to say that it is — like all novels written after 1982 — a post-liberation novel. Its essence is to be belated, to be a reaction to something that preceded, whether clone culture, or a particular kind of novel. It is both defensive and aggressive in pursuing its quite different goals, seeming to say at many points: *My* character will choose love, not infatuation; he will not only love, but be loved by his family; he will not give up everything — career, friends, citizenship — for "love." It will be a novel, each sober patient page promises, not of ecstasy and despair, but of Freud's "ordinary unhappiness."

Most gay novels have been coming-out stories of one kind or another, and their main character has been the gay man discovering his homosexuality, falling in and out of love, and (after Stonewall) joining or leaving the gay ghetto. *The Lost Language of Cranes* is unusual, first of all, because it has not one, but two gay characters; and second, because those characters are father and son. But the deeper novelty of the book is its refusal to treat the coming-out of Owen and Philip as cause for rejoicing. The final peculiarity (and genuine interest) of the book is its attempt to do justice to the coming-out story as taking place within a whole family. Indeed, it is because Rose, Philip's mother and Owen's wife, is given such an important role that many critics have liked *Lost Language* so much, especially if they were women. After all, here is a coming-out story that includes *them*.

The novel centers around a group of simultaneous events. Owen Benjamin, Philip's father, has been for some time a distant, depressed man who every Sunday disappears from the Manhattan apartment he shares with his wife Rose. She does not know where he goes — they have led increasingly independent lives over the years — but the reader finds out at the very beginning of the novel: Owen goes to the Bijou, a gay porno movie house. (Thirty years after Mr. Krupper's visits to the Joy Rio, however, Owen is still not enjoying it.) At the same time that this betrayal is going on, there is a second: the apartment Rose and Owen have inhabited for twenty-five years, and in which they raised their only child, Philip, is going co-op. Can they afford to buy it, or must they move? Rose is the one primarily horrified by the prospect of moving. Third, Philip is seeing his first serious boyfriend, Eliot, and this change in his life seems to demand that he come out to his parents for the sake of honesty, but also for the pleasure of sharing his happiness with them.

While Philip is the character with whom the reader identifies, he is not the character to whom the most important things are happening. His affair with Eliot, a feckless charming downtowner who abandons Philip halfway through the book, is nicely observed, of course (everything in Leavitt is), but doesn't seem to go anywhere fictionally any more than it does erotically. He is, so to speak, a "lesson," "an experience" for the young Philip, a step toward growing up. At the end of the book Philip is inching toward what may be a more serious affair with a college friend, Brad, who is as dowdy as Eliot was glamorous. (At one point he greets Philip, who has stopped by unexpectedly, in his bathrobe, eating cinnamon toast, and I don't *think* we're meant to find this funny.)

Of his two parents, Owen has the more melodramatic role in the novel, as we watch him slink, or blank-mindedly *glide,* to the Bijou Sunday after Sunday, overhear a funny embarrassing phone call to a dirty-talk phone service, and — best of all — watch him flirt via Philip with a handsome young teacher, Winston, over dinner with Rose and Philip. (This last scene would have made a wonderful farce sequence in other hands.) Owen bursts into tears at unpredictable moments. When, in the most dramatic moment of the novel, Philip comes out to his parents, Rose is tight-lipped and angry, Owen dazed and guilty. He goes to the bathroom where Rose can hear him sobbing while the shower runs. It is this very profusion of tears that suddenly awakens her to the knowledge that Owen, too, is gay.

Rose is the tough one and, one warily suspects, the "moral center," the one who's mature. A proofreader for a publishing house, she is patient, meticulous, resigned to hard repetitive work, and accustomed to small — and diminishing — rewards. (Isn't this what "maturity" is all about?) Her shock when Owen reveals his homosexuality to her at the end of the novel is not just surprise, but disgust. (It is also somewhat self-protective, for Rose, too, has been unfaithful, if heterosexually, to her marriage.) She, too, then is guilty, though not *feeling* it as much as Owen. To the extent that she does represent a moral touchstone, her comparative guiltlessness implies that perhaps heterosexual affairs simply *are* less evil.

In a way, it is Rose who has the most to lose as the defining events of this novel hit home. She stands to lose her home, her husband, and her son; or rather, her illusions about all of them. And it is she whom both her gay husband and gay son want desperately to "understand" them — and who, perhaps rightly, refuses to give them the easy forgiveness they really seek. As the one with most to lose, she is an anomaly in a gay coming-out story: how odd to make one of the few who is not gay so central! She is a pitiable figure — all of them are — because she is a victim, because she has done nothing "wrong" and yet must suffer. The novel is in fact an indirect praise of all such people who manage to get through life with some dignity, despite the gradual erosion of comfortable beliefs, youthful hopes.

The novel ends inconclusively. After the disastrous dinner party with Winston, during which both Owen and Philip flirt outrageously with the straight

Winston, Owen finally confesses his secret gay life to Rose. She is as tight-lipped and unforgiving as she had been toward Philip at a similar moment. In flight from her seemingly just anger, Owen finds himself at Philip's apartment, where he confesses the truth also to his son, then falls asleep on Philip's bed as Philip watches over him: "He would lie awake for a long time, he knew, looking at Owen's white ankles in the bright moonlight" (319). An inconclusive ending because it is uncertain what Philip, Owen, or Rose will do with their new and unwelcome knowledge. Will Rose divorce Owen? Disown Philip? Will Philip guide his father into the gay world or help him stay in the straight one? In a sense the question seems a moot one, for if the family members begin to pull away from one another, how could that separation be any greater than what they have all undergone already? Could Owen be any more distant from Rose and Philip than he already is? Is any of them capable of a happiness that extends beyond a stoic calm? Philip, perhaps. He at any rate is still young, still goofy about love, and of course has the enormous good fortune to be growing up in the post-Stonewall world. Homosexuality is for him a So what? as it will never be for Owen or Rose. For Philip, Eliot, and Brad it is not homosexuality that is the problem, but sex: they live in the age of AIDS, rather than in the hedonistic seventies so ambivalently celebrated by Holleran.

But actually, I don't believe that even AIDS can explain the sense of being hemmed in that afflicts all the characters in this novel. The barriers, rather, are their very virtues: moral decency, sincerity, need for Freud's "love and work." Leavitt's novels and stories never get beyond these categories, can't imagine any others. What has been left out of this picture? Passion, joy, arrogance, triumph in one's youth, vindictiveness, anger. AIDS alone isn't enough to explain the cautiousness of Philip, Brad, Jerene, and the rest of them. For the cautiousness extends well beyond "safe sex" to a generalized fear of experience. If Eliot can represent "experience" on the strength of wearing "cool socks," what on earth can "innocence" be?

Leavitt as a man, as a writer, and as hero of his own books strikes one as a decent, likable man: indeed, not merely likable but desperate to be liked, fearful of being disliked. (His correspondence with Stephen Spender over the plagiarism of Spender's *World within World* was full of wide-eyed hurt that anyone could mistake his *hommage* for a theft.) But the niceness comes at a price — he doesn't press anything home. One of the things that is most noticeable about Leavitt's fiction is how full it is of lost opportunities: tiny little moments that are intensely "there" but go nowhere, and great big moments that find him emotionally and artistically at a loss. Characters appear and disappear at the drop of a hat, their stories no longer useful once the main character's heart has been successfully pinned to his sleeve. Crucial incidents (for example, Owen's coming out to Philip) are breezed through, while others (such as the dinner party with

Jerene and her new girlfriend), which are structurally insignificant, receive a full-dress scene-setting, pages of mediocre dialogue, and a sad and/or goofy little moral. Leavitt's niceness is everywhere felt, but is it enough? For all his good manners, there is something self-centered and narcissistic about his fiction; we are meant to like much of it because it's by *him*. It tends to turn us into doting parents.

Take a completely irrelevant incident—one of many—at the beginning of *The Lost Language of Cranes.*

Philip and Eliot are in a cab going from Philip's apartment on the Upper West Side to Eliot's glamorously edgy dump in the East Village. As they travel downtown, the cabbie suddenly slams on his brakes:

> Then Philip looked out the window and saw that the intersection was full of white mice. Thousands of them. They swarmed the street in panicked hordes, like tiny indistinguishable sufferers in a fourteenth-century vision of hell. They cascaded over the sidewalk curbs and plunged after each other into gutters. Against the new snow they were nearly invisible, small quakings of motion.
>
> "My God," Philip said. The driver opened his door and got out of the cab, and Philip and Eliot followed him. . . . "I hope no one was hurt," Philip said. "There'd be ambulances if anyone was hurt badly." In the distance, police sirens wailed. . . . The cab parted the sea of mice, and turned onto Ninety-sixth Street. Philip closed his eyes, fearful that he might be compelled to look behind himself for small clots of blood in the snow. . . . "Well, in any case, we can read all about it in the *Post* tomorrow," Eliot said, as if in conclusion. "The *Post* will put this on its front page. MICE ATTACK UPPER MANHATTAN."[8]

And that's that for the mice—with the exception of one, infinitesimal later mention: when the winter comes, Philip wonders briefly if all the white mice have died of cold.

What on earth would make an author write such a scene? Is it to be filed under New York: Crazy Things That Happen In? Are we meant to take it as a sign of Philip's moral fineness that he worries about the mice and can't bear to think of them being crushed (although he completely forgets about them within five minutes)? Or more portentously, are these mice to be taken as parallels to Eliot and Philip themselves? Are these two gay men similarly trapped? Are they, too, on their way to a terrible fate (the mice to the labs at Columbia, Philip and Eliot to, well, the East Village)? Will Philip's liberation prove as ironically brief as that of the white mice: freed from homophobia and shame, is he only to suffer some dismaler destiny? ("O, the mind, mind has molehills," as Gerard Manley Hopkins might have said.) None of these solutions is satisfactory, of course. But that is not the real problem with the scene. The real problem is that the novel does not depend, in even the smallest part, upon our coming up with a solution. (The *Post* never put it on the front page. The event has literally no consequences.) It's there, not for "local color," but for fictional color: it's a "nice piece of writing," to be slotted in *somewhere*. It's as respectable and empty as a nineteenth-century British fugue.

Sometimes these set pieces give more away — or something different away — than Leavitt intends. Let's look, for example, at a love scene. It is the first time we have seen Philip and Eliot together and a great deal, fictionally, rides on our accepting their relationship as important enough to shake the Benjamin family to its roots. Here, too, however, Leavitt gives way to unnecessary writing. The randomness is less obvious than it was with the escaped white mice, but has far worse consequences, either distracting our attention from the lovers or making them unappealing.

> Philip was in love. He lay pinned under the body of Eliot, his lover of almost a month, and he couldn't move. His left arm felt like part of Eliot — alien and heavy — but he did not dare reposition it. He must have woken Eliot up ten times during the night with his thrashing (love made him thrash), and he wasn't about to risk doing it again. Instead he lay still, trying to flex his fingers to get his blood running, and watched a sliver of gray cloud pass between the sagging curtain rod and the frame of his one window. Eliot's breath tickled the hairs under his arm. The radiator wheezed, the super's Dobermans barked, rain clicked against the roof. He tried to identify the room's generally unpleasant smells — dirty dishes, sweat, old socks — and wondered what time it was. Probably around noon, he guessed, but could not bend around to look at the clock. (25–26)

What is the point of this gratuitously unromantic paragraph? Is it meant to be grotesque? If so, why? Their love is genuine. Is it meant to show how crazy love is, that you feel happy even when surrounded by Dobermans and "generally unpleasant smells"? If so, it seems merely cute. Is it a foreshadowing of the unhappy ending of this affair? If so, it's ineffective.

As often with Leavitt — we will see it in his treatment of Owen and Rose — it is the *body* itself that gives rise to these nervous fictional tics, this midge-swarm of shrugs and blushes and smells. In particular, it is Leavitt's desire to avoid sex — even here, where sex is plainly in the offing — that leads to another oddly italicized event. The first words the lovelorn Philip speaks to Eliot are "I have to go to the bathroom." Once again, there is something disingenuous about the treatment of Philip's nerdiness. We're meant to find his squeamishness *charming*. But it's not charming, it's embarrassing, not because Philip is embarrassed but because Leavitt is. It is sex itself he is ridiculing, by turning our attention to that other, vaguely ridiculous function of Philip's penis, urination: "He trembled as he urinated, and tried to calm his erection, which was sending the urine off at wrong angles, making it hit the rim of the toilet bowl and splash onto the floor. Finished, he flushed, wiped up what he had spilled, and went back out the door" (26). The next thing Philip is made to do is wash the dishes (apparently, love makes him not only "thrash" but scrub). When Eliot understandably tells him to come back to bed, he gives up this unconvincing act and says, "in a voice he had never heard before, a voice that belonged to Greta Garbo, 'I am yours' " (27).

There is absolutely nothing wrong with taking sexual embarrassment as a fictional topic, but Leavitt isn't going to do that. Instead, he's getting some mileage out of Philip's being *cute* in his squirmy fastidiousness. This scene turns Philip into a prig. The priggishness, the asexuality that Leavitt pretends to find funny, goofy, and charming are potentially serious topics, but they are not taken seriously. To Leavitt, it is enough to *notice* them (another writers'-workshop tic), then get rid of them when they become a liability — when, for instance, he wants to turn Philip into a vehicle for "deep" emotion.

If Philip is turned into a cute prig, the reader is turned into an unwilling voyeur. Not, obviously, a voyeur of sex, but of Leavitt's adolescent deflection of sex: dirt, bad smells, excretions. Like the episode of the mice, the scene of Philip's urination is terribly "observed." But do we really need to be shown what it is like to spray urine on the floor? Or to have the difficulty of peeing while erect treated so solemnly (mightn't it be funny)? Would a young man newly in love really steady his forehead like a fifties housewife and start doing the dishes rather than take that erection right back to bed? Would the sober, uncampy Philip really speak in Greta Garbo's voice? Would the nastiness of the body really be uppermost in his mind?

If Leavitt were a different sort of writer, the answer might well be Yes. Indeed, there was the promise in this mini-scene of both farce and fetish. But once again, neither promise is fulfilled, perhaps even noticed. Like his main character, Leavitt is a nice narcissist who thinks anything he does must be interesting by virtue of the fact that *he* does it. Nor can he see that, to a disinterested reader, Philip's sexual shame might seem either ridiculous or perverse. To Leavitt it is neither, but rather an occasion for showing off. He's *proud* of that passage on the urine, just as Philip, that rascal, is proud of making a nasty mess on the floor. Without meaning to, without even being aware of it, Leavitt is literally rubbing our noses in it.

It is strange how often and automatically Leavitt strikes this note of physical squeamishness. It is not just sex that brings it out in him, but reference to any appetite. Here is a passage, for instance, about Philip's parents. It, too, is curiously anticarnal, though here the primal scene is eating.

Owen and Rose are sitting across the living room from one another in the twin corduroy La-Z-Rockers they had once rented a car and drove all the way to

Jersey to buy. It is late at night. Through the crack beneath the door to his bedroom, the light of four one-hundred-watt bulbs glares. There is no sound but that of pages turning, bodies shifting, an occasional stretch. "Two hundred pages to go," says Owen. He is reading a densely footnoted biography of Lytton Strachey. Then he moves into the kitchen and opens the refrigerator door. The cake is there, the icing gleaming in the light that goes on when the door opens, one or two slices already missing and the knife — coated with white silk and yellow crumbs — lying on the plate next to it. Rose joins him. She takes the plate out of the refrigerator, puts it down on the counter, and sinks the knife into its softness. He stands by, helpless, watching her as she hoists two pieces of cake onto dessert plates and carries them to the table. All without a word. Then they sit down, prop their books open in front of them, and eat. (5–6)

Every detail in this description is meant to put Owen and Rose in the wrong, to imply that there is something pathological in their relationship — and this is not true. The worst you could say about Owen and Rose is that they're bored with each other, as middle-aged couples often are. So what? Leavitt, however, is determined to make their twin midlife crises ponderously "important," and thus bestows on his poor creatures the contemptuous gift of "twin corduroy La-Z-Rockers" they had driven "all the way to Jersey to buy." He makes menacing even their love of books — don't read those footnotes, Owen!

And then there's "the cake," led up to by a series of ominous drum rolls and tremolos. The description of Owen "moving" to the refrigerator, as if hypnotized, of Rose cutting into it like a priestess sacrificing an infant, is ludicrously italicized. The last two words, "and eat," reduce Owen and Rose to ravenous chewing mouths. The prose is pornographic in its breathlessness, its silence, the intentness of its gaze. (If only Leavitt could have described Philip's and Eliot's sex life like that!) But when Owen stands by "helpless," I always want to ask "Why? What's to be helped?"

The point of this elaborate set piece is to imply tension, depth, unspoken secrets where there are none. (Unless, of course, Leavitt secretly believes that Owen's secret, that homosexuality itself, is such a horror. Ah, but *that* must never be conceded, even hinted at.) It suggests that Owen's and Rose's life is one not merely of uneasy accommodation to middle age and marriage, but of actual despair. But is that despair ever truly justified by their actual situation, or by anything that happens to them? Is Owen's guilt or Rose's anger commensurate with the emptiness that seems to stare out at them from that frighteningly well-lit Edward Hopper refrigerator?

If these three examples of lost, or mishandled opportunities turn on Leavitt's giving us more information than we need, others turn on his giving us far less. When Owen finally comes out to Philip after the disastrous dinner party where both of them have flirted with the straight Winston, the dynamite goes off as prettily as a sparkler:

> "I'm not sure," he said quietly, "how much you've figured out about me."
> "What do you mean?"
> He was quiet. "I'm a homosexual," he said. "I'm a homosexual, too."
> Philip stared at the neat rows of garbage cans in the alley, listened to the hiss of the radiator.
> "Does that news surprise you, son?"
> "No, not really," Philip said. His eyes began suddenly to tear.
> "It's just I — I guess I never let myself see it before." (314)

Since this very revelation has been lying in wait from the first page of the book, the reader has a right to expect more. Instead, the trap is sprung and (to our astonishment) hurts no one. I consider myself up-to-date, but surely it is not every day that a twenty-five-year-old son hears his father tell him he's gay. It is a tribute of sorts to Leavitt's incurably clean mind that the incestuous power of this scene is so blandly neutralized: Owen even falls asleep on Philip's bed (his bed!) while the sadder-but-wiser Philip simply watches over his father like a wounded guardian angel. Even the Hamitic crime of looking on his father's nakedness is made simultaneously cozy and deflating: "He would lie awake for a long time, he knew, looking at Owen's white ankles in the bright moonlight." One final slap at the unloved male body, reduced here to the white ankles of a middle-aged man who has never had much pleasure in his life.

The tendency to lose opportunities as well as oversell them is not limited to the end of the novel. It can be seen in numberless plot twists that are carefully set up, then go off with a wet little sputter. It is carefully prepared, for example, that both Philip and his father go to dirty movies at the Bijou Theater. Given the fact that this story is largely about their shared homosexuality and their eventual admission of it to each other, one expects they will accidentally run into each other there, or that in the cinematic gloom they might unknowingly be groping the same person — or even each other! The possibilities are endless; the merest sitcom writer would have known what to do with them. Leavitt for some reason ignores them. A similar complaint could be made about the phone call Owen places to the Gay Hotline, a potentially touching and/or funny scene in which he tells the counselor on the other end that his son is gay and that he is, too. A promising scene, made even more promising by the fact that it is Jerene, Eliot's lesbian roommate, who answers Owen's call. We think we know how this scene will go: something Owen or Jerene says will tip them off as to each other's true identity . . . our breath pleasurably quickens. . . . Instead, nothing happens; rather, we're left with another shower of tears from Owen, and some embarrassing social-workerese from Jerene. There's nothing exactly *wrong* with this scene except that it's so much less than it could have been: so much less funny on the one hand, so much less moving or suspenseful on the other.

A final example of inconsequentiality, of free-floating emotion untethered to probability, Jerene and Philip meet in a coffee shop because Eliot has decided he doesn't love Philip and has stopped returning Philip's calls. Philip wants news of him from Jerene. She supplies it, and thereby makes Philip cry: " 'He says he can't face you,' she said. Philip's eyes widened, and he leaned forward in his seat. 'Can't face me!' he said. 'Can't face me!' And cried harder." Jerene is briskly sympathetic: "Please don't ask me to justify him . . . He does this to people. He's done this to other boyfriends. He can be a real bastard at times." This doesn't reassure Philip, of course: "He was really sobbing now" (189).

Tears are the one bodily secretion Leavitt thoroughly approves of. He thinks that they are always healing, always truthful, and always *somehow there*. We shouldn't be surprised, then, that Philip's tears are so contagious that "across the way, a long-haired woman wearing dark circular glasses, as if inspired by him, began to cry as well" (189). What power there is in this nerdy lovesick boy! But we shouldn't be surprised. This is a book, after all, that takes weeping as a sort of default emotion; so much so that even lust, that powerful drier of tears, gives way to it. In a particularly ridiculous scene, Leavitt takes Philip to a dirty bookstore in Greenwich Village, where "it seemed appropriate that at the end of the night he should find himself in a curtained booth . . . crying. As at the coffee shop with Jerene, no one seemed all that surprised that he was crying. Other people were crying. A lot of people apparently came here to cry" (199).

I have visited many peep shows in my time, and I have heard many sounds in them. Never have I heard tears. But the adroit reader understands the real reason for their presence: they are clues as to what we ought to feel, the equivalent of the movie soundtrack that swells up under an otherwise unmotivated kiss to give it "depth." What we may fail to notice at first, in an understandable eagerness to have some kind of big emotional discharge, is how many possibilities Leavitt has left out: for example, the possibility that people might go to peep shows out of some complicated mixture of longing, shame, need, and laughter; that they might, conceivably, have a good time there and even meet someone to go out with or befriend. (All these have been known to happen.) But in this book about "lost languages," the one most fatally lost is that of irony.

It is a loss that Christopher Isherwood, in *A Single Man,* never allows to happen. With much of Leavitt's own desire to show a gay man in the round, neither to italicize his sexuality nor make it symbolic of anything super- or sub-human, Isherwood nonetheless writes with seriousness, accuracy, and humor. There is none of the carelessness that marks Leavitt's storytelling: the invention and dismissal of characters, the descriptions that serve only to show the writer's cleverness. Instead there is a thoughtful attention to his main character that pays George (and us) the compliment of taking him seriously but never solemnly. The result is an unforced pathos, an unsleeping sense of the ridiculous, and a dry objectivity that can make your hair stand on end.

CHRISTOPHER ISHERWOOD'S *A SINGLE MAN*

Isherwood has dared to take for his hero a character far less cuddly than Philip: a cranky middle-aged transplanted Briton who shirks his job, meditates lurid but impotent revenge, avoids his friends except when pinned down by them, holds forth on subjects he barely understands, sucks his belly in at the gym, has spasms of grief and self-pity, tries with drunken passion and little success to pick up one of his students — and possibly dies at the end. He is a man whose life (like this novel, which takes place over the course of a single day) is full of restriction: will he really go to Mexico for Christmas vacation and have wild sexual adventures? ("*You won't and you never will,* a voice says, coldly bored with him.") Will he find a replacement for his dead lover Jim, and if so what kind of "love" will that be? Will he ever weigh less than 150 ("in spite of all that toiling at the gym!")? Will he ever leave the house he and Jim bought years before?[9]

For a book by a practicer of Vedanta, *A Single Man* is unrepentantly full of love for the ego, that mask of self which turns out to be so oddly adequate to life — to the daily encroachments of hypocrisy, cruelty, sexual shame that make friendship and love so hard and so worthwhile.[10] Another object of its love is George's battered, unreliable body with its aches and pains, its pyloric valve and vagus nerve, its lusts and imminent death. By doing critical homage to these selves which are so limited, so transient, and in a way so false, Isherwood performs a radical act of transvaluation: every word of this remarkable nonmoralistic novel pings with selfishness and triumph, rather than sentimental moral uplift.

But *A Single Man* speaks also with a deep pathos and a justified rage at George's limits. Despite the book's structural equanimity (it begins with George waking up, follows him through the day, and ends with his falling asleep), and despite its comparative uneventfulness, it packs a punch of suspense. The nearly palpable enemy throughout is Time: George is running out of it. As he tells his student Kenny, drunkenly but not falsely at the end, "The time is *desperately* short" (175). Will George make it? The huge obstacles in his life — obstacles to being "out" as a gay man, to making contact with his students, to finding a new Jim — have been made unnervingly visible. He is one man against all these impossibilities, against time, a "single man" who will not win, even though he may have momentary triumphs. But not for that reason will George give up, for he is, as he realizes at one point, still a "contender."

But there is so much to contend with, including himself. The almost shocking urgency of the novel comes not from the invention of improbable melodramatic events, but from Isherwood's clear view of the forces that lie just under the surface of George's life — larval personae of which George himself is nervously half-aware. Some of these ghostly presences are benign, some horrifying, and some humiliating or ridiculous. Some are roles he half-chooses to play, others roles that have been thrust upon him and that he can no longer escape. The widowed George, for instance, is constantly looking for love and is arguably pitiable. But the sadistic "Uncle George," a vengeful imaginary person who surfaces as the respectable professorial George is driving to work, is so angry and alienated that it has a fantasy of taking revenge on "three-quarters of America" for Jim's death. The vain George is given free rein to ogle himself at the gym, the lonely George to make himself maudlin at the supermarket, the drunken lustful George to try unsuccessfully to seduce his student Kenny.

To live with so many rebellious selves requires the tactical skill of a general, and one of the metaphors Isherwood keeps coming back to is military. When George wakes up, "the entire intercommunication system . . . issue[s] the first general order of the day: UP" (10). As he drives to work he daydreams of punishing the right-wing homophobic state senators with "brute force," the only language they understand. "Therefore we must launch a campaign of systematic terror" (38). When he strips in the gym and looks at himself, he must admit "he has abandoned the neck altogether, like an untenable military position" (105). And in fact one way to grasp the novel as a whole is to see it as a war novel without the name. George is a warrior — a "single" one and unlikely to win. And his heroism lies in his willingness to fight back against time, his body, the sentimental hypocrisies of his society, the cult of sexual normality, the multiple untamed selves that coinhabit his psyche. His combativeness — though not his success — is what makes him a new man: the first modern gay man in literature.

The novel is almost impossible to summarize, because (like a poem) its effects are all local. I would like to concentrate on the beginning and end of the novel, and a telling scene from the middle.

The novel begins unforgettably with a description from within of the terror, the unreality, of the most ordinary event in the world: waking up.

> Waking up begins with saying *am* and *now*. That which has awoken then lies for a while staring up at the ceiling and down into itself until it has recognized *I*, and therefrom deduced *I am, I am now*. *Here* comes next, and is at least negatively reassuring; because *here*, this morning, is where it has expected to find itself: what's called *at home*. (9)

How easy it would have been to fall into an exaggeration: to make the point of the passage a self-consciously arty presentation of "stream of consciousness" or to go for the effect of self-pity and "lostness." Isherwood does neither. His voice is flexible enough to encompass George's and his own: the comatose George would hardly say "*Here* . . . is at least negatively reassuring." And at the same time, how powerfully the effect of self-alienation, of disquiet is created: "That which has awoken then lies for a while staring up at the ceiling." Finally, how economically the sardonic tone that will come to be George's is established: "what's called *at home*" plainly distinguishes what George would call this from what the world forces him to call it. Ironically, indeed tragically, "at home" is just what he is not, what no one ever is.

After waking up, it empties "its" bladder and weighs "itself" (for George is still, in his semiconscious state, more a body than a mind). Then it looks into the mirror.

> What it sees there isn't so much a face as the expression of a predicament. Here's what it has done to itself, here's the mess it has somehow managed to get itself into during its fifty-eight years; expressed in terms of a dull, harassed stare, a coarsened nose, a mouth dragged down by the corners into a grimace as if at the sourness of its own toxins, cheeks sagging from their anchors of muscle, a throat hanging limp in tiny wrinkled folds. The harassed look is that of a desperately tired swimmer or runner; yet there is no question of stopping. The creature we are watching will struggle on and on until it drops. Not because it is heroic. It can imagine no alternative. (10)

Unlike Leavitt, Isherwood is not exploiting George's physical decrepitude for some sentimental purpose, but trying to see it for what it is. Thus, the grim picture—coarsened nose, mouth dragged down, cheeks sagging—is modified by a tone of amused disgust: "Here's what it has done to itself, here's the mess it has somehow managed to get itself into." The voice is that of someone addressing a drunk or a child—Look at you!—but is neither contemptuous nor preachy. And if the face shows signs of wear, there is pity for it too: "Staring and staring into the mirror, it sees many faces within its face—the face of the child, the boy, the young man, the not-so-young man—all present still, preserved like fossils on superimposed layers, and, like fossils, dead" (10). But it is not only one's own toxins that have so soured one's life, but the necessity of pleasing "the others." "[T]he cortex orders it impatiently to wash, to shave, to brush its hair. Its nakedness has to be covered. It must be dressed up in clothes because it is going outside, into the world of the other people; and these others must be able to identify it. Its behavior must be acceptable to them" (11). To be in the world of "the other people"—odd disquieting phrase—is to be in disguise, a pitiable but also a welcome disguise. ("It is glad that it has its place among them.") That disguise is only part of who it is, but a needful part, the part one can know.

However much George dislikes or mocks "the other people," however much he perceives the many other selves that co-occupy his body, he also knows that without this body, this outward self, he has no identity. It is this electric ambiguity — loving and hating identification — that runs like a thread through this novel. To awaken is to accept (with mixed feelings) the burden of a name: "It knows its name. It is called George."

George now walks downstairs, pausing only at the kitchen door where he and his lover Jim would always bump into each other. This reminds him that "Jim is dead. Is dead," and causes him a pain so intense that he can only grunt like an animal and wait for it to pass. "These morning spasms are too painful to be treated sentimentally. After them, he feels relief, merely. It is like getting over a bad attack of cramp" (13). (I can only imagine what Leavitt would have made of this "cramp.") When Jim was alive, "breakfast . . . used to be one of the best times of the day." They would talk about "everything that came into their heads — including death, of course, and is there survival, and, if so, what exactly is it that survives." But even if "something approximately to be described as Jim can return to see how George is making out . . . would this be at all satisfactory?" Wouldn't it be like "the brief visit of an observer from another country" seeing "this figure who sits solitary at the small table in the narrow room, eating his poached eggs humbly and dully, a prisoner for life"? (15). Once again, the tone is just right, neither sliding into bathos nor dismissing the question of "what survives," a question which will occupy George, and Isherwood, throughout the book.

One of the limits, one of the identities that is George, is the body: it signifies to him both vitality and decay. And because this is a book so candidly about the body, it is natural, or at least plausible, that one of the things it describes would be George taking a shit. How different this is from Leavitt's description of Philip urinating, which was pointless because Philip's body is never again found interesting. In Isherwood, the scene is neither naughty nor squeamish, but funny. George, feeling "a bowel movement coming on with agreeable urgency" — what exact, witty words! — "climbs the stairs briskly to the bathroom" with (of all things) a volume of Ruskin, which he "misuses . . . quite ruthlessly" to "trigger the conditioned reflexes of his colon" (16–17). Isherwood uses George's bowel movement to as good effect. As George sits on the john he looks out over his neighbors — "they can see his head and shoulders from across the street, but not what he is doing" — and (as befits one sitting on a throne) passes judgment on them. But if George is saying, "I shit on you," he is also saying "I belong to this place, too." Indeed, this comic scene permits Isherwood to commit the rhetorical trope of topographia, description of a place.

The very neighborhood George lives in has changed, his house has become a last bohemian (and queer) outpost. The original colonists' "utopian dream" was ridiculously, touchingly contradictory: "a subtropical English village with Montmartre manners: a Little Good Place where you could paint a bit, write a bit, and drink lots." It was a place where a gay couple like Jim and George could fit in. After the war, however, came "The Great Change," when the vets—and worse, their wives—came out west "in search of new and better breeding grounds.... And what better breeding ground than a hillside neighborhood like this one, only five minutes' walk from the beach and with no through traffic to decimate the future tots" (18). Now "they"—always an important word in George's paranoid vocabulary—have taken over, the tangible symbol two signs: "one of them told you not to eat the watercress which grew along the bed of the creek, because the water was polluted.... The other sign—those sinister black silhouettes on a yellow ground—said CHILDREN AT PLAY" (19).

"They" are in one sense heterosexuals, nuclear families, "children at play." But sexuality is merely the kernel of their otherness. For with culturally privileged heterosexuality comes (according to George) a kind of blindness: unawareness of people's difference; fear of change and risk; complacent participation in the social lies concerning everything from work to extramarital sex; and the universal preference for hypocrisy, "blandese," that covers everything with a smog of phony tolerance and friendliness. "For breeding"—note the contemptuous animal-husbandry term!—"you need a steady job, you need a mortgage, you need credit, you need insurance. And don't you dare die, either, until the family's future is provided for." It is a world that must forbid direct experiences such as eating the "delicious" watercress which Jim and George ate without harm. It is the world of what Isherwood himself called "the heterosexual dictatorship," a world that fears direct experience, strong feeling, and plainspokenness.

As he sits on the toilet George divides up the typical day of his neighborhood with a general's attention to spheres of influence. First comes the children's hour (when the proto-psychopath Benny Strunk pretends to murder a broken bathroom scale with a hammer), the Mothers' Hour (when Mrs. Strunk, "smiling evasively," tells George "'I never hear the noise children make—just as long as it's a *happy* noise'"), the adolescents' hour (the boys "kick and leap and catch with arrogant grace . . . If a car ventures along the street, it must stop and wait until they are ready to let it through"; the girls "will do the weirdest things to attract [the boys'] attention: for example, the Cody daughters keep fanning their ancient black poodle as though it were Cleopatra on the Nile"), then finally the men's hour, when "the ball-playing must stop" because the men are so tired of their vaguely sleazy jobs that they "can bear no more noise" (24).

As he looks down from his toilet throne, George imagines that the husbands "doubtless look at him and growl 'Queer'." The wives, "trained in the new tolerance, the technique of annihilation by blandness," perhaps bring out their psychology book — "bell and candle are no longer necessary." They pity him, as if Jim had been a poor substitute for a wife. But "your book is wrong, Mrs. Strunk, says George,

> when it tells you that Jim is the substitute I found for a real son, a real kid brother, a real husband, a real wife. Jim wasn't a substitute for anything. And there is no substitute for Jim, if you'll forgive my saying so, anywhere. Your exorcism has failed, dear Mrs. Strunk, says George, squatting on the toilet and peeping forth from his lair to watch her emptying the dustbag of her vacuum cleaner into the trash can. The unspeakable is still here — right in your very midst. (29)

"The unspeakable is still here — right in your very midst." This is George's battle-cry, it is his weapon. For what he is saying is true. He is a reminder in the flesh of the unspeakable that the Strunks would like to "exorcise" from their world, Mrs. Strunk by bland tolerance, Mr. Strunk by macho bluff ("I don't give a damn what he does just as long as he stays away from me" [27]). He is at least two monsters: the gay monster Mr. and Mrs. Strunk think him, and the more frightening monster that is "unspeakable" because it is bodily. And the two go together; his homosexuality is an unavoidable reminder of all sexuality, of our bodily condition. He is, as sexual — or excreting — body, the monster that Mr. Strunk and Mr. Garfein have to get drunk to ignore: "the fiend that won't fit into their statistics, the Gorgon that refuses their plastic surgery, the vampire drinking blood with tactless uncultured slurps, the bad-smelling beast that doesn't use their deodorants, the unspeakable that insists, despite all their shushing, on speaking its name. . . . Among many other kinds of monster, George says, they are afraid of little me" (27).

The Strunks and Garfeins *think* they understand George but don't. It is the other way around. *He* understands, for instance, that Mr. Strunk and Mr. Garfein, drunk at the end of a long cocktail party, are not brave but cowardly; that they are like boys "calling to each other as they explore a dark unknown cave, growing ever louder and louder, bolder and bolder. Do they know that they are afraid? No. But they are very afraid" (26). Isherwood implies by his setting of this scene that one reason George understands them is his willingness to be a "monster," to be anus and brain together, to be *aware* of his body and its desires as they are only frightened of theirs. (They pinch each other's wives only when they get drunk enough.) He sees his own — but also their — monstrosity.

This monstrosity has two aspects, a daytime and a nighttime one. The former, it seems to George, can be managed, honored, harnessed. If one only acknowledges the parts of one that are antisocial or irrational, one can be empowered by them. But there is also a nighttime view of monstrosity, as when George wakes up or becomes suddenly enraged or notices that he's been on "automatic" for long periods of time: this monstrosity is more closely related to things completely out of one's control: sex, death, the unconscious.

One of the most characteristic moments in *A Single Man,* and one bearing directly on the question of George's "monstrosity" and "difference," comes in the classroom scene. In it, not for the first or last time, the surface George is taken over by something in him that is quite different, something angry, combative, and almost-gay. George is teaching Huxley's *After Many a Summer Dies the Swan,* and one of his students complains about Mr. Propter's claim that the "stupidest text in the Bible is 'they hated me without a cause' " and asks, baitingly, if Huxley is anti-Semitic. George says no, then (to his own surprise) takes off on a half-eloquent, half-confused defense not only of Huxley, but of himself. "No — Mr. Huxley is *not* antisemitic. The Nazis were *not* right to hate the Jews. But their hating the Jews was *not* without a cause. No one *ever* hates without a cause. . . . Let's think about this in terms of some other minority, any one you like, but a small one — one that isn't organized and doesn't have any committees to defend it . . ." (70).

George is plainly thinking of homosexuals, and even looks at the "unappetizing" sissy Wally Bryant "with a deep shining look that says, I am with you, little minority-sister." Though we think he might be about to confess his homosexuality, or at least explicitly use homosexuality as his example, he dodges away: the "something about to happen" doesn't happen. He explains that to be a "minority" a group has to be perceived as a threat: hence, the freckled are not a "minority" to the unfreckled. Furthermore, the difference between the minority and the majority must be real: we mustn't simply wish it away:

> "Sure, minorities are people — *people,* not angels. Sure, they're like us — but not *exactly* like us; that's the all-too-familiar state of liberal hysteria in which you begin to kid yourself you honestly cannot see any difference between a Negro and a Swede. . . . So, let's face it, minorities are people who probably look and act and think differently from us and have faults we don't have. We may dislike the way they look and act, and we may hate their faults. And it's *better* if we admit to disliking and hating them than if we try to smear our feelings over with pseudo-liberal sentimentality. . . . We all keep trying to believe that if we ignore something long enough it'll just vanish. . . ." (71)

Like many of George's speeches, this one deflates itself, partly because George gets carried away by it and partly because to make himself perfectly clear he would have to come out. But notice the argument George is half-persuasively improvising. Being a member of a minority means being genuinely different from the majority, not just superficially. Or rather *especially* superficially. For the surface in Isherwood is always important. If it is the cause of prejudice and of difference, it also provides the condition for the possibility of friendship and love. Looks are not deceiving here. This theme of difference is echoed time and again in the novel: George, it is made clear, is different from the world around him; he is *not* the Strunks, is *not* the other middle-aged men at the gym, *not* his friend Charlotte (though she might think so) and *not* his student Kenny (though he lusts after him). In a sense he's not even *George* — as we have seen from the beginning and end of the book, when "George" is reduced to "Cortex, that grim disciplinarian" and the tweakings of "the vagus nerve." There are selves within selves at work in George, including the "chauffeur" and the vengeful "Uncle George." *A Single Man* sees very clearly the paradox of personality; of our being at the mercy of forces we barely acknowledge, let alone control; and the necessity of humoring them.

Indeed, if there is a philosophy implicit in *A Single Man* it is that implied by Montaigne in "On Experience": "Between ourselves, these are two things that I have always observed to be in singular accord: supercelestial thoughts and subterranean conduct."[11] Isherwood's eschewal of the supercelestial frees him from the subterranean. Paradoxically it is because he refuses to punish or ridicule the body that he is free of its tyranny. It is notable that one of his happiest moments comes in the gym, where George is naked and (contentedly) reduced to his body, that very index of all stubborn irreducible differences.

At the end of the novel, there is a more complex and touching presentation of George's monstrous difference. Here, the topic is the "monstrosity" of being an older man, of being still lustful, of being almost on the verge of coming out without quite having the nerve. George has at this point gone through an entire day — teaching his English class, visiting a dying woman who was once a rival for Jim's love, working out at the gym (the high point of George's bodily day), and having dinner with an old friend, Charlotte, like him a transplanted Briton who (unlike him) wants to go "home." At the end of this alcoholic dinner, George at first "gives himself a stern talking to. You are drunk. Oh, you stupid old thing, how dare you get so drunk? Well, now, listen: We are going to walk down those steps very slowly, and when we are at the bottom we are going straight home and upstairs and right into bed, without even brushing our teeth" (146).

But the next thing he knows he "suddenly turns, chuckles to himself, and with the movement of a child wriggling free of a grownup — old guardian Cortex — runs off down the road, laughing" (146). He ends up at the Starboard Side, a squalid seaside bar that (like George himself) is a holdout, a throwback to the old unreformed days:

> Oh, the bloody battles and the sidewalk vomitings! The punches flying wide, and heads crashing backwards against the fenders of parked cars! . . . Hitch-

hiking servicemen delayed at this corner for hours, nights, days; proceeding at last on their journey with black eyes, crab-lice, clap, and only the dimmest memory of their hostess or host. . . . And then the beach months of 1946. The magic squalor of those hot nights, when the whole shore was alive with tongues of flame, the watchfires of a vast naked barbarian tribe — each group or pair to itself and bothering no one, yet all a part of the life of the tribal encampment — swimming in the darkness, cooking fish, dancing to the radio, coupling without shame on the sand. George and Jim (who had just met) were out there among them evening after evening, yet not often enough to satisfy the sad fierce appetite of memory, as it looks back hungrily on that glorious Indian summer of lust. (147–48)[12]

George ends up at the Starboard Side because he hopes at least once more to find another Jim. In this unillusioned optimism ("He believes he will because he must"), he is different from the other men he had seen that day at the gym: "What's wrong with them is their fatalistic acceptance of middle age, their ignoble resignation to grandfatherhood, impending retirement and golf" (105). George realized even then that he was different from these men "in some sense which can't quite be defined but which is immediately apparent when you see him naked, *he hasn't given up*. He is still a contender, and they aren't" (106). The indefinable sense in which George is different is his homosexuality — which in this book implies also his conscious attention to the body, to sex, to looks.

Sure enough, he does find someone there — his student Kenny, goofy and unpredictable, whom George sometimes nervously suspects of "knowing the secret of life." Kenny has earlier shown an anomalous, unreadable affection for George, talking to him after class to ask George whether he had ever taken drugs, whether he ever "saw God." Kenny has also given him a casual present: a red pencil-sharpener, a gift that made George feel that "even if all this doubletalk hasn't brought them any closer to understanding each other, the not-understanding, the readiness to remain at cross-purposes, is in itself a kind of intimacy" (82). This "kind of intimacy," George's kind, reaches its climax in the penultimate scene of the novel.

Kenny is writing poetry at the bar, and George starts talking to him. The two of them get drunk ("Kenny fairly, George very") and have what George calls a "dialogue," "but not a Platonic dialogue in the hair-splitting, word-twisting, one-up-to-me sense; not a mock-humble bitching match; not a debate on some dreary set theme" (154). Rather, "there the two of them sit, smiling at each other — oh, far more than that — fairly beaming with mutual insight" (155). Kenny, to test George's claim to be much "sillier" now than he ever was when young, dares him to go skinny-dipping in the Pacific with him. To Kenny's delight and surprise, George immediately says Yes. In a marvelous, slightly sinister scene, the two of them swim in the dark ocean, George almost being drowned by a "great, an apocalyptically great wave" (163) — note the elegantly compact drunk talk — from which George is dragged out, laughing, by Kenny. The two of them go back to George's house.

The scene is now set for a seduction, for both George and Kenny have been flirting shamelessly with each other — though only George knows it. What follows is a masterpiece of "not-understanding" in which nonetheless some kind of communication happens, if an equivocal one. Kenny is curious as to whether George lives here alone. "As a matter of fact, I used to share this place with a friend," says George, dropping a hint for Kenny to follow up. "But Kenny shows no curiosity about the friend"; to him, living alone is simply the most desirable of all things (166). George tries once more to bring up "the friend": "This friend of mine had lots of animals. . . . Of course, it's different when there's two of you . . ." (167). But Kenny still isn't biting. George switches the topic to Lois, Kenny's girlfriend. This time it's Kenny who (inadvertently?) drops the hairpin: "'Anyhow, I'm in no rush about marrying anyone. There's a lot of things I want to do, first — '" The pause is extremely erotic; what else could those "other things" be than sex with a man, perhaps with George? And indeed, Kenny *is* thinking about sex, but not quite the way George wants him to: "'I think you want to ask me something different. Only you're not sure how I'll take it.'" Does George really want to know, for instance, "if Lois and I — if we make out together." "'Well, do you?' Kenny laughs triumphantly. 'So I was right!'" (168–69).

George uses (as he must) even this unwelcome heterosexual topic as a wedge; and for reasons touching in their helplessness and comic in their self-interest, makes Kenny an offer. He tells Kenny that from now on, every week on this night, he will go to dinner at his friend Charlotte's. The house will be unlocked and empty. "If that bed were ever used while I was out, and straightened up afterwards, I'd never be any the wiser" (172). If Kenny, in other words, wanted to bring Lois not to a motel (which she would reject) but a real house, he could. There is humiliation, but also self-satisfied cleverness and sexual heat, in this procurer's offer.

Kenny is faintly embarrassed by George's proposal, and in the final turn of this conversation George attacks that very embarrassment with a funny, desperate passion. The only reason, George says, we fail to communicate with each other is that we're all "miserable fools and prudes and cowards. Yes, you too, my boy. And don't you dare deny it! What I said just now, about the bed in the study — that shocked you. . . . Oh God, don't you *see?* That bed — what that bed *means* — that's what experience *is!*" (174–75).

And now his own mask comes off. In a painfully botched coming-out, George makes his awkward move: "Here am I. Here are you — in that damned blanket. [Kenny has showered at George's and is naked under the blanket he's wrapped in.] Why don't you take it right off, for Christ's sake? What made me say that? I suppose you're going to misunderstand that, too . . ." (175). How piti-lessly Isherwood mimes this fifty-eight-year-old's throwing of caution and self-protection to the winds, his erupting with "Why don't you take it right off, for Christ's sake," then immediately repressing it ("What made me say that?"), and finally saving face by disingenuously throwing the burden back on Kenny ("I suppose you're going to misunderstand that, too"). The normally smooth George is suddenly in the power of another "apocalyptically great wave" of passion and long-stifled candor. The effect is complex: we both laugh at and pity him, for he is speaking truly and at the same time self-deceivingly.

> "All right, let's put the cards on the table. Why are you here in this room at this moment? *Because you want me to tell you something.* That's the true reason you came all the way across town tonight. You may have honestly believed it was to get Lois in bed with you. . . . But you can't fool a dirty old man; he isn't sentimental about Young Love; he knows just how much it's worth — a great deal, but not everything. No, my dear Kenneth. You came here this evening to see *me* — whether you realize it or not. . . . I know *exactly* what you want. You want me to tell you *what I know.* Oh, Kenneth, Kenneth, believe me — there's nothing I'd rather do! . . . But I can't. I quite literally can't. Because, don't you see, *what I know is what I am?* And I can't tell you that. You have to find it out for yourself. . . . Instead of trying to know, you commit the inexcusable triv-iality of saying 'he's a dirty old man,' and turning this evening, which might be the most precious and unforgettable of your young life, into a *flirtation!* You don't like that word, do you? But it's the word. It's the enormous tragedy of everything nowadays: flirtation. Flirtation instead of fucking, if you'll pardon my coarseness. All any of you ever do is flirt, and wear your blankets off one shoulder, and complain about motels. And miss the one thing that might really — and, Kenneth, I do not say this casually — *transform your entire life —* " (175–77)

This scene, the climax of the novel, could easily have failed by falling into pathos (the poor old queer trying to get someone to love him) or into a sermon about "communication" or even, I suppose, into a happy or tragic love scene. None of these happens. George is so drunk at this point that he barely notices Kenny is there (it's a little like the scene when he is driving to work and the vin-dictive "Uncle George" fantasy takes over, wanting to punish the entire straight world for Jim's death: "When George gets in as deep as this, Jim hardly matters any more"). Indeed, he passes out immediately after, only to wake long enough to find a note from Kenny saying he's left, a comic and deflating moment.

At the same time, what George has said is not false, only partial — and partial because, for all his spunk, George *can't* tell Kenny "who I am." Who he is is, of course, a gay man. I don't think Isherwood is saying that that is *all* George is. At the same time, sex — "that bed" — is very close to "who I am." Knowing him must mean knowing (as people nervously say) in the "biblical sense." The body and its lusts are not divisible from the mind; George, whom Kenny has thought "spiritual," doesn't choose the supposedly more tranquil blue pencil-sharpener Kenny offers him, but the red one — red for "rage and lust." Nor is George's inability to tell Kenny "who I am" entirely within his power. The world he lives in, the Strunk world, makes self-revelation nearly impossible, not only for George but for everyone, including the Strunks themselves, including even Kenny. And yet the pity of it, the waste! George is berating himself as well as Kenny when he accuses him of "flirting," not "fucking." If both of them could speak the unspeakable, which has been virtually on their lips the entire evening, it would indeed *transform their entire life.*

But it doesn't happen, and Isherwood is never greater than when rising to George's fall. When George passes out and wakes up again, reading Kenny's (still-ambiguous, still-flirtatious) thank-you note, he "lets the paper slide to the floor" "like a general who has just glanced through an unimportant dispatch. . . . Little teaser, his mind says, but without the least resentment" (178). Right! You can't fool a dirty old man! He's still here, with his tough battered survivor's body; he'll survive this minor failure as he's survived so many major ones. Young Love, he knows, is worth "a great deal, but not everything" (175).

After taking a piss (how many of them there are in this book, and how eloquent!), he goes back to bed and before going to sleep decides to masturbate. But even his fantasy won't obey him, or tells him a different story from the one he thinks he desires:

> Lying in the dark, he conjures up Kenny and Lois in their car, makes them drive into Camphor Tree Lane. . . . No — it won't work. George tries several times, but he just cannot make Lois go up those stairs. . . . But the play has begun, now, and George isn't about to stop it. Kenny must be provided with a partner. So George turns Lois into the sexy little gold cat, the Mexican tennis player [he'd watched at the college]. . . . No. That won't work, either. George doesn't like Kenny's attitude. He isn't taking his lust seriously: in fact, he seems to be on the verge of giggles. Quick — we need a substitute! George hastily turns Kenny into the big blond boy from the tennis court. Oh, much better! Perfect! Now they can embrace. Now the fierce hot animal play can begin. George hovers above them, watching; then he begins passing in and out of their writhing, panting bodies. He is either. He is both at once. Ah — it is so good! Ah — ah . . . !
> You old idiot, George's mind says. But he is not ashamed of himself. He speaks to the now slack and sweating body with tolerant good humor, as if to an old

greedy dog which has just gobbled down a chunk of meat far bigger than it really wanted. (178–80)

Isherwood catches the imperiousness of lust with lethal, unsentimental accuracy: George "makes" Kenny and Lois drive up his street, "hastily turns Kenny into the big blond boy." But the scene is neither whimsical nor unnecessary; perfectly echoing and completing the "dialogue" Kenny and George have had in the bar, a dialogue where "you and your dialogue partner have to be somehow opposites." Here, the "gold cat" and the "big blond" are such opposites, their sex a form of fierce dialogue, "impersonal" and "symbolic." The kind of communication that George longs for from Kenny is itself half-battle, half-sex, full of the "not-understanding" that is "a kind of intimacy." Best of all, perhaps, truest to the completely grown-up vision of sex and separateness in this novel, is the coda of George's "tolerant good humor": "You old idiot. . . ." Everything is respected here, even the semifailures of fantasy and lust. "Yes, I *am* crazy," he thinks as he falls asleep. "That is my secret; my strength."

Kenny is George's favorite pupil, the one he has hopes of communicating with, precisely because he's willing to have George be different from himself. In a brilliantly uncliché moment, Kenny, commanded by George to say why he calls George "Sir," admits that he *likes* it. "What's so phony nowadays is all this familiarity. Pretending there isn't any difference between people — well, like you were saying about minorities, this morning. If you and I are no different, what do we have to give each other? How can we ever be friends?" (158).

Can friendship be the clue to what Isherwood means by "singleness"? I think so. George sees love itself as friendship, and the metaphor has political and literary implications. Marvelous and brave as Tennessee Williams's stories are, they almost never represent friendship, and when they do, friendship only with a woman, as in "Two on a Party" or "The Mattress by the Tomato Patch." The gay characters are looking not for friendship, but for love; and not married love, but romantic love. Such a love demands the total fusion of one person with another, as is grimly, comically caught in "Desire and the Black Masseur," in which Anthony Burns is willingly beaten to death and eaten by a nameless black man. What this preposterous cannibalism signifies is the phase of romantic love that demands *incorporation* into the beloved, a secular Eucharist. Mr. Krupper, too, who "expired in an attitude of prayer," has not only consumed the Host, but been killed by it, like a priest who achieves his dream of dying while celebrating Mass.

Isherwood is far different. Even in love, he says, George and Jim remained at opposite sides of the sofa, each absorbed in his own reading, yet each so intensely aware of the other. This intense awareness of separateness is echoed in Kenny's "not-understanding," which is nonetheless to George "a kind of intimacy."[13] It is echoed also in "that bed"—a good metaphor for George's and Isherwood's version of "what unites us" precisely because it is not too ethereal. Like George's "experience," love is stubbornly personal and opaque, one's *own*, though one may find indirect, crafty ways of communicating it to someone else. Being grown-up means just this acknowledgment of one's own stubborn untransparent personality, painfully tied to the need to share it with someone. In this way one can be a father without having a son—George angrily denies the subpsychoanalytic guess that a homosexual lover is no more than a son in disguise—"Jim was not a son"—and realizes that he "doesn't need Kenny," who *is* like a son. In this way one can be homosexual and an adult man—something the American neo-Freudianism of 1964 thought quite impossible.

But something David Leavitt's quite un-Freudian, superficially "liberated" version of homosexuality finds impossible, too. For it would seem that in Leavitt a gay man really *is* still a perpetual child. (This is Rose's bitter complaint after the dinner party at which both Owen and Philip have outrageously flirted with the handsome, straight Winston Penn: "Jesus Christ, I thought, does he have no dignity at all?" [*The Lost Language of Cranes,* 306].) The "optimism" that Eliot sees in Philip is also present in Owen; or rather, not optimism, but childishness: that foolish if understandable hope that one will be forgiven, that one can start from a clean slate, that one need never be entirely defined. Owen's guiltiness is in fact only superficially different from Philip's guiltlessness, for both are premised on the possibility of "innocence." Only Rose sees that innocence may not be an option; which is why only Rose seems like an adult at all.

Leavitt's might in fact seem an anti-gay novel if the reader thought he were aware of how unattractively he has presented his two gay protagonists (not to mention the feckless Eliot), of how he has turned them into moral children. It is not simply a question of prudishness; Leavitt is not a prude. It is a question of what George says of Kenny in his masturbatory fantasy: "He is not taking his lust seriously," that is, not taking one's own selfishness and aggression seriously. Leavitt's gay men are so polite, so self-effacing, that they seem unreal. At the same time, this self-effacement is itself a deception: a fundamentally narcissistic way of preserving one's own fantasy of innocence. For despite the promise of a story about Rose's anger, *The Lost Language of Cranes* is mostly about Philip's and Owen's "bravery," about the importance of sincerity and true love. It is thus sentimental. It is somehow no accident that this sentimentality goes together with a presentation of sex that is either seamy (a peep show) or nervously deflected (urinating) or out of focus. Leavitt can make sex nasty or make it "romantic," but he can't *see* it. To the extent that an open-eyed acceptance of one's sexual life is essential to adulthood, no gay man in Leavitt's fiction is quite grown up.

Isherwood's 1964 novel turns out to be a far more uncompromisingly gay book, a far more liberating one, because George is *not* innocent. His is not the "ignoble" false adulthood he sees in his age-mates at the gym who have simply given up, resigning themselves to grandfatherhood, impending retirement, and golf. Nor is it the false manhood of Mr. Strunk and Mr. Garfein who, as they get drunker and drunker, sound like scared boys in a dark cave. To Isherwood, as perhaps to George, fatherhood — being a grown man — means precisely the repudiation of innocence, especially in the forms of ignorance and inexperience. "That bed" — the tragedy and farce of sexual desire — is the fitting symbol of Experience, and requires no "supercelestial thoughts" nor "subterranean conduct" to be meaningful. One can even, if necessary, be "single" on that bed, though George does not enjoy it. "That bed" is the rock on which George's life and the truth of Isherwood's great novel rest. The absence of such a bed is the fatal weakness of Leavitt's.

Chapter Six

HOMEWARD BOUND

Much has been made in gay literature of the metaphors of family and home. The communitarianism of the late sixties spilled over directly into the language of "community" in the post-Stonewall ghettoes like the Castro in San Francisco, the West Village in New York, the South End in Boston. To be sure, the phraseology is sentimental, even sometimes grotesque (as when HIV-positive people are said to be "members of the AIDS community"), but for men who felt estranged from their biological families, the idea of being part of a new one was intoxicating. The attractiveness is reflected in titles of such popular books as Michael Cunningham's *A Home at the End of the World,* and John Preston's essay anthology, *Hometowns.* Lost homes — so poignant and continual a part of American culture — appear in indirect metaphors of Atlantis (Mark Doty, Samuel Delany) and of language: Philip Gambone's *The Language We Use Up Here,* or Leavitt's *The Lost Language of Cranes.* As Frank Browning has shown in his own quirky contribution to the genre, *A Queer Geography,* gay men have been no less eager than the rest of the American populace to seek those contradictory things, independence and community.[1]

As the gay ghettoes began to form in the big cities, stories gradually began to be told about these urban hometowns. The earliest, most charming and most durable were Armistead Maupin's *Tales of the City,* a series of (eventually) six novels that began as newspaper columns in the *San Francisco Chronicle* in 1976. While these tales were not exclusively gay, they *were* set in San Francisco, a city which seemed at the time virtually one huge gay ghetto. And the gay characters, especially Michael Tolliver (Mouse), his lover Jon Fielding, the transsexual Anna Madrigal, the lesbian Mona (her daughter), all play central roles. While disease, death, age, and careerism eventually overtake the Maupin series — Michael's best friend Mary Ann becomes a ruthless self-promoter, his lover Jon dies of AIDS — what remains permanently enchanting is the configuration of foolish lives in a home that so effortlessly includes *everyone*. This home, 28 Barbary Lane, is a minor utopia, a "good place" where your mother (Anna Madrigal) positively *encourages* you to smoke dope and have sex, whether with man or woman. It is a bastion of fantasy and at the same time of moral uprightness, a place where your heart can be nourished and protected. Maupin's *Tales* have a kind of magic that it would be pointless to explain. In their ditzy cheerfulness, their resolute assumption that all forms of love are equally good, their boundless tolerance, their zany plot complications, these books are the quintessence of San Francisco. At the time they were written, they were glimpses of a good gay life that seemed more possible in California than anywhere else. The first time I went to San Francisco, *Tales of the City* was left as bedside reading much as Mrs. Madrigal used to leave joints taped to the doors of her new tenants. For those of us living in the post-AIDS world, they have become a sort of dream factory: were we once so silly and hopeful?[2]

But "family" has served more than nostalgic or sentimental purposes. One of the funniest transformations of the theme can be found in Ethan Mordden's stories (collected as *I've a Feeling We're Not in Kansas Anymore, Buddies,* and *Everybody Loves You*). These are also "tales," but set in that most un-Maupinian place, New York City. Mordden's "home" is far less cozy than Maupin's and much fuller of loudly squabbling siblings. It is parentless — no Anna Madrigal here — and deliberately so. Mordden is more of a ghettoite than Maupin, and believes in a sort of gay brotherhood that makes its own rules and takes its own risks. Unlike the laid-back residents of Barbary Lane who, when things get too squirrelly, kick back with some Maui Zowie dope, Mordden's gay men harangue and argue. So while this, too, is a sort of "good place," its goodness is based on the "readiness to be at cross-purposes" that Isherwood described between George and Kenny and claimed to be "a kind of intimacy."

A second transformation of "family" is like a combination of Maupin and Mordden: Michael Cunningham's elegiac *A Home at the End of the World* (1990). This novel also presents an artificial "family" composed of one gay man, one bisexual one, one older straight woman, and eventually the baby they all have together. In this novel, the gay Jonathan Glover escapes from the dying city of Cleveland and his own shamed homosexual adolescence to New York. But unlike Mordden's or Maupin's refugees, Jonathan experiences no joy as a result, only at best a sort of dignified disappointment. To him, New York does not represent freedom but aimlessness, or (as Cunningham put it about himself) the freedom to "amount to nothing."[3] It is there that he meets Clare, a woman eleven years his senior, who oscillates between being a smart, eccentric sister and a consoling mother — a sort of postmodern fag hag. They constantly fantasize (and joke) about having a child, and soon get one, in two senses. The first child comes in the form of Bobby Morrow, Jonathan's oldest friend from Cleveland, a lost, ambitionless boy with whom Jonathan had had a sort of affair when they were teenagers. Bobby, like Jonathan and Clare, is untethered in life, but even more incurably so. He is a spiritual and literal orphan whose parents both died in his youth, following the freak accident that killed his adored older brother, Carlton. He desperately needs a family and finds it, first, in Jonathan's mother and father, and then in Clare and Jonathan.

This whimsical family becomes a more literal one when Bobby and Clare become lovers and Clare gets pregnant. With Clare's inheritance, they buy an old farmhouse in upstate New York, open a café, and raise "their" daughter, Rebecca. The trilateral union of Jon, Bobby, and Clare is, however, an unstable one for all sorts of reasons, and Clare eventually breaks it by striking out for a new life with her daughter. A new, all-male, and oddly defeated, triangle remains the only memory of this seminoble experiment: Jon and Bobby are joined at the end by Erich, Jon's ex-lover, who is now dying of AIDS. The last image of the book is of these three standing in a frigid pond in early spring: life has come down to "the chance to be one of three naked men standing in a small body of clear water."[4]

It is interesting, though not perhaps surprising, that all these "families" eventually fail. In the case of Maupin and Mordden, who have not written a continuous novel but a sort of saga of interleaved tales, we are given only a partial understanding of why they fail. Maupin's characters are simply overtaken by middle age, the mid-seventies by the late eighties. As they gradually move out of Mrs. Madrigal's chummy household, the magic of their lives disappears — at least for this reader. It was only so long as they formed a "home" that their stories were magnetic; by themselves, these "children" are winsome but feckless. In Mordden, too, events overtake the characters. In his case, the event is specifically AIDS, which leads to the endangerment of the gay ghetto and the small microcosm of it that is Mordden's circle. As in Maupin's tales, the fantasy of a good life lived by a group of witty, sexually adventurous "brothers" cannot be sustained in the face of the plague.[5] Cunningham is the most thorough of these three explorers of gay family; in him, the failure *is* the story. Indeed, all of his families — whether artificial or biological, gay or straight — are doomed from the start: there is not a single successful one depicted in his pages. For Cunningham the failure of "the Hendersons" — Bobby, Jon, and Clare's mocking name for themselves — is only part of a much larger failure: the decline of America in the Reagan years, the absence of love between husband and wife, between father and son.

Thus, though these families all fail, the authors' attitudes to that failure are very different. If failure seems to be built into Cunningham's vision, it is not in

Mordden's, who consequently is violently outraged by the failure. In this respect, it is significant that Cunningham sees homosexuality itself as a less defining identity than Mordden does. Unlike Mordden's stand-in Bud, Jonathan
Glover does not take part in or enjoy the gay world around him. His homosexuality provides him only a negative identity: he's *not-straight*. Mordden's characters, by contrast, hold tenaciously to the gay identity they have forged for
themselves, and furiously fend off attacks on it by straights, closet gays, and
"crossovers" who try to breach the Stonewall battlements. Cunningham shows
the worm of dissolution working from within every family, Mordden the vulnerability of a gay one to attacks from without. Cunningham has, finally, no
vision of what the good family might be, whereas Mordden definitely has.
The two then offer a particularly clear view of what one might call second-
generation Stonewall fiction, asking "What do you do once the revolution has
been accomplished?"

MICHAEL CUNNINGHAM'S *A HOME AT THE END OF THE WORLD*

Every time I read *A Home at the End of the World,* I find myself first entranced,
then hypnotized, finally bored. I am entranced by the first part of the novel,
which in a series of vignettes eerily recaptures the strangeness of the past, my
past: of the suburbs, the Midwest, the middle class, childhood, the sixties. It
concerns three people primarily and is told from their points of view. The
pivotal character is Jonathan, a boy who grows up to be gay; his best friend,
Bobby; his mother, Alice. (The fourth main character, Clare, will not be introduced until Part 2). What is most noticeable about these three characters is that
they are all struggling to recover from some event that influences them still. For
them, and later for Clare as well, the struggle is unavailing, and their reaction to
their helplessness both comic and pathetic. The comedy and pathos have a
peculiar elegance, perhaps because the events all are trying to escape or reform
are so nugatory, often not even identifiable *as* events. But *A Home at the End of
the World* is not the sort of novel in which a psychiatrist steps in at the end to
solve the problem once and for all. Whatever has gone on in the past is both
pervasive and invisible, like carbon monoxide. The characters themselves sense
their progressive enfeeblement but can do nothing about it except to laugh
wryly and make occasional panicked attempts to get out of the lethal house.

Of all the characters, the one who has the clearest "event" behind him is
Bobby, Jonathan's best friend. An impressionable boy with two terminally
vague parents and an older brother he worships, he is from the very beginning
vulnerably plastic. He longs to go to Woodstock (which would have happened
just before the novel begins), even though (at age nine) he can hardly imagine

what it was. The important thing is being with his brother, Carlton, who dies, shockingly and for no reason, not long after the beginning of the book. Bobby never recovers from his death.

Bobby's love for Carlton is touching and funny as we watch them take acid together (Bobby then nine, Carlton sixteen). "It was the sixties — our radios sang out love all day long" (20). And love radiates from these pages. Carlton is already a hippie, a free spirit, the older brother of one's dreams, encouraging Bobby to take risks but also accompanying him in them. As the acid begins to come on, for instance, he says "Stay loose, Frisco [Bobby's 'new' name]. There's not a thing in this pretty world to be afraid of. I'm here" (23).

This scene could go so many predictable ways and doesn't: for instance, into a freak-out — after all, what nine-year-old can handle acid? — or an unconvincing psychedelic rapture or even a Dennis Cooper–like apathy. Cunningham spares us all of these: the trip is a tremendous success, Bobby's happiness real. As they come down, Carlton and Bobby are back home in their little suburban house while their mother fixes dinner. The combination of strangeness and familiarity strikes the reader as it strikes them: "We both know we have taken momentary leave of the earth. It does not strike either of us as remarkable, any more than does the fact that airplanes sometimes fall from the sky, or that we have always lived in these rooms and will soon leave them" (24). They are both "home" and not at home; or rather, home has expanded to include the wide psychedelic sky while keeping intact — though fragile — mother, father, brothers.

Yet airplanes do sometimes fall from the sky. When Carlton dies in a freak ac-cident, it happens so suddenly the reader is almost physically shocked. Bobby's parents are holding a party for their friends. But it turns out to be a party for Carlton, who shows up with his girlfriend and a few friends and, to everyone's surprise, charms the grown-ups. Everyone's dancing to the Doors, Bobby is sneaking drinks and staring with admiration at Carlton. At one point a friend of Carlton's yells for everybody to come outside to see a "flying saucer." Carlton runs all the way out across a gully to the cemetery at the back of the house, and stays there after everyone else has gone back in. The sliding glass door to the living room has been closed, and when Carlton runs back to the party he doesn't see it and bursts through the glass. "Carlton reaches up curiously to take out the shard of glass that is stuck in his neck, and that is when the blood starts. It shoots out of him." Within five minutes he is dead.

It is a tremendously daring move, and Cunningham makes it work, neither grandstanding nor ironizing the horror. He is perhaps at his best in showing what happens to the family afterward: Carlton's father, an amiable, quietly desperate music-teacher, turns into a drunk; his mother establishes "her life of separateness behind the guest-room door" (35) and kills herself a few years later. As Bobby says, with devastating understatement, "Years have passed — we are living in the future, and it's turned out differently from what we'd planned" (36). (But this will be the refrain sung by every character in this novel.) With Carlton's life went all life. He was the only one in that doomed ordinary family to imagine there might be something beyond "Cleveland," the daily round, the safe compromise. Now that he is dead, mother, father, and younger brother more or less give up; though Bobby (forever looking for a new home, another brother) arguably finds what he needs in the family he eventually forms with Jonathan and Clare.

Jonathan's youth, too, is beautifully evoked in this first section, though the story has far less "profile" than Bobby's and it is far less clear what we are to feel about him. The story is mostly about his love for Bobby, which seems to spring from a frustrated love of his handsome father, Ned. Ned himself, like so many fathers in this novel (Bobby's included), remains a shadowy figure. And though Jonathan says "I want to talk about my father's beauty," he never quite does, apart from a few lovely sentences ("the potent symmetry of his arms, blond and lithely muscled as if they'd been carved of warm ash; the easy, measured grace of his stride" [6]). But why does he want to speak of his father's beauty? To undo the primal curse on Ham for looking upon his father's nakedness? To "explain" his own eventual homosexuality? Oddly, and noticeably, he gives up on this topic before it ever quite begins — and never returns to male beauty again, even after his adulthood has brought him sexual experience of it.

Equally open-ended is the story of his sissyish boyhood when his favorite toy was a doll, which leads to a potentially dramatic but thwarted encounter with that beautiful father. (The drama *is* the thwarting.) It happens after Jonathan's mother has miscarried, and his father is in despair because they will never have another child (she's had a hysterectomy). The family dynamics at this point are all tortured. Jonathan himself is both triumphant and fearful — glad that he's alone, without a sibling rival, and afraid of being punished for it. Sucked into his mother's "more ravenous sorrow," he never makes emotional contact with his father again. His parents (like Bobby's, after Carlton's death) also turn against each other. During a fight, Jonathan suddenly sees his father as frightening: "For a moment it seemed he had left us after all; his fatherly aspect had withdrawn and in its place was only a man, big as a car but blank and unscrupled as an infant, capable of anything" (17). (Notice the construction of "manhood" here: big, dangerous, amoral. Anything powerful, anything emotional is dangerous.) Dad sends Jonathan to bed, Jonathan won't go, there is another fight. Suddenly Jonathan, in a rage over he doesn't know what, grabs the doll that is his toy and screams "This is mine," in "a nearly hysterical tone of insistence." His father simply gives up on him at this point: " 'Fine,' he said more quietly, in a defeated tone. 'Fine. It's yours.' And he left" (19). Jonathan thinks later that if his father had "picked me up and taken me onto the bed with him," it might have "rescued us both" (17). Because he does not, Jonathan is stuck for the rest of his life in the rage and humiliation he felt then. From them spring his hopeless love for Bobby, his determination to leave home and never return, and perhaps his inability to satisfy either of Freud's requirements for "love" or "work."

The story is recognizable, even cliché. The son, rejected by his father, is colonized by his mother: no wonder he becomes gay. It's what I remember reading, tremblingly, in the psychology section of Carnegie Library in Pittsburgh in 1965. Is Cunningham simply endorsing Irving Bieber's etiology of distant father, close-binding mother?[6] Not exactly. He is plainly not going to *condemn* Jonathan, Ned, or Alice for anything — the book is a sort of monstrosity of nonjudgmentalism. But neither is he going to *overturn* that story, for it looks very much as if Jonathan *is* damaged, after all, by his father's refusal to "rescue" him, and his mother's increasingly "ravenous" intrusion into his life. (In his adolescence, she listens to music with him and Bobby, smokes dope with them, and in a climactic scene catches them in the front seat of the family car with their pants down.) But this "story" of causation is never insisted on but rather left as a mere possibility. It explains, in the sense of making probable, Jonathan's emotional closedness and his flight from his family. But it is a story without an ending or even a clear purpose.

In fact, Cunningham's novelistic technique is much like Jonathan's eventual accommodation to the world: ironic, sharp-eyed, intensely aware of pathos, but profoundly unwilling to attach a meaning to it. The understanding must remain forever in play, forever tentative: this is perhaps what most captivates the reader at first. Like Jonathan in his aimless life, Cunningham is unwilling to shut down any possibility in his novel. What is the "story" of Jonathan's flight from his family? A coming-out story? Hardly: that part of his homosexual life is left completely unexplored, as if uninteresting. Is Bobby's choice to live for eight years after high school in Jonathan's parents' house about his need for new parents? (Yes.) Or about his incapacity to choose a career? (Yes.) Or about the ravages of drugs? (Yes.) Or is it, like the story of Ned's theater, about the failure of the American economy, especially in the Rust Belt? (Again, yes.) Is Clare's drifting eccentricity attributable to the long hangover of Woodstock? (She was at the Woodstock concert, and it is what makes Bobby fall in love with her: she turns into another Carlton.) Or to her parents' mutual antagonism? Or to her being a rich kid (she will eventually inherit half a million dollars with which Bobby, Jonathan, and she buy their farmhouse in upstate New York)? Or to her being a woman in the aftermath of the sexual and feminist revolutions, an aftermath that leaves her, nonetheless, marginal, a sort of updated fag hag?

All these are perfectly possible answers, but none is decisive. There is some ur-gloom hanging over all these characters that seems forever out of sight, unexaminable. Resignation is the default emotion, irony the default attitude. (Irony infects even the solemn, dumb Bobby.) The novel seems to take these emotions and perceptions as a sort of given — as though every reader would understand them. I do understand them, of course; but as the story goes on, I become more and more befuddled, even as I am wrapped in more and more layers of gorgeous prose. The book imitates its characters by getting lost. Is the novel an eighties story? A New York story? A Gen-X story? A gay story? A bisexual story? An AIDS story? A family story? I never find out, but am instead piqued — or rather, lulled — by the impossibility of finding the answer.

There is of course a kind of master plot implicit in all these possibilities, and it is one that interests us as gay readers. This plot is about the need to free oneself from precisely the *anomie* and drift of one's life, whether the cause is economic or psychological depression. Two characters do free themselves, out of all the characters in the book: Clare and Alice, the two older women, the two mothers. The gay Jonathan and the bisexual Bobby do not. Clare, against her will, allows herself to be talked into moving to upstate New York, opening a café, and raising her and Bobby's child, Rebecca, with Jonathan. But it becomes clear that this pretend "family" is the men's fantasy — even the supercilious Jonathan's — not her own. Even though they are living the upright free life promised by the sixties, demanded by the seventies, even though Jonathan is the one to get up at four in the morning to change the baby and soothe her to sleep, even though Bobby is (to say the least) the most motherly of fathers; still Clare realizes that she's fundamentally in this baby thing by herself. Further, she realizes (though for reasons that are never quite exposed) that at age forty, she can't continue living her marginal life. In a move that is both foolish and brave, she takes Rebecca to California, telling the boys she's going to visit her mother in Washington, D.C. In the West, she will set up a new life on her own. Jonathan's mother, Alice, was right, in other words, when she warned her poor "unfinished" son that this family he was so proud of, the family of his choice, would not last: "That woman is not going to let you have equal rights to her baby" (291). Biology finally wins out over choice.

And Alice herself is freed at the end. She and Ned have moved to Arizona for the sake of his emphysema. He dies eventually of a heart attack on the way to his front door from his mailbox: the absurd, pathetic death of a "beautiful" man who made no impression on anyone. Ned's death frees Alice in unexpected ways. She meets a new man, with whom she begins not merely a "golden age" love affair, but a sexually passionate one: "he'd begun teaching me a range of pleasures I had hardly imagined while married to Ned" and "kissed me in spots Ned had hesitated even to call by their names" (287). Like Clare and unlike her son, Alice manages to put the past behind her. In beautiful words that might stand as the moral of this novel, she learns that "we owe the dead even less than we owe the living, that our only chance of happiness — a small enough chance — lay in welcoming change" (294).

It is this piece of disillusioning wisdom which she wants to share with Jonathan, but which he cannot bear to hear. In a touchingly exact scene, she summons Jonathan to Arizona for the express purpose of scattering Ned's ashes, getting rid of the past. But Jonathan, the ironist, turns out to be far more upset by his filial duty to a man he never knew than one would have thought. He is strangely dutiful toward this handful of incinerated bone, refusing to scatter it in the tiny flowered oasis he and his mother pass on the way to the airport. And yet Cunningham is absolutely right about this, for Jonathan is only a half-baked ironist. He is sentimentally attached precisely because he can't deal with being emotionally attached. Even when he does eventually scatter the ashes, back in upstate New York, we know him too well to think that this simple act will settle things for him. He "decides" to do it in the middle of the night, on a whim. (A less spontaneous decision would perhaps seem too calculated to him — too final, too adult.) His life is still "unfinished," perhaps unfinishable.

Alice's new love affair and Clare's escape from Bobby and Jonathan's incestuous brotherhood are the only glimmers of hope in this novel. Their hope is of course wry: "a small enough chance" of happiness — but it is real. It's as though Cunningham, seeing the end in sight, relents and gives at least two of his characters something they want. And it's interesting that what Alice wants is sex. For sex as a pleasure, indeed as an identity, is what Cunningham has denied to any of the others, especially Bobby and Jonathan. And it is sex, with its imperious demands and glimpses of heaven and hell, that has been excluded from the novel. Jonathan and Bobby first have sex almost in a trance: you feel that for Bobby, especially, it's barely happening. For Jonathan, of course, it is, but Cunningham deliberately avoids making this a novel about Jonathan's sexual desires. We know he's gay — so does his mother — and we know he feels vaguely ashamed of it. But the story of his homosexuality never takes center stage. The same is true of Bobby, even more weirdly. One of the things that is odd about him is the detachment from his desires. We learn for instance that when he is finally seduced by Clare, at age twenty-six, he has never had a girlfriend, never had sex with a woman. Even after he begins having sex with Clare — and Cunningham catches brilliantly his goofy pleasure in doing so — he is never a demanding lover, and indeed sex quickly ends between them. What he needs, apparently, is the comfort of a woman, not her sexuality.

It is this indifference to sex that can stand for what's missing from this brilliant, depressing novel. It's not that Cunningham avoids talking about sex (in fact, a prissy gay reviewer actually found the book obscene).[7] But he seems to have excluded any of the stronger passions, of which sex is so decidedly one. We don't recognize this at first, partly because some of the incidents, like Carlton's death, are so violent. Cunningham is seductive: his sentences are so ravishing, his irony so delicate and fleet, his pathos so lovely that one feels oneself in touch with the real day-to-day sadness of life. But the effect is cloying. Why is New York — so promisingly shimmery to Bobby — so dead and dull to Jonathan and Clare? Why has desire not seemed to faze Jonathan for good or ill? Why do books and movies not give them any idea of other ways to lead their lives? Why do they have no friends, nor even any lovers?

The bohemian life seemed to Henri Murger "a gay life, but a terrible one" — portentous words which are quoted by Puccini at the beginning of Act 4 of *La Bohème.*[8] Rarely has it seemed so merely sad. This tone of sadness is virtually what the book is about, substituting for the cruder pleasures of a plot and real characters to whom something can happen.

Indeed, it is Cunningham's very style — for which he has been rightly praised — that gets him into the most trouble, for all of the characters' first-person voices sound the same, or rather sound like Cunningham. The result is an exquisite, mournful monody that sometimes reads like a fictionalization of Sir Thomas Browne's *Urn-Buriall.*

This uniformity is most unconvincing in the passages supposedly spoken by Bobby, who has been presented as virtually inarticulate — either stoned, stupid, or terrified; someone who can barely make conversation except in minimal units of "Okay" and "Uh-huh." But when he comes to tell his own story, his prose takes off. Here's a passage when Bobby, having just arrived in New York, is taken by Jonathan to a record store to buy a Van Morrison tape:

> He took me back out of the apartment, and we walked to a record store on Broadway. He had not been lying about that store. Nothing shy of the words "dream come true" would do here — it was the cliché made into flesh. This place spanned a city block; it filled three separate floors. In Ohio I had haunted the chain store in the mall, and the dying establishment of an old beatnik whose walls were still covered with pegboard. Here, you passed through a bank of revolving doors into a room tall as a church. The sound of guitars and a woman's voice, clean as a razor, rocked over rows and immaculate rows of albums. Neon arrows flashed, and a black-haired woman who could have been in perfume ads browsed next to a little boy in a Sex Pistols T-shirt. It was an important place — you'd have known that if you were blind and deaf. You'd have smelled it, you'd have felt it tingling on your skin. This was where the molecules were most purely and ecstatically agitated. (134–35)

Some of this sounds like the Bobby we know — the short phrases "this place spanned a city block; it filled three separate floors" — but some sound like, well, Michael Cunningham: "it was the cliché made into flesh," for instance. Bobby doesn't think linguistically; he doesn't identify phrases as "cliché" or "original." Nor would he engage in what Fowler called "elegant variation" ("rows after *immaculate* rows"). Nor has he read, and remembered, Fitzgerald or Holleran: "This was where the molecules were most purely and ecstatically agitated." The passage is ravishing but out of character.

To a lesser degree this is true of Jonathan, Clare, and Alice as well, who tend to blur in one's ear. Apart from some factual details, can one tell the difference between the voices in these three passages?

I'd get my money in a little over a year, more than half a million, but at thirty-eight you can't think of your life as still beginning. Hope takes on a fragility. Think too hard and it's gone. I was surprised by the inner emptiness I felt, my heart and belly swinging on cords. I'd always been so present in the passing moments. I'd assumed that was enough — to taste the coffee and the wine, to feel the sex along every nerve, to see all the movies. I'd thought the question of accomplishment would seem beside the point if I just paid careful attention to every single thing that happened. [Clare] (161)

We'd hoped vaguely to fall in love but hadn't worried much about it, because we'd thought we had all the time in the world. Love had seemed so final, and so dull — love was what ruined our parents. Love had delivered them to a life of mortgage payments and household repairs; to unglamorous jobs and the fluorescent aisles of a supermarket at two in the afternoon. We'd hoped for love of a different kind, love that knew and forgave our human frailty but did not miniaturize our grander ideas of ourselves. It sounded possible. If we didn't rush to grab, if we didn't panic, a love both challenging and nurturing might appear. If the person was imaginable, then the person could exist. And in the meantime, we'd had sex. [Jonathan] (172)

He didn't permit himself much in the way of gloom or pessimism. Perhaps he was incapable. His demonstrated emotions ran the gamut from rueful acceptance to mild disapproval, and as I bid my own farewells to the Cleveland kitchen and the pear tree in the back yard I realized I had always planned, in some understanding way, on leaving him. Or, rather, I had planned on someday having a life beyond our mild domestic comedy, the cordial good cheer of our evening feedings and our chaste, dreamless sleep. . . . Few fates are wholly disagreeable. If they were, we might do a better job of evading them. Ned and I set up housekeeping in those small white-painted rooms, hung curtains and set the copper pans against a new kitchen wall, where they shone just as brightly in the desert light. I realized that in no time this place would take on its own inevitability. Indeed, it was assuming that quality even as we debated the arrangement of chairs and pictures. . . . We are adaptable creatures. It's the source of our earthly comfort and, I suppose, of our silent rage. [Alice] (181–83)

One of Cunningham's tics is his love of that most Chekhovian tense, the past perfect: "I'd always been so present in the passing moment," "in the meantime, we'd had sex," "I had planned on someday having a life beyond our mild domestic comedy." What this grammatical fondness signifies is the way the characters see themselves: constantly comparing their present with their past, with several layers of their past, in fact. Their main consciousness is of regret. All three display Cunningham's gift for the casually poignant turn of phrase. But Ned's narrow gamut (from "rueful acceptance to mild disapproval") is the gamut of the novel itself. "Few fates are wholly disagreeable," Alice says with a tartness that has an audible sigh behind it. But this is also, *mutatis mutandis,* her son Jonathan's voice: "We'd hoped for love of a different kind, love that knew and forgave our human frailty but did not miniaturize our grander ideas of ourselves." And also Clare's: "I'd assumed that was enough — to taste the coffee and the wine, to feel the sex along every nerve, to see all the movies." The regret is, indeed, Cunningham's own: how witty and well bred his sorrow is — and yet how automatic, even comfortable. As Alice says truly, "We are adaptable creatures." One of the things Cunningham can "adapt to" is failure, and the melodious expression of it.

When "White Angel," an excerpt from *A Home at the End of the World,* appeared in *The New Yorker* in 1988, it received almost universal applause.[9] It was applause that was not only deserved but, so to speak, needed. Cunningham himself alludes to the "hard times" that had preceded its publication, episodes of poverty and political distress: the Reagan years, the AIDS years.[10] The success that followed his perseverance was doubly welcome as both acknowledgment of a personal triumph and vindication that there was a story to be rescued from the endless bad news of that decade. Cunningham was a good guy who had suffered and finally won.

For gay readers, too, *A Home at the End of the World* was an occasion. For here was a book that, while not exactly *gay,* told the story of a love between men that originated deep in the past and survived far into the future. Here was a book that found a different story to tell from the already passé one of coming out on the one hand, or of disco-dancing on the other. Here, finally, was a book that the intelligent reader could take seriously. Beautifully written, with a constant wry wit and perfectly judged tone, it did for American gay readers what *The Swimming Pool Library* had done two years before for British ones — show the possibilities of telling a gay story that was literarily sophisticated. It was the sort of book you could give your smart straight friends.[11]

Cunningham himself has been clear that the book he wrote was not intended as a "gay" book, and told me in an interview that he didn't want to be considered a merely "gay" author.[12] (In this reluctance he joins other authors like James Purdy and Gore Vidal.) His book therefore poses an interesting, Morddenian problem to the chronicler of gay fiction. How "gay" does a book have to be to fall into the canon? What does it mean for a gay author to write a "crossover" book — one, that is, that addresses a straight audience as much as, or more than, a gay one? What does it mean for a gay author to choose to make his gay character peripheral, or unheroic? To leave him as confused at the end as he was at the beginning?

One answer is simply: it means gay fiction has finally grown up. No longer the product of a ghetto mentality nor aimed at one, it is free finally to examine the question of homosexual life in the largest possible context — a context which will inevitably place the gay character somewhat off-center. (Statistics alone suggest that the larger world, even of bohemian New York, is composed of far more straight people than gay ones.) Jonathan's story in *A Home at the End of the World* is not "privileged" above that of the mostly straight Clare, the bisexual Bobby, or Jonathan's asexual mother and father. The result is a disinterestedness like that of George Eliot in *Middlemarch,* where no one character dominates the story, but rather the life of the whole village is the subject; and indeed Cunningham strikes repeatedly an Eliot-like note of submission to duty and acceptance of diminished possibility.

Another answer is: it means Cunningham is a traitor, a quisling, one who has deserted the flag of gay liberation. Even his personal history (he did not come out until later in his life and was heterosexually involved in his twenties) might suggest to some that Cunningham was "hiding something from himself" or remaining in some literary as well as sexual closet. And it is true that he does not harp on the preoccupying questions of Stonewall literature: gay identity, coming out, sexual exploration, or friendship with other gay men. It is possible to see Cunningham's deviation from these earlier inaugural stories as evasive or even homophobic.

While this second reading is crudely political, it has a kernel of truth. Is it an accident that the only grown-up characters in *A Home at the End of the World* are Alice and Clare, straight women? It is Clare who pays for a house in the country ("a home at the end of the world"). It is also she who makes the only decisive move in the novel, when she picks up Rebecca and leaves. Alice is able to get on with her life after the beautiful Ned's death; Jonathan can't. Where do their courage and stoicism leave Jonathan, the only gay character in the story and (it would appear) the central one as well? Is he, as both his mother and Clare suspect, "unfinished," a moral adolescent? To say so flirts with a certain discourse of homosexuality which concludes that there's nothing exactly *wrong* with gay men, they're just not quite "grown up." This is the Freudian "arrested development" theory.

It is also, curiously, the substance of the one harsh review Cunningham got for this book, by Richard Eder in the *Los Angeles Times:* "Once she is a mother, [Clare] can no longer avail herself of the refuge, the escape from fundamental choices provided by this comically warm and funky ménage à trois in upstate New York. Lovable and user-friendly to the ultimate degree, it is producer-hostile and as stifling as any unduly prolonged childhood must be."[13] What Eder misses is that this is Cunningham's *point*. It was certainly not *his* intention to create a "comically warm and funky ménage à trois" in the manner of Armistead Maupin, but rather to expose the roots of our longing for it. Nevertheless, it is not surprising that Eder should have said what he did. He assumes understandably that it is Clare who is the main character. After all, is it even possible to write a story about the petulant Jonathan, the lost Bobby, the dying, seldom-alive Erich?

One is charmed by Cunningham's fictional demonstration of the possibilities of "family" and "inclusion," but one wants also to ask: Who is including whom? I see Cunningham as continuing a story begun only after Stonewall made it possible: namely the story of a gay "family." We have seen it in Maupin, where the "includer" is the decidedly fey Anna Madrigal. We will see it in different form in Mordden's attempt to show what an all-male gay family might look like (and indeed *did* look like). In Mordden no one includes because the larger authority is the group itself, or more generally, the gay ghetto. Cunningham takes both earlier narratives seriously and combines them in a novel that is as depressing as it is accomplished. *A Home at the End of the World* seems to me a work it would be profoundly unjust to call anti-gay or "self-hating" — any of the usual spluttering responses to a mentality that tries to go beyond accepted categories. Though the gay characters (Jonathan and his bare-minimum lover Erich) are indeed shown to be childish, the alternatives are not much better among the heterosexuals. Bobby and Clare have drifted through life as aimlessly as any Malone "looking for love." If gay culture is no better, it is also no worse than the mainstream that surrounds it. Indeed, it is precisely the *counterculture* that proves the downfall of all four.

Nevertheless, in *A Home at the End of the World,* what little happiness there is occurs in the realm of biology, not choice. The real, that is, heterosexual family — Clare and Rebecca, Alice and her new lover Paul — offers a satisfaction beyond the mere daydreams of Jon, Bobby, and Erich. Though the future is limited for everyone in this novel, it is only the heterosexual women who stand any chance of happiness in it, because only they have been courageous enough to see and accept its limits.

ETHAN MORDDEN'S SHORT STORIES

Ethan Mordden's "tales of gay Manhattan" first began appearing in *Christopher Street* magazine as a monthly column called "Is There a Book in This?" and

I remember reading the first ones and thinking, No. He seemed to be working too hard at appearing casual, and he hadn't figured out that casualness wasn't his métier, and further, wasn't even necessary for the story he needed to tell. It took Mordden awhile to find his voice: that of a gay man in his thirties living in New York (it couldn't be anywhere else), well educated (but not an academic), a cultural, not a social snob, militantly gay (but not a politico, clone, or queen); solitary but surrounded by a sort of club of friends that becomes for Mordden a simulacrum of "family." Begun in the third year of the Plague, his stories are an odd mixture of essay, harangue, vignette, and documentary: scenes of gay life from the twilight of the Age of Clones. They are also paeans to friendship, the great Stonewall virtue, and by the end of the series form a remarkable because hard-won tribute to a world of friends that seems to him Stonewall's *raison d'être*.

"Bud," Mordden's spokesman, is a new gay man. Aggressive, judgmental, and loyal to his new family, he is a sort of warrior. He thus bears some resemblance to earlier avatars like the queen or the dandy, but is far more likely than they to take the offensive, not defensive side. He sees himself and the small group of friends around him as a sort of raiding party: avengers of slights, defenders of honor, Gay Musketeers. (Indeed, there is a decided boys' book feel to his stories.) He believes that the Stonewall world is precious and must be made secure, that no quarter must be given to those who would abridge its freedoms. His preferred weapons are an encyclopedic culture, a withering scorn for ignorance and naïveté, and a prurient interest in male sexual behavior, which is the topic of most of his stories. Like a gay Dr. Johnson, Bud talks for victory, to convince, to encourage, to understand and enlarge the boundaries of the Stonewall nation. The charm of his persona is its unexpected, if sometimes unconvincing, toughness.[14]

One of the unspoken themes of these stories is the loner's discovery of friendship, friendship with *men* — one of the last frontiers of the post-Stonewall gay world. (As was the case with preliberated women, many gay men half-believed that friendship with another gay man was an impossibility — they were either rivals or sexual marks. With women, of course, friendship of a kind was possible — as in the familiar dyad of fag and fag hag.) In this he is both like and unlike Isherwood's George. Like George, Bud is a believer in friendship. Unlike George, Bud actually *has* friends: it is one of the new possibilities of the post-Stonewall world. (George wants to find a friend in Kenny, but can't bring himself to speak the words that would make friendship possible: "I am gay.") Bud is able to find a circle of friends that not only tolerates but loves him. He is in this respect, too, like Dr. Johnson, who discovered in his sixties that younger men (Boswell, Topham Beauclerk) enjoyed his company. Bud's gradual realization of his dependence on the group, signaled in the last collection, *Everybody Loves*

You, by a quite improbable new boyfriend bestowed on him by the group, becomes almost the *point* of that collection. But all his stories partake of the same fantasy: a brotherly Eden, a gay good place. His characters sound like gay men of the second Stonewall generation, men who are neither queens nor waifs, but adventurers and brothers—or in his own old-fashioned term, "buddies."

As Michael Schwartz has shrewdly seen, Mordden's mind and art are taxonomic: they are concerned with what is, and is not, "gay."[15] This would seem a mere parlor game, but becomes in Mordden's hands a convincing fictional argument about the possibilities of a good gay life. Until you know who is "in," and why, you don't know who you are as a gay man. It is for this reason, for instance, that Mordden loves not only the gay ghetto of New York but the hypergay resort, Fire Island. Unlike Holleran, who is ambivalently in love with it, Mordden praises it unreservedly: Fire Island is where we go to see "who our people were, who we are . . . Manhattan is ours, too, in a way—in several ways—but Manhattan we must share. In The Pines, we are the majority."[16] Indeed, in story after story, whether set on Fire Island or Manhattan, Mordden tests the categories of gay and straight, to see if they can be made to work in ever-changing circumstances. We must mean something by the word *gay,* but what? Opera? Sex? A place at the table?[17] The "beauty of men"? Depending on your answer, you will have chosen to be a certain kind of gay man.

Who's in and who's out is thus crucial to him, not because of snobbery (though, as he says, "Mention elitism and all gays are transfixed"), but because you must constantly *work* at yourself as a gay man. Gay identity isn't simply handed to you. In this respect, homosexual identity is problematic exactly as masculine identity is: both are achieved only with a fair amount of anxiety, even though both seem at the same time perfectly natural.[18] This anxiety is more than personal or psychological; it is also political. And for Mordden in these stories, the big question is: How much diversity can the gay community absorb (dilettantish wannabes, younger gay men who don't understand gay history, conflicted older men who don't understand the new possibilities of gay life) without dissolving? This is almost an ethnic question: who is "pure"? Mordden, a Jew despite his assumed Celtic name, thus continues in gay language the arguments American Jews had in the postwar period about marrying out of the faith.

Mordden's solution to the problem is the creation of an expandable but not infinite gay "brotherhood," and for once the metaphor does not seem a cliché. For one thing, these "brothers" are as quarrelsome as real ones; their "fraternity" no tensionless calm, but a constantly shifting balance of power. (If Bud's best friend and sparring partner Dennis Savage is, in a sense, the ideal gay man of the post-Stonewall age—sexual, intelligent, warm—he is also complacent and must be constantly tested and taunted by Bud.) Further, the brotherhood is forever challenged by what Mordden calls "crossover": that is, by the sexual behavior of men who do not call themselves gay but who do perform homosexual acts and even — horror of horrors — fall in love with men. Sexual crossover is both exciting and threatening to Bud. Exciting because the undefinable straight man (of whom there are many in these stories) brings with him a scent of the wide world; threatening because he threatens to engulf, neutralize, dissipate the gay minority. Mordden's obsessive interest in what "gay" means is thus both the subject of his tales and an indirect statement about what gay "tales" ought to be.

One of the most typical Mordden stories, although not one of the best, is "I Am the Sleuth," in *Buddies*. This "Case of the Questionable Straight," as Bud terms it à la Erle Stanley Gardner, concerns a waiflike young man named Ray Holgrave who is having an affair with Bud's best friend Dennis Savage, "the gayest man in New York." Ray claims to be straight. What puzzles Bud is the suspicion that Ray is only *pretending* to be straight — an impersonation that puzzles the reader, too. For why would a gay man pretend to be straight when he's in a gay world? Why not take off the mask? To Bud's mind, Ray must be playing a deep game. For instance, he must be pretending to be dumber than he really is when he responds to dandyish quips with "Hey, that's for sure!" As "the sleuth," Bud tries to snare Ray with high-cultural bait ("the Odessa Steps montage, *Zuleika Dobson*, June 16, 1904, Rosebud, the Mapleson cylinders").[19] Ray never bites. And yet he's "emotionally available" to men — Mordden's rough-and-ready definition of "gay." He isn't gay and yet he *must* be.

The story, like many of Mordden's, ends in an aporia. Ray Holgrave is on Fire Island, where even the most devious or conflicted gay man would surely show his true (gay) colors. Ray is still coolly playing the role of the heterosexual kept boy, when a straight couple comes up and asks him "if he was the Mr. Hamill who was the graduate assistant of Dr. Copelman's Hawthorne and Melville course at Bucknell two years before." This is the opening Bud has been waiting for, because if Ray is really Perry Hamill, then he is most certainly not as stupid as he has been pretending. Furthermore, Bud now holds a piece of strong suggestive evidence. Clearing his throat dangerously, he addresses his friends, none of whom has shared his suspicions: " 'In *The House of the Seven Gables* . . . there's a character named Maule who takes a pseudonym. . . . Would someone like to guess what pseudonym this guy named Maule takes in Hawthorne's *The House of the Seven Gables?*' " The answer is Holgrave, "and it's pronounced with an Anglo flip on the vowel: Hahlgrave, just the way Ray pronounced it" (*B*, 96–97). Ray, however, still won't admit to being Perry Hamill, and the scene is over without a revelation. Ray eventually drifts away from Dennis Savage to a straight couple who take him under their wing for a ménage à trois. However, Bud sees Ray once again and decides to ask him directly: " 'Are you Perry Hamill, a former teaching assistant in a Hawthorne-Melville course at Buck-

nell?' " Ray "smiled and looked me spang in the eye and whispered, as he turned
to go 'Wouldn'st thou like to know?' " — thus hinting strongly that the answer is
"yes" (*B*, 99).

Does this prove anything, and if so, what? Furthermore, what earthly difference does it make whether Roy is who he says he is or not? Bud and Dennis
Savage have a conversation on this very topic, and the answers Bud gives are as
confusing as the question:

> "Why does it matter so much?"
> "Because I believe culture is finite and taste is fixed. I've built life and art on
> those precepts. I have to know what is true in the world."
> "Why?"
> "Because I am the sleuth!"
> He shook his head. "When you write it all down," he said, "I hope you make
> it clear to everyone just how irritating you've been about this."
> "You only say that," I told him, "because you think this was Ray's story. 'The
> Tale of the Drifter,' or something like."
> "Whose story was it, then, may I ask?"
> "Mine." (*B*, 98)

Why is the story Bud's? Partly because he's "built life and art" around the idea
that gay is gay, straight is straight, and to pretend otherwise is to play the
oppressor's game. Partly because Bud's circle of friendship depends on the story
of a heroic exodus that Ray has not participated in, yet benefits from. But also
because "Bud" is as much a self-creation, a mask, as "Ray Holgrave." Bud
knows Holgrave is not what he seems because he isn't either. Bud is "the sleuth,"
that is, because he is also the criminal. He has invented his past — his family — by
turning himself from a Jew into a Celt, and analogously, by turning himself from
a straight "son" into a Stonewall "brother."

As the sleuth, Mordden plays one of the perennial gay roles, that of spy or
double agent. He is not closety or ashamed, but he is *aware* of his homosexuality in the highly self-conscious way that so many gay men of his (and my)
generation are. "Will we ever know what is true in the world, especially about
sexual crossover?" he asks himself rhetorically. "I guess not. The data is secret,
the informants are inarticulate, and they are probably too shaken by their
experiences to report fairly on them. We have to take the word of writers . . ."
(*B*, 98). But Bud's "word" as a writer is considerably less straightforward than
at first appears. Indeed for Mordden writing is a form of perverse theater — of
voyeurism, self-excitement, and self-control. Only *he* knows all the truth, and
often (as in "I Am the Sleuth") he teases and doesn't tell. And what he is most
fascinated by is not even men's sexual lives, but their emotional lives. His stories

are astonishingly full of tears, the tears of someone giving up a long-held secret. They are about understanding men who do not wish to be understood.

But it is not Ray Holgrave alone who wishes not to be understood. We know that Mordden is fascinated by straight men and the slippages of their straightness; is it possible that he is equally fascinated with slippages of his own gayness? When he's trying to figure Ray out, Bud tells his friend Carlo that "Straights have no feelings," and Carlo corrects him: "*Gringos* have no feelings. Straights are something else" (*B*, 95). What if Bud is (like Ray) "something else" — accessible but not exactly gay? Or to put it a different way, what if he's gay but "has no feelings" — a possibility in these stories of intense masculinity and (in Bud) emotional imperviousness?

The "case of the questionable straight" is thus about more than Ray Holgrave's concealments; it is about what makes a man desirable. Indeed, at first it is not Ray himself that is so provoking to Mordden, but the fact that Dennis Savage has fallen for him. Does this mean Dennis Savage is falling into the pre-Stonewall trap of self-hatred? That he can only love what is unavailable to him? But if so, isn't "the gayest man in New York" homophobic? Gay culture has been particularly adept in shaping existing sexual-difference stereotypes to its own ends: through the exaggerations of drag and queenliness on the one hand, of leather and butchness on the other.[20] Ray Holgrave represented to Dennis Savage the attractiveness of the innocent youth. To these ways of understanding sexual attractiveness Mordden has added a category that is peculiarly his own — or rather, his own as a post-Stonewall clone: the "buddy." Unlike metaphors for gay eros that turn one partner into "the man," the other into "the woman" (or "the child"), in this metaphor for the desirable, the turn-on is the quasi-incest of sex with a "brother." He is intrigued with "brothers": his first novel, *One Last Waltz*, is about four brothers, only one of whom is gay.[21] A number of his stories feature a straight brother of Bud's named Jim, a construction worker who has strangely fervid friendships with other straight guys. And of course Bud's own circle of friends is a group of self-chosen brothers as well.

It is perhaps no accident that the final story of *Buddies* should be about a literal fraternity. In this tale, "Sliding into Home," Bud's friends are once again at the Pines. Once again into the "family" comes someone unknown, almost unknowable: a straight-looking forty-year-old man "in an outfit one rarely sees at The Pines, slacks and the kind of striped shirt you wear with a tie." He radiates the out-of-it decency of the heartland. He seems to know Dennis Savage's goofy boyfriend Little Kiwi — though not well enough to know that "Little Kiwi" is his real, that is gay, name. (Dave, the Midwesterner, calls him Virgil.) It turns out that Dave has moved to New York from the Midwest and promised Virgil's father he'd check up on him. Who was Virgil's father (Seth) to Dave? Well, he was Dave's "paddle brother." "*Paddle brother?*" shrieks Bud in audible italics. "Our fraternity, St. A's. It's just a . . . term. Read 'big brother.' Or 'sponsor' " (*B*, 216).

As usual, Mordden goes into sleuth mode: "It occurred to me then that I really had no handle on Dave — had no idea why someone so oddly out of tune was there at all. Who was he, besides a friend of Little Kiwi's family?" (*B*, 218). A gay man who discovered he was gay after being married twenty years is what he is. Bud is loudly incredulous: "Nobody discovers his sexuality after being anything for twenty years. . . . And anyone who says otherwise is a bloody fucking liar" (*B*, 218–19). In these infringements of endogamy, Bud's first instinct is to repel the challenger. Dave is not to be allowed into the sacred Stonewall precincts just by presenting himself at the gate. Despite his homosexuality — indeed because of his failure to acknowledge it sooner — Dave is tarred with one of the fraternity's worst slurs: *gringo*. "What's the idea of bringing that gringo clown out here during my stay?" (*B*, 219).

The reason Dave is so concerned to look after "Virgil" is that he regards him as the son he never had — more, the son he wished he might have had with "Virgil's" father, Seth. Indeed, Bud the sleuth turns out to be right in his guess that Dave did *not* suddenly "discover" his homosexuality at forty, but knew long before: "Dave admitted that he'd had the knowledge all along, but could not accept it till the night he got into bed with a man he wanted sexually. 'What man was that?' asked Little Kiwi. 'Your father,' said Dave" (*B*, 230). After that sexual episode, Virgil's father denies ever having been in bed with Dave: "He was very calm about it. So we stayed friends. But it had never happened. There was nothing between us except . . . except . . ." And Bud thinks: "if that *except* could be explained to the world, George Will" — his favorite homophobe — "would be out of business" (*B*, 236).

Once again, Mordden is deeply implicated in the story, for explaining that "except" has been *his* life's business. But he has a wonderful ambivalence about the explanation. Was Ray Holgrave gay or straight? What happened *really* between the dominant and submissive man in "Rope"? What happened between Bud and Harvey Jonas (in "The Homogay")[22] that so shamed Bud that he can't speak of it even now? What happened between Dave and Little Kiwi's father? Mordden is half in love with the very inarticulateness he so decries in confused sexy man like Dave and Little Kiwi's father, Seth.

But Dave's revelation (and Bud's grudging acceptance of it) is not the end of this story. In an unexpected coda, another exile from Stonewall "slides into home." It is Bud's hunky friend Carlo, the echt-clone; the man who left Manhattan because to live a safe sexless life there was "dishonorable"; a gay man "so imbued with the liberty of the sexy brotherhood that he offered to give it up rather than see it dully survive" (*B*, 237). But Carlo's return is now fraught with sadness and even despair. For if "home" is where you always wanted to be, your goal, it is also simply the end, death. Carlo comes back having solved nothing. Going home to his birth family was no solution. But being back on Fire Island with his gay family is a stopgap. Though he himself is not dying, his world is.

The final image of this story is movingly complex. Carlo and Dave, two exiles from Stonewall (though for opposite reasons), fall for each other instantly: "Carlo grabbed Dave and took him so fervently Little Kiwi asked Dennis Savage if he ought to take Bauhaus for a walk" (*B*, 237). But though it is Carlo who might be thought to be initiating Dave, he is as much in need of consolation, as we see when Bud goes downstairs for a drink and finds Dave and Carlo in bed. "As I turned, drink in the right hand and candle in the left, Carlo wheezed and squirmed and hugged Dave in a hunger of death" (*B*, 239). The image is disturbing. "Gay" has never been, for Mordden, easy: it is not, he says somewhere, a club with "open admissions." But it has not been so threatened since Stonewall. Everything Carlo represents (and Mordden admires) is under attack: from the political right (George Will), AIDS, and the "blasted morale of . . . no-fault cruising of look-but-don't-touch" (*B*, 231). If being gay means (as Mordden says in "The Dinner Party," a later meditation on the same theme) establishing a "man-to-man system that doesn't fear sex" (*ELY*, 221), then what becomes of gay life once sex becomes something that *should* be feared? Carlo's "hunger of death" thus reads both ways: hunger to evade death, and a hunger for it, for extinction. He has gone to South Dakota to forget about Stonewall and freedom and himself. He has returned, it would seem, to die as much as to live — and indeed we hear little of him in the third collection (though he reappears in the fourth, *Some Men Are Lookers*). But what place can someone like Carlo occupy in a frightened, asexual world?

It is hard to remember that *all* of Mordden's tales were written in the post-AIDS period, because Mordden's seems like the very voice of the ghetto itself; and the ghetto, with its happy triumphs, seems (like its icon, Carlo) incompatible with disease and death. And yet it is precisely this threat to the gay community which compresses Mordden's fiction to diamond hardness. We see this clearly in one of his very best stories, "The Dinner Party," found in the third collection, *Everybody Loves You*. First published in *Christopher Street* in 1988, it is a strange merger of an AIDS story with a Fire Island story, like Alan Barnett's "The *Times* as It Knows Us," also set in the Pines with a cast of dying friends.[23]

I find Mordden's even more moving, perhaps because it comes as more of a surprise. (Barnett was himself HIV-positive when he wrote the story and died shortly after its publication in 1992. Mordden, so far as I know, is uninfected.) The opening line of "The Dinner Party" invokes Jane Austen: "It is a truth universally acknowledged that a gay man in possession of a fortune must be in want of an oceanfront house in The Pines." This waspish opener seems to promise a light bright story in Mordden's first *Christopher Street* manner. It is followed, however, with dips into two different patois. First urban queen-talk: "And I *told* Colin: east of the co-ops is the chic quartier. But no. No, he found what he wanted so far west that when we're still, we can hear people coughing in Hoboken." But then a different voice altogether: "But we are seldom still this weekend, for the usual Pines reasons — a lot of guests, a lot of dropping in, a big dinner planned, and there has been another death. Greg was diagnosed, went right home, and decided to choose in a no-choice situation. Heroin overdose. Are you with me so far?" The dandy rewrites Jane Austen and the urban fag speaks the lines about the "chic quartier," but someone else tells us why the group is "seldom still this weekend." With a heartlessness that exceeds even the dandy's, this voice airily includes death itself as one of the "usual Pines reasons" for being "seldom still," as though he were complaining about a bad deejay at Tea Dance. Then, before we've had time to shake ourselves awake, he's laid on the circumstances of that other death, circumstances that neither Austen nor Wilde could have imagined. Mordden caps it with that single insulting line, "Are you with me so far?" (*ELY,* 205) in which he turns on the reader as if to say: You want plot, I'll give you plot. In a passage of fewer than a hundred words, we have gone from marriage comedy to farce to accusation, and it is not only the journey but the dazzling, furious swiftness that is new.

The story, like so many of Mordden's, is a meditation on what it means to be gay but also to be "family." How could Greg's biological family not have "Known" Greg was gay, as Mordden writes with exasperated capitals? "Straight sons are survived by a wife and kids, not by a porn star, an opera impresario, an ad man, and an airline pilot." The straight world does not understand such unmonogamous, loose families: "the five of them passed into a second honeymoon of casually devoted friendship, a state unique to gay — penetration without sex" (*ELY,* 206). Indeed, Mordden pivots on his angry lashing out at Greg's family to praise these gay "families": "What is a striped-tie-and-vest ad exec doing in the company of a man whose work clothes are chest hair? What did the opera maven and the pilot talk about? Ah, but was not this very sophistication of identities one of Stonewall's revolutions? Have we not made the received bourgeois discretions of status and culture irrelevant?" And he enunciates his credo. In Stonewall, "Sex outranks status. Friendship purifies culture" (*ELY,* 207). The taxonomist whom we've seen in "I Am the Sleuth" and "Sliding into Home" is still hard at work, but his questions have become more urgent. What if such "family" is never again reconstituted? What could ever take its place?

Poor Greg is in fact no more than what Henry James called a "*ficelle,*" the thread that serves to connect us to the main story, which is about the fourth of Greg's "widows," the airline pilot Cliff Dickerson. Cliff is one of the few characters in Mordden's stories whom Bud finds almost *too* gay: his "slashing moral clarity [makes] brunch with Cliff as exhausting as the Royal Shakespeare *Nicholas Nickleby*" (*ELY*, 208). Even Bud, who is no slouch in the slashing moral clarity department, is upbraided by Cliff. When they first met, Bud reports, Bud was complaining (in true dandy fashion) of the etymological mésalliance of the word *homophobe*. " 'Homo,' from *homos*, denotes 'same.' . . . Thus a homophobic lawyer would hate not gays but lawyers." Cliff will have none of this pedantry: " 'You will use this word,' he told me, 'because it's our word' " (*ELY*, 208–9). From this description we first fear Cliff is a dreary political gay, as much fun as a sour washcloth. But this is not the case. He is very handsome, with the looks of a "Swedish lifeguard." But he was "better than handsome or sexy: he was exciting" (*ELY*, 210). Cliff is the final embodiment of all of Mordden's fantasies of Stonewall life: the place where sexual heat, masculine aggressiveness, and intellect come together. He is in many ways the longed-for other of Bud's own fantasies, what *he* would be if he were a Swedish lifeguard, an airline pilot — except that Bud's role, ultimately, is to be alone, the chronicler, not the embodiment, of the ghetto.

Cliff *is* the embodiment of the ghetto. Cliff initiates newcomers — and does so in the time-honored ghetto way, by means of sex. When he sees at the baths a confused hunk he recognizes from the Eagle, he calls out to him, " 'Hey, buddy! This is where,' and the Eagle guy went into Cliff's room and Cliff had him shouting for joy, and a small crowd pulled up to know more about this, and the Eagle guy came out literally staggering, goofy with pleasure. Then Cliff stood in his doorway and said, 'Big cock, slow fuck, deep intention' " (*ELY*, 210). Promiscuous sex is — was — the ghetto sacrament, and Cliff is its theologian. He educates newcomers to the Stonewall country, reforms them, gets them out of their hedonistic self-destructions (like drugs), and sets them on their feet — all through the eucharist of sex. "Why else do you think I've been stuffing your ass?" he once asked the young, now dead, Greg (*ELY*, 222). If they won't listen, he beats them up — for their own good, of course. He is another one of Mordden's sexy, unpredictable older brothers: gay but straight, friendly but tough, articulate but inaccessible.

Cliff and Stonewall suggest, indeed demand, a revision of our limited expectations of gay life. Promiscuity itself is not an end but a means: sexual friendships like Cliff's are what build up a post-Stonewall community, one in which the "sophistications" of Greg's multiple lovers are possible. Mordden has a lovely, nasty passage on this "success" that looks like a digression but isn't: "The left-out gay writers who have to publish in porn slicks or local newspapers of occult circulation try to cheer themselves up by hating what they think of as the Pines School of Fiction: all about good-looking men finding themselves, so to say. And yes, I can see why tales of men getting men threaten them, because they don't get anything. (A homophobe hates what he is.) However, the primary theme of my particular Pines fiction has been friendship. Not sex: a kind of eroticized affection. Not cruisers: buddies" (*ELY,* 211).[24]

I love Mordden's argumentation with himself in these sentences, and the way he both tells his "Pines School of Fiction" story and at the same time neurotically stands outside it, justifies it, defends it. It is this story that is threatened by AIDS, and with it Mordden's own sense of who *he* is, what his vocation as a writer is. What would it mean to have rooted all this while for a losing team? In "The Dinner Party," Mordden does not just talk about Cliff, but *becomes* Cliff, bullying the reader with his own "slashing moral clarity": "I've been trying to tell you about something else in story after story; is it taking? I've been trying to tell you that a man-to-man system that doesn't fear sex creates the ultimate in man-to-man friendships. This is what I mean by penetration" (*ELY,* 220–21). The "I've been trying to tell you something" is not casual or conversational, but urgent — and new in Mordden's fiction.

Like "Sliding into Home," "The Dinner Party" introduces an interloper, a rich smug faggot "who owns an art gallery in Soho, *the* art gallery in Soho, really," (*ELY,* 218, 223), "an enraged schmuck with a suave façade." He is so isolated from the Stonewall sense of community that he makes the mistake of praising Roy Cohn, the self-hating gay "sneak." Cliff becomes instantly enraged, jumps on him, and starts choking him. The dreadful guest of honor flounces out and the party, needless to say, is over. In the aftermath Bud goes down to the shore to sort out this new complication: even for Cliff, this attack is unusual. As he sits on the beach listening to the wind, Cliff joins him and starts reminiscing about earlier times: "So many nights sitting like this, or on the deck of someone's bedroom, huh? I'd listen for the messages. Accusations. Warnings. Best wishes on a memorable occasion. I don't understand the right language, though, sure. Back when All This got started, I would listen really careful, because I thought . . . Well, there ought to be some interpretation in it, you know? *Purport.* Maybe no purport a gay man wanted to hear. Nothing we'd like, right? But something to know. Something that I could hear most clear here in this place. Something in the wind out there, ace" (*ELY,* 226).

"All This" is AIDS; and, as often when Mordden is most serious, the dialogue gets stilted: the man who uses the word *purport* would not "listen really careful" or "most clear"; he would not call anyone "ace." It's like Cliff's being an airline pilot: a gesture rather than a convincing fact. What Mordden is trying to convey is the sheer masculine *attractiveness* of post-Stonewall gay men. "When I first came to New York," Bud tells Cliff, " 'I was afraid that all the gays were going to be like the ones in *The Boys in the Band,* full of self-hatred and cultivating phobias.[25] You know what I saw instead?' He is smiling. 'What, chief?' 'You. And the people you knew. . . . Your friends all took their sexuality for granted, is the thing. . . . It wasn't a cross to be borne, but their gift. They were great examples for someone like me'" (*ELY*, 230–31). There is a silence, and Cliff wonders aloud why he never had sex with Bud. Then he drops the bomb: "'Maybe just as well, my good friend . . . Because I've got it too, now, and who knows if I wouldn't have given it to you?'" (*ELY*, 232).

That Cliff has AIDS come out of the narrative blue, and Mordden is resourceful in exploiting not just our shock but what it means for his ongoing theme of gay community. He has mentioned earlier someone known jokingly as the Midnight Rambler, a man who apparently walks through the Pines by night, leaving gates ajar, never arousing dogs or suspicion: a sort of ghost. This man now actually materializes, a "woozy preppy with a southern accent." This man, like the voice of the ghetto itself, asks

"Aren't you Cliff Dickerson?"
"Yeah. How would you know that?"
"Everyone knows *you*."
Cliff shook his head. "Nobody knows me."
The stranger very gently touched Cliff's face. "If you're Cliff Dickerson," he said, "how on earth can you be crying?"
"Because I'm going to die." (*ELY*, 233)

It is a surprisingly successful moment, one that is hard to bring off in AIDS fiction. But the Midnight Rambler's ghostly conversation with Cliff serves more purposes than simply that of pathos. He acts rather as a confirmation of what Bud has just said about Cliff's importance to himself, by continuing: "'There was one night in the Eagle. You were standing with an unbelievably beautiful man. Laughing. And then you were quiet. Just looking at him. And he opened up the buttons of your shirt, very slowly. One button after another, right there in the bar. He ran his hand down your chest. And I thought if I could know you, I would give ten years of my life. Just to be your friend.'" Cliff whispered, "'*Is that what I'm going to be remembered for?*'" (*ELY*, 233–34).

A heartbreaking question, but an unsentimental one, for in a sense, all Cliff *has* done is to befriend other men, and it has gotten him nowhere; it has gotten him AIDS. Like Holleran's Malone, Cliff's "adventurous ideal of homosexuality" has failed him. All the ideas he so militantly advanced, all the Gregs he so resolutely fucked and saved, have landed him right here on this beach, "known" only by strangers. But his sad question, *Is that what I'm going to be remembered for?* is one for Bud, too. And as the wind rises one last time, the long-deferred tears are released: "Cliff began to sob, and it was like the end of the world" (*ELY*, 234). This phrase looks melodramatic at first, but it too is connected to an earlier conversation. For earlier, Bud had said to Cliff: "'You're not afraid of

anything . . . The day you're afraid of something will be the end of the world' "
(*ELY*, 214). Without underlining it, Bud has now told us that Cliff is very afraid
and that this fear is, for both of them, the end of a world.

There is a special charm in the literature that seems written "for you," literature
like Mordden's, and it is useless to pretend that one reads it dispassionately.[26] I
now find some of Mordden's stories unconvincingly precious on the one hand
and unconvincingly butch on the other: he often explores his main theme — gay
"families" — without exposing much of *himself.* At the same time, I cannot say
his obsession is much different from my own, or that it doesn't reflect what
many of us were thinking and saying in the seventies and early eighties. Childish
as the conversation about who and what is "gay" seems, it exerts a powerful
pull on my imagination. One reason is simply that I am old enough to remember
the days when homosexual men who were attractive and talented were thought
to be thin on the ground; when like Mordden, you entered a gay bar fearing to
find nothing but the haggard characters of *The Boys in the Band.* The truth
turned out to be different; and the seventies were years when fantasy and reality
vied to outdo each other, when gay men turned out to be handsome, sexually
magnetic, available, and good friends to boot. It was like growing up poor and
suddenly inheriting a million dollars. Mordden, above all others, is the recorder
of that moment.

He is consequently — and memorably — the recorder of a certain gay arrogance. This too was no mere fantasy, but a palpable truth, at least if you lived (as
Mordden did) in the gay ghetto. As Neil Miller says, quoting a gay man of
Mordden's (and my) generation: "Before AIDS, he said, 'the future was always
bright. Things were always looking up.' " Now he is " 'in mourning.' "[27] Mordden does not falsify the experience of joy so many of us had at that time, even
from the bitterness of hindsight. His joy manifests itself in crowing over the
supposed stupidity of the straight world, the superiority of the "sexy brotherhood" to "gringo" dullness. Again, a somewhat undignified trope, but a truthful
one: we all did talk, and some of us still do, about the dreariness of our straight
friends' lives and the pleasures of gay sex and friendship.

Whistling in the dark? Of course — and not very subtle at that. But one of the
most endearing things about the Bud persona in these stories is his lack of
subtlety, his being not quite as in control of his material as he pretends. It is like
the cover photo on the back of his first book. In it our author, almost pre-
posterously clonelike in his Adidas running shoes, tight jeans, and leather
jacket, sporting a regulation moustache and dark glasses, is caught by the camera trapped between two cars, his back up against a brick wall. He looks like
he's in a police lineup. Criminal and sleuth; out but unknowable. The best
moments in his fiction are not merely those in which he is victorious, though

those are often very funny and satisfying; but those in which he is at a loss for words or overplays his hand or gets trapped in high-sounding rhetoric. In these moments when the mask of control slips, I find myself drawn to Mordden more than ever. Even the clumsy triumphalism, the exaggerated cleverness seem then touching and attractive. At such moments, one hears not the carefully constructed "Bud" voice, arrogant and deaf, but precisely the sound of someone whistling in the dark.

But why not? The world we now live in, the AIDS world, *is* dark. The possibilities for a gay family were always slightly unreal—hopes for the future as much as satisfactions in the present. In "The Dinner Party," when Bud is talking to Cliff on the beach, he says of their host, "He's of the great world. We're ghetto boys. Inside" (*ELY,* 231). His stories have the limitations and the thrill of the ghetto. They are the closest thing in fiction to the experiment the gay ghetto was, both in style and subject. As the ghetto wanes, with all its excesses and folly, its self-indulgence and materialism, its unthinking self-satisfaction and vanity, only Mordden's stories remain as a testimony to its bravery, imagination, and beauty: most of all, to its friendships.

[Part Four]

IMAGINING DEATH

Chapter Seven

A WEDDING AND THREE FUNERALS

FOUR AIDS NOVELS

Like Ethan Mordden's "The Dinner Party," many of the most successful pieces of AIDS writing have been in short forms: the lyric poem, the play or film, the short story. I think of the poetry collections by Mark Doty (*Atlantis, Bethlehem in Broad Daylight,* and *Turtle, Swan*), Thom Gunn (*The Man with Night Sweats*), and Paul Monette (*Love Alone*); of the plays of William Hoffman (*As Is*), Larry Kramer (*The Normal Heart*), and Tony Kushner (*Angels in America*); of the films *Parting Glances* and *Longtime Companion*; of stories by Edmund White ("An Oracle," "Palace Days," "Running on Empty"), Andrew Holleran ("Friends at Evening"), Alan Barnett ("The *Times* as It Knows Us"), and Adam Mars-Jones ("Slim").[1]

By contrast, when I was considering what novels to discuss in this chapter on AIDS fiction, which ones had meant something to me when I needed them most, I drew a surprising blank. Where were the novels for a representative gay reader who had lived through the beginning and middle of the AIDS epidemic? In an obvious sense, *all* gay novels of the last fifteen years were AIDS novels. Thus, characters with AIDS appear in Michael Cunningham's *Home at the End of the World,* although it is not exactly an "AIDS novel." AIDS even makes its way into works where it is not mentioned at all: Andrew Holleran's *The Beauty of Men* is unthinkable without AIDS, even though its main character is well, and the only dying person is his mother. And there certainly were dozens, probably hundreds of novels written in the eighties and nineties that dealt openly with AIDS, but very few have remained with me, unlike many poems, short stories, and plays. Some of these well-intentioned but unsuccessful titles would include Oscar Moore's bathetic *A Matter of Life and Sex; Some Dance to Remember,* Jack Fritscher's gay *Gone with the Wind;* Tim Barrus's hollering *Genocide;*

Felice Picano's *Like People in History.* Even Ethan Mordden's own long novel *How Long Has This Been Going On?* is less successful in this regard than stories like "The Dinner Party."

Holleran put a finger on the problem when he wrote, "I really don't know who reads them for pleasure."[2] Alan Barnett said the same thing to Michael Denneny: "Who wants to read this AIDS fiction? It hurts me to reread them [his own stories in *The Body and Its Dangers*]."[3] I remember refusing to read Randy Shilts's *And the Band Played On* for the same reason. The only book I wanted to read about AIDS, I said at the time, was the one that (like an old-fashioned murder mystery) divulged the culprit and the cure. Denneny himself astutely compares AIDS writing to the writing of the First World War, only to note the differences as well: "It is as if Sassoon's poetry were being mimeographed in the trenches and distributed to be read by men under fire — the immediacy of these circumstances precludes the possibility of this being a merely aesthetic enterprise."[4]

Two opposite responses can and have been made to this dilemma. One can choose to write directly polemical works whose intention is to awaken guilt and indignation, and to lead to legal reform and medical treatment. This has been the more or less open intention of works such as *The Normal Heart,* the first great agit-prop piece of AIDS theater; Sarah Schulman's *People in Trouble* (1990), which was the gritty pedestal for the glittering musical *Rent;* Tony Kushner's *Angels in America,* which draws provocative connections between AIDS, self-oppression, anticommunism, and the millennial fantasies of America; and Tim Barrus's *Genocide.* The usual canard that political works are somehow less "artistic" certainly doesn't apply in some of these cases, but in any case, their *immediate* function is to wake people up.

Exactly the opposite tack was taken by the British novelist Neil Bartlett, who, overwhelmed by the dilemma of AIDS, retreated from it entirely, choosing to translate and mount a production of Racine's most mannered tragedy, *Bérénice.* In a sense this has been Joe Keenan's and Paul Rudnick's solution, too; only they have opted for the perfect machinery of farce rather than that of classical tragedy. (I am not thinking so much of Rudnick's somewhat maudlin *Jeffrey,* but of his brilliant pseudonymous column "If You Ask Me" by "Libby Gelman-Waxner.") Keenan and Rudnick write, of course, to amuse;[5] but as the circus owner Mr. Sleary says in Dickens's *Hard Times,* "People mutht be amuthed."[6] For these writers farce is a useful sponge for mopping up misery and self-pity, as well as a powerful diversion. Bartlett's choice is surely understandable as well, though the "entertainment" is of a ludicrously high cultural altitude:

> Two years ago, a lot of people were saying to me, either directly or indirectly, "You have to write a play about AIDS." And what I did was the translation of

Bérénice for the National Theatre. It's the most beautiful play ever written, it's the most accurate description of how loss operates, what it means to say good-bye to someone over an extended period of time. Having to deal with that, we need a shape for that sensation. And that may seem like an incredibly perverse way of addressing the situation, but it was the only way I could speak of those things without losing my voice. Because what happens is, you want to speak but before you start speaking you cry. Racine forbids tears, there are no tears on stage. It becomes a very appropriate language for me to use.[7]

Despite these counterexamples—Bartlett's mandarin retreat from AIDS, Kramer's attack on it—AIDS and "the aesthetic" have not been completely contradictory. It may be, indeed, that even for the writers, readers, and critics Denneny hypothesizes, for whom aesthetic "distance is not available," aesthetic power can nonetheless be achieved. Thus, Paul Monette—a trench poet who compares himself explicitly to Wilfred Owen—says in the Preface to *Love Alone* that "I would rather have this volume filed under AIDS than under Poetry, because if these words speak to anyone they are for those who are mad with loss, to let them know they are not alone."[8] It may be, however, that the very compression of time, the very urgency of the need to speak before dying, speeds up the poetic process, compresses the coal of feeling and word all the more powerfully—it certainly seems to have done so for Monette. His beautiful elegies will indeed be filed under "Poetry," despite his wishes.

But the question still remains: why has it not turned the coal of fiction into more diamonds? Is it that fiction-writing simply requires more time—time which an HIV-positive writer may not have? Or that neither writers nor readers want to inhabit the "world" that we conventionally say we enter when we pick up a novel? Or simply that the vignette, the lyric poem, the short play goes to the heart of loss so much more efficiently? For whatever reason, the number of successful AIDS novels, works that cause, as Nabokov said, "the sudden erection of your small dorsal hairs," is still tiny.[9] In this chapter, I will discuss four that strike me as exceptions.

At least one of these books—Christopher Davis's *Valley of the Shadow* (1988)—is not at all well known. It is of all AIDS novels I know the most full of pity. (As Wilfred Owen tells us—and he should know—"The poetry is in the pity.")[10] What I admire in Davis's book is its unrelenting focus on this emotion, and the only odd thing is how seldom it has been attempted. Over and over again, the narrator of *Valley* (identified only once by his name, Andrew) starts telling a story, his only story really, about his poor dead lover Ted. Again and again he comes back to the contradictions that formed their love and the horri-ble gap in his life made by Ted's death. Again and again, he returns—with pity, not self-pity—to his own imminent death. There is very little that happens in this novel of reminiscence except for this memory of what he has lost. It ends without quite ending, its last unpunctuated words being "I remember" — a sigh which is followed only by an announcement, obituary-style, of the narrator's death.

I am not sure whether *Valley of the Shadow* is a great book or even a good one. I do know it is one of the few AIDS novels that has ever made me sob. Many of us have had the taste for tears trained out of us — to weep is "sentimental" — but there must be room for this emotionality in a literature whose very subject is overwhelming loss. To ignore it, or automatically to sublimate it into something supposedly nobler — political outrage, spiritual insight, aesthetic purity — may be just a phobic flight from grief. To read *Valley of the Shadow* is, for me anyway, to reexperience the power of *pathos* — the emotion touched so often by Puccini. And if we are tempted to become impatient with it (finding it "sentimental," "exaggerated," perhaps "effeminate"), let us be honest enough to recall our tears for Mimì, before we claim to prefer our dry-eyed sympathy for Verdi's Otello. There is, there has to be, room for both.

Another, Samuel R. Delany's "pornotopic fantasy" *The Mad Man,* both is and is not about AIDS. The subject is certainly mentioned — announced, indeed — in the first sentence: "I do not have AIDS. I am surprised that I do not."[11] Delany's book is by far the most ethically interesting and intelligent of the texts I will discuss, and also the one that will push most readers' buttons the hardest. It is (like his earlier *Hogg* and *Equinox*) an outrageous book, raunchy to the point of disgust. But the shock of the book is really something other than its raunchiness. In *The Mad Man,* Delany neatly sidesteps the fictional conventions of writing about AIDS, especially the necessity of the tragic, or at least pathetic, ending. His main character dismisses the normal counsels of good sense and "safe sex," or rather reinterprets them to suit himself. This cheerfully sluttish protagonist, John Marr, neither gives sex up, nor practices monogamy, nor (oppositely) abandons himself to doom. *Yet he does not die.* His story is, in part, a tribute to and a fictional preservation of the glory days of the Mineshaft and other sex venues of the discredited seventies. If for no other reason, *The Mad Man* is remarkable for daring to recontextualize the whole question of promiscuity. The trick and power of this book lies in Delany's courageous, witty, and imaginative treatment of the *ending* of AIDS narratives. Like *Longtime Companion,* it solves the problem of the obvious morose ending by imagining a happy one, though *The Mad Man* is bracing and impudent where Lucas's film was lyrical and tender.

A third book — John Weir's *The Irreversible Decline of Eddie Socket* — attracted modest attention at the time of its publication (1990), but has generally been forgotten.[12] The reasons for its comparative oblivion have less to do, I think, with its own strength or weakness as a novel than with its deceptive similarity to other, more initially engaging or imposing works: especially Stephen McCauley's 1988 *The Object of My Affection* and Michael Cunningham's 1991 *A Home at the End of the World.* By these comparisons, Weir's novel seems a runner-up. Eddie Socket is neither as cute and smart-alecky as McCauley's hero nor as blessed with a perfect prose style as Cunningham's four depressed narrators. Weir's quips are good but not great, his examination of family sadness is a bit superficial. Indeed, the book is very much like Eddie's face, as it is described in the opening lines: "neatly arranged but lacking authority, he felt, because of his chin. It wasn't square enough or strong enough to carry the rest of his face, which was boyish and fine. It hadn't emerged. Neither had he."[13] (A quick look at the author's jacket photo reveals that Eddie in turn looks like *him.*) Add to this unemerged quality Eddie's smugness and you might expect fictional trouble: the smirk on Eddie's face often crosses Weir's, and you long to slap both off. Nevertheless, as I later found, this novel turns out to have strong "legs." It is a far more interesting, indeed eccentric book than I remembered. The good thing about it is what it *doesn't* do: namely, make a big case out of Eddie's suffering. Weir's pity for Eddie's "irreversible decline" comes with very little special pleading, without gods (or demons) ex machina. It is so unpredictable a mixture of dryness and humidity, irony and pathos, that it regularly takes one's breath away.

Finally I will look at a writer who has the best claim to canonical status: Dale Peck. His 1993 novel *Martin and John* is far more sophisticated and far more beautifully written than any of the three books I've mentioned. An intricately structured series of interleaved stories that comment on one another, it passes the most exalted tests of postmodern self-referentiality. Its supple prose pays itself out flawlessly, a silken rope of hypnotic sadness. Like all other AIDS writers, Peck has had to solve for himself the "problem" of the ending (Does one make the main character live or die? Does the death "mean" anything?). Peck solves it by imagining a sort of metamorphosis of one character into another: the names, places, ages, even sexual orientations change, but the ongoing story remains the same — incest, violence, longing, and loss. In one sense no one dies, in another, everyone does. Is the way to write about AIDS to think the whole world a site of loss? To imagine oneself both dying and not-dying?

AIDS appears explicitly in the second half of the book, when the book's principal narrator John has moved to New York, met his (eternal) lover Martin, and lost him to AIDS. As he brings his series of stories to a close, he wonders aloud what he has just done: "Now I wonder, Has this story liberated anything but my tears? And is that enough? I want to ask. . . . In this story, I'd intended semen to be the water of life. But, in order to live, I've only ever tasted mine."[14] I will return to this conclusion in a moment, but perhaps it will be enough to point out that this poignant passage asks one of the enduring questions of all gay male fiction: what is the role of sex, not only in our lives but in the stories about them? Peck is saying, among other things, that not only is life in the age of AIDS different from what preceded it, but so is literature. (What would it mean to write a single decorous "elegy" for Martin?) The glorious literature of lust, too, he fears — perhaps hopes — to be unwritable. How can he, as a young gay author, possibly tell a story about gay desire when that desire is death? Does sex become purely theatrical (as in the S and M scenes)? Or does it consume itself in bitter idle longing (and thus signal a bizarre return to gay stories of the forties and fifties)? Does it turn, as in the final story, to sex with a woman? And if it does, has the heterosexual master narrative finally taken over, as Peck himself fears: "Even as Susan takes John inside her he knows that this baby means something, though I've fought against that." What kind of story can the gay writer possibly tell, when the water of life has become poison? In this respect, AIDS becomes not just a story, but a commentary on previous gay stories.

JOHN WEIR'S *THE IRREVERSIBLE DECLINE OF EDDIE SOCKET*

One of the pleasures of writing a book like mine is that of discovering novels for which you had no time at first. One in particular, *The Irreversible Decline of Eddie Socket,* I read when it came out in 1989 but it made no impression on me. Indeed, I moderately disliked it — all that Gen-X whining, the ridiculous anti-hero in his ridiculous slum apartment dying his ridiculous death! In 1989, when AIDS had finally surrounded me and my friends, I wanted to hug my grief to myself and not share. I certainly didn't want to hear it come back to me in John Weir's quirky, resentful slacker's voice. Now, eight years later, I very much do.

What's happened since is the death not only of my friends and the community we once formed, but of a foolish heroic vision. As an Andrew Holleran character says in "Friends at Evening," explaining why he cannot move back to New York: " 'I can't romanticize this,' Ned said, nodding south. 'I can't romanticize taxicabs, or men with Spanish names. I . . . can't romanticize *me*' " (*Men on Men,* 113). *Eddie Socket* is genuinely unromantic, refusing much meaning at all to the suffering of its hero without falling into the counterromanticism of nihilism or cosmic gloom. In this it resembles Eddie himself, who is a strange throwback to the forties and fifties, identifying with Montgomery Clift and Doris Day. His attitude toward life (and eventually death) is a strange mix of the vulnerable and the wacky. Both are masks for a self so embryonic as barely to exist, and Eddie's short life is very nearly a pure loss.

The story concerns a guiltily privileged Gen-Xer named Eddie Socket. (Born something else, he takes the name "Socket" as a deliberately bad joke when he moves to New York with his college friend Polly Plugg.) When we first see him, he's in his lukewarm bath whiling away time. This is something he apparently does a lot, but he feels vaguely guilty about his inactivity nonetheless. In fact when we first meet him, he's having an imaginary conversation with his "punishing pig," a sort of cartoon embodiment of self-reproach:

> He was having a pig attack. Mirrors always activated the pig, the punishing voice inside Eddie's head, which he had tried to neutralize by giving it a size and shape, a constant perch on his left shoulder, and a voice like Mercedes Mc-Cambridge forcing obscenities through Linda Blair's innocent mouth in *The Exorcist.* . . . He was tired of spending his time with a pig, but this was part of his own performance, the quotes he had set around his life. He had his little devices to keep himself out of the world. He was afraid of the world, ironically, because of how much he felt he deserved. He was a white boy, after all, an American, and he secretly had the greatest expectations. He was trapped between an overwhelming sense of entitlement and the paralyzing suspicion that his actions, whatever they were, wouldn't reverberate. . . . He didn't believe in actions; faithful imitation of real events, the exact sequence of motion and fact carefully recreated, was the closest he felt he could come to an earnest response to the world. To give himself the illusion of having a connected emotional life, he had created his punishing pig. (4–5)

Waiting for life to happen to him is Eddie's métier. But in this story of a minor Rodolfo, all the romance of Bohemia is rejected, and with it all the gorgeous tunes of hope, ambition, and courage. Despite having done all the right wrong things, despite having "taken acting classes, written poetry, and failed at a series of real jobs . . . gotten by on quantities of brown rice, wrapped ties at Brooks Brothers at Christmas . . . been in therapy, done affirmations, marched in rallies, voted for Jesse Jackson, . . . come out of the closet, and had sex with men he liked, or didn't like" — despite all these certificates of demerit, Eddie is still a misfit. "He had been poor in New York, without feeling gilded, or glamorous" (5).

As he's lolling in his lukewarm bathwater, his roommate Polly zips in with a Bloomingdale's bag. Despite living in the deepest Lower East Side, she's still midwestern or middle-class enough to enjoy a good shop, and tells Eddie about her upcoming date with "Brag," a handsome young stockbroker, then speeds out to meet him. In the wake of Polly's bustling activity, Eddie makes his own decision, the only one that will "reverberate," though he hardly knows it at the time. He decides to go to a Montgomery Clift retrospective to see — perfect choice — *The Misfits*. There, he runs into a man he knows, an art appraiser, whose dictated tapes he has occasionally transcribed in one of his many dead-end jobs. Saul recognizes Eddie, speaks to him, then (fatally) introduces him to his lover, Merrit Mather. Merrit, who turns out to be a moral black hole, absorbing all light and giving none back, quickly, almost invisibly seduces Eddie — for good as it turns out. The two are ill matched, Merrit favoring preppiness in clothing, propriety in behavior, and quick sexual flings. Eddie has never possessed a Shetland sweater in his life, is a kneejerk antiauthoritarian, and, unbeknownst even to himself, is looking for love.

As this unhappy affair develops, so does Polly's equally unlikely affair with Brag: a terminally straight-arrow (though not, as it turns out, straight) young stockbroker with a big dick and a small, unimaginative heart — a sort of Merrit-in-training. (When it turns out that Brag is actually more gay than straight, the reader is smugly satisfied to learn that he has been going *out* with Merrit, behind both Eddie's and Polly's backs.) Both affairs are failures — though, as so often happens in gay fiction, heterosexuality triumphs. Brag may be a jerk, but Polly doesn't break her heart over him.

Neither, of course, does she die, and Eddie does. Halfway through the book, after a few mostly miserable dates (including a trip to Merrit's cabin in New Hampshire which is almost funny, and almost fun), Eddie gets AIDS. Just like that. We open Part 2, entitled in audibly ironic quotes "Alas," ready for some more wry whimsy. What we read is the following sentence: "Eddie Socket got it. AIDS" (99). It sounds at first like a joke or a children's song; and I laughed in advance, waiting for a punch line that never came.

At first, I didn't know how to take Weir's casualness: How can our bona fide Great Tragedy be happening to someone as tragedy-free, as *undeserving* of tragic dignity, as Eddie Socket? But on the other hand, how else, given Eddie's general haplessness, could AIDS appear in his life? How could it *not* be comic and unformed? Weir's narrative move shocks the reader because the emotional weight of Eddie's illness is (like him) so touchingly small: there is no drum-roll leading up to Weir's announcement, no funeral march leading away from it. Even Eddie barely takes it in, and except for a sudden panicky flight across the country to look at his parents' old house in California — Eddie is always a sucker for an origin, *any* origin — he dies having done as little with AIDS as with his expensive Oberlin education. Eddie himself, trying to make sense of his foreshortened life, tells his father: " 'I haven't felt much about anything, you know, for a long time. Not until this. I mean, you left, and there was Mom, and then there was Merrit — I guess you don't know about Merrit, he was this man, I sort of liked him — and then there was this. I sort of wonder where I was in all of that, it all just sort of happened, and I thought, all right, try this, try that, I tried a lot of things, but none of them — oh, fuck it, I don't know' " (233). Having always felt he was living his life "in quotes" (as he puts it), he dies in quotes too: he dies *literally* quoting an early Yeats poem (not very well) just before he dies in Polly's arms. But as Polly had realized, the real quotation has been his pretend-heartlessness: "If anything about Eddie was in quotes, she thought, listening to his records, it was his nihilism, which was merely his defense against his need to be wanted, and loved" (217).

The story continues past Eddie's death, at once dignifying and placing it. The novel ends like a seventeenth-century comedy, with a *vaudeville* in which the actors each say good-bye to the audience: first Merrit, then Polly, doing a "combination lost object–preoccupation–fourth wall–phone call exercise" in her acting class, then Saul and Merrit going to a ridiculous perfectly Eddie-ish spreading of the ashes at the Penn Central railyards on the West Side, and finally Saul realizing that his life with Merrit is over. The last words of *Eddie Socket* are Saul's, in a chapter called (echoing Elizabeth Bishop's "One Art"), "The Art of Losing": "So many things are lost, I think. Door keys are lost, and wallets are lost, and houses and cities are lost. Friends are lost, too, eleven in the past nine months, and lovers are lost. Even grief is lost, finally, then you mourn the loss of that.... Even losing Merrit, I think, is easy enough, if only I put him in his place in the room, among the fixtures of a life that I no longer lead, there at the table, preserved, wearing a sweater that doesn't belong, nursing a tooth, and drinking heated milk" (275–76).

There are so many ways this novel might have gone wrong and didn't. Saul, for instance, who faithfully tends Eddie in his death, is very nearly forced to become a sort of Jewish Mother Teresa. (Weir, like Eddie, idolizes Jews to the point of stereotyping. As Polly tells Eddie: "That's so reductionist.... A stereotype is a stereotype. It's nice that yours is so exalted, Eddie, but still" [7].) Certainly his lover Merrit Mather is a stereotyped WASP villain, all tweed on the outside, ice on the inside. Eddie's father, whom he refers to as "Joseph Stalin" because of his rigid Catholicism, almost becomes a standard-issue "distant father" who never showed his single child any love. But, because of his weird ultramontanist theology — he is always sending Eddie "cautionary, epigrammatic postcards . . . on all the major religious holidays" — he is himself almost as charmingly lost as Eddie himself. And even *were* he the villain of neo-Freudian nosology, where is the "close binding intimate" mother? She turns out to be a rather butch woman much happier on her own than with her husband or her son, raising dogs in the country.

But the biggest surprise is Eddie himself. I worried when I opened this book that it was going to be a simple repeat of Stephen McCauley's popular and whimsical *The Object of My Affection* (1987), which I hadn't much liked. As in *Eddie Socket*, the hero of *Object* is a gay man in name only. His best friend is a straight Jewish woman; they have parallel love affairs, and ambivalently flirt with each other. Their relationship is defined by smart-alecky one-liners and a distaste for people less hip than they are. Even the typography is similar. For both *Object* and *Eddie Socket,* the book designer shrewdly chose pretend-handwritten characters, with loops and swirls like the trailer for a Doris Day movie. The only thing missing is a champagne glass with stylized bubbles fizzing out of it. "Wacky" is what they say in all but words.[15]

But there the similarities fade. George Mullen, the hero of *Object of My Affection,* is intended to be cute and winning. Eddie is just the reverse: he's a waif, but an obnoxious waif. (George *thinks* he's obnoxious, is indeed rather proud of that fact, but is actually a reader-friendly pussycat of a character.) Eddie is harder to grasp, harder to take, harder to forget. His endless vacillations, his self-created *anomie,* his self-righteousness are all enough to put the reader off. But then he dies, and the death, while hardly noble, asks insistently the question of who Eddie really was — and asks it without offering an answer. Eddie both was and was not the tough, hardhearted New Yorker he'd tried to be; he both was and was not "in love" with Merrit. His life has very little profile, whether tragic, comic, romantic, or grotesque. Unlike earlier AIDS stories, for example, his infection with the disease does not come (in good Sophoclean fashion) as a result of his passionate willfulness (i.e., lots of sex), but of boredom and bad luck. As he tells Polly just before his death, "I was never really very good at it, you know . . . The wild thing" (248). Eddie is, in his own small way, a mystery; George Mullen remains as "lovably" surly at the end as he was at the beginning.

Eddie's tenderness — as opposed to his ostensible passivity — comes as a surprise, perhaps because we're waiting for it to be rejected. But the truth about Eddie's life turns out to be very simple: "For a man who could sing as much of 'I Didn't Know What Time It Was' as he could manage between gulps of oxygen — well, there was no getting around his sentimentality. Eddie Socket was a sentimentalist. He was not 'in quotes,' as he claimed, not at all. He had merely been embarrassed by his own romanticism. . . . He wanted to live without hope, he said, because hope disappointed, but he sat in his hospital bed and romanticized his mother, idolized Merrit, turned Polly into the world's most charming woman" (217). In poor Eddie's case, the three great loves of his life — his mother, Polly, and Merrit Mather — are touchingly obvious, just the ones you'd expect. He has modeled his rather unconvincing "toughness" on his mother; his punkish *anomie* comes from Polly; and he has projected onto Merritt the sophistication, masculinity, and romance he and his mother both seek in a "husband." This then is the truth about Eddie Socket, and it comes with the sort of surprise felt by a reader of Chekhov's "Lady with the Pet Dog," in which a bored middle-aged philanderer and a neurasthenic married woman not only have an affair — love in quotes, so to speak — but simultaneously fall in love — love for real. What is astonishing is that Chekhov gives up neither the irony nor the genuine romance, that we feel un-ironic love stealing into the characters without their being aware of it.

Even Merrit turns out to be surprising. The beautiful high–New England façade he maintains at such emotional cost to others has a childishly simple origin: social insecurity. Why does Merrit make people fall in love with him, then dump them? Why is he such a cold fish? Because it turns out that he has invented his "aristocratic" self quite as much as Eddie or Polly have invented their Lower East Side selves, and is terrified of being found out. He's a fake. The following lovely and unexpected paragraph tells us this simple unexaggerated truth about Merrit, and indirectly, a less-flattering truth about Saul:

> Saul . . . thought that Merrit had a secret. He always wanted to know what it was — had he slept with his mother, murdered his father, what could it be that kept him so quiet, so cool and withheld all his life? [Merrit] could never tell Saul that his secrets were easy, and small. He read books not for plot or character, but page number — he liked to count the pages more than he liked reading them. When he sometimes ran in the park, he told himself that he had a fence attached to his spine, with which he marked off lands as his own, with each successive stride. His grandfather used to operate a junk shop in his dining room, collecting damaged goods in fire sales and evictions, and Merrit thought as a child that he had been gotten in a similar way. When his parents first started out, they ran a motel, which was where he grew up. Now they operated a chain that stretched from Massachusetts to California; Merrit got his money from the kinds of places seventeen-year-olds went to lose their virginity. He didn't like sex very much. Those were his secrets, which wouldn't have satisfied Saul. (260–61)

Even Merrit's most obviously unacceptable behavior — his refusal to visit Eddie when he is dying — is seen in an understanding, if not a sympathetic light. Merrit turns out to be precisely the character who is *most* aware of death, and therefore of Eddie: aware, so to speak, from the inside. "*For I know what death feels like,* he thought, the coffee smell in his nose, the saddle shoes under his coat. Death is relentless, and dull. You wait for people to die. You sit and wait, and sometimes they get better, for years, and sometimes they go very quickly, and you're almost surprised. But the whole time, you rehearse. A little bit at a time, you go through the feelings of loss. And then when they finally go, you've already lost them in stages, and there isn't any grief to be aware of. How do you let go of a person, Merrit wondered, a relationship? You just rehearse the losing carefully, until it doesn't matter anymore" (261).

It would not seem (from what we can guess of his own alliances) that Weir would be the type to let Merrit get away with his high-handedness. He is politically left-wing, constantly reminding us that Eddie is living a "white boy" fantasy of romantic failure which is not available to those who aren't white. Like

Eddie, he feels guilty about his privilege. Nor does he have much good to say about the gay world, especially in its erotic aspect. (It isn't just Merrit who dislikes sex. Eddie has given it up two years before his "irreversible decline" begins; and the only sex scene, between Polly and Brag, is clumsy and unerotic.) But for all these reasons, his willingness to understand Merrit strikes me as positively heroic. It makes this novel something other than we expect from its two main voices — those of Eddie and Saul, the cynic and the romantic.

The Irreversible Decline of Eddie Socket is the best of several novels that have taken as their subject not the horror or outrage of AIDS (though there are some memorably awful hospital scenes in *Eddie Socket*), but the loss which is heart-breaking because it is so small. I think, for example, of Christopher Bram's *In Memory of Angel Clare,* about a boy roughly Eddie's age who doesn't die himself, but whose older, more interesting lover does.[16] The strength of Bram's book, as of Weir's, is its patient imagination of a life that is not very important to anyone, certainly not important enough to justify a big tragic statement. Both are for that reason strangely touching.

SAMUEL R. DELANY'S *THE MAD MAN*

Samuel R. Delany's novel *The Mad Man* is what the French, with their flair for intellectual theater, might call a "provocation." Indeed, it is hard to imagine what reader would be unprovoked by it. Not only is Delany's depiction of John Marr's sexual life graphic, it verges on the pornographic. The novel itself is awkward, encyclopedic, long-winded, and like nothing so much as an un-believably raunchy *Magic Mountain.* But though a hyperbolic work, it is hardly (I think) an untrue one. And it is shockingly radical, though in an unexpected way. Its radicalism is grounded not in its protagonist's alienation (an alienation to which, as a black gay man, he is certainly entitled), but in his insouciant claim to be includable, and indeed included. Marr presents himself at the door of middle-class white America and doesn't so much demand entrance as announce it. There is something so breathtakingly confident about this act — an act of what one might call self-inclusion — that it leaves the reader only one possible response: an amazed and acknowledging laugh. John expands our "common-sense" notions of what is possible, desirable, good.

But if the reader arrives at such an expansion, however, it is after a great many other sensations, not all of them so uplifting, as a brief plot summary will show.

The Mad Man begins with a startling and tantalizing statement: "I do not have AIDS. I am surprised that I don't. I have actively had sex with other men weekly, sometimes daily — without condoms — for the last decade and a half" (5). This sentence deliberately echoes Harold Brodkey's self-justification in *The*

New Yorker ("I have AIDS. I am surprised that I do").[17] What one hears in Delany's sentence is the sound of a gauntlet being thrown down, for he wants to completely reverse the story Brodkey tells: the story, that is, of an "innocent victim" who may have played around a *little* but *very long ago* and certainly not doing *those things*. John Marr, by contrast, is presented as a "guilty victor," so to speak, in that he *has* done all those things (though not, it is true, unprotected anal intercourse) and has yet survived.

The speaker, a black graduate student in philosophy, while completing his dissertation on Timothy Hasler—a Korean American philosopher who seems a conflation of Foucault, Wittgenstein, and Delany himself—finds himself living in Hasler's old building in New York. Seeking to understand Hasler (and ultimately solve the mystery of his violent death about a decade earlier), he begins replicating Hasler's "degrading sexual experiments" by cruising Riverside Park, where he has sex with homeless men.

As it turns out, Hasler's fantasies were far tamer than John's actualities. (He *was*, however, an ardent foot-fetishist.) Because he died in 1973, his life was, as John Marr says, "largely pre-Stonewall." John's is not. John's first "experiment," with a white bum called "Piece O' Shit," is paradigmatic of many that follow. Piece O' Shit, like nearly all of Delany's bums, is a diamond-in-the-rough, physically wrecked though sexually alert, and fundamentally kind. He is sexually imaginative and, though straight himself, is only too happy, indeed grateful, to have John suck him off. He praises John's oral service by saying "Nigger, you got a nice touch there!" He is also, of course, dirty, which John thoroughly enjoys—and Delany thoroughly describes. As John removes the first of six "yoni rings" which have kept Piece O' Shit's foreskin stretched, he naively asks: "What's the stuff all over it?" "What the fuck you think it is? . . . You got you a good, grade-A quality goat here. And that's grade-A quality goat cheese! I mean that's the *real* gorgonzola!" (37). He then pisses in John's mouth.

I do not recount this brief episode to shock or disgust—and neither does Delany. Or rather, knowing his story *will* shock, he writes in the plain belief that it ought not to. Indeed, *The Mad Man* constantly forces the reader to reexamine the whole question of sexual desire: how it should be expressed, whether it should be restrained, and if so, by what means. The most shocking thing about this book is not its presentation of extreme sexual acts, however, but its assumption that even they can be occasions of friendship or love. Paradoxically, if the sex scenes had been written with and for what Judge Woolsey called "the leer of the sensualist," if they depicted John and Piece O' Shit as desperate, compulsive people, most readers would be perfectly content with them. But this is precisely the sort of smug judgment Delany will not permit. He and his hero are heart-warmingly aboveboard in their pursuit of pleasure—John in his life, Delany in this deliciously dirty text. (As one gauge of John's mental health, one could take his sense of humor: he describes his philosophy department as so uptight that the "idea of 'publishing prematurely' was tantamount to walking down the hallowed halls with your dick hanging out your fly.") As a result, we are not allowed the easy escape of moral superiority to these "desperate" characters.

Part 2 of the novel ("The Sleepwalkers") skips ahead a few years to the first hints of the AIDS epidemic, which is to send John into a series of panics and depressions:

> In the years between 1982 and 1986, the world (that American hyperbole for urban U.S.A. plus the suburban residents concerned with what goes on there) changed. The cancer Mossman [John's graduate adviser] had mentioned in his third PS was not a skin cancer at all, but rather a cancer of the mesodermic capillary linings called "Kaposi's sarcoma" — till then almost unknown but, during those years, one of the most mentioned diseases in the American press. Soon, from time to time, I'd see men walking around the neighborhood with its purple lesions on arms, shins, and faces. Then, in papers like the *New York Native* and the *Village Voice,* it was joined by "pneumocystis carinii pneumonia" and "oral thrush" and "toxic plasmosis"; and, as statistics mounted from three thousand to six thousand to twenty thousand to sixty thousand, we entered the age of Acquired Immune Deficiency Syndrome — AIDS. (95)

As this untheatrical passage reminds us, *The Mad Man,* while a fiction, takes place in a specific time and place. And one of the places Part 2 memorably recaptures is the Mineshaft, with its orgies, bathtubs, and camaraderie. This section also includes Marr's meeting with Pete Darmushklowsky, a student with whom (or rather, with whose feet) Hasler was once in love. Like all people in this book who have accepted their sexuality and its kinks (his is an exclusive desire for Asian women), Pete is helpful, kind, and nonjudgmental. (The kindness of the sexually satisfied, like the deliciousness of natural bodily secretions, is one of the assumptions of the book.) And at the very end of Part 2, John gets a surprise: his first HIV test is negative.

This surprise is not only epidemiological but narratological: the story of promiscuous sex is supposed to be fatal. But the fact that John gets away with it merely fictionally confirms a far more important assertion made by him in the great centerpiece of this second section: a seventy-page letter to his adviser Mossman's now-ex-wife. A remarkable, almost separable document, it is a confession of sexual faith and a defense of promiscuous sex. I will return in a moment to this letter, which both describes a turning point in John's life and is the turning point of the book as a whole.

The third, fourth, and fifth sections take us into progressively deeper sexual waters. In the third, "Masters of the Day," Almira Adler, the "old Poet" who was Hasler's friend, tells John that, at his death, Hasler's apartment was a "sty," his books and walls pissed on, and a Heraclitean term meaning "conflagration" daubed on a mirror in shit. Though Hasler was not killed there, it was from this scene of filth that he went unknowingly to his death at the Pit, a hustler bar downtown. Two new characters lead John indirectly to solving the Hasler mystery: Crazy Joey, who masturbates relentlessly (and publicly), and Tony, who devours Joey's shit every night. Together they lead the reader into Part 4, titled "The Place of Excrement."

For those who don't remember their Yeats, "the place of excrement" — the vagina, the anus — is where "Love has pitched his mansion."[18] In this section Marr descends — or ascends — into "degrading sexual experiments" with excrement and promiscuity which Hasler could only have dreamed of. But once again, the truly shocking assertion is that these can be, and are, acts of love: "The remainder of this tale is a love story," says the outrageous opening line of Part 4. It is a love story because in it John meets someone he loves, a bum named Leaky. Leaky is a white hillbilly (the racial mixing of *The Mad Man* is one of its compelling charms) who — not surprisingly — likes to take his leaks on John, in John, around John, it scarcely matters. Leaky's own story is enough to make a social worker's hair curl, as he was "abused" — willingly, if that is not a contradiction in terms — by his father back in West Virginia. But as elsewhere in this book, Delany deliberately refuses to take the beaten path to moral indignation, and instead implies that Leaky is a better man for his paternal love. (For Delany in this novel — though not necessarily in his earlier *Hogg* — consent is essential. But his most button-pushing passages are those which question our automatic assumptions about what constitutes consent, who is capable of it, at what age, and in what circumstances.)

This section dovetails with the fifth and final one ("The Mirrors of Night"), in which the solution to Hasler's murder is almost casually revealed, a new murder is committed, Leaky and John agree to become a couple, and John gets his first teaching job. Though more or less "married" to John, Leaky "still hasn't had any regular work for more than a few weeks at a time. But daily he pisses on his hands to keep them hard — and goes down to Forty-seventh Street and Sixth Avenue about every third day to panhandle. He says he likes to pay for his own beer; he drinks enough of it. I say, I get about as much out of it as you do. He says, well, since that's the diamond-sellers' neighborhood, panhandling there he keeps a hard, monstrous, nail gnawed thumb on a certain pulse and rhythm to the city's glittering dream" (550). The final sentences, the "happily ever after" of this "pornotopic" fairy story, have an almost Fitzgeraldian sound to them, and thus serve to remind us that *The Mad Man* has been a New York as well as an AIDS, or a love, story. Indeed one of the many old-fashioned things about this novel is its vision of the city (quite unlike Eddie Socket's) as a place of glamour, hunger, and hope.

Why is *The Mad Man* so outrageously sexually graphic? Does it intend to horrify? to educate? to arouse? Can it be called "pornographic"? Is its gutter slang about race and sex self-oppressive? politically retrograde? Is it the testament of a "sex addict"? an unconscious plea for "rescue" from these degrading passions? Why, in short, should we read such a disgusting book?

We should read it because it makes a serious and rare attempt to justify sexual exploration in the age of AIDS. The sexual adventurousness of Delany's main and most admirable characters is never punished, and is indeed rewarded. Second, it envisions a homosexuality that does not so much receive a "place at the table" (to use Bruce Bawer's metaphor) as offer one. Delany's characters make us at least *conceive of* a realm of satisfactions that can encompass intellectual, emotional, and sexual pleasures: a sort of reassociation of sensibility. They shake up our commonsense assumptions about the danger of strong appetites and make us wonder if we haven't sold ourselves short.

The character who has sold himself shortest, and thus speaks for most readers, is Irving Mossman, John's graduate adviser. A student of Hasler's work, Mossman has been trying to write a biography of him for years. But when he comes across Hasler's pornographic stories (about a creature half-bestial, half-human whose dung he eats), when he reads about Hasler's fantasies of sex with bums, he throws his hands up in well-bred timid dismay.

> Really, John, I have to consider seriously whether Timothy Hasler is a man I want to be writing about. . . . What sort of compassion can I be expected to have for a man who writes an eight page description in his journal about finding a Doberman loose in the park, bringing it home, feeding it, sucking its penis to orgasm four times, then turning it loose again. . . . What compassion can I have for a man who, once a week, bought a bottle of cheap wine, went out and hunted up an old black wino in the park, the two of them getting blitzed together, till he got the wino to urinate in his mouth? (He has the nerve to call this man his "friend." . . . What sort of compassion am I supposed to have for a man who fills up pages in his journal, fantasizing about sex with nightmarish creatures who aren't even human. (21, 50)

John thinks in retrospect that "Mossman's moment of confusion, disillusions, and degradation . . . mark[ed] a kind of beginning for me" (21), the beginning of his emancipation as a thinker and a grown-up gay man. The emancipation has everything to do with taking his own risks, staking his own claim, not only to Hasler but to sex. As he says to himself at a moment when Mossman has given up the biography altogether, because he's not certain Hasler is yet important enough:

> Irving, you're doing this all wrong — and you've been doing it wrong for years. With someone like Timothy Hasler, you can't *gamble* on his fame! You read his

work; you study it; you even teach it — and *you* decide if within the systems of the world, that work is of major importance or not. If you decide it is, you write your book, and your essays, and your articles, and your lectures — in which you *say* that! You write them because *you* believe in the work. You don't spend all your time looking around you, counting how many other people are saying this stuff is great — or not saying it. You don't keep counting the footnotes in which the name appears, wondering if you should abandon the project because there aren't as many this year as last. . . . The gamble, Irving Mossman, is *not* on Timothy Hasler. The gamble is on *you.* (75–76)

Marr speaks in this passage of Irving "gambling" on Hasler's reputation. But "gambling" is, in another sense, just what Mossman *won't* do; or rather, he is willing to place only a *sure* bet. But life cannot be lived like that, even if one is a philosopher, and this brings us back to John's long letter to Mossman's wife, Sam; a letter which describes, defines, defends, and justifies Marr's own gamble — on life, sexual happiness, and intellectual pleasure.

There are many remarkable things about it, but let us consider only the most obvious. It is written by a young gay man to an older straight woman who is, to make matters worse, married to his teacher. Think of the Freudian complications that would ensue in most novels! But John is unintimidated by Sam or by Freud. His letter is fueled in part by anger at the bland liberal ignorance which unintentionally keeps him and other gay men in the closet.

It begins quickly, decisively: "Some months ago I went down to 'GSA Night' at the Mineshaft — stayed out till six-thirty in the morning. (Rare for old nine-to-five me.) On the first Wednesday of each month, my friend Pheldon told me, GSA (The Golden Shower Association) sponsors a Wet Night — catering to guys with a taste for recycled beer" (116). For readers unfamiliar with the scene, the Mineshaft was the premier sex club of the late seventies and early eighties; recycled beer is urine; and the "golden shower" fell on more mortals than Danaë.

When I first read this passage, my heart lurched. Was he really going to talk about *that?* How much? With what degree of irony? (The answers were: Yes; A lot; and None.) Mine was a self-protective question as well as a thrilled one. I, after all, had also gone to GSA Nights at the Mineshaft. I felt as though my own life, my own gamble, was being exposed. I have no idea whether Marr's experience is also Delany's, but does it matter? One can only assume that anyone who has written in such loving detail about the Mineshaft has been there. Furthermore, for most readers (even most gay readers), even to imagine what Delany has so lusciously described is to damn yourself as a pervert.

The letter is remarkable (like so much of this book) for its candor and complete lack of defensiveness. Not once does John attempt to "justify" (in the defensive sense) his orgies of piss-drinking, cocksucking, and promiscuity. This is its greatest virtue. At the very end of the letter he makes only the following concession to Sam's sensibilities: "I really wonder, Sam, what all this must look like to somebody so outside this particular life as yourself" (191).

But though he is not "defensive," Marr certainly makes a de facto defense of his actions. The defense is very simple: pleasure, indeed sanity. At one point, after a particularly excessive bout of piss-drinking, John realizes suddenly that he "felt . . . good!"

> Incredibly good!
> And peaceful.
> And content.
> I didn't feel any need to talk to anyone. The feeling that gets you up, looking for this and that, that starts you off doing one thing or the other, just to have something to do, was in abeyance — an abeyance I usually associate with tired-ness; only, though it was after three in the morning, I didn't *feel* tired. I thought about that strangely and rarely attainable condition Heidegger called "medita-tive thinking" and wondered if this was it. (125)

Perhaps only Samuel Delany would have permitted his hero to think about Heidegger at this point; but doing so allows him and us to draw some useful conclusions. The most important is (to put it too crudely) that sex is good for you. Like many notions in *The Mad Man,* this idea is not so much argued for as exemplified. John Marr is the prime example; but even a minor, rather sinister character like Big Buck, a latecomer to the "place of excrement" in Part 4, is humanized by sex — and "degrading" sex at that. While taking a shit in another man's mouth, Buck's voice "filled out, even as I heard him take a breath that, for the first time sounded as though it were complete and full and human" (470). No less important, however, is the idea that the free exercise of sexual desire is good for society as well. Not only the comparatively middle-class world of the Mineshaft, but the definitely lower-class world of dirty movie theaters is re-markably safe, remarkably unviolent: "Most of [the men who go there] can be mildly annoying to someone at one time or another. But given any ten days in their lives, including their time here, you will not find them annoying anyone" (165–66). The dangerous people in this book are not the bums, not the cock-suckers, not the transvestites, but the fearful "city fathers." Such people — more pitiable than evil — have swallowed the myth of sexual scarcity: they control sex because they cannot believe that it is so freely available to all. Enslavement to this myth has resulted literally in Hasler's death, and symbolically in the death of philosophy itself.

But can sex really be "good for you" during a sexually spread epidemic? Yes — as we and Sam learn at the long letter's climax: a moment that Marr calls, with some embarrassment, "a mystical experience." What has happened? During a routine afternoon of cocksucking at a porno theater, John Marr suddenly and completely *stops being afraid of AIDS.* "When I entered the Variety Photoplays Theater, I was, doubtless, like half the men there, terrified of AIDS. As I walked around the theater, doing what I did, like most of the men there, I thought about AIDS—constantly and intently and obsessively. But when I left (and in this aspect alone, perhaps my experience is—not unique—but certainly rare), I no longer had any fear of the disease. At all" (184). Marr himself is not quite sure what led him to this reversal, but what he says is that there is no way around the "gamble," and that coming face to face with that terrifying fact paradoxically "obliterates the terror" of AIDS: "Still—until much more is known—any course of action is more or less a gamble—even unto cutting out all sex entirely. And in such a situation every one of us must put up our own stakes and know that the outcome can be death. . . . Yet it is the realization that one is gambling, and gambling on one's own—rather than seeking some possible certain knowledge, some knowable belief in how intelligent or in how idiotic the chances are—that obliterates the terror" (189). This is, in other words, the same reproach he has made to Irving: make *your* choice, stake *your* claim.

His new fearlessness enables Marr to make a powerful defense of sexual promiscuity: "When sex is so available and plays such a large part in life, sexual activity ends up fulfilling many, many psychological functions—as chosen recreations often do: It helps you deal with any number of tensions and becomes a stabilizing and balancing force—and it provides an object for as much or as little intellectual analysis as anyone by temperament might require" (184). He can also see that in a strange way AIDS has put us all back in the closet, in "the same situation I'd been in when the only information I had about homosexuality was what I'd found in an outdated psychology book by Erich Fromm from the 1950s on a shelf of the local library, whose appendix told me that to indulge one's homosexual urges was to foredoom oneself to an unavoidable career of alcoholism, devoid of any rewarding or mature relationships (whether sexual or any other kind), with an almost certain probability of suicide sooner or later!" (185). To recall Fromm's exploded certainties makes us realize that even the most immutable truths (such as the "sickness" of homosexuality) change. Why not the received wisdom about AIDS, then? Notice that in all this, Marr is not (like some "doomed queen") *looking for unsafe sex,* is not seeking self-destruction. To the contrary. What he is doing is choosing to live despite the omnipresence of death. He has seen that sex is enlivening and that it may therefore be worth gambling on, even though "the outcome can be death."

The Mad Man is itself a vivifying gamble, both for what it says and for what it is. How unpretentious it is, how enjoying, how generous! (I wanted to grab John Weir and Dale Peck and rub their noses in it till they agreed to smile.) It is a gamble on the body and on the language we permit ourselves to use about it. All the "dirty" talk about the body in fact pays homage to its beauty. No one in this book forgets he is "embodied." The blackness or whiteness of skin which plays such an important part in the fantasies and language of these characters is for once salient — an interesting but not determining fact: thus, "white" is a color as well as black, and the characters make fun (and lust) of whiteness as of blackness. Delany is on the side of the body, which means being also on the side of all its beautiful, tragic, and arbitrary concreteness — of race, age, looks. And like the bodies he admires, Delany's speech is direct, funky, unhypocritical, and lively.

Most important, it is a gamble on the imagination. In John Marr, Delany has dared to create a character — a black intellectual faggot — who with every strike against him gets everything he wants: career, love, raunchy sex, and even a clean bill of health. And the fact that John's life does not seem *entirely* improbable forces us to reopen the question of our own erotic desires, a question we usually close off by terming them "unrealistic," "immature," "self-destructive." But are they? Or have we merely inured ourselves to doing-without? The fact that John can think of addenda to Russell and Whitehead (!) while drinking his lover's urine suggests that we, too, might start asking for more pleasures, rather than fewer.

The book implicitly asks "Why not?" Why not satisfy every appetite that is not violent or destructive? What prevents our doing so but custom and inattention? After a marathon session of piss-drinking with Leaky, for example, John thinks: "people feel guilty about wanting to do stuff like this. But this is the reward of actually doing it, of finding someone who wants to do it with you: the fantasies of it may be drenched in shame, but the act culminates in the knowledge that no one has been harmed, no one has been wounded, no one has been wronged" (419). *The Mad Man* is, in this respect, a surprisingly old-fashioned justification of seeking your own pleasure and development, provided they do not harm others. Similarly, liberation comes not as permission but as confirmation of what one has already permitted oneself to do: "But it was only through a few years of doing what I was doing and looking at the people I was doing it with, many of whom seemed no less happy than anyone else, that I began to ask that most empowering of questions: Could all these people around me be both crazy and damned? When one is dealing with the satisfaction of an appetite, you relegate the Erich Fromms *et alia* to the place where one stores those abstractions that don't particularly relate to the systems of the world around you. I did that" (185).

In the introduction to *The Mad Man,* warily called a "Disclaimer," Delany refers to his novel as a "pornotopic fantasy." It took me a moment to figure out what the phrase meant. But then I realized that "pornotopic" was a neologism based on "utopic" or "utopian": he has written a fantasy of "the good sexual place." But I take the disclamatory word *fantasy* with a grain of salt. The book does not seem to me primarily fantastic, though (like many comedies) its happy ending does. The Mineshaft, after all, was real, and my memories of it are of the fondest — even though I have to admit they include a nasty case of amoebiasis as well as an incurable case of joy. Nevertheless, my experience of gay life is that John Marr's combination of high and low pleasures, while extreme, is hardly uncommon, certainly not impossible.

Nonetheless, the good news of Delany's gospel went largely ignored, even in the gay press. I can only imagine that its questioning of white-bread safer-sex clichés was too dangerous for many readers to accept — not to mention its refusal to conform to "good gay" conventions, whether of literature or life. It is for that reason a useful case-study for the question of "political" fiction. Delany is as "political" a writer as one could hope to find. Not only in this novel, but in his science fiction, his memoirs, and his essays, he has constantly addressed issues of race and sexuality. The fact that he is a black gay author has never escaped his mind and doesn't escape his reader's either. At the same time, like the hero of *The Mad Man*, Delany is winningly cheerful in his political assumptions. Unlike many embattled authors, he actually expects success. In a charming essay called "Coming/Out," he describes taking his daughter ice-skating in Central Park with other members of the "Gay Fathers." "As I wobbled across the ice, a large black woman in a sweeping purple coat, far steadier on her blades than I, asked, 'Excuse me, but who *are* you all?' and I explained, falling into her arms, 'We're a group of gay men, here with our children!' "[19]

If John Marr is "self-included," so is Samuel Delany. A less resentful writer would be hard to find. Does this make Delany cowardly or deluded? I don't think so. What he has done is to infiltrate all sorts of usually white, usually straight institutions — whether science fiction or membership in the intelligentsia — and to plant himself there. I do not claim that Delany's work of infiltration has been easy, or that his method is the only one. But it has tremendous power, precisely because it is positive, showing us what a free life would look like, not simply what our prison address is. His achievement, while "pornotopic," is also entirely plausible and indeed politically necessary. He usefully corrects the oppositional stance of other political writers like Larry Kramer or Sarah Schulman. To the extent that we admire John Marr, we become heirs of his sexual adventurousness. To the extent that we admit we are no different from him, we widen the scope of our sexual, racial, and intellectual categories.

This is, very simply, the revolution from within.

CHRISTOPHER DAVIS'S *VALLEY OF THE SHADOW*

Jane Austen said when writing her greatest novel, *Emma*, that she was "going to take a heroine whom no one but myself will much like."[20] Christopher Davis may have worried about the same thing when he wrote a novel that is probably not "great" by any standards, let alone Jane Austen's, but which has nonetheless surprising power. One reason many readers might be expected to dislike Davis's hero is that he is, like Emma, "handsome, clever, and rich." He has friends, muscles, a lover, and a job; and has (like her) lived most of his years in the world "with very little to distress or vex [him]." His happiest memories are trivial: dancing and fucking on Fire Island. His family adores him and takes care of him in his illness. He even finds it in his heart to forgive the universe for his premature death.

Well, if *he* can't who *could,* one may want to disgustedly ask. And indeed, this description might make Andrew seem a dreadful narcissist, a yuppie in the moral as well as the financial sense. He is not. He might also seem "childish," and this would be closer to the truth, for he is utterly absorbed by his grief. Can one take seriously (especially from the political vantage) a book whose narrator and main character is, well, so privileged? If one does, is one merely flattering the already powerful? Why, in other words, should we take the highly self-indulgent suffering of a gay yuppie as in any way representative of our own?

In fact, there are two plausible reasons (besides racism and classism) for why some of the best stories — including *Valley of the Shadow* — were told about successful gay men. The first is simple: these people were among the very first to be struck by AIDS. And as Vito Russo wrote, rebutting similar squeamishness about the film *Longtime Companion*:

> *Longtime Companion* will be criticized on many counts by the same people who always want films like this one to cover all bases and be all things to all people. Aside from the fact that such a thing is impossible, I'm tired of people who demand political correctness in art. Not only isn't it possible, it isn't desirable. . . . Virtually all the characters in *Longtime Companion* are white, handsome, and upscale professionals — and rightly so, because this is exactly the population first identified with this disease in exactly the setting in which it happened. . . . By the end of the film, they're talking about sit-ins outside city hall, wearing ACT-Up buttons and T-shirts, and working the phones at the Gay Men's Health Crisis. That's the way it happened, and it's insulting to tell these people that their experience is somehow not valid because they're white.[21]

The second reason is literary. The suffering of the fortunate makes a good story, a "tragic" story in the simplest meaning of the word. (In "The Monk's Tale," Chaucer tells us straightforwardly enough: "Tragedie is to seyn a certeyn storie, / As olde bookes maken us memorie, / Of hym that stood in greet prosperitee, / And is yfallen out of heigh degree / Into myserie, and endeth wrecchedly." Sounds like AIDS to me.) It is paradoxically easier to pity someone of "heigh degree" than someone of low — or even ourselves. We invest such creatures with all the luck we secretly wish we had, then gleefully, fearfully watch as the gorgeous vessel is dashed on the rocks. Andrew's descent from the top of Fortune's wheel to the bottom is thrillingly steep: he had everything, he loses everything; if it happened to him, it could happen to us. The outline of his story is satisfyingly simple, his suffering satisfyingly pure.

Andrew's is, to say the least, a very different story from that told of or by poor women who have gotten the disease because they turned to prostitution to pay their bills; or heroin addicts who have gotten it from sharing needles; or hemophiliacs who have gotten it by the negligence of the government. These are all stories well worth telling; but while the suffering may be objectively as great, narratively it is less exciting. The fall is not from high degree, but from a degree already low. When one reads, for example, a poem like Rafael Campo's "Age 5 Born with AIDS," one's reaction can only be a sort of numb helplessness.[22] "Jaime" in this poem not only did nothing to "deserve" AIDS — not that anybody does, exactly — but did nothing at all. He was just a child, as close as one can come to a pure victim. The pathos of Campo's poem is built into its subject: in a sense the title says all we need to know.

Because of Andrew's precipitous destruction, and the patient clear-eyed view he has of it, *Valley of the Shadow* offers a great gift to the reader: pity. It allows us to shed tears for what surely has a right to be mourned: a happy life. Given the losses of his young life, one might expect Andrew's memoir to be bitter and angry. It is not. Andrew so unguardedly *misses* his old life that he gives us permission to miss our own. He knows he was complicit in his illness (after his problematic lover Ted left him, he started going to the baths and getting fucked every night) but still does not regret the many fugitive joys that have so inexorably led to his present appalling loss. The uncomplaining tale he tells shows us a way to die not only with dignity but humorous regret. These emotions, which will strike many readers as inadequate or "sentimental," are indeed the limits of Davis's book.

What *has* he lost? The simple answer is "Ted." But, as in all good love stories, to say this is only to begin. Ted is not only Andrew's beloved companion, first love, hotly desired sex partner, and best friend, but the very force that makes Andrew's tight-budded flower open to the sun. He is impetuousness and brashness (not caring who sees him naked), bohemianism (living in the East Village as a mostly out-of-work actor: Andrew by contrast is a banker); promiscuity and sexual adventurousness (he is fascinated by S and M); intoxication (he's often drunk or stoned); pleasure (he loves dancing and eating and sex); gay pride (he refuses to kowtow to Andrew's grumpy fundamentalist grandfather). He is also, of course, self-absorption, destruction, and death, not just for himself but for Andrew. With Ted, a whole world of beautiful and dangerous desires invades the safe, upper-middle-class Andrew and changes him completely. As he writes of a summer at Fire Island halfway into their relationship, "At the beginning of that summer I seldom drank, I didn't take drugs, and I didn't much like to dance; but by the end of summer I loved them all."[23]

It is lucky that Andrew is writing a memoir rather than a novel about Ted — lucky for Davis that is, because it would take a greater pen than his to make Ted as magnetic to a disinterested reader as he is to Andrew. The reader has to take a fair amount on trust. He's mostly an awful jerk: drunk, abusive, truculent. Andrew himself, for that matter, would not be a believable, perhaps even a likable character if excerpted from this monologue and displayed under the pitiless light of a third-person novel. Although Davis has provided perfectly plausible characterizations, motives, and actions for these two lovers, the "objective correlative" details of their lives are only approximately sketched in. Ted and Andrew are — in a good sense — ciphers, placeholders. There is no mystery in them. They signify grief and love, and permit the reader to remember his own. The characters serve here an analogous function to the words in an opera: they focus and name an experience that is really wider than they.

But the novel doesn't depend for its power on a belief in Andrew or Ted, but in a voice. It is the voice of a man younger than his twenty-eight years: someone young enough to be full of hope, and thus also of despair. It is not a voice remarkable for wit or style or profundity, but it does not need to be. Its greatest characteristic is transparency, as Andrew's greatest gift is his capacity to register joy and pain. It is a *bewildered* voice — bewildered as children are — one which can speak with a sort of devastating wonder of the changes wrought by AIDS in his life.

> I can remember when I was young, not very young, not an infant as some people claim to remember, but still young, when my body was weak and small. I remember my father teaching me how to swim. I was afraid of the water when I was young and small and I remember my father taking me out into it and holding me under my stomach and then letting me go. I cannot remember any more than that: I cannot remember if I gasped and choked and sank and had to be lifted out of the water with strong arms or if I somehow made it to the shore, but I know that now I love the water; I love to feel my body moving through it and I love to feel the surf of a roaring ocean breaking over my head and I like the feeling of swimming out until I am enervated and then drifting back, exhausted but strong enough, strong enough. (1–2)

As this opening passage shows, Andrew's voice is naive and affectless as a child's; the pathos of the book resides in his sheer devastated surprise that these things are happening to him. But of course naïveté is in fact a sophisticated literary device, just as pastoral is an aristocratic poetic form. The author has to create a context (or a pretext) for naïveté, and this Davis has successfully done. A dying man who knows that his memory is quickly slipping from him, Andrew is forgiven for "wandering." Indeed, once we concede that he has the right to wander, we begin to hear a characteristic meandering music. He rarely tries to second-guess himself; rather, the self-corrections are made *en passant* ("when I was young, not very young, not an infant as some people claim to remember . . ."). The naïveté also permits Davis the cliché of the implied simile (swimming in deep water = dying) and the "obvious" contrast between then and now (signaled by the repeated word *young*). The effect is of unpremeditated, unedited reminiscence — which is precisely the conceit of the book.

One advantage of such a voice, besides its melody, is ethical: *Valley of the Shadow* is never judgmental. It sees without blinking the treacherous pleasures that land its two main characters in such terrible trouble. It never uses the word *alcoholic,* for instance, even though the term would be applicable to Ted. It does not regard Andrew as a "sexual compulsive," though that would be an easy and conventional way to understand his reckless promiscuity after Ted's disappearance. This strategy enables Andrew/Davis to tell a story that surprisingly few gay writers have attempted: the *why* of sexual promiscuity and drug use, the reasons these men with everything to live for risk death.

Here, for example, is a beautifully unguarded passage on Andrew's second coming-out:

> Before then I had been gay, of course, but only in that I preferred to have sex with men instead of women; gay culture did not touch me, and if it did I scorned it. I had had sex with many men, as I have said, but Teddy had been right, I did think I was somehow better than they were: *I* wasn't in the gay ghetto; *I* didn't dress like a clone; *I* wasn't effeminate (not that being effeminate is equivalent to being gay); I was not interested in what I considered to be *their* petty little world. And then do you know what happened, I became part of it, and I could not get enough. Life for me, at the time I met Ted on the steps of the Plaza last year, had become a complicated landscape of parties, gyms, beautiful men, knowing the right people — the *in* people, going to the opera, the symphony, the ballet, rushing off to the Island in a seaplane in order to make Friday Tea. And I do not apologize for that; it was an interesting and satisfying way of living and one that I miss. And it all began that first summer Ted took me to the Pines. (115–16)

This passage is far more shocking to most readers' sensibilities than Samuel Delany's raunchiest descriptions of piss-drinking. How dare Andrew call his drinking, drugging, dancing days "interesting" and even "satisfying"? But even worse, how dare he admit to enjoying the "complicated landscape of parties, gyms, beautiful men, knowing the right people"? The one thing that is unforgiv-able in most serious American writing (as in American culture) is to *enjoy* one's privileges. (They ought rather to be guilty secrets.) How dare he say as he does twenty pages later, "there cannot be a finer thing than to be a young openly gay man in this wonderful city"? (138). Doesn't he know how elitist that sounds, and is?

And yet, Davis is in the right. Like *Dancer from the Dance* and *Ready to Catch Him Should He Fall, Valley of the Shadow* is audacious — and therefore necessary — because it imagines (if it does not grant) success for its heroes. "Success," here, takes the form of pleasure. Because of pleasure Andrew is a bigger person at the end than he was at the beginning. Ted may indeed have killed his body (directly or indirectly), but he liberated his spirit. And because of the long history of gay oppression and sadness, even to imagine success is revolutionary. Nor is Andrew's story so strange to me, at least. He has (like so many gay men I have known) a peculiar gift for pleasure. To read his reminis-cence is to have awakened in ourselves many disremembered joys: the love of one's parents and family, excitement over music and books, the exuberance of first love, the incomparable realization that one is now in flower. "Awakened" in the simplest, most naive sense: Davis had to do little more than name the joys; he trusts the reader to do the rest.

The book could have gone wrong in so many ways at so many points that the fact that it doesn't is a kind of miracle. In one embarrassing scene, for instance, it is Christmas, and Ted (already very ill) is visiting Andrew's family once again. In an earlier Christmas scene — Davis *believes in* Christmas, as he believes in loving your family — Ted had won over Andrew's homophobic grandparents by reading aloud St. Luke's account of the nativity. In this later scene it happens again, but with the plangency of imminent death: "Last Christmas, when Teddy was so sick but insisted on going to Maine with my family and when Grand-father was no longer with us, I asked Teddy if he remembered reciting the Bible to Grandfather and he was quiet for a long time, lost in his own memories, but then he found the right thread and followed it and he said quietly, looking at me: 'And it came to pass in those days, that there went out a decree from Caesar Augustus, that all the world should be taxed'" (77–78). He then recites (and Davis quotes) the entire passage, right up to "Glory to God in the highest, and on earth peace, good will toward men," after which "when he was finished I had to leave the room so I wouldn't cry" (79).

The moment risks mawkishness of the worst sort. And most editors would, I am sure, have slashed it out or, had they permitted it, would have cut the direct, unironic quotation of fourteen verses. They would feel, doubtless rightly, that the sensitive reader should be spared such embarrassingly sincere proclama-tions of feeling.[24] (Suggest! Suggest!) But Davis, like Andrew, is not "sensitive."

He likes emotionality. One of the ways he often seems "naive" is his uncomplicated, unironic enjoyment of good feeling—whether for your childhood, your parents, for Chopin, or for men's bodies. He delights in what is delightful. It is his lack of embarrassment which is itself embarrassing to us, but also such a pleasure—a refreshingly guilty one. He is not afraid to *dirty* himself with the sloppiness of sentimentality. As an artist, Davis eschews the controlling mode preferred by highbrow writers from Henry James to Edmund White and Dale Peck—the obsessional need to manipulate the reader's reaction down to the smallest detail. Like Dickens, Davis is willing to trust the reader to supply either the emotion or the detail himself. Davis's lack of aesthetic shame is actually a liberating willingness to *be* shamed. And it echoes his main character's enjoyment of certain sexual acts, as when he discovers that "I really did enjoy what is usually referred to as S and M." In another scene, again at Andrew's family's Maine house, Ted and Andrew have particularly loud sex: "I'm laughing as I write this, but I can remember that the next morning, Christmas, I felt terribly embarrassed when I woke up and I didn't want to see my parents, who could not have helped hearing their son getting fucked if they had had their heads under their pillows and plugs in their ears (I admit it, I liked it)" (81–82). Andrew's embarrassment is completely understandable, and yet I don't recall ever having seen it in print. Notice that neither Andrew nor Davis *corrects* the shame: to the contrary, "I admit it, I liked it." He does not censor either his feelings or his parents'. Davis enjoys the shame, as we all sometimes do. And it *is* shameful—if anything is—to have sex in your parents' house, within their hearing, especially if you are "their son being fucked." It is like the moment I have quoted when Andrew admits—without self-justification—that he went from not liking to drink, drug, or dance to loving them all. One is not *supposed* to like these things if one is a serious person! But even more, one is not supposed to admit liking them in so casual, unironic, and enthusiastic a way. As with *Ready to Catch Him Should He Fall*—written in a similar voice—the twin shames of sex and sentimentality are linked in *Valley of the Shadow*. And as both are experienced, both are vindicated. The book is a defense of weeping and of coming: a defense, one might almost say, of homosexuality itself, that shameful erotic disposition in a man to be penetrated and to gush.

Andrew says at one point that what started as a simple memory of his life with Ted has turned into an "autobiography about a gay man who loved life, who loved being gay, who loved Ted as much as one man can love another, and who will be dead before thirty" (199). This seems an unexceptional, even maudlin statement. What could be easier to write or drearier to read? And yet the book is not dreary, partly because the ambition is bigger than it may first seem. How many AIDS novels have focused on the sheer happiness of life? Jack Fritscher's *Some Dance to Remember* does so, but so defiantly and loudly, with so exaggerated a style that one resists his perfectly genuine grief. (The opening paragraph portentously begins: "Something there is in love that rules out amnesty. For everyone. For every word and act. For every promise and betrayal. For every reason and passion. For all sins of omission and commission.")[25] Though I like the story Fritscher wants to tell — the rise and fall of the gay ghetto and the shattering of a dream of "homomasculinity" — the voice is too grandiose to be touching. David Feinberg's kvetchy *Eighty-Sixed* is as funny and knowing as a *New York* magazine article, but is all about BJ's conventionally comic failure to find a boyfriend.[26] Bruce Benderson's *User* isn't so much an AIDS novel as a novel in which AIDS surrounds the down-and-out characters like the dirty New York air they breathe.[27] But happiness is hardly on their mind. (The characters are so down-and-out as to remind one of Campo's infected five-year-old.) Holleran's *Nights in Aruba* and *The Beauty of Men* are both *pentimenti* which see the past as full of illusions, and the present as full of nauseating regret.[28]

If we smile, then, at the naïveté of Andrew's memoir, perhaps we should consider that his attempt has not often been made.

DALE PECK'S *MARTIN AND JOHN*

In an interview with Tim Long, Dale Peck said that

> the only piece of criticism that ever bothered me about *Martin and John* was one line in one review when the reviewer said that I was anti-narrative. I thought that was the most wrong-headed thing you could say about the entire book, that the whole book was a way of reexamining one's relationship to narrative without ever rejecting it. In fact, I, for years, referred to myself as a slave to narrative, because I could see no way around it. As I said earlier, I see there's just one narrative, it's birth and death and the journey between, and it's a one-way, irrevocable journey. I've always wanted to subvert it, I've always wanted to say death is not inevitable, but, of course, death is inevitable, and, failing that, I've wanted to reexamine it from different ways.[29]

The line in the review is indeed "wrong-headed," though one understands what the reviewer meant to say: namely, that *Martin and John* frustrates our ordinary sense of narrative — as Peck himself concedes by saying that though there is "just one narrative" — "birth and death and the journey between" — he "always wanted to subvert it . . . to say death is not inevitable." In other words, by breaking up the expected narrative patterns, by allowing us to imagine multiple endings to the same life, he can in a sense undo the power of mortality. This is a sort of inversion of the eternizing conceit of some of Shakespeare's sonnets: you can't change the "one-way, irrevocable journey," but you can redefine the person who is on it so as to keep him eternally traveling.

In this quasi-novel (arguably a book of thematically connected short stories), Peck does indeed show himself a slave to narrative. A slave, indeed, to two kinds of narrative. In the most ordinary sense, *Martin and John* is crammed with *stories,* so many that one gets lost in them, can't connect them with a particular character, can't find them when one is looking for them. Peck has an astonishing generosity, especially by comparison with the rather stingy attitude of many contemporary novelists toward "plot." But *Martin and John* is enslaved in a second sense to the narrative of "birth and death and the journey between." Not only do various characters meet their deaths, but the book as a whole describes John's growth from infancy to adulthood and possibly death. It begins with a baby crying in his mother's arms and ends with a man taking AZT.

The story of John's life is told in snippets of italicized prose, individual vignettes that mark John's childhood, his abuse by his father, his leaving home, his love of Martin, Martin's death and perhaps his own. Interleaved with these (italicized) vignettes are longer stories which either comment on that life or invert it in some way. They are stories John has either remembered or made up, depending on how much you believe him. Some are openly fantastic, such as "Driftwood" (about a boy who suddenly appears in the narrator's barn, and as suddenly disappears) or "The Gilded Theater" (in which the narrator, a young man now, jumps from the penthouse of a tall apartment building and lands without a scratch). He claims at the end of the novel that, whether remembered or made up, they are stories he began telling himself as a child, to drown out the sounds of his parents fighting or fucking. They are also "created" in a different sense — because his dead lover Martin has urged him to write them down. One of the puzzles of the novel is deciding whether it matters if these stories are memories (autobiography), tales (fiction), or words by which the author brings the dead Martin back to life (magic).

These interleaved tales recapitulate in kaleidoscopic fashion the "one narrative" of life as it moves to death — "kaleidoscopic" because in them the same few shards of glittering glass are restlessly rearranged. The one still point, the peephole, is "John." That is, there *is* a "John" in every one of these stories, and he is always approximately the same person: waif, abusee, observer, masochist, innocent victim, complicit victim. It is this "John" who in the final long story "Fucking Martin" breaks the proscenium to be identified openly with "Dale" — presumably our author.

The narrative motion in *Martin and John* is as illusory as that of the arrow in Zeno's paradox, for in each new story (and each embedded substory) we have not only people with the same names endlessly repeated, but the same situations endlessly enacted. It's as though Peck — a virtuoso — has set himself the artistic challenge of using the smallest number of characters and motives to achieve the largest number of stories. (It is a bit like the single-subject Haydn piano sonatas which must create drama without contrast.)[30] Thus the same names — Martin, John, Henry (Harry), Bea, Susan, Johnson — keep recurring, only in different positions. Martin (though always the beloved/friend) is in "Driftwood" the mysterious barn-boy, in "The Gilded Theater" an obscenely rich older man who essentially "buys" John, and in "Three Watchmen" a young man of John's own age trapped with him in a grim job in a grim Kansan town. Henry is generally the abusive or domineering older man, as in "Driftwood" or "Someone Was Here," but sometimes the abuse is desired, as in "The Three Watchmen," where Henry is an older man who was John's "first lover," or the Henry in "Fucking Martin" who, not cruel himself, does John a favor by treating him to a weekend of desired sadism. Sometimes on the other hand the loved/hated user/abuser is *not* Henry: in one of the most touching of these stories, "Transformations," the narrator's *stepfather* is a kind man named Martin, who seduces John. Bea is the fourth of the major arcana. She is usually a mother figure (once a stepmother, but hardly a cruel one), usually abused in some way and the parent whom the boy most likes, though not the one he most loves. (One of the unexpected twists of *Martin and John* is that John plainly adores the tormenting older man, just as his fictional epigones will.) There are smaller figures who also recur. Susan is mentioned in the first story, "Blue Wet-Paint Columns," as John's first girl-friend/sexual partner. She reappears in the last story as a friend of the dead Martin who wants to have sex with John in order to get pregnant and thus "preserve" Martin in some sort of life. Even a virtually invisible figure — known only by his last name, Johnson — comes in at least three times (I may have missed some): as a rival in Henry's construction business in "Driftwood," a homophobic supervisor in "Three Watchmen," and a mugger in "The Gilded Theater." What we have, then, are recurring figures one would be tempted to capitalize and dignify by the name "archetype" if the word did not seem *deep,* and thus false to the nature of Peck's cool fiction. They could be enumerated as follows: Father, Mother, Son, Lover, Other Woman, and Male Enemy.

Events, too, have a family resemblance. John in "Given This and Everything" explains how his right hand came to be broken: his father in a rage deliberately crushed it with his foot. In "Tracks" (a later vignette) he meets a boy whose hand is also mangled, though by himself: "Red lumps deformed every knuckle, and at the center of each lump was a tiny brown scab; a few oozed pus. . . . They were self-inflicted. It was something I'd never thought before: that people might hurt themselves on purpose."[31] Even Dad's dog Major in "Driftwood" partakes of the same wound: one of his paws "had been ruined by one of my father's traps two years before" (36). (In Dale Peck's world, "men" — that is straight men —

have a bad track record with pets, children, and wives: they hate them, beat them, fuck them, kill them.) In two stories there is an odd detail of the narrator, an adolescent boy in both cases, lying in bed and lifting his legs up to put his feet on the floor, and seeing a desired, dangerous father-figure in the V of his legs: his real father in "Blue Wet-Paint Columns" and his stepfather/lover Martin in "Transformations." In "Always and Forever" Martin and John, lovers, are coming home from the opera and admiring flowers in a shop when they're attacked by three men. In "The Gilded Theater," Martin and John, lovers, coming home from a "Nuyorican performance" in the East Village, get lost and on a long subway ride home are attacked by five men. Twice, John has sex with a woman named Susan (who may or may not be the same person) out in the country in Kansas. Twice, John has rather dramatically abusive sex with an older man (once in "Lee," an italicized and therefore "real" vignette, and in "Fucking Martin," the final long story). In his love of symmetry, Peck is as elegant and insistent as Debussy.

And finally there are purely stylistic echoes and symmetries. In one story it appears that Justin, John's brother, has drowned while under John's care. Imagery of drowning both precedes and follows this story. In "The Beginning of the Ocean," a brief vignette, John, Mother, and Father are at the beach. John has been sleeping, then wants to get up, but he's held down by his father's arm so his father can continue to masturbate his wife without John's seeing: "*in that second I see my father's other hand low on my mother's abdomen, and I see that the bottom of her swimsuit is pushed down as well. . . . Then I fall asleep again, and this time the water does invade my dreams. I'm swimming, diving down, looking for the beginning of the ocean, but soon I realize I've gone too far.*" As the dream ends, John wakes up at the same moment that his father comes: "*just as I start squirming, my father's hand flies up and he groans loudly. . . . [Then] something comes to me from my dream, some half-human shape crawls out of the dark water, and I realize that my father has been drowning my mother as well*" (34–35).

Again, in "The End of the Ocean," John recapitulates this image: "*I turned in my chair and put my hand, my big clumsy hand, on his chest. Each finger took a rib like shipwrecked swimmers clutching at life rafts, but my thumb danced over his heart, alone, uncertain. And then I gave in and moved close. I rested my ear against his chest, encircled him with my arms, and lay like a swimmer who has at last reached the end of the ocean*" (142).

But the most pervasive, haunting repetitions are not so easily pinpointed. It is the narrative voice itself which is the greatest constant in this book. This voice can partly be identified with "John," but is not confinable to any one character. At the same time, it barely shifts register over the course of dozens of characters, dozens of ways to *be* John or Martin, Bea or Henry. It is not indeed the voice of a character, but the voice of a desolation whose origins are everywhere suggested and nowhere found: infusing into every character and event a mood of impotent desire and aimless regret.

Like Hemingway, whose style he "adores," the core of Peck's style and story is his sense of place; and the place he most remembers is the open prairie of Kansas, with its beautiful, terrifying sparseness, so devoid of human narrative.[32] (By contrast, New York, the setting of half of these stories, barely comes into focus.) One short passage will have to stand for many one could choose. In the first story, "Blue Wet-Paint Columns," John and his father move to Kansas from Long Island, having left John's mother in a nursing home after the onset of a devastating neurological disease that has left her paralyzed:

> Our town was tiny and there was nothing to see in it; inevitably, the prairie drew me. Nothing on Long Island had prepared me for the long wind-smoothed rolls of land which surrounded our new house. Tall brown grass covered everything. The grass had a dull side and a shiny side, and when the wind blew, the grass rippled and the sun flashed as though off glass, or water. Seeing that, I reached back and imagined the prairie as the sea it once was, and I imagined myself on the first island to raise itself about the water's surface. I stood there in mud fast drying under the sun. As I watched, all the water retreated under the land around me, and then for a time there was nothing except me and the naked wet soil, and we waited for the wind to carry the first seeds there, we waited for the grass to grow and cover us like a blanket. (19–20)

Here, in Peck's most immaculate, bleakest prose, is a Noah without wife or child or any other living thing.

Despite the difficulty of connecting the dots, the story of *Martin and John* can be told. It is about a gay kid from a violent midwestern family: father abusive, mother abused (maybe drunk), son guilty, smart, vengeful, and self-destructive. He moves eventually to New York (thrown out of the house by his father perhaps), where he becomes a hustler, a porn actor, the lover of Martin, and a writer. He is a masochist working off some ancient guilt. The lover dies of AIDS and John himself may be infected.

Much of what I have told is fully present in the first vignette "Here Is This Baby," though it is scarcely two pages long. This Tillie Olsen–like monologue introduces us to the three main characters of the novel and their three moral positions of innocence, guilt, and complicity. The narrator is a young mother, probably poor, probably uneducated (she says "it don't" and "he don't"). Her baby, John, has been crying all day, and she's at the end of her rope: "there isn't a woman I know can listen to her own baby cry for eight hours straight and not pick it up once in a while, and not get mad sometimes, and have to bite her lip to keep from yelling." In her desperation she calls her husband at work — a mistake, for Henry is a grim old-fashioned father who doesn't want to be bothered. We hear the anger in his voice: "*Bea, I told you not to bother me at work. Ain't nothing wrong with John. Ain't nothing wrong with* my son" (3). What is he angry at? Women? Marriage? His job? The heat? As the monologue ends, with the sound of a car door being angrily slammed, we know Henry has come home in even worse temper. Oddly enough, it is at this very moment that John stops crying: "*And I'm not saying that John heard this, and I'm not saying he understood it either, but I'll be damned if he's not shutting up at just the right time, lying in my arms with his eyes wide open and innocent like he hasn't done a thing, and don't he just know* who's *going to get it now?*" (4).

Here the story ends. What will happen? The father is furious and will (we guess) get into a fight with her, possibly hit her or John or both. Whom will he blame? "My son," about whom he is so defensively proud? Or his wife? His wife is both relieved — for she's gotten a response from Henry and silence from John — and afraid: did she call Henry for nothing? And what about John himself? He stops crying, it would seem, *because* he's heard his angry father's return. Henry's rage translates to John as joy. He longs for his father's return no matter what it means: blows, kisses, or a combination of the two. But one way or another, he will be responsible for whatever is about to happen.

This responsibility, this innocent guilt or guilty innocence, will remain at the core of John's personality over the course of this novel. In one sense, he is always the innocent, the naïf, the waif. In another, he is always the provocateur, the bad boy who needs and wants to be hurt because he has hurt, even killed, others. As he reminds himself when he's about to have sex with Susan in the final story, "Science says I have nothing to protect her from. But still" (218). He might kill her too, or kill the baby, if he does have AIDS. And the title "Fucking Martin" suggests that he may also have killed Martin with sex, just as the father in "Blue Wet-Paint Columns" has killed his wife by causing the miscarriage that leads eventually to her degenerative paralysis.

In *Martin and John* "responsibility" is not quite guilt; it can never be paid off. While it is operative in every story, every character, it is seen only out of the corner of the eye. What is it that Peck, as well as John, can't bear to look at, what guilt? (That he does, *or does not,* have AIDS?) One of the ancient Greek words for guilt, *aitia* — blame — is also a word meaning "cause" (as in *etiology*); and the conjunction of meanings may help us see that what Peck has most "left out" is causation. In John's world, quite as much as in Eddie Socket's, action is treacherous. In Peck's fiction, it is slightly vulgar to boot. Thus, John loves men who abuse him as he loves the father who stepped on his hand. But the former love does not exactly *cause* the later.

At one point in the final story, Peck (having stepped into the story himself) looks at what he's done and assesses it in a characteristically melodious but puzzling way. "The sum of life isn't experience, I realize, isn't something that can be captured with words. Inevitably, things have been left out. Perhaps they appear in others' stories. Perhaps they were here once and John's forgotten them. Perhaps some things he remembers didn't really occur. But none of that matters now. Even as Susan takes John inside her he knows that this baby means something, though I've fought against that; even Martin has become something abstract. A symbol, like the rose John once put in Martin's lapel, like Susan's African violet, like the fern in the shower. But after tonight, Martin's face will be inseparable from Susan's, from John's own, which is just a mask for mine. How can this story give Martin immortality when it can't even give him life?" (220).

Who is speaking these profoundly dejected words, to whom, and why? This passage, adroitly mixing fictional "I's" and inviting us to step back from the series of stories we've now read, brings Peck himself down to the footlights. A disillusioned Prospero, he now realizes that "experience . . . isn't something that can be captured with words" and seems to abjure his smooth magic. The passage is beautiful, like much of *Martin and John*, but slippery. Who ever thought that experience *was* something that could be literally caught in language? Are we willing to be fobbed off with "None of that matters now," a phrase which presumably means that something, perhaps the very need for an ending, is forcing a cause and an explanation on the reluctant author? The sexual act by which John and Susan will create new life *may* tend to "mean something" — to Peck's dismay — but why should it mean that the characters we have met will now become inseparable from each other and their creator? Finally, poignant as the last sentence is, how seriously can we take the author's rhetorical surprise that the present novel fails to confer not only immortality but even life on poor dead Martin? What if, remembering some of the vivid, actual "Martins" in this novel, we disagree? What if we agree, but weren't expecting "life" (in any common sense) in the first place?

Peck answers his own rhetorical question about the possibility of giving life to Martin with another, in an interesting passage which may tell us at least what his affective intentions are: "Now I wonder, has this story liberated anything but my tears? And is that enough? I want to ask. To which I can only answer, Isn't that enough? I thought I'd controlled everything so well, the plants, Martin, John, Susan. Even the semen. In this story, I'd intended semen to be the water of life. But, in order to live, I've only ever tasted mine" (220–21).

Tears, it appears, were his destination! But while sadness characterizes many of these stories, it seems odd to me that Peck thinks they would "liberate" tears, his or ours. (If it's sobbing one wants, a tear-jerker like *Valley of the Shadow* succeeds better.) Peck's sadness is so deep it has no specific cause or termination;

and I do not know who he is or what he wants of his reader. Indeed, "I don't know" is the subtext of every page of *Martin and John,* a book filled with tiny moments of joy, or more usually pain; moments which are so brief, so unconnected with *knowledge* that they have the silent sadness of old photographs.[33] The numb sad voice is the sepia, and the sepia is the story.

And what does it mean that he'd intended semen to be the water of life, but that he has only ever tasted his own? The passage is about more than an act of sexual intercourse between John and Susan; it is about the possibility of writing about desire in the age of AIDS. Semen is deadly both to the writer and to the man. "How can we sing the Lord's songs in a strange land?" lamented the Psalmist. Peck, like many belated gay novelists, wonders how to sing the sex song in a land where sex is death. It is a question that has passed through John's mind earlier (as it should, for he is a richly gifted pornographer). In "Always and Forever," after an AIDS funeral, he wonders whether his love affair with the rich, still-healthy Martin hasn't kept him from having a life: "Sometimes I think we have been betrayed by our safe lifestyles, and have missed a time of easy, base, pure love, the period of our greatest freedom" (159). But how do you follow the path back to that time of "easy, base, pure love" without betraying the present? How do you contemplate the gray grim present without wanting to beautify it out of recognition?

AIDS stories pose a terrible dilemma to the writer: in Andrew Holleran's honest words, "I really don't know who reads them for pleasure." Most fiction, even the grittiest, most naturalistic or grotesque, flatters the reader in some way, offering if only by implicit contrast a vision of a good life. What happens, then, when the reader cannot be flattered, cannot be pleased, even indirectly, as is the case in so many stories about AIDS? Not only the joy of living, but the joy of reading and writing seem oddly to have vanished.

Peck's solution has been to turn the problem itself—How can I be honest about AIDS without falling into a lie?—into the subject of his novel. Whether this is a profound "re-examination" of narrative (as Peck boasted in his interview), or merely a clever device, it is too early to say. But frankly, Peck's defense of "narrative," even if it is true, strikes me as beside the point. He is, to my mind, a mannerist writer whose greatest achievement so far is not narrative, but style. His style enables him to say certain things better than anyone, but also traps him into saying the same things over and over, and perhaps prohibits his saying more than a few things. (The first-person voice—the way sentences fit the writer like a glove—can become a treacherous echo chamber.) And despite Peck's comparatively harsh moral reference points (sexual abuse, for example), the language he uses seems rather as dreamy and unreal as that of lyric poetry. How often, as I read *Martin and John* (or rather drifted on its soft black waves), I thought of Tennyson's self-justification in the fifth poem of *In Memoriam:*

> But, for the unquiet heart and brain,
>   A use in measured language lies;
>   The sad mechanic exercise,
> Like dull narcotics, numbing pain.[34]

And in fact, *Martin and John* is exactly like Tennyson's obsessive, circling poem; constantly returning to the same loss in different forms.

It is Tennysonian, too, in its near-addiction to grief and the blurred edges of its "plot." Consider, for example, the last paragraph of the book: "*Everything tells me that if I want to survive I have to find a middle ground, a place where I can stand and not feel as if on one side a sea rages to consume me and on the other side a vast open prairie waits deceptively to engulf me in immense emptiness. I don't know what the place is I'm looking for, I only know what it's not, and it's not that, it's not all or nothing. It's something, but it's not that*" (228). This is a good example of Peck's gifts, with its virtuosic, almost frugal manipulation of the words *all, nothing,* and *something.* At the same time, how dodgy it is, both in its reference (what is it exactly about? what are the sea and prairie between which he wants to stand?) and in its affectional intentions (how are we to respond to this gorgeous music of resignation?). This passage has all the movement of a final statement, but there may be less to it than meets the ear. Is it grand or grandiose?

Another passage poses the question even more uncomfortably. At the end of "Transformations," a sad sexy story about John's seduction of (rape by?) his stepfather, the stepfather writes him many years later and John comments on the letter:

> "Dear John," he wrote. "Do you remember our time together?" Sometimes I don't know what I remember, what's real and what's been transformed with time. "I've never forgotten you or your mother, but I had to leave for my sake, and yours and your mother's." All he ever wanted was both of us, and of course he could have neither in the end. That's like Martin, like his tears, his touches, his other empty words. You can have your dreams, he'd said in the kitchen, of how life should be and what your ideal lover should look like and how your first time should go, but he knew — and I do too, now — that you'll never get it, or never be able to hold on to it if you do. Not in this life, he'd told me: only when you're dead. (81)

This passage is so beautiful, so musical, that one wants to believe it. And yet I found upon rereading it, reading it with an appetite for dissonance, that it let me down. If we knew more about the person speaking these bathetic and exaggerated words, we'd perhaps be able to excuse or understand them. But we do not.

And in any case, the language here is quite indistinguishable from that of any other "John" in any other story; or indeed from the final lines of "Fucking Martin" spoken (it would seem) by Dale Peck himself. Consequently, the plangent tones, so muted, so sad, came to seem at least partly fraudulent. "You'll never get it, or never be able to hold on to it if you do" — these are the words of a spoiled adolescent, not a writer as intelligent and emotionally austere as Peck. Are we meant to pick up on their fraudulence, ironize them, or simply ignore them? Or (more direly) are we expected to find them "true"?

Where in AIDS fiction does *Martin and John* fit? While the plague can be said to dominate the second half of the novel, it is really (to Peck's mind) part of a huger canvas of sorrow and loss beginning with, and inseparable from, the story of betrayal, hunger, and love in the very first story, "Here Is This Baby." AIDS adds nothing but a modern, perhaps a personal reference. In this respect, *Martin and John* reminds me of Michael Cunningham's *Home at the End of the World,* another ravishingly written novel in which AIDS is merely a particularly awful instance of futility. But to call either an "AIDS novel" *tout court* seems to me a mistake. *Martin and John* is a novel of death: of the "one-way, irrevocable journey" on which we have all already set our first and fatal footsteps.

[PART FIVE]

LOOKING BACK

Chapter Eight

BOY'S LIFE:

NEIL BARTLETT'S *READY TO CATCH*

HIM SHOULD HE FALL

The boy lives in "the incompletion of desires" both longing for the fulfilment of simple lust and longing for that fulfilment to have meaning. He goes on the long random walks of adolescence looking for a someone, the ideal who is also on such a long searching walk, whose random wandering may suddenly intersect one's own, and whose needs would respond to one's own needs.

Thom Gunn, "Homosexuality in Robert Duncan's Poetry"[1]

If Dale Peck's *Martin and John* is a minimalist novel, Neil Bartlett's *Ready to Catch Him Should He Fall* (1990), is a maximalist one. It is big-gestured, big-hearted, and (I am tempted to say) big-dicked: a book that revels in pleasures and is easy to love.

It is also the only British novel I have included in my canon. (Isherwood's *A Single Man* is of course set in California — as was Isherwood.) A more respectable choice might have been Alan Hollinghurst's *The Swimming-Pool Library* (1988), an elegant fantasia on themes of exploitation, colonialism, and the last gasps of sexual libertinism before the age of AIDS. Unlike most critics, however, I have been unable to love *The Swimming-Pool Library*. It is of course immaculately written, and clever in the dual perspectives that invite us to compare the behavior of the young dandy Will Beckwith and that of his older gay counterpart, Lord Nantwich, sixty years earlier. But it seems a safe book, one that (despite its occasional hot sex scenes) is emotionally constrained. My favorite scene in it is the one in which Will is waiting in his friend James's flat for James to return. Like any good immoralist, he immediately goes through James's drawers, finding dirty magazines: "The Third World Press specialised in blacks with more or less enormous cocks, and in leaden titles like *Black Velvet, Black Rod* or even *Black Male*." As he leafs through them, Will thinks, with his aristocrat's disdain for the middle-class James, that "the fact that even in his own home he kept them neatly hidden away . . . showed I suppose the secret and illicit power they still had for him." (Class is *much* more interesting than "enormous cocks.") Bored, he sits down with James's diaries: "James's diaries were always a good read and at Oxford I had made no pretence of not knowing what was in them." What made me laugh out loud (in recognition, I must admit) was the way Will not only read the diaries but did so *looking for references to himself*: "Will adorable," "W. looked fabulous."[2] Here, as in few other parts of this brilliantly accomplished novel, I heard and relished Will's hugely self-satisfied voice. I didn't hear it often enough. Perhaps because Hollinghurst chose a narrator who was only *slightly* shallow, the novel came to seem heartless in the wrong way: not truly heartless as Wilde, Vidal, and Boyd McDonald are, just narcissistic. I never felt really permitted to *loathe* Will, as I'm sure I should have.

In any case, *Ready to Catch Him Should He Fall,* a far less guarded, an unabashedly romantic, even sentimental book, moved me more. It is the novel I would now give to any reader, gay or straight, who wanted to know what gay life since the Second World War was like. It evokes many dead or dying worlds, especially that of the bars which were our first refuge and rallying point, but also the first glimmerings of gay liberation, of disco, of AIDS. In part a defense of the gay traditions of theater, promiscuity, and sexual worship, it is not, however, merely nostalgic. Indeed, the note it strikes with repeated success is that of survival and hope—a note, however, which rings true precisely because it is enunciated in the voice of someone excluded from the bright gay future, an older, solitary gay man. The narrator of *Dancer from the Dance* saw that, even at the end of his career, Malone's face could shine with "radiant exhilaration": "It was his joy that there were men who loved other men." So too, despite his own exclusion, Bartlett's narrator finds himself proclaiming the dazzling possibility that a man might "choose another man, or men."[3] Indeed the novel is about such a choice, treating it in luxuriant, voyeuristic detail.

It is our greatest novel of requited love. What's so great about that? the contemporary reader might ask: surely *we* know (even if this dreary old queen doesn't) that a man can "choose another man, or men"? Yes: but do we know, even yet, what that choice means? Just as *Dancer* imagines not just what coming out means, but staying out; just as Purdy's *Narrow Rooms* imagines what "love" might include; so *Ready to Catch Him* is a disciplined reverie about what it might mean to declare yourself gay, to love a man, not a woman, to be fatherless and yet a "son," to combine fidelity and promiscuity in even the deepest union. In so doing, *Ready to Catch Him* performs one of the essential tasks of fiction by helping us imagine the task of love between men. It shows why choosing homosexuality might not be easy, even now; and why it might entail suffering, ingenuity, and disguise.

The book, like *Dancer,* both tells a tale and frames the telling. Consequently, we can't be sure what or how much has been made up; and even more than in *Dancer,* we don't know whether the main character is Boy, or the older narrator who so raptly remembers — or invents — him. Nor do we know at first who his listener is, though he seems to be a younger gay man who ignorantly believes those old days were simply self-oppressive. He eventually turns out to be a "boy" himself, a young man in bed with the narrator, to whom this improbably long *récit* has been told. The whole novel, then, is pillow talk — with the seriousness, tenderness, and loneliness of such postcoital confidences.

While the world represented by the older narrator and the Bar may be dead — for the Bar has closed its doors by the end of the book — he does not crow over that death. Life is indeed better for gay men now than it was in the fifties (which the narrator seems to remember), but that does not mean gay life was only, or even primarily, terrible before. And indeed, nothing in Bartlett's world is ever quite dead. Like the tales of Isak Dinesen, *Ready to Catch Him* takes place both *in illo tempore,* once upon a time, and in various particular times, ranging from Oscar Wilde's London to the fifties to the present; and it evokes from all of them a peculiar, haunting sense of recognition. In one of its boldest moves, it celebrates Boy's wedding night by imagining him and his lover O literally surrounded by the ghosts of gay men from three centuries: *revenants* come back to watch over what has become possible only in our own time, the physical and spiritual marriage of two men.

One of Bartlett's assumptions is that the history of gay life cannot be told only from the pitying perspective of more enlightened days as a story of mere victimization — as though gay men never fought back or as if they totally regretted their sexual fate. Even in those bad old days, he claims, the Bar was less a place of misery than of ingenious transformations of misery — transformations so witty, beautiful, and sexy as to deserve the name of art. In this praise of gay men's ingenuity in transforming their circumstances, *Ready to Catch Him* reminds one of Tennessee Williams's "Hard Candy" and the old and ugly Mr. Krupper's hopeful journeys to the Joy Rio. Surely there was nothing very remarkable about the Joy Rio or about Mr. Krupper, Williams says poker-faced, but then he slily adds: "To notice something you would have to be looking for something."[4] And that is Bartlett's claim too. Indeed, to look properly is to see that the boundaries we draw between realism and romance, between lust and love, are interpenetrable; for as he says, "just look round any bar and you'll see that everybody there, myself included (you too if it's your kind of bar), has in their time been both The Boy and the Older Man, both Banker and Domestic, Ingenue and Other Woman, booted Prince and stirrup-holding Groom."

Thus, although the narrator is a man whose life has not been nearly as happy as that of the younger couple whose story he tells, he does not repine. Indeed, Boy and O's story (imaginary or true) becomes a version of his story, and an instantiation of all its moments of fleeting happiness. Boy and O are *good* reasons to be gay. In a surprising outburst, he cries: "There are such men in this city, and even to see them, never mind to touch them or have them kiss you, or see them just before dawn, or to have them as one of your dear friends, is one of the great pleasures of our life, and it is commoner than most people think. In the part of town where I live I see strangers who I would call truly beautiful at least once a day" (15).

"There are such men . . ." reminds me, in its enthusiasm, of the line in *Dancer* about Malone's long-delayed erotic awakening: "The long years of dutiful behavior fell away." Here, too, tears come to my eyes as I think of what he is saying. That "part of town" is the gay ghetto, the streets and friendships of my own life. And the beauty of Boy, like the possibility of love, is *not* just confined to the stage or sound-set, but has a place in my world, too.

Ready to Catch Him Should He Fall is divided into three parts: "Single," "Couple," "Family." In the first, we trace Boy's coming out, especially his enormous need for sex. (Even in overt coming-out novels how easily this need is passed over as if trivial or vaguely unpleasant!) In it, we are also introduced to "Mother," the owner of the Bar, and to the handsome "O," who will become Boy's lover. The second part is both the most unnecessary and the most beautiful. It depicts in loving, perverse detail Boy's initiation into homosexual manhood. It is unnecessary in the sense that it has only one event, and that long foreseen: the marriage of Boy to O. But in order that this marriage be more than a "dumb and dark ceremony," in the words of the Prayer Book which Bartlett quotes at the beginning of this section, Boy must gradually be brought to a full consciousness of the burden and glory of loving another man. As Bartlett said in a talk at the University of Sussex in 1995, "Something I very rarely hear talked about but which I think is very true and a truth of great influence, is that whether your body is habitually one which penetrates or which is habitually penetrated must make a difference to the way you perceive your body and therefore describe your body. Even worse, to be someone who can choose to do either, on different occasions and for different reasons, that is a terrible and joyous burden to bear."[5] For Bartlett this "terrible and joyous burden" is what it means to be specifically gay; and his purpose in this section is to understand and dramatize the stages of a gay man's self-development, his facing of shames and reluctances within, of hostility and violence from without. The third section, by far the most problematic, attempts that most difficult of tales: "happily ever after." Not only does Bartlett take us past the wedding night of Boy and O into the unromantic realm of domesticity, but he burdens the new couple with a dying man called "Father," whom Boy tends almost neurotically until his death.

When the story of Boy begins, its hero has made his way to a metropolis (London — though the city is never named). He has no past: for it is unimportant where he came from; what counts is where he is now. All that we need to know of him is that he is nineteen and handsome and desperate to be with men. "Boy was like that, he was hoping that somebody would take him to the place where everybody else was" (18–19). He is hungry and thirsty and "at the point of exhaustion," when he finds himself in front of a small black door: "Over the doorway was a small plaque. It said, *In this house* (and the ceramic of the plaque had broken and the name was missing) *stayed on his first visit to the city, and it was here that he wrote the opening pages of his greatest work.* There was no name painted up over the door. . . . The door was shut, locked in fact. Boy could see the scuff marks around the doorhandle where other men (Boy knew it couldn't be *people,* he just knew it was *men*) had opened and closed it. On the black paint of the door was chalked a message: *eleven o'clock.* The street was empty. Boy had an erection. He promised himself that he would come back later no matter how tired he was" (21, 23).

Bartlett has deliberately made the details of Boy's hero-journey vague, for the story he wants to tell is a symbolic one. He knows the door he has found is the gateway to an unborn part of him that is sexual. Symbolic without being ethereal, however. Indeed, the door and the bar it leads to couldn't be more down-to-earth. We too have seen those handsome oval plaques on London houses commemorating the astonishing achievements of so many writers, scientists, and explorers. And as anyone would, Boy gets a very unsymbolic erection at the mere thought that *men* have been behind that door.

In keeping with Bartlett's desire to make the scene real but not too real, the name of the great writer has been effaced. Even so, especially in this work about the persistence of the past in the present, how appropriate that the *genius loci* of the Bar should *be* a writer; for behind its black door the most enchanting yet empowering illusions are nightly "written" and acted out. These illusions are the drag shows, torch songs, and *tableaux vivants* we will later see, but also the unwritable, evanescent text of cruising and promiscuous love. All are images of a fully sexual and humane life for men who love "another man, or men" — images which eventually create what they first only imagined.

In those days, says the narrator, "if somebody arranged to meet you for a date there, and it was their first time and they weren't sure how to find us, you'd joke with them, and you'd say well first there is a wedding, and then there's a death, and there's the news, and then there's us; meaning, first there's the shop with the flowers, the real ones, and next door to that is the undertaker's with the fake flowers in the window, china, all dusty; and then the newsagent's and magazine shop, and then right next door to that is The Bar. You can't miss it" (16–17). Like the rest of Bartlett's scene-setting, the joke is both realistic in its teasing queen-talk and symbolic in its placement of "The Bar"—gay desire itself—within the context of marriage, death, and politics. But sex is the point, the goal. Even "the news" is sexual to Boy; for in its window he sees a "single magazine whose cover displayed a naked man instead of a naked woman or a smiling mother" (20). It is not the nakedness alone that matters to Boy, but the *fact* of pornography. And indeed Bartlett has said that for him, too, pornography was the gateway to a conscious gay life: "for me and most of my friends and gay colleagues you read about doing dirty things or see pictures accompanied by text of dirty things before you do them."[6]

Boy imagines buying this magazine, imagines opening it "perhaps in the privacy of his room or perhaps right there on the street at five o'clock." He imagines what he might find in the magazine: "cheaply staged pictures of sexual tortures," "a full-page black and white photo of two barechested men . . . photographed in daylight, walking down the street," "men photographed in colour . . . doing extraordinary things but in ordinary rooms," and "personal messages." Even here, in the realm of sexual fantasy, it is the real which Bartlett eroticizes: "Boy imagined sleeping with these men, actually sleeping, sharing a bed with them for the night. And then Boy could imagine having a cup of coffee with them in the morning, but he couldn't imagine anything else after that." But Bartlett's book, like the pornographic magazine Boy sees, does not draw a firm line between the imaginary and the real, and sees imagination as leading to experiments in pleasure—art, pornography—which effectively create a new reality. The men engaged in "sexual tortures," who do "extraordinary things in ordinary rooms," will prove to be the very same men who are "photographed in daylight, walking down the street" (20). But Boy must learn to make the fantasy real, to imagine what comes after "sharing a bed" or "having a cup of coffee."

The Bar which Boy stands outside of and vows to return to is, seen from the inside (the narrator's vantage), an old-fashioned place populated by old-fashioned gay men: "Ron Ackroyd; Terry and Bobby (and Bobby's Mother); Awful Hugh Hapsley; Teddy, Tiny, Leaf, Minty, Winter; Madge, also known as The Troll; Miss Public House; and, of course, Mr Mortimer." Not only do the men have campy nicknames, they still talk a camp talk which even the narrator knows to be archaic: "And there was the way of talking, as well. Stella again: 'Good evening, Sean. Remember what I told you; the first lesson's free'" (24). The narrator who is telling this story is aware that the younger man hearing it may not understand or approve of such language or such men: "People criticise this style and say it's all a lie, they take one quick look in through the door and they say that we are all acting madly to conceal some great sadness from ourselves. All I can say is, I think they must never have spent a night in The Bar if they think that, or never a good night. I want to say to them, when they talk like that, *well, where do you go in the evenings?* Playing like we played wasn't lying at all, it was nothing to do with lying. What did you expect us to do? Sit around and be depressed?" (26).

Within this wonderful queenly exasperation is contained an implicit defense of art, and an observance of the Wildean distinction between unimaginative "misrepresentation" and full-blooded "lying." Wilde, the narrator, and Bartlett are all apologists for *play,* a word whose many meanings (childish, theatrical, and sexual) the novel exemplifies. The "play" of art is a way to show things without explaining them (and to be forced to "explain" is the fate of the weak and oppressed). Even younger gay men like the supposed listener can become oppressors: "giving an account of it like this makes me feel as though you're asking me to account for it, explain it for you. Explain our lives there — as if they needed explaining, and the whole point was that when you walked in the door of The Bar you knew you didn't have to explain anything to anyone who was there, not anyone" (23). Here the narrator puts his finger on the peculiar nature of our oppression and self-oppression: having constantly to *explain,* to justify one's sexual desires. This compelled justification is related to sexual shame: both are forms of intense and painful self-awareness. Play will be the antidote to shame — not because it ignores self-awareness, especially sexual, but because it changes that awareness from being painful to being pleasurable.

Like Malone, Boy has a great smile, full of "a welcome and a promise." He is someone capable of, oriented toward, delight. And he spends his first weeks in The Bar exploring that capacity. He goes home every night with one of the bar's regulars, as though it were a job. (But isn't it? Don't we have to teach ourselves about these things?) He is "still amazed and fascinated by the fact of two men being together at all" (37). He goes home almost always with older men, men who have something to teach him. For this reason he doesn't mind being called "Boy," either: "He loved to be called Boy. He smiled whenever the name was used. He loved it that we had christened him and he knew that he was special to us" (13).

Boy's education is an education in sex, of course; but sex conceived as *service.* This fact may seem as archaic as the Bar itself to contemporary readers — though it wouldn't to James Purdy. What is it these older men teach him? On one level sexual technique, but on another acceptance of sexual need. Though Boy's sexual acts are never described in detail, we know that by the end of his education Boy will have experienced everything a man can do to another man. When one of the older queens, Miss Public House, tells him not to get forced into anything he doesn't want to do, "Boy honestly could not imagine anything he would not want to do with a man" (35). By not blinking Boy's promiscuity and perversity, Bartlett pronounces a refreshing literary judgment on books that do. The narrator speaks for him when he says, "And I will say that myself I was very promiscuous sexually, I will say that because I think a lot of people want to leave that out of the story, well not me thank you very much" (24). In this tart sentence perish half the gay novels of the last ten years.

But Boy's real education goes beyond sex. It is an education in *being with men*. In an almost painfully honest sentence, Bartlett writes "Boy thought all the time about men being together" (121). It is this which gay men have to learn, this for which we have no mental picture and which yet holds the key to our future. Even with his roommate, with whom he doesn't have sex, Boy is fascinated to watch him. "Of course Boy had seen inside a lot of men's houses, but this was the first man's life he had ever watched at such close quarters, the first time he had ever seen a man taking care of himself, the first time he had ever seen another man living day after day after day" (44). When he goes home with a couple, it isn't only to discover how two men make love with a third, but how they talk in the morning over coffee. If he goes to a smart dinner party, he is learning not just how to hold a knife and fork, but how men, gay men, talk to each other.

This story, how Boy learned to be with a man, is new. We've seen older men longing to have sex with a boy: Mr. Krupper, for instance. Williams also showed us a very knowing boy (Clove) seducing an older man (in "The Killer Chicken and the Closet Queen"). We've seen two boys trying to "be with each other" in every form from David and Giovanni to Dennis Cooper's waifs. We've seen a sort of rough male democracy in the circle of nonsexual friends described by Mordden. We've seen the neutered "marriages" of David Leavitt's good boys. But the desire of a beginner for guidance, of youth for erotic experience, has not been told. In Edmund White's novels of betrayal and abandonment, the younger man is filled with so much ambivalent love toward the older that he must destroy him or leave him. White's characters in fact never *do* learn "how to be with men." They fearfully desire men without ever loving them.

Boy's chief characteristic besides physical beauty is his capacity for wonder; imagination is his gift as hope was Malone's. After he starts going to The Bar, he moves in with a man, from whose flat he looks out at the mysterious city spread out beneath him. With photocopies of maps of that city from earlier times, he tries to locate The Bar on them (as if to say: where were gay men, where would *I* have been in those days?).[7] He also has a collection of letters that he has apparently found, letters from gay men who sign them (as did Holleran's correspondents) with the names of famous courtesans, celebrities, or queens. He has photos of handsome men scrawled with (fake?) signatures of Wilde and Reginald Turner across them. He has also scraps of paper, which in their incompleteness speak poignantly of loss: "*Darling, it's going to be alright, really it's going to be alright*" (54). Boy spreads these scraps of former gay lives around his bed like a card-reader, trying to combine them into a meaningful tale. Finally, he has letters that seem to be his own: letters addressed to him signed only "Father." These are the scattered leaves from which he is trying to construct his identity.

The Bar is an all-male world with one important exception, Madame, its owner. She is a woman of indeterminate age, but well over forty. A woman, it would seem, *of* the forties as well, in her severe white makeup and sharply etched "*Rogue Extrême*" lipstick. Paradoxically, it is this hyperbolically feminine woman who provides the framework within which men discover other men. Madame lives above The Bar with her twelve copies of her good black dress, her Waterford crystal glasses for neat gin, and her shelves of books on famous successful women: courtesans, abbesses, wives. She wears many rings: on the right hand eighteenth-century cameos, on the left, a diamond: "very big and very real: Madame believed in money." In a marvelously perverse scene later on, Boy sees those rings dripping with O's semen.

Every night, clad in her black dress, Madame ascends the six steps of the Bar's small stage to Gary's piano accompaniment, where she sings an old-fashioned torch song, "All of Me": "Why not take all of me?" It is her theme song, and the theme of the bar—as "Make Me Believe in You," sung in Patti Jo's "metallic, unreal voice" was for Malone and Sutherland. When you heard Madame sing it, you thought, "This woman knows what she is singing about." Like everyone else in The Bar, she has less a personal history than a role: her history *is* that role, perfected but never fundamentally changed—like her black dress. She is "Madame" or "Mother," and her life is about surviving in the teeth of opposition and on the resources of cunning and art. The fact that Madame is a woman enables her to enact the necessary role of victor for these beaten men. If *she* can do it, so can they. (And unlike Maupin's kindly Mrs. Madrigal, another mother figure, Madame is ruthless, capable of rage and lust. She is thus a much more complete role model for gay men.)

It is fitting that when Boy finally meets O (for "Older Man"), who is to become his true love, their courtship should be conducted semitheatrically. During their first weeks of love, for instance, they are as thoroughly scrutinized by The Bar as any actors: when they come in together after a week's absence, and Boy is showing bruises on his arm and rope burns on his wrists, everyone is aware of it. So is he. And in the perfectly serious initiatory scenes that come in Part 2, Boy enacts—always to an audience—every possible relationship with men. The narrator fears the boy he's telling this story to will laugh and defensively tells his listener (our stand-in): "You, of course, living in a rather different time or in different countries, will find all this hard to credit now, everything they went through, it all seems so elaborate, but anyway you get the point which is that O only had Boy's best interest at heart when he was training him like this.

I've always loved those adverts that say, *strict tuition given*" (202–3). Bartlett, too, must have feared and overcome this fear. To enact seems so . . . childish. But the "strict tuition" of art is older than that of psychoanalysis or politics. It instructs us in the necessity of speaking the truth to another person, speaking it out loud, sounding it for its depth of pain and shame.

This is what Boy's initiation — "Couple," the second section of the novel — is all about.

This section, though strictly unnecessary from a plot point of view, shows Bartlett at his best — as a contriver of erotic ritual. In the first enactment, for instance, Boy is forced to play the part of a disgraced daughter from a Victorian melodrama who is pleading with her father (played by O). Bartlett, himself an actor and inventor of melodramas, provides a resonant text for them to speak: O, as the father, begins "in a voice thickened by rage": "You are very hard-hearted, my dear." Boy, kneeling at his feet, returns: "I cannot ask you to understand, and I will not ask you to forgive me. My behaviour has indeed been perfectly disgraceful, but believe me, it has not hardened my heart. . . . Since nothing I do or say can shock you further, I will end this interview by asking you to lend me money. . . . I need sixty-eight pounds to get to Paris, and I need it tonight" (161). After rehearsing this scene for Mother, Boy is smiling "because he had at last and so clearly and with such force said what he had wanted and waited so long to say" (163).

What is it he had wanted to say except that he is gay, and that he loves O, will run away from home to be with him, will risk disgrace? Mother, watching this charade, is impressed. "But splendid as it is, it is not enough. . . . Boy, I want you to go back upstairs now and to take off the dress and the wig, and to come back down here dressed as a man. . . . Nothing else will need changing, except . . . except that, of course, O, your first line will of course now read, 'you are very hardhearted, *sir*' " (163). In other words, Boy will now enact the role closer to his own situation, will avow his disgrace to his father *as a son*. His "disgrace" is never named, but it doesn't need to be. We know, and Boy knows, what it is: the disgrace of being gay, of desiring another man. When we add to that the perversity of declaring his desire not just to a "father" but to an actual lover, and doing it before an audience, the harvest of shame is rich indeed.

Even after Boy and O have successfully performed this melodrama of shame and defiance, Bartlett does not relinquish his rituals. In a thrillingly porno-graphic sequence of scenes, he continues Boy's "initiation" by transforming a heterosexual marriage ritual, the "robing of the bride," into a gay initiation. The bride, of course, is Boy. For Boy to be properly "married" to O, indeed for him to become a complete gay man, he must undergo further tests. These tests involve his assuming the roles of other despised creatures.

One of the roles he must play, for instance, is that of a sexually ashamed schoolboy, with O as his sadistic teacher/interrogator. The interview consists of explicitly sexual questions, questions "that would have mortified Boy at fourteen; at nineteen, they made him realise how little he still knew, how easily he still blushed, how hard he found it to look in a man's eyes, how he still didn't have a way of talking about these things" (191). The "despised" person he enacts here is himself at an earlier age. In another, he has to dress as a "small town queen." "This time they smoked Marlboro and drank milky instant coffee; Stella [a queen from The Bar] had the television on all evening too. She put cushions covered in green dralon with cat hairs on them on the sofa, and put a copy of *Dance with a Stranger* on the coffee table" (192). This despised person is everything Boy is not: self-hating, weak, resigned to failure, closeted.

In a final charade, Boy must learn to dress, speak, and move like a woman — to smile and ask no questions; and is taken out to a straight dinner club with O. Before they go out, however, Stella concludes her instruction with an unexpectedly violent speech: "Stella sent O out of the room and closed the door, and then very quietly, and with great bitterness, and at great length, she described being on a night bus with a friend and seeing a man pull out a screwdriver and use it like a knife, bringing it down and pushing it in for no apparent reason, just with pure crude hatred, saying, while he did so, *you cunt, you cunt*. Then she filled her lungs with a single deep, sudden breath and in that one breath she called Boy all the names she herself had ever been called, beginning *you cunt, you bitch, you stupid fucking bitch, you stupid queen, do you know what I would like to do to you, you stupid fucking queen?* She repeated all the foulest and most humiliating insults that men and women had ever thrown at her. When this was done Stella was white faced and exhausted. She said, *I've taught you everything I know*" (198). If being gay means, in part, being a woman, then this too is a role Boy must learn to play.

In order to discover your perfect role you must recognize other, less glamorous ones. There is nothing whimsical or cute about these charades, which is the difference between them and the theater scenes in *Nocturnes for the King of Naples*. Love between men, Bartlett seems to say, is inherently unstable, violent, fraught with shame. One ignores the instability at one's peril. To survive, Boy must learn to face facts, which means acknowledging the despised parts of himself. Those despised parts are both personal and historical. It is as though Boy must undergo *in propria persona* the growth of the entire gay community. His ontogeny recapitulates gay phylogeny.

By experiencing the shaming power of earlier archetypes — sinful daughter, impure schoolboy, "tragic" homosexual, beautiful woman, drag queen — the gay man stands a chance of happiness. Gay culture is more than a story of victimhood. We have the power, Bartlett always insists, of changing the story not by evading history but by finding ourselves in it. Hence the importance for him, as for many gay men, of myths and fantasy, which have given many of us our first glimpse of ourselves.

O, for example, talks in his sleep. One night, he describes the place he and Boy will live. This is perfect in its indirectness. His inability to say "I love you" except in analogy — the analogy of lovemaking or dream — makes his speech the more truthful. Here, he expresses his adoration for Boy by means of a vision of a Great Good Place for men like themselves:

I'm going to do up this apartment. I'm going to sand the floor twice and bleach it and seal it. In the centre of the floor I shall have painted a copy of the mosaic panel from Hadrian's villa at Tivoli representing the Ascent of Ganymede, all properly done in the correct seven coloured marbles, and lapis for his eyes. I'll fix the bedroom window. The dado will be of seven different woods; and on the top of the dado will be a gilt rail, and on the rail will be perched a life-sized and perfectly realistic lion marmoset carved in white cherry wood; clutched in his left paw will be two stolen cherries carved in red mahogany; between his teeth of stained ivory the marmoset will be carrying a grape carved in ebony. Press this, and the staff will be summoned by a hidden electric bell. Above the dado I shall cover the walls with hammered and lacquered Spanish leather, and in the centre of each wall hang a grisaille panel depicting scenes from the lives of great men: Antinous drowned and perfect at the age of nineteen (I will commission the artist to make Antinous's body a copy of yours, and no one will know this but me); Will Hughes playing the gilded boy mentioned by Piers Gaveston in Marlowe's Edward the Second; *Rimbaud in the house of glass which he built in Addis Ababa; Federico Garcia Lorca on his first night in New York; Robbie Ross lifting his hat to the passing prisoner in the corridor of the Old Bailey. Pendant to each of these scenes will be a naked male figure representing each of the seven virtues: Charity, Promiscuity, Generosity, Dignity, Honesty, Beauty and Courage.* (145; italics Bartlett's)

Like the charades of the Robing of the Bride, these are not mere fancies, but the indirect, complicated visions of art. O is expressing his love for Boy, his hopes for a future, by means of this dream. There is nothing amusing or whimsical about the scene or the imagined room, on which Bartlett has lavished every resource of a historian's memory and a mythographer's imagination. The language is so beautiful and the reference so exact that we may at first be surprised to hear them in the mouth of O, a man of presumably working-class background (he works at a video store, never mentions an education). How does he know about Hadrian's villa or Aretino's engravings? But, as in so many of this book's richest details, the question is irrelevant. Bartlett is not interested in the likelihood of O's saying these things — indeed the point is that, educated or not, he *couldn't* say them directly, for they are too revealing, too shaming for speech. The gay man, perhaps any man, invents an indirect language for his passion because he must. What Bartlett is doing is building an adequate language for speaking of eros between men — a "joining," in Robert Duncan's phrase, which is "not easy."[8]

The joining of Boy and O, at any rate, is "not easy." It is a complex mixture of shame and shamelessness: for in no way does this book betray gay passion by neutering it, by making it (in the words of a grimly uplifting seventies film) "a very natural thing." Perhaps all human sexuality is tainted by such self-consciousness, but certainly homosexuality is: our history has been a series of battles with and for unnaturalness. We do not have the option afforded most heterosexuals of thinking that what we do in bed is merely natural, or in accord with some cosmic plan of the universe. It can't be made pretty, though it can be made beautiful; and (as Bartlett, like Purdy, believes) it can be, perhaps must be, violent or shaming.

One of the most arousing scenes in this section isn't even homosexual. In this scene the narrator imagines Boy climbing the staircase to Mother's sanctum. There he sees O, stripped naked and sitting on a chair. Mother, fully clothed, is behind him. They are watching themselves in a mirror. As Boy looks on, Mother masturbates O to orgasm. "Boy is not horrified to see this but fascinated." "O slowly arches back in the chair, and then he comes and his come splashes over Mother's hand and flows down over her rings. . . . Now Boy sees Mother slowly looking up from her task; as she looks up her hair is pulled out of O's mouth and away from his face, and in fact both of them are now looking at Boy standing there in the mirror; from the way they look it seems that both of them knew all along that he was watching" (182). Everything in this scene is about pollution, from the transgression (in gay male terms) of O's sex with a woman, to O's and Madame's self-display, to the incest implied in Mother's name, to the semen gathering on her rings. *Ready to Catch Him* is a novel that dares to praise such pollutions as necessary and therefore beautiful. They are seen not as naughtinesses, on the one hand, nor as mere mechanical fetishes; but as visions of the shame-drenched life which, acknowledged, becomes shame-free, or (perhaps more accurately) shame-rich. Adult love, he is saying, must be able to be unclean.

So too, even on their wedding night, "O gave his boy a real hard time. He gave him real dirt. He talked real dirty to him. He didn't touch him too much at first. He made him bend over and spread his buttocks with both hands. He made him display the marks on his back, display his armpits, the soles of his feet and the roots of his hair; as if Boy was an animal and O was deciding whether to buy that animal or not. O made Boy pull back his eyelids, his lips and his foreskin . . ." (215). But "when all that, the violence, was over," they make love "with a tender concentration and a complete lack of fear" (217). It has been to achieve this "lack of fear" that all the initiatory rites have been performed. It was done in order to break through the male armor which is at once so beautiful and so imprisoning, the armor of self-sufficiency, stoicism, hardness of heart, embarrassment.

Break through it, but not, perhaps, ever destroy it. For, as Bartlett has seen, sex — perhaps gay sex especially — is full of unavoidable shame. He has a wonderful passage, for instance, on being fucked: "Boy began to think that there are two kinds of sex: the kind of sex where you say *do this, do that,* or you man-oeuvre yourself into position for a particular kind of pleasure; and then there is the other kind of sex, where you want to say, *do anything. Do anything you want to me, you can do anything you want, I give you entire permission over me.* This feeling and especially these words cannot actually be spoken, because the words are too shaming; but for the men I know and for myself certainly I know that it usually comes out as *fuck me, please fuck me* . . . This is all so hard to tell someone, so you try to do it with your body. When you see a man bury his face in his pillow, he is doing it to avoid saying all this; to escape from the words he hears himself wanting to say, to silence himself, because he knows that your face is just six inches from his but still he cannot look at you or say what he means" (108–9). Pornography is, as Bartlett said at Sussex, the way out of shame because (like other forms of art) it shows possibilities.[9] "Pornography," not "erotica." Boy's and O's sexual rituals are meant to be *dirty,* and sex without dirt is only possible through the blurred lens of "erotica."

The pollution applies to more than sex. It applies to literature itself. If this novel is partly a defense of pornography, it is also a defense of romance, ritual, melodrama, and sentimentality: all the despised forms of art and feeling. By refusing to condemn them, Bartlett is saying: this, too, must be accepted; this, too, is part of the story. The narrative of post-Stonewall gay fiction (whether the coming-out story, the tale of friendship, the AIDS jeremiad, the cool postmodern ironies of Dennis Cooper or Dale Peck) must be allowed to become tainted with these forbidden subjects. The book will not permit us the usual comfortable ironic distance we expect as modern readers. It turns us into voyeurs. The narrator is himself a voyeur, and it is a book that defends the necessity of voyeurism as an analogue of the self-consciously sexual life. And for Bartlett, to be homosexual is necessarily to be self-conscious about sex: for one is aware constantly as a gay man of the transgressions one is making.

It is this narrative pollution which Bartlett carries, with tremendous audacity (and mixed results) to its logical conclusion in the third part of the novel, "Family." In this section an old, unhappy, resentful gay man, "Father," comes to live with Boy and O, or rather comes to die with them. His presence threatens to undermine not only their love, but the voyeuristic theater that Bartlett has so profoundly imagined. It is not only his dying, but his lack of imagination, his nasty spiteful envy, that Boy and the reader must endure. In a sense Bartlett wants to see if he can preserve the narrative of eros within an anti-erotic narrative; to make passion and gritty, unromantic sickness meet. He pollutes his own romantic story with a very different one. In a sense, he's added an AIDS story to a jerk-off book.

"Father" is an unknown quantity, to the reader, to O, and also (perversely) to Boy himself. He is the man who has sent Boy every week a letter telling of his garden, or indeed of damage to his garden. He is a man thus exiled in every sense from Eden, someone who (it turns out) may not ever have lived there: for it turns out that many, if not all, his letters are deceptive. He doesn't live in the country for instance, as we were led to believe, but merely in another part of London; the past he repeatedly recalls as being shared by him and Boy is equally unreal.

We never do learn who or what "Father" is. Boy hints at one point to O that he is the surviving member of a gay couple, the other of whom was killed in World War II. (The Second World War is the inaugural point of modern gay history for Bartlett.) Has "Father" then raised the child left abandoned at the other's death? A pretty story; but (as O and the reader realize) Boy is not old enough to be that child. Was Boy, then, a trick, or a kept boy? In what film of "Father's" is Boy playing the starring role?

But even more puzzling: in what film of Boy's is *Father* playing a part? And why is that part so central that at the very acme of Boy's happiness — the achievement of marriage to O — Boy threatens it by bringing "Father" into their new flat, and tending him there until he dies? Why, further, does Bartlett risk squandering the enormous emotional capital he has invested in Boy — the reader's *desire* for him — by turning a hot young man into a harried housewife who earnestly reads booklets on how to care for the elderly? Why does he risk the damaging comparison of Boy to the Virgin Mary in a reverse *pietà*, holding a dying parent in his lap — a comparison that is made overt by Mother's seeing herself as "St. Anne," Mary's sister?

However awkward this final section may be, the awkwardness may be the point; a strategy to prevent the novel from seeming too easy. It is as though there is a deeper humiliation which Boy must go through before he can be a complete man, a complete lover, a complete homosexual. Hercules' thirteenth labor, arguably the greatest, was to be dressed as a woman and spin flax at the court of Queen Omphale. Another reason for this sudden dizzying descent into something like the "real world" may be precisely to test the assumptions of the previous story, a testing analogous to the testing of Boy. Can the homosexual novel Bartlett has been writing survive, meet the challenge of, a world outside the safe confines of art, of the Bar? Can a gay union like O's and Boy's survive the invasion of bodily morbidity? To these questions Bartlett wants to answer Yes. But I'm not sure how completely he succeeds.

After Father's death, Mother disappears, The Bar closes, and soon the money she has been sending Boy and O dries up (she needs it for herself). This vanishing act obviously signifies another stage in Boy's maturity. As Mother herself writes, "*I realised you didn't need a Mother any more*" (302). With the symbolic deaths of a mother and a father, Boy is, well, a man. Clumsy though it is, this is Bartlett's version of Dante's moment of liberation in the *Purgatorio* when Virgil leaves him and he is "crowned and mitred over himself."[10] In a parallel incident, Boy and O, surrounded by potential gay-bashers, fight them off by sheer self-assertion: "*not a hair upon his head you fucker!*" shouts O (247). Between them, these two incidents tell us their love story is over.

And as he finishes this long story of Boy's coming of age, the narrator shows his listener a photo of Boy with his shirt off and a new tattoo: "And it was for him [O, that is] and at his request that Boy made this mark on his body, and not for any whimsical or ordinary contract but as a sign of his faith in the love of men, in the fact that it is indeed possible to choose a man, or men, and you be quiet now and sleep and don't ask me any more questions." These sad words, addressed as much to the reader as to the narrator's bed partner, break the novel's proscenium. In a sudden moment of pathos, the narrator cries out: "Oh how I wish there really was a picture like that for me to give" (310), as much as admitting that this photo, perhaps this whole story, has been made up. Indeed the final "photo" that he "wishes" he could show his bed partner (someone, we imagine, who is *not* Boy, not the lover he has always wanted to meet) is of something that has not happened yet: not really a photo at all, but a visionary glimpse. Once again, art is less a reflection than a revelation of life. Once again, he creates an image of what it would mean for two men to be together, for their desires to be publicly acknowledged, for bashers to be abashed, for ravaging diseases to be cured, for the captives to be set free, and for Boy and O and all men who love other men to be "perfect, perfect, perfect" (301).

Another imaginary scene crosses the boundaries of past and present, six-hundred-year-old celebrations somehow present in fifty-year-old ones, or ones that have not yet come. When you imagine such a possibility, the narrator tells us, "Let it be the night of the sacking of the palace of John of Gaunt, when the looters in their pride and their fury cast a whole dinner service of solid gold into the dark river; let it be the night when the war was over and men kissed in the streets; let it be the night Franco died and the two Spanish queens I was with got drunk and started making out right there on the dinner table, let it be Riga, let it be Budapest, let it be Berlin." And then in a touching voice that is almost a plea: "but let it be in our own country, right here in our city, this city, let it be a night to remember, a night to say, *I was there.* Let it be the night we raised a hundred thousand pounds, let it be the night they changed the law and we danced all night, spilling out of The Bar and dancing our way into the street, and nobody stopped us . . ." (331). The scene need not be grander than that; and if the joy he speaks of cannot be naturalized in "our own country, right here in our city, this city," then all the dreaming in the world is of no use. It must be *our* celebration, not somebody else's: a reality rather than any mere glamorous dream.

And in the final scene, the narrator *creates* the photo he was "looking for." In this picture, Boy and O, now older, help an ancient Madame onto the

> makeshift stage in the middle of the square . . . walking with a silver-headed cane now but still, just for old times' sake, still wearing the silver beaded dress . . . And there is silence, you can hear the hush spreading through the crowd, and then she sings, or rather half speaks, the words which we all know, the words we all knew and loved so well: *Your goodbyes, Left me with eyes that cry, How can I go on, dear, without you?* And from the great crowd comes rising the whispered chorus, a great, strong, slow, gentle sound, everyone now holding up a candle or just a hand or a photograph of a person who couldn't be here tonight:
> *All of me,*
> *Why not?*
> *Take all of me;*
> *Can't you see?*
> *I'm*
> *No good*
> *Without you?* (311–21)

How honest he is, even here, recognizing that even in the utopian future there are those who are alone, who hold up a candle or a hand or a photograph for "a person who couldn't be here": for all the men dead of gay-bashing attacks or AIDS, for all the resentful "Fathers," for all the men from other times who have (like the narrator) been left behind. The last scene is not a mere feel-good fantasy, but an epitaph and memorial. And how grateful I am that Bartlett has risked this last theatrical gesture of Mother singing one last time to her audience. It is fitting that the narrator's last words, murmured as if he were himself dropping off to sleep, should be themselves a mixture of gratitude and sorrow: "*Goodbye Boys. Goodbye Mother. Goodbye Father. Goodbye, and Thank Your, Thank you and Goodnight*" (313).

For much of this novel, Boy and O are figures in a dream-landscape: their true home The Bar, their city unnamed, their very identities reduced to archetypes of youth and manhood. The Bar is terribly important to them because it offers ways of imagining their future. It is significant in this respect that they and all the Bar-goers are lovers of illusion: readers, amateur actors, operamanes. In the "secondary worlds" of art, and nowhere else, these gay men see adumbrations of themselves. Even on Boy's and O's wedding night, O, quite speechless with love, puts a record of *Don Giovanni* on the stereo and plays Boy "*Dalla sua pace*," letting it speak for him. He then translates—and improves—the text to suit their situation: "*You know that when you come that makes me come too*" (213). Again, a crucial step in Boy's education as a gay man comes when Madame gives him half a dozen books to read, books in which he might catch a glimpse of himself not as he now is, but as he might be. And, as Boy says wonderingly to himself: "*I am acquiring a library. I must have a future*" (81).

Boy's touching amazement at the possibility of a future is more than a joke. It is a recognition that having a future depends upon having a past. The theatrical roles so endlessly and enchantingly acted out on these pages are not "playful" in the common academic sense. They do not invite their participants to see through those roles and thus to dematerialize their notion of "identity." They do not hold out the promise of limitless freedom in one's "choice" of roles. Quite the reverse: they demand an intense identification with a few roles, just as Mother wears only copies of the same good black dress. Boy's initiation involves painful or humiliating *expansions* of identity, rather than dissolutions of it. His frequent donning of women's clothes makes no statement about the arbitrariness of gender roles, let alone effeminacy. It is far closer to the audacities of drag than to the permissions of gender "performance." According to Bartlett, it is precisely by playing roles that we gain knowledge of the world and ourselves. For that reason, such play is not whimsical. For Bartlett, to choose a role is a serious undertaking, a declaration of intent and a means of self-discovery, just as Boy's decision to enter the blank door of The Bar is serious. By contrast, Edmund White's theatricals in *Nocturnes* are "fun" in the negative, whimsical sense: they come unaccountably (why are the boys living in a theater at all?), have no consequences (the actors are unchanged by the experience), make no one laugh or cry (there is no audience). Boy's impersonations, on the other hand, guarantee his future and that of his spectators.

Ready to Catch Him also guarantees—gives warrant of—a past. Such a warrant is particularly needed by gay men of the post-Stonewall period, who have been unsure what to make of their history, which has been one of humiliation and danger. Much seventies liberation rhetoric explicitly urged us to shake off the fetters of the past: any sympathy for the life of the queen or the hustler was taboo, a virtual admission that you were in love with your suffering and wanted to reenter the closet. Bartlett, perhaps because he is not an American and thus less given to revolutionary befores and afters, has a different view. The negative things that have been, are, and will be said about homosexual desire may never disappear, but they can be transformed and used to your advantage. Can be, and are. There's something beautiful in the ridiculous exaggerations of the past—in the quasi-archetypes of queen and butch, trade, soldier, golden boy, etc. These roles are, so to speak, works of popular art, to which pornography is a better guide than high literature. Here, too, *Ready to Catch Him* has been faithful as few books are to its origins in shame-filled private fantasy.

By telling this story from the point of view of an outsider, someone left behind by the sexual revolution, Bartlett smuggles into the reader's consciousness all the shames and envies — but also all the ingenuity and courage — that we have conveniently forgotten in our desire to be self-made free gay men. To identify oneself with this narrator is to befriend a despised part of oneself, something like Jung's "shadow." The result is a massive return of the repressed, a flood of feelings and thoughts we may have forbidden ourselves to have, including pity and self-pity, pornographic desire and sexual envy.

Ready to Catch Him Should He Fall is obviously about coming to terms with our parents, with "Mother" and "Father," with all the immediate limiting past. But it both deepens and broadens our sense of what that past, those contingencies are; and (like a successful analysis) reveals surprising beauty in the very limits we have struggled to escape. It places our modern gay life in the context of the past; not letting the past dictate its story, but allowing that story to be enriched, made human and believable by all the previous stories that are its soil. The victory that Boy and O achieve is thus — despite huge improbabilities — made probable and convincing, not a mere fantasy or wish-fulfillment. This is, I think, what Bartlett was trying to do with the somewhat unconvincing incorporation of "Father" into Part 3.

Ready to Catch Him Should He Fall is thus more than a simply nostalgic novel. It looks back on a hundred years of gay culture and finds in it not merely a quaint whiff of the past, but beauty and hope for the future. In a marvelous, unexplained festival Boy and O attend in the Park, for instance, whose theme seems to be the world of 1895, someone like Oscar Wilde is being hauled off to jail, jeered (as Wilde was) by female prostitutes: "'E'll 'ave to get his 'air cut regular now . . ." (124). At the end of the novel, this incident is echoed and changed: when a potential gay-basher mocks and threatens Boy ("*oh, oh such a pretty boy*" [297]) and raises his hand to caress his hair, the mockery is interrupted, the jeer thrown back, and Wilde's tragicomic fate given a happy ending. We can rewrite history to some extent, we need not repeat it.

As a novel, too, *Ready to Catch Him* gathers together the preoccupations of earlier gay writers such as Genet, Tennessee Williams, James Baldwin, Christopher Isherwood, Andrew Holleran, and James Purdy, recapitulating their great themes of promiscuity, sexual worship, and theater. Holleran asked "Can one waste a life?" and answered, ambivalently, Yes. Boy can be thought of as a Malone who gets it right. The narrator says of Boy: "I was so scared for him, so scared that he'd get it wrong, that he'd waste himself" (12). But Boy, unlike Malone, does not waste himself in the least: like the lover in some metaphysical poem, he grows by spending. Boy and O are also the luckier descendants of Williams's horny old men and his beautiful younger ones. Even when most faithfully married, Boy and O are never chaste, but practice what Bartlett dares to call the "virtue" of Promiscuity. They are descendants of Isherwood's unromantic George, another stubborn, unrespectable Englishman. They are younger brothers of Purdy's agonists, but their agony has a comic victory at the end. They are descendants, most of all, of fiction itself, and vindicate its power to create something real in the world by making up beautiful images of something that does not yet exist.

But if Bartlett's novel gathers together all of these gay stories, it also implicitly *ends* them. What comes after The Bar? This we never learn. Boy and O become older, that is all. Perhaps the institution of The Bar, like that of the ghetto and its image of gay separateness, has come to an end. Perhaps one day even Boy and O's relationship—presented here as the crown of homosexual success—will seem old-fashioned and pointlessly self-conscious. Perhaps that time is already here, as the narrator of *Ready to Catch Him* implies when he asks his listener (and reader) to forgive the flights of his fancy: "You, of course, living in a rather different time or in different countries, will find all this hard to credit now, everything they went through, it all seems so elaborate" (202). In an age of queer, rather than gay, identity, his defensiveness is understandable.

Since the present book has taken for its subject the gay literature of the very period traced by Bartlett's novel—the fifty years since World War Two—it is a question for me, too. The stories I have discussed, and those I have most loved, may well seem "elaborate" to a younger generation of readers, gay or straight; not necessarily elaborate in the baroque manner of Bartlett's novel, but in their obsessive fascination with what it means to be a gay man, how gay men differ from straight men or women or from lesbians. It is a literature, in other words, of gay identity—a concept that has come under increasing suspicion. We are far more aware at the turn of the millennium than we were at the time of Stonewall of the variety of constructions of sexual life.

One of the books that has called sexual identity into question for many gay Americans, Frank Browning's *A Queer Geography: Journeys toward a Sexual Self,* quotes an apposite review by Edmund White of Marjorie Garber's book on bisexuality, *Vice Versa,* in which White admits that Garber "browbeat me into wondering whether I myself might not have been bisexual had I lived in another era."[11] Here, as in his essay "The Politics of Gender: Michel Foucault"[12] and the introduction to the 1983 edition of his own *States of Desire: Travels in Gay America,*[13] White shows himself acutely aware of the difficulty posed by the language and culture of just such a gay "identity" as Neil Bartlett and I have been describing. At the same time, like many gay men, White has mixed feelings about Garber's, Foucault's, and Browning's distaste for a reified sexual self. He correctly notes in his foreword to the *Faber Book of Gay Short Fiction,* for instance, that, despite the possible falsity of the assumption that "sexual identity is profound, hidden, constitutive, more a matter of being than doing," he and other gay men "continue to believe their gayness is in fact something they are rather than something they do. . . . If gays tell each other — or the hostile world around them — the stories of their lives, they're not just reporting the past but also shaping the future, forging an identity as much as revealing it."[14] And more recently, White has made an analogous claim for the continuing, if shifting, relevance of gay identity in the form of a defense of the centrality of sex in gay fiction: "the word *homosexual* contains the word *sexual* and . . . when pundits ask what exactly is it that unites our community, what single principle can we erect that might rally all of us, rich and poor, black and white, young and old, the answer is right there staring at us with its single, slightly rheumy eye."[15]

White, our most lucidly self-aware writer, poses these questions in his fiction as well as his essays; and I can think of no better way to close my survey of the — possibly waning — literature of gay identity than by turning to its most skeptical, but perhaps most faithful, practitioner.

Chapter Nine

WHITE LIES

EDMUND WHITE'S GAY FICTION

By common consent, the most distinguished American gay writer is, and has been for twenty-five years, Edmund White. And "distinguished," with its faintly Edwardian overtone, is the right word for someone who is, like him, an old-fashioned man of letters. (In "Watermarked," a late story/reminiscence, White cites Thornton Wilder as "the only contemporary 'man of letters' I knew about and a model for the career I hoped to have"). He has been not just a writer but a *professional* writer since leaving graduate school at the University of Michigan, where he had been studying Chinese. When he first arrived in New York in 1962 he worked for Time-Life Books, and later was an editor of the magazines *Saturday Review* and *Horizon*. He has since written in many forms with astonishing fluency and ease: the biography (his award-winning *Genet*, 1994), the novel (*Forgetting Elena*, 1974; *Nocturnes for the King of Naples*, 1978; *Caracole*, 1985), the autobiographical novel (*A Boy's Own Story*, 1982; *The Beautiful Room Is Empty*, 1988), the occasional essay (many of which have been collected by David Bergman as *The Burning Library*, 1994), the short story (*A Darker Proof*, 1988; *Skinned Alive*, 1995), the travelogue (*States of Desire*, 1980; *Our Paris*, 1994); even the sex manual (*The Joy of Gay Sex*, written with Dr. Charles Silverstein, 1977).

He has been the Liszt of our time: not only a magnificent virtuoso, but a kind friend and a generous sponsor of other artists. The best word to apply to him might be "unprovincial." Through him, we see our lives placed in a larger, more luminous perspective, one not limited to our time or place. If a group of gay Venusians were to present themselves at the White House for a state dinner, Edmund White would be everybody's choice to negotiate with, interview, and captivate them. In being so unprovincial, White is of course very American: like

Henry James and T. S. Eliot, the less provincial he gets, the more clearly he shows his American roots. The laborious self-fashioning, the scrubbing oneself free of birthmarks of style, class, philosophy, identity, history is arguably as much an American obsession as the more familiar one of claiming that one is *entirely* American (the claim sometimes made by Hawthorne, Twain, and Whitman).

There is an illuminating comment apropos of this self-cleansing by Auden:

> "Tradition," wrote Mr. T. S. Eliot in a famous essay, "cannot be inherited, and if you want it you must obtain it by great labour." I do not think that any European critic would have said just this. He would not, of course, deny that every poet must work hard but the suggestion in the first half of the sentence that no sense of tradition is acquired except by conscious effort would seem strange to him. There are advantages and disadvantages in both attitudes. A British poet can take writing more for granted and so write with a lack of strain and overearnestness. American poetry has many tones, but the tone of a man talking to a group of his peers is rare. . . .[1]

White's achievement, and his most characteristic style as a novelist, is precisely that of "a man talking to a group of his peers."

But who are his peers? The question isn't just a rhetorical one. To the degree that he has identified himself as a gay man (that is, mostly but not entirely: *Caracole* has no gay characters), his peers are of course other gay men. But which ones? The reader of *The Joy of Gay Sex,* for instance, was just about everybody who was having sex with another man, and could afford the price of this coffee-table book with its elegant pen-and-ink drawings of frottage and fellatio. But it's hard to imagine this comparatively midcult reader picking up *Genet,* whose audience might be less homophile than francophile: the book is much too heavy to be read in bed. Who are his peers in the fictional autobiographies *A Boy's Own Story* and *The Beautiful Room Is Empty?* As installments of a projected tetralogy on growing up gay, they are seemingly destined to any audience of gay men — but not the group of happy warriors who needed advice about crabs in *The Joy of Gay Sex.* Its audience might be the generation that came of age just before Stonewall — White's generation — a middle-class, well-educated group for whom White's horror stories of psychoanalysis will ring a bell. To take yet another kind of work, who are his peers in *Forgetting Elena* or *Nocturnes for the King of Naples?* Readers of these difficult, Firbankian novels are a much smaller group than that which might read *Genet,* let alone the autobiographies, for they are very hard to follow, as White himself has ruefully admitted. ("In *Nocturnes,* I thought I had been almost perverse in how few clues I gave to the reader, and I was amazed by how much was made of so little.")[2] One wants to say that this group is composed not of homosexuals, but of *intellectuals.* If these are books, as some have claimed, that helped put gay fiction on the map, the reason is that they take seriously what intellectual map-makers of all sexual orientations take seriously, especially the need to escape from clichés of thought, emotion, or language. White's peers here include any-one, gay or straight, male or female, who has learned to live without distorting illusion. Finally, who are his peers in his latest short stories and memoirs, many of them about AIDS? The HIV-positive? The mourners of those who are dead? Survivors?

At the present, White has reached an apogee of respectability and even affec-tion: so much so that the line he once applied to a certain kind of urban gay man — "Thank *God* for Stephen Sondheim!" — could now be rewritten as: "Thank *God* for Edmund White!"[3] Thank God, that is, for a gay writer who is an adult, who doesn't confine himself to earnest coming-out sagas or sweaty porn! Thank God he is so witty, so wise, so candid — so like us! As a writer White's manners are perfect, both relaxed and polished. You pick up one of his books — whether essays, short stories, or memoirs — knowing in advance you won't be embarrassed by anything in it. And if (as sometimes happens in the more experimental fictions such as *Forgetting Elena* and *Nocturnes for the King of Naples,* you aren't quite sure *what* he's talking about, at least you know he's talking *well.*

He has, in other words, been appropriated by gay men, with a certain proud fondness. This appropriation is on its face very odd, considering his extremely highbrow past, and most readers' decidedly lowbrow present. He has never been an easy writer and is only superficially more so now. He does not write romances, cookbooks, or detective stories. He refuses to cheerlead for gay liber-ation. So the question remains: who reads him and why? What sort of pleasure do so many gay men take, or think they take, in his highly eccentric fiction?

Perhaps I should confess at once that this is my question as well. I have read Edmund White for twenty years now, yet I have no clear idea of what I find there; indeed, when I think of the many pleasures White has given me, I notice that they are unusually tangled (in my memory) with reservations. In the follow-ing remarks, I will be trying to disentangle these complicated reactions to our greatest, our most *complete* author. And if an occasional exasperation makes itself heard, if I sound sour or thick (like standing milk), I plead the master's own excuse. In the introduction to *Our Paris,* a memoir of his love affair with France and a young Frenchman, he writes: "Despite the sometimes catty sound of this book, its name-dropping and archness, I hope at least a few readers will recog-nize its subtext is love. Hubert loved me with unwavering devotion. . . . I loved him, too, in my cold, stinting, confused way."[4] I hope to pay a fellow gay midwestern WASP the same grudging, heartfelt compliment.

In his introduction to *The Burning Library,* a collection of occasional essays and reviews by Edmund White, David Bergman reports that "one of White's longtime friends and co-workers warned me when I began work on this book, 'Don't trust anything Ed says.' It was good advice that White himself frequently gives the reader, if somewhat indirectly, for many of these essays celebrate the value of irresponsibility. The reader of his essays must expect to be betrayed."[5] "Betrayed" sounds a bit ominous: if we really felt we should be betrayed, or if we thought it mattered, would we read further? And yet I laughed aloud at the cheek of putting so damning a statement in the introduction to the book. It smacked of the very betrayal it claimed to find in White himself, for Bergman is himself a loyal friend of the supposedly traitorous author.

What Bergman calls "betrayal" (irresponsibility, a Barthesian *jouissance*) one might call by other names: elusiveness, hypocrisy, charm. I think of it as shamelessness: the frequent tone of virtuosi like White toward an audience eager to be tricked. Impudence is also one of the great gay tropes. We find it classically in *The Importance of Being Earnest*.

> ALGERNON: Why is it that at a bachelor's establishment the servants invariably drink the champagne? I ask merely for information.
> LANE: I attribute it to the superior quality of the wine, sir. I have often observed that in married households the champagne is rarely of a first-rate brand.[6]

This brief exchange has often struck me as a touchstone of gay wit, based as it is on self-exposure, not self-concealment. It is funny because the self-exposure is completely unmoralized: Algernon doesn't pretend to be indignant, and Lane doesn't pretend he hasn't drunk the champagne. How one's heart leaps up at the spectacle of so much shamelessness! And how useful a tool it has proved to gay men, whose only hope of disentangling themselves from the knots of social contempt and religious damnation was shamelessly to cut them.

White is not "impudent," as Algernon's servant is, for he is far less confident. His shamelessness reveals itself not in Lane's glorious black-and-white, but in a thousand rueful shades of self-depreciation. Nevertheless, there *is* an impudence in White's frequent "good advice" that we not take him too seriously: an impudence all the greater when one thinks how seriously he gives it. How earnestly he warns us he can't tell stories, or has no subject, or is boring, or can't remember! He is like Chaucer's Pardoner (that quasi-gay forerunner), whose shamelessness leads him to tell his fellow pilgrims that he's a terrible fraud, then to hit them up for money. But unlike Chaucer's Host, who threatens to cut off the Pardoner's balls he's so furious at being mocked, White's pilgrims hear the terrible confession and beg him to continue. We never believe his "advice." Why? Because the advice is given so apologetically and whimsically that we skate right over its impudent (indeed radical) implications.

Two passages, one from *A Boy's Own Story*, the other from *Nocturnes for the*

King of Naples, will illustrate this. Chapter Four of *A Boy's Own Story* (a fictional autobiography of White's adolescence) begins like this:

> Like a blind man's hands exploring a face, the memory lingers over an identifying or beloved feature but dismisses the rest as just a curve, a bump, an expanse. Only this feature—these lashes tickling the palm like a firefly or this breath pulsing hot on a knuckle or this vibrating Adam's apple—only this feature seems lovable, sexy. But in writing one draws in the rest, the forgotten parts. One even composes one's improvisations into a quite new face never glimpsed before, the likeness of an invention. Busoni once said he prized the most those empty passages composers make up to get from one "good part" to another. He said such workmanlike but minor transitions reveal more about a composer—the actual vernacular of his imagination—than the deliberately bravura moments. I say all this by way of hoping that the lies I've made up to get from one poor truth to another may mean something—may even mean something most particular to you, my eccentric, patient, scrupulous reader, willing to make so much of so little, more patient and more respectful of life, of a life, than the author you're allowing for a moment to exist yet again.[7]

And in *Nocturnes,* en route to a meticulous evocation of the narrator's days in boarding school, White says:

> We label the feelings of our childhood with the names we learn as adults and brightly, confidently, refer to that old "anguish" or "despair" or "elation." The confidence of liars. For those words meant nothing to us then; what we lacked as children was precisely the power to designate and dismiss, and when we describe the emotions of one age with the language of another, we are merely applying stickers to locked trunks, calling "fragile" or "perishable" contents that, even were we to view them again, would be unrecognizable. But come, let us jimmy the hasp and lift the lid.[8]

Both passages are making an alarming claim, especially when we consider that White's main genre is always the memoir. In the first, he claims that a blind memory "lingers" selectively over certain details, and that writing, and writing alone, must connect the dots between them. An artist is best seen in the connective tissue he has to "invent"; and the object he makes is the "likeness of an invention"—a tricky phrase meaning both "the sort of resemblance we expect from inventions," and also "resemblance *to* an invention," that is to other works of art. So it is that he claims the story of his life to be little more than a humble sequence of "poor truths," and that what touches the reader are lies. (This is exactly the opposite claim of Samuel Johnson in the *Preface to Shake-*

speare, which asserts that Shakespeare "holds up to his readers a faithful mirrour of manners and of life. . . . His persons act and speak by the influence of those general passions and principles by which all minds are agitated, and the whole system of life is continued in motion.")[9] To White, by contrast, it is in the "improvisations" and "inventions" that he manages to convey meaning at all to "my eccentric, patient, scrupulous reader." Beneath this assertion is a belief (or fear) that no "general passions and principles" do in fact "agitate" all human minds.

In the passage from *Nocturnes,* it is not the power of art that he discusses, but the weakness of memory. Here the alarming claim is not that memory lingers selectively, but that it lingers in vain. The feelings of childhood are spoken in a language unknown to the adult; conversely, adult terms for those feelings are *faux amis:* terms in two languages that only *seem* identical. "Anguish," "despair," "elation" are concepts that "meant nothing to us then." Childhood and maturity are then radically incommensurable; we have no common measure by which to judge the former by the latter. Even words in the mouth of an artist like White "betray" what they are to describe. Here it is not art that lies, but the mind itself. Nor is it clear what, or even if, the artist can hope to communicate to another.

In one sense, I suppose we could look at White's claims as a later version of Wilde's defense of mendacity in *The Decay of Lying.* ("For the aim of the liar is simply to charm, to delight, to give pleasure. He is the very basis of civilized society, and without him a dinner party, even at the mansions of the great, is as dull as a lecture at the Royal Society. . . .")[10] But they don't sound like Wilde, and I don't think they mean what Wilde meant. Wilde's idea of mendacity was more outrageous and baroque. He was for grandstanding, for *big* lies: we recall that it was he who sued the Marquis of Queensberry, not the other way around. White hardly aspires so high. Indeed, he is grateful to the "eccentric, patient, scrupulous reader" for *putting up with* his lies, for being "respectful" of a life the author himself claims to find dull. But though he has asserted the impossibility of speaking the foreign language of childhood he obviously has no intention of taking his own advice. Thus, in the passage from *Nocturnes,* he writes (memorably!) about a scene he has declared to be literally unmemorable. When he has finished describing such a scene — he is a teenager waking up at boarding school — it doesn't seem foreign at all. The lie he is telling, then, has to do with lying itself. He rather likes the idea of being a liar, as of being a "betrayer."

And why shouldn't he? It confers on the rather mild-mannered Clark Kentish author a raffish villainy that is very attractive. He's like the man who warns you in conversation that he's a terrible drunk or has just gotten out of jail. He may or may not be lying, but you are certainly enjoying being lied *to.* Second, the admission that his life is "poor" unless pieced together by gorgeous swatches of invention disarms the reader's criticism: we can hardly say we hadn't been warned, or that he's, well, *lied* to us. Indeed, it makes the lies more effectual, for who will disbelieve so "honest" a speaker? He comes before us with the crafty resignation of some Levantine merchant: "I will not deceive you, my pet," sighs the gold-toothed seller of the dubious rug. "It is a little torn."

Further, the untruthfulness perfectly suits White's peculiar gifts and minimizes his weaknesses. It enables him to escape various inconvenient vulgarities: suspense, character, and conclusiveness. ("My plots are rather primitive," he shamelessly "confesses" to an interviewer in the *Paris Review*.)[11] Conversely, it enables him to be "sensitive to the way things look." ("I agree with Conrad that fiction is primarily a visual medium, and that there is something very concrete and valuable and eternal in any accurate description of the way things look.")[12] Finally it allows him to be sensitive to the way *words* look, to use them with a kind of symbolist precision and unreality, as if they were gems, not transparent panes of glass. Even his colloquialisms (while perfectly correct) seem to have the delighted strangeness of a second language as written by a foreigner of genius. Not surprisingly, Nabokov was one of White's earliest important admirers, and White is on record as saying *Lolita* is his favorite novel.[13]

So yes, Bergman is right to warn us against White's lying. At the same time, he may have fallen for a White lie by dignifying as "betrayal" White's gabby irresponsibility. For even if we begin to see "lying" as not only a favored style, but even the *subject* of White's most characteristic work, the quality of those lies is very special, peculiar to him. As lies go, White's are modest to the point of scrupulosity. (The most he dares, in *Nocturnes*, is to turn the kaleidoscope of the family romance in a melodramatic direction: the abandoning father is turned into a heroin addict; the abandoned mother kills herself.) Further, they serve despite his best intentions — his worst, I mean — the cause of a deeper honesty. Indeed, no matter how much White may or may not have made up in his stories, essays, and autobiographies, their *tone* is patient, meticulous, unexaggerated, and — despite the gorgeous colors of the prose — rather drab. The overall effect is anything but peacocklike: he apologizes even as he fans his feathers.

This is true even in the earliest, most outré, of his novels, *Forgetting Elena*. (Unlike Verdi, and like Richard Strauss, White is an example of the artist who begins his career obscure and ends it comparatively clear. His career has been one of disembarrassment, in both of its senses.) *Forgetting Elena* is quite literally the "memoir of an amnesiac," to quote Oscar Levant, though the joke isn't particularly funny. (Is it meant to be? Anxious questions always follow any assertion about White, as they haunt the writer himself in *Elena*.) It concerns a young man who awakes to find himself on a beautiful island, surrounded by people who seem to expect something of him — but what? Their leader seems to be a young man named Herbert, who is apparently of great authority on the island. But not to everyone, it turns out. At one point, thinking he must be a servant, the narrator goes out to rake pine needles and cart them off. (White also describes having to rake pine needles at his father's house in *The Beautiful Room Is Empty.* Ought we to read backward through this palimpsest? Is Herbert really Dad? No, no: that way madness lies.) As he is doing so, a beautiful woman appears, accompanied by Billy, a handsome young man whom the narrator has assumed to be Herbert's "valet or nephew or perhaps lieutenant." The woman and Billy, themselves haughty, shock the narrator by making fun of Herbert — "I'm sure Herbert will codify *that,* too" — and convince him that he ought to leave off raking and take a walk with them.[14] As they walk down the beach, they are approached by a messenger from the "old Minister of the Left," who wishes to invite them to his house to "discuss the subtleties of language with you over drinks." The older woman laughingly refuses: "*Drinks!?* . . . But we don't want drinks. We were just going on a little stroll down the beach. Invite him to come along if he likes" (49–50). Soon the "Little Stroll" attains processional status: "In only a few minutes about twenty young men have joined our promenade," including someone the narrator thinks of as The Pale Stranger who turns out to be the owner of a house that had burned down the previous night (51).

"The woman," apparently flouting some unspoken but rigid etiquette, abruptly breaks off the procession, inviting only the narrator, Billy, the Minister, and the Pale Stranger to her house. There the Pale Stranger gets a nosebleed and must lie down on the counter, while the woman fondles the "small breast" of Maria, a "negress" staying in her house. Casually asking Maria to slip her dress down to her waist, the woman places a "pink shrimp on her brown belly. They both contemplate the shrimp and then slowly their studiousness turns into laughter" (63). The Minister, inspired, takes a paper doily and, dipping his index finger in brown sauce, "sketches the Negress." The Pale Stranger, recovered from his faint, pronounces the sketch "adorable." At this point, however, the narrator calls out "in a ringing voice," "Not adorable." " 'If not adorable, then what is it?' The room is quite still. Billy looks delighted. A dozen words flash through my mind, none of them right or even sensible, and I repeat, huskily, appalled at myself, 'Not adorable.' " (64–65). It is on the strength of this sudden negative that the narrator begins to be known on the island as a wit: "it's the best laugh we've had in months. Herbert's amazed at your erudition and your powers of instant recall. He had no idea that you even knew that old poem" (107).

Gradually it begins to dawn on the narrator that people are seeking *him* out, rather than vice-versa. Later that afternoon, for instance, after the nosebleed and the "not adorable" sketch, the Little Strollers find themselves at the Minister's house, where the mysterious woman reads a book she's writing, "about us," she tells the narrator pointedly. The story concerns a family, tribe, or group named the Valentines. The woman, a Valentine herself, had arrived on the island years before and determined to dominate it by incorporating some, but not all, of the fastidious customs of the Valentines' "Old Code." She met a man who was "perfect" for her, who would allow her to master the island. The narrator anxiously wonders if *he* was the perfect man. Another possibility suggests itself: "Am I her brother? Could my name be Valentine?" (74). ("Valentine" *is* in fact White's middle name.)[15]

His explicit doubt — "Am I her brother or her lover?" (87) — does not prevent him from making love to her; though like everything else on the island, sex is complicated and governed by fear and second-guesses. "Even if what we're doing is quite customary, I'm certain I'm not pursuing it in the right way. I'm wrong, it's wrong, this will come out badly" (95). In a sulk (or a panic? or embarrassment?) he interrupts their lovemaking and leaves, still uncertain of the woman's identity or his own.

On his way home from this *coitus interruptus,* the narrator is invited to stop for a drink by Jimmy, who lives apparently in the company of Daryl, Doris, and a man known as The Hand. As Daryl is introduced to him the narrator begins to realize a bit more about who he is: "So. I'm a neighbor, a permanent neighbor, and not Herbert's guest, not a newcomer. Daryl was introduced to me, and not I to him; I'm more important than he" (105). Doris, it turns out, is (like the mysterious woman) a Valentine, and thus a representative of the Old Guard. Eventually they all (including Herbert and the narrator's roommates) end up at "the hotel" where everyone is dancing the "Fire fire who" (steps inaugurated the night before as the Pale Stranger's house was burning down). There the narrator dances with Jimmy, then invites the Minister and Maria to join them: "Great powers are surging through me. I must express them or burst. Everyone in the room, or at least a face in every group, is familiar, has been propitiated. Doris, Daryl, Jimmy and the Hand lie vanquished. The *fatalia* singers? Placated with poems. The woman has fled the hotel. Tentative lines of good will have been cast to Kay and Sys; . . . Herbert's smiling. He's in love with me. Billy, the mirror girls, the Minister and Maria are my own dancing partners; they have to stand behind me. Tod and Hunter, chatting with a stranger next to the bar — they're my roommates, after all! And there's Bob by the passageway to the lavatory, we've found him at last, a servant taking *two* nights off, still in his green shirt and blue pants, harmless, uncritical" (126–27).

Then, in an extraordinary passage among so many others, he begins to dance — and in words as exact as they are minatory describes the evolution of a wordless art. It's like describing air. "Four notes rise, stop, repeat the ascent, rise again. I have firmed up my circle, confirmed suspicions, found due Herbert, rendered him his due. 'What. Do. You. Want?' as the four rising notes. 'What.

Do. You. Want.' Each note's equally spaced, similarly sounded, neither louder nor faster than the rest, the entire interrogation uninsistent. 'What. Do. You. Want.'" To his surprise, he finds himself in a circle "*occupying the center*" (128; his italics).

On his way home he runs into Herbert, who is composing a "dawn poem." Together he and the narrator exchange poems, containing a single identical word: "love." Just as Herbert is on the verge of declaring his love more openly, "the woman" suddenly appears and Herbert rushes off. The narrator runs to her, seizes her hands. "As I fold her in my arms my astral self, trembling with joy, covers her with kisses in the gold light" (140). He and the woman spend the following day making love, which this time is hardly interrupted. (The only sex in this book is heterosexual.) As they awaken they begin discussing the upcoming Royal Arrival — a joke? — as well as Herbert's sinister role in the arson of the Pale Stranger's house. The narrator figures out that it was no accident, and the woman confirms his suspicions. But why should Herbert *wish* to burn down the house? More teasing revelations follow at a party that night at Jason's.

The party, like many pleasures on the island, seems at once refined and menacing: concealed speakers are playing Vivaldi and Scarlatti, for instance, but the tapes have been redubbed so that the phrases come out absurdly: "Devoid of connective passagework, divorced from their familiar settings, the traditional questions and answers, the themes and inversions, the false resolutions giving way to the true, the interlocking voices — all stutter and break off, then rush hysterically into a dense fog of noise, slow to a hypnotic grind, finally bark at each other in tiny, stifled yaps" (140–41). A model of "the woman's" black companion Maria stands on the terrace. It suddenly explodes.

As the narrator goes for drinks, he is quizzed by Billy and Herbert: who are the drinks for? Elena? (So! The mysterious woman's name is "Elena . . . Elena Valentine" [151].) He overhears Herbert explaining to two "mirror girls" the niceties of picking pubic hair out of one's teeth after sex: "It should be done *en douceur,* should be a way *de dire des douceurs à* whomsoever" (152). The narrator, still looking for Elena, remembers their afternoon of lovemaking, when she had said "I can imagine our going away. Or even staying here, but staying together. Becoming different people. Forgetting all codes, old and new. Walking out of a room in a simple, natural fashion instead of *recessing*. No more arch comments. No more mystification." Was she serious? Was she even capable of unironic speech? "I don't think she trusted me. I didn't trust her" (156).

At this moment a hand is laid on his shoulder: Doris. Why has he come here with Elena? Is he out of his mind? The narrator is still mystified. Doris explains that when the narrator went off with Elena rather than Herbert, Herbert was wounded. As a result she and Herbert (Old and New Codes, Valentines and others) have reconciled with each other, given up their "ridiculous pride."

Armed with this information, the narrator finally gets back to Elena with the paper cup of "delicious punch" (Jason's awful specialty), only to suggest they "circulate" the party, "independently."

A bad decision, apparently, for Elena is never seen again: when the narrator wakes up the next day, Herbert tells him the shocking news: "Elena killed herself last night." The narrator, horrified, retires to his room to read Elena's book "on us": it seems to be a further account of her "perfect man": "He hated the island and constantly made fun of the lame little verses, the fancy clothes, the mechanical production of 'shocking' remarks." Even the introduction of "the New Code," meant to humanize and simplify the rigid court etiquette of the island, has merely moved it underground, made it more exquisite: "Under the New Code the islanders, forbidden to ridicule people for their low birth or humble position, have resorted to rejecting their inferiors for some supposed insensitivity to beauty or for some social blunder" (172). But Elena's love affair with the perfect man had been broken up by Herbert: "But how did Herbert do it, regain control? It wasn't very difficult. Herbert had created him after all, had trained him to catch allusions, invent poems, adjust to whims, smile, bow, conform. The odd thing was that Herbert had never converted to the New Code he had himself invented. Herbert is a realist, as I am not, as his creature could not be. For the perfect man, who was Herbert's creature, our adventure in sincerity must have been only one more novel sensation, a delicious *frisson*. When he tired of me, or when what I demanded of him became too much of a strain, he put me out of his mind. He forgot me" (173).

The final scene of the novel is that of the Royal Arrival, the last remaining ceremony of the Old Code. The narrator, Herbert, Jason, and others are on a barge landing at the dock of the island. The narrator has no idea what part he is to play. "I step off the barge. All the other men in my party back away from me, their shirts fluttering in the giant centrifuge. And then, in a single motion, as though responding to a signal, the entire population of the island sinks slowly to its knees, facing me, yes, I see, facing me, a prince, *the* prince" (178).

So! The riddle is now solved! After a tour of his "palace" (including the very room where he and Elena first made love), the narrator's last act is the symbolic burial of the past. Or is it symbolic? It is the real Elena — whoever she is — who is to be buried; it is not a mere ceremony. Or so we think. But in the final lines of the book we read: "I look around at this ring of strangers and wonder what this man [Herbert] expects from me. Is there a dead person in that box? Am I a newcomer to the island? I remember nothing. Who is Elena?" (184).

It is hard to read *Forgetting Elena* tranquilly. It is like the music at Jason's party, "devoid of connections." (We will see the same thing, though less like a bad acid trip, in *Nocturnes*.) Not only is the book an elaborate tease, it is one that deliberately (insultingly?) excludes most readers, even oneself. Nor are you permitted to throw it across the room: such a temper tantrum would prove you to be "of low birth or humble position," "insensitive to beauty." You grit your teeth and bear the unrelenting feather touches that eventually make you want to scream.

The novel has been explained, given a key, by White himself, who claims in a 1991 Afterword to *States of Desire* that *Forgetting Elena* was a satire on the new gay community, the community that is that had grown up post-Stonewall. To White the anthropologist nothing had really changed, however: the rules governing behavior were just as strict, and as irrational, as ever. New Code just excluded different people: "The old polarities that had functioned in an earlier period of gay life (butch/femme, older/younger, richer/poorer) and that had been patterned after borrowed social forms (husband/wife, teacher/student, gentleman/worker) had been rejected in favor of a new tribalism. To be sure this equality was only apparent (the subject of my first novel, *Forgetting Elena*), but on a sweaty disco floor at dawn, surrounded by a congeries of half-nude bodies, the interchangeability of human beings did seem real enough."[16]

If this is the *clef* to unlock the *roman*, you could have fooled me. For one thing, Old and New codes scarcely seem differentiated: both are so ridiculously remote from ordinary manners that the reader can be forgiven for failing to see that their differences are *only superficial*. (In this novel, they aren't even that.) Consequently, *Forgetting Elena* does not seem satirical, despite this explanation.

Second, if it is some kind of allegory, how is it to be read? What does it mean that Doris and Herbert, Old and New codes respectively, Valentines and non-Valentines, reconcile? What does it mean that the narrator accepts (remembers? inures himself to?) his role as *"the* prince"? That he rises to the "stoicism" of public office (as Herbert has suggested a royal must do), or that his heart and memory are merely hardened? What does it mean that the cycle of forgetting is about to begin again? ("Who is Elena?")

If this is an allegory of homosexuality specifically, exactly how are old and new gays different from each other according to this book? When the narrator says he was "too much of an islander" to read Elena's book after her death without the thought that the gesture was a cliché, is this a statement about being gay? Does "islander" = "faggot"? And if so, is it good or bad to be one? Or does "islander" rather = "outsider," "waif," or even "artist"? What does it mean that Herbert (who has challenged the Old Code) is capable of ruthlessness (burning down the Pale Stranger's house, perhaps even causing Elena's death)? That post-Stonewall gay culture is ruthless? When he succeeds in separating the narrator from Elena (before the story begins, and perhaps after Elena has died), does this signify the sinister power of the homosexual to separate the otherwise straight man from "the woman"? What does this seduction allude to — the artificial segregation of the sexes in seventies gay life? Finally, is the "gay" element in this book its hyperbolic language? Its occasional camp sensibility? Or its perception of sex as "always already" *wrong:* "Even if what we're doing is quite customary, I'm certain I'm not pursuing it in the right way. I'm wrong, it's wrong, this will come out badly."

All these are ways of asking my first question: What pleasure does this book aim to give? Who is supposed to be pleased, and how? The mutual admiration of reader and writer which lubricates most books turns out to be one of the "traditional questions and answers" disrupted by this novel, as Vivaldi and Scarlatti are disrupted by having the ends of phrases patched onto the beginnings. The narrator *himself* is strangely immune to pleasure; I can think of no moment, even when he is making love to Elena, when he is happy. One might think that having no responsibilities, that being "*the* prince," would make one blissful: it merely makes him anxious. He forgets not only Elena, but his own desires. It strikes me as interesting that the dance he creates at his moment of triumph at the hotel is based on a text that ought to be a question, but is presented as a statement: "What. Do. You. Want." But if the narrator doesn't know what he wants, the reader is balked of the pleasures of identifying with him; and I at least feel a certain resentment mixed with admiration of his audacity.

The anhedonic quality of this text reminds me again how different White is from an earlier gay writer he otherwise resembles, Ronald Firbank. The two share many things: an extremely indirect way of telling stories, a preference for closed, quasi-aristocratic societies, and an almost imagistic use of language. (Just as Firbank invents such marvels as "The Madonna of the Mule-mill" or the basilica of the "Blue Gesù," so White invents the "five brushstrokes used to do rock: the Sheer, the Veined, the Pebbled, the Beautiful and the Cold," and the names of bygone beauty-marks: the "Tornerò" and "Il Dottore.")[17] In both authors, language itself becomes the main pleasure of reader and characters alike.

No one invents a world from the ground up without (partly) wanting to dwell in it, and one senses in Firbank a tremendous relish for the ridiculously artificial world he creates. ("I suppose *The Flower beneath the Foot* is really Oriental in origin, although the scene is some imaginary Vienna.")[18] White, by contrast, seems to take his pleasure sadly, like the Englishman in the French witticism. And the world in *Forgetting Elena* is so full of terror, aggression, and madness that the "beautiful details" seem like makeup on a cadaver. The silver spades used to bury Elena, for instance, are grotesque, horrifying precisely because they're "beautiful." So is the dance invented on the spot as the Pale Stranger's house burns to the ground, the "Fire fire who." The islanders, Elena reflects, are so jaded that only the most minute discriminations are any longer of interest to them: they wish to be "*not quite human.*" This is literalized in Jason the "decrepit" pedophile, who was seen two nights before wearing an *insect* costume.

Maria is turned into a statue that explodes. Music is deliberately ugly, and consciousness itself becomes hostile: it takes the narrator five pages to get down three steps after the dance at the hotel, as it does when you are horribly stoned.

In Firbank, by contrast, the invented world is a great good place — or at least a small one. In *Concerning the Eccentricities of Cardinal Pirelli*, the cathedral city of Clemenza, with its orange trees and opera, is a *locus amoenus*. So is the Cardinal's luscious garden, or indeed the Church itself, which despite machinations of sober-sided papal envoys, tolerates and even nourishes "eccentricities" like his. (They include not only baptizing a Duquesa's German shepherd — "I do call thee Crack" — but chasing a lovely adolescent boy around the darkened cathedral at night.) Sex, too, though talked about indirectly (as in White), retains an enormous charisma. Firbank's comedy in fact resides in the contrast between its power and the utterly bland respectability of its practitioners (that is to say, absolutely everyone).

> Mrs. Montgomery sighed.
> "Once," she murmured meditatively, "men (those procurers of delights) engaged me utterly . . . I was their *slave*. . . . Now . . . one does not burn one's fingers twice, Mrs. Bedley."[19]

White's characters are terrified of sex — it kills Elena, after all — and it rarely strikes them as pleasurable. Firbank's find it beautiful, dirty, melancholy, but never boring or inhuman. In White's world, sex is *unheimlich*, uncanny. In Firbank's, it is a shared and rather tender private joke — truly a way *de dire des douceurs à* someone, rather than a new way to be "wrong."

While action is never exactly the *point* of Edmund White's fiction, it is even less the point than usual in *Nocturnes for the King of Naples. Forgetting Elena*, for all its abstractness and mystery, is at least about a young man's waking to find that he is "prince of the island." It is fey but consecutive. The autobiographical novels have, if not plot, chronicle: the coming to consciousness of one gay man. *Nocturnes* is like neither, and is for that reason the most radical of White's fictional attempts. In a sense, it takes place in a kind of numinous present — the present in which one would address a god — except that the god being addressed is known to be dead. In *Nocturnes*, there turns out to be no paternal god to forgive or punish, and in the absence of such a god, the sinner's sufferings and rebellions are literally without meaning, without weight. They don't quite form a story. Indeed this is the discovery finally made in *Nocturnes*: "Experience has taught me you were kind but powerless and that my struggle to make you punish me, save me, stop me, teach me was misguided" (139). This "struggle," which sounds very much like a plot, is the plot of a novel that can never be written because the narrator of *Nocturnes* is not sure what the power of such a narrative would be.

Most of the novel is told in flashback — but one from which very little can be, or needs to be, reconstructed. The central event is a love affair with an older man about whom we know little except that he *was* older. (Michael Denneny told me that the older lover was intended to be White himself and the entire novel an exquisite revenge for having been abandoned by a younger man.) It begins with a baroquely elaborate description of the sex-piers of seventies New York, where the narrator has picked up a man he turns out to know: "the crazy one who gave you the dog." But instead of having sex, they have an "orgy of talk" about "you." "You" was apparently a man of some intellectual or artistic accomplishment, though we don't learn what. He had a "genius for friendship," and is survived by a wide circle of friends who are devoted to him, even after his death. The narrator's feelings about his lover are decidedly mixed. On the one hand, the older man rescued him from his father, a coldly boisterous heroin addict who lives mostly abroad. For that act, the narrator is grateful. On the other, he feels always excluded from the charmed circle of the older man's friends: they, like "you," were somehow already in place, already loved *first*. ("His Being is his anteriority," as Roland Barthes says of Racine's fathers.)[20]

In order to escape this anteriority, he runs away from the older man: "When we lived together I devoted my nights to fleeing you" (32), he writes in a neat paradox. He forsakes this older man for a series of charmless youths: Robert, a provincial gawk, "a man who purports to be the mayor's younger brother" and who "dust[s] his swollen feet with lilac-scented talcum powder" (34); Peter, who transforms him into a "cock-ass." At the same time, he wants to be re-united with this man and makes occasional trips back to his apartment, only to find him gone. His life, even more than Malone's, "drifts." The book ends with a party on an unnamed island at which friends of the dead man are gathered, bringing him back to a sort of life by imitating his mannerisms, his smiles, his jokes. The narrator remains as included, and as excluded, as he ever was: to come "home" to the island is to lose himself in a garden where "the sultan and his beloved" are "besieged by mist and the howls of two lost dogs" (148).

In between the pier and the island, *Nocturnes* is a series — not quite a sequence — of events that neither lead up to, nor away from, this failed love affair; events that are presented in no particular order and are thus hard to emotionally define. The moment of greatest pathos, for instance, is the death of the narrator's dog — even though that occurs far in the past, in the context of his mother's suicide (the dog is found dead next to her in the closed garage). Is our pity for the boy, for the dog, *meant* to supersede that which we feel for his mother, who remains a shadowy figure? It is hard, again, to figure out the reaction we are meant to have when the narrator goes to stay with his father in Italy. His father turns out to be a drug addict whose need for reassurance is even greater than his son's. In a particularly grotesque vignette, the narrator ends up in bed with his father, who passes out sucking the boy's thumb. Is this meant to horrify? To amuse? To explain? To evoke pity? David Bergman claims in *Gaiety Trans-figured* that this is an act of symbolic fellatio.[21] If so, what does it imply about the father? That he's gay? Probably not. That he too is needy? So what? Like much in this novel, it seems a pattern without a point.

It is the same with many of the flashbacks to a city which I suppose is Naples, although it is never named. The narrator spends a fair amount of time cruising, but we seldom feel he desires the men very much. (Imagine what Andrew Holleran would have made of the Mayor's younger brother with his "lilac-scented talcum powder"!) He is taken up by a couple of highly eccentric Neapolitans — Didi and her estranged father, who live next door to each other but speak only on the phone — but his feelings about Didi don't go much beyond a general shame at being American and thus unsophisticated. (When he starts dressing flashily and cruising the streets, Didi mockingly calls him a "Cockass," her portmanteau term for male peacocks whether gay or straight.) Toward the end of the book, the narrator recalls hanging out with a neurotic boy named Sergius who cannot, for instance, bear to hear the numbers three or seven, which "became 'two plus one' and 'six plus one.' " This peculiar obsession, and the narrator's toleration of it, are never explained. Indeed, to ask why the narrator befriends Sergius is to ask an unanswerable question: "Being with Sergius that long summer provided me with another life — not an alternative to my real existence, which has no character, but to every evening's round of parties and melancholy adult pleasures" (129–30). What distinction is he making between "another life" and "an alternative to my real existence," especially when that very existence "has no character"? Why, if he is bored, does he hang around with the ineffably boring Sergius? Later on in his life, the narrator finds himself living in a theater in New York, indeed on its stage, with two boys he is in love with who are not (alas) in love with him. There they enact scenes from Victorian melodramas or Shakespeare in an attempt to spell out their feelings for one another. ("Perhaps if we staged it. Put it on somehow. Then I could see it" [70], says one of them in a recitative that could not call more loudly for a corroborating aria.) But nothing is understood as a result, except the old tale of being unwanted: the various roles are mere costume changes, not discoveries of something new.

In all of these "events," what is most obviously, even defiantly missing is any sense of purpose. By "purpose" I do not mean moral but narrative direction: why *this* detail rather than that? Why Naples? Why a theater? Why make his father a heroin addict? Why give the Mayor's younger brother "lilac-scented talcum powder"? Why invent Sergius or Didi? What light does any of these vignettes or characters throw on the narrator or his story? White acknowledges these questions in a beautiful but disingenuous sentence: "Moralists say that our actions and not our intentions define us, and by that harsh rule I lose all definition. I longed away my childhood, resisted my youth, regretted the rest . . ." (133). Gorgeous prose, and a damning admission. For whatever "moralists" may say, novelists at any rate have usually found that actions, not intentions, constituted their work. White is one of those authors whom Flannery O'Connor described as "a person of really fine sensibility and acute psychological perception trying to write fiction by using these qualities alone."[22] And if he's confessing to some fatal flaw — living on intention, not action — I'm not sure I believe it. How secretly proud he is of that flaw!

A more troubling question for me is: *has* he "intended anything"? In all the scenes I have described, what comes across is some exquisite *impotence* to intend or even desire. (He is a master at evoking the fizzy ennui of adolescence when we first realize that time may have to be "killed.") Few of White's promising scenes are told from a strong emotional point of view. They rather evoke the inhibited emotions of regret, embarrassment, and boredom. We are left to guess at what these secondary emotions conceal or suggest. Is it because, for a gay man of White's generation, desire is so fraught with contradiction that one evolves a weirdly imaginary persona who seems all but sexless, or a prose style that is "sensuous" without being "sensual"?

In *Nocturnes* (as opposed to *Forgetting Elena*) the gay element is at least explicit, whereas in the former novel it had to be elaborately inferred. But though the novel begins with a scene of sexual riot on the piers, desire in this novel is mainly *pretty*. In the masterful description of the pier scene, for instance, acts of sex are turned into extended and improbable metaphors: "A moment before the barge's beam invaded the cathedral we were isolated men at prayer, that man by the font (rainwater stagnant in the lid of a barrel), and this one in a side chapel (the damp vault), that pair of celebrants holding up a flame near the dome, those communicants telling beads of buttons pierced through denim, the greater number shuffling through, ignoring everything in their search for the god among us" (4–5). Not only is this not quite a description of sex, it isn't even a description of a sexual state of mind: lust does not speak in mini-allegories. And when I read of the men "telling beads of buttons pierced through denim" (i.e., opening the fly of a pair of 501's), I am reminded of Dr. Johnson's complaint about *Lycidas:* "it is not to be considered as the effusion of real passion; for passion runs not after remote allusions and obscure opinions. . . . Where there is leisure for fiction there is little grief."[23] White stands at an angle even to himself, and one of the things he sees ironically is desire, as though it were happening to someone else.

To the extent that desire lies at the heart of gay fiction from Tennessee Williams to Andrew Holleran and Neil Bartlett, White seems oddly marginal. But he is even marginal to a gay tradition one might have thought more congenial: the tradition of camp. Or if we think of gay fiction as establishing a narrative of separateness, even superiority — the strand represented by Christopher Isherwood and Ethan Mordden, for instance, and visible beneath the baroque façade of Firbank — then White is again the odd man out. He is temperamentally too reserved to cheer, lacking Isherwood's English bloody-mindedness and Mordden's Stonewall triumphalism. If Holleran is a lapsed Catholic, White seems a lapsed Protestant: a Milton both in the artificiality of his style and in his reluctance to sign on with any team. (Milton ended his life a member of no church but his own.) The three marginalities — of style, skepticism, and sexuality — interlock to form a constellation of undefinableness.

It is this undefinableness that is his pride, his sorrow, and his story in *Nocturnes for the King of Naples*. Despite being written during the heyday of the gay ghetto, it barely mentions that world or evokes voices that might exemplify it. The cast of characters is an extremely vague one, but none of them is living, even mentally, in 1978. His characters seem like throwbacks to the fifties, the age of anxiety, rather than inhabitants of their own decade.[24] Despite White's agreement with Conrad that "a novel should show how things look," therefore, I find that it doesn't succeed in this respect. Or rather, it succeeds only in small ways, not the large. *Nocturnes* lacks a sense of place and time which far more vulgar works like *Dancer from the Dance* effortlessly achieve. While much of it surely takes place in New York — the opening scene on the piers, for instance — it might as well be set in ancient Alexandria. Indeed, this vagueness is almost the point of the book, like the vagueness of the narrator and his older lover, neither of whom have names, dates, or visible means of support.

What comes across most strongly from both early novels is a sense of longing born of an obscure, nameless deficiency: the attentiveness to people like Herbert or the older lover is a way of figuring out what to do next, what is expected of one. Such a person as the narrator of either book is necessarily self-aware (even self-absorbed) and at the same time self-abnegating. He is a chameleon who changes colors for self-protection. So far, the changeableness *is* his color. But as we come to the second group of White's fiction, the autobiographical *A Boy's Own Story* and *The Beautiful Room Is Empty*, we begin to get closer to the chameleon. We begin to see him *in situ*, with a history, a family, a future, a routine. He begins to share some characteristics with readers who do not, for instance, live in a theater or on a mysterious island.

In these works (written in 1982 and 1988, and thus separated by as much as sixteen years from the earlier), more changes than the setting. The language itself, for instance, while still capable of wry and recherché puns, has trimmed down. It's as though the style had undergone the change described in the Afterword of *States of Desire* between sixties queenliness and seventies butchness: "Whereas such earlier gay esthetic sensibilities as dandyism or camp had proceeded through indirection and puzzling, deliberately intimidating reorderings of traditional values, the new esthetic, which I dubbed the Pleasure Machine, was frank, hedonistic, devoid of irony. It was lived out not in secret, twilit chambers tufted with purple velvet and containing a rotting, jewel-encrusted tortoise, but rather in airy lofts outfitted with chrome fixtures and industrial lamps and carpets and glossy photos of stylized sadism."[25]

White's new style has plainly gone to the gym and gotten itself a V-shape. But, like the difference between Old Code and New, the difference between the earlier novels and these "autobiographies" is at least somewhat illusory. For we have the same cast of characters, only given an American, indeed midwestern, field of action: the waif/sissy-boy, the inaccessible straight man, the brutal father, the helpless mother, the sister one loves and violates. There are also a few new ones, especially the "good" female twin — Maria in *The Beautiful Room Is Empty* — with whom one can temporarily form a successful version of the doomed incestuous marriage in *Forgetting Elena*.

What's new here is history, something the earlier novels cavalierly did without: who can tell "before" from "after" in *Nocturnes?* In *Aspects of the Novel* E. M. Forster neatly captured the difference between history (which he calls "plot") and mere chronicle (which he calls "story") this way: " 'The king died and then the queen died' is a story. 'The king died and then the queen died of grief' is a plot."[26] If as White himself has said, he's more interested in "controlling the mood" than in his "rather primitive" plots, there is nonetheless a fundamental change wrought by the autobiographical genre of these later novels. The main character has to have a youth, an adolescence, a young manhood; and they have to proceed in order. Despite White's frequent recourse to music as metaphor, his first two novels have the atemporal placidity of pictures rather than the intense suspensefulness of music. His new ones, however, begin to sing a tune.

Plot in Forster's special sense also makes *character* possible, indeed necessary. The boy who "had no character" in *Nocturnes* and therefore put up with crashing bores like Sergius, the young man who literally did not know who he was in *Elena,* now becomes someone who has a *bad* character, one of which he is ashamed. This character has everything to do with his homosexuality. He becomes a schemer, a concealer, a betrayer. He wants more than the earlier narrators. Love is focused on terminally unavailable straight boys or revoltingly available gay ones, but at least it has a name. The characteristic unspoken emotion of the autobiographies is rage, as anxiety was of the first novels. And if the characteristic action of the earlier books was abandonment (largely unconscious and unintentional), the action of these is seduction. *A Boy's Own Story,* for instance, ends with White seducing a gay teacher at his prep school, then betraying him to the headmaster. (The scene of White's quaking journey to see the headmaster is a sort of antiheroic parallel to Stephen Dedalus's trip to protest his unjust pandying in *Portrait of the Artist.*) Between being betrayed and betraying others — the trajectory defining "manhood" in White's fictional world — comes a series of attempts to be acceptable.

Among these hopeless attempts, the most hopeless and most doggedly pursued is psychoanalysis. As a gay adolescent trying desperately not to be gay, "White" first decides that what he needs is "an all-male environment," and bullies his father into enrolling him at "Eton," a pretentious midwestern prep school evoked also in *Nocturnes for the King of Naples*. To no one's surprise, the all-male environment doesn't do him much good — *please* don't throw me in that briar patch! — so White now talks his reluctant father into sending him to a "famous analyst," Dr. John Thomas O'Reilly.

As his first two names suggest, Dr. O'Reilly seems to be the very embodiment of a priapic Lawrentian heterosexuality. In truth, he is unhappily married: having divorced his wife in order to marry a patient, he was forced to un-divorce her when she was discovered to be dying of cancer; the former patient then flipped out and had to be institutionalized. He is an amphetamine addict who barely listens to his patients: "To save time, O'Reilly unfolded his ideas at the outset and then rehearsed them during each subsequent session" (168). He feeds White's sense of self-importance and at the same time, of miserable deficiency: "Don't you realize," White screams hysterically to his mother in *The Beautiful Room Is Empty*, "Don't you realize I know I'm neurotic, that I'm a brilliant person saddled with a terrible disease [sc., homosexuality], that I'm working day and night feverishly to cure myself, and that anything you can say against me I've already analyzed in depth with Dr. O'Reilly?"[27] But even though White quickly figures out that O'Reilly is a fraud ("I was ashamed of him," he writes at one point), he always goes back: "the wolf in me trotted away from the campfire, threw back a finely modeled head, and howled — but the sheep went to O'Reilly, because I didn't know how to say no" (97). Indeed, the dependence on O'Reilly becomes yet one more thing to be ashamed of.

The preoccupation with *being fixed* lasts through the second autobiography. The climax of this book (the long awful journey of a gay man to *some* kind of freedom) is a chapter about yet another quack therapist. Dale "specialized in a treatment based on the idea that everyone at all times was playing a game" (209). It is now at least a dozen years since White first encountered psychiatry, but he is no less dependent on or wounded by it. He and his then-boyfriend Sean, an unhappy man who wishes he weren't gay, are put in separate groups, all the better to coerce the "truth" out of them (i.e., get them to give up their homosexuality). "Under pressure from the group to date girls, Sean told me the sexual part of our relationship was over. He looked so pitiful, so *flayed,* that I didn't object" (213). Eventually, Sean goes crazy under the pressure of the group, is committed to St. Vincent's, then "bloated from suffering and pills and completely silent . . . shipped home to his parents in the Midwest" (215).

Sudden pity for Sean overwhelms White, and the feeling spreads to the reader: "I missed Sean so much I started to fester with it. I'd lie in bed and cry *it* and turn in *it* until I'd soiled myself with *it*. Everything, feebly, spoke *it*, even the neighbor's laundry palpitating shadows on my blinds" (215). He tries to write about Sean, but fails because he can't maintain the "appropriate irony and understatement and objectivity" (216). Somehow what has happened to Sean, poor midwestern Sean who was never smart enough for White, and no better able than White to reconcile his homosexual longings with love and self-respect, somehow Sean's completely undeserved suffering awakens his sense of injustice.

By this point in his story, it is the late sixties, and White is living in New York and begins going to the new gay bars that are opening in the Village, including "a new dance place, the Stonewall, which had the hottest jukebox" (216). But he is still unable to see his sexuality as anything but a ridiculous joke, a point-less, disgusting curse. How could he? Even "the magazine I worked for pub-lished an editorial on homosexuality for no particular reason. It denounced the 'chic new trend toward treating homosexuality as though it were a *different* way rather than a *lesser* way. . . . We must make certain that in this era of drugs, free sex, and sloppy liberal rhetoric the Homintern, that conspiracy of bitter inverts who already have a stranglehold over the theater, fashion, and fiction, does not pervert the lives of decent people by glamorizing vice, neutering the female body, and making the fine old art of being a mature man or woman look dull — or as *they* would say, campy'" (219). He goes to Cherry Grove, where he stays with an alcoholic queen and eats burned chicken at midnight to the tune of bitter "dish" about every other gay man in the place. He comes back to the city and wakes up in the middle of the night "gasping for air." Why? He himself barely understands, but the reader does. Who could *ever* have breathed that poisoned air?

At this nadir of his life — hasn't his experience at Cherry Grove *confirmed* the editorial's denunciation of "bitter inverts"? — a final backbreaking straw is laid on him. "When I cried in group therapy about Sean, about the helplessness I felt now, Simon [a fellow-patient] said, 'I wanna hear about de goils.' A rage I couldn't control boiled up inside me. The other men in the group had to pull me off Simon. I knocked his chair over and was sitting on him, choking him with both hands and shouting, over and over, 'Don't you *ever*, don't you *ever* — ' but I didn't know how to finish the sentence" (220).

This rage has been the subtext of not only this book but its predecessors. Irony and distance no longer suffice the man (or indeed the author); and this reader at least lets out a huge sigh of relief. (We too have been "gasping for air" as we read the thousand plausible reasons to find our lives third-rate and squalid.) At last the right answer has been found — rage, choking someone else rather than yourself — even though we, too, may be unable to finish the sentence.

This scene is the climax of *The Beautiful Room Is Empty,* though the coda, too, is satisfyingly flashy. White and his former lover Lou find themselves, of all places, at the Stonewall Inn on a hot June night in 1969, just after Judy Garland's death:

> Then the music went off, and the bar was full of cops, the bright lights came on, and we were all ordered out onto the street, everyone except the police working there. I suppose the police expected us to run away into the night, as we'd always done before, but we stood across the street on the sidewalk of the small triangular park. . . . Lou was already helping several black men pull up a parking meter. They twisted it until the metal pipe snapped. . . . Lou, a black grease mark on his T-shirt, was standing beside me, holding my hand, chanting, "Gay is good." We were all chanting it, knowing how ridiculous we were being in this parody of a real demonstration but feeling giddily confident anyway. Now someone said, "We're the Pink Panthers," and that made us laugh again. Then I caught myself foolishly imagining that gays might someday constitute a community rather than a diagnosis. (225–26)

To come upon the Stonewall riots from the retrospective angle of someone who didn't know they were going to happen, who was too timid to have *wanted* them to happen, makes politics real by translating them into a language we can understand. The rage of the men who battered down the door of the Stonewall *names* the rage White felt while strangling Simon, enables him to conclude the sputtering sentence that began "Don't you *ever*." White's hitherto "terrible disease" can now be understood, was only ever understandable, as a *political* grievance. "The personal is the political," we said in the sixties, but White's splendidly melodramatic *coup de théâtre* makes me understand the slogan as I never did at the time.

Even at this climactic moment, however, White is faithful to his honest muse, when he describes "knowing" that this was not, and could not be, a "real demonstration" but only a "parody." In those days, one of the most effective devices used to keep our anger at bay was that perfected by homophobic shrinks like Dr. Bergler: homosexuals were not *victims* of injustice, they were "*injustice collectors.*"[28] (Just like Lalique!) In White's description of the voice in his head telling him this was not a "real" demonstration we hear the last gasp of the "wrong" gay man, the one who "knows" he has a "terrible disease," who is incapable not merely of love but even outrage; the sheep who heads back to O'Reilly. And how clingingly subtle the poison must have been for that well-trained voice to have spoken even then, when victory was at hand, saying with weary contempt: You protest, yes; but your protests are childish. You suffer, yes; but your suffering is a fraud. You have no right to suffering, therefore none to redress of suffering. It is also the birth gasp of the "wronged" gay man, that is, the one who perceives that an injustice has been done. Even so, when White and Lou (sleepless that night for thinking of new possibilities) search the morning papers "to see how the Stonewall Uprising had been described . . . we couldn't find a single mention in the press of the turning point of our lives" (227).

This is the final sentence of the novel, but how glad I am that White preceded it with Stonewall (who cares if he was there or not, he *ought* to have been). The "plot," the "history" which had hovered just out of view throughout the first impressionistic novels and much of the autobiographies allows the reader a new emotion, triumph, and a new possibility of understanding based both on history and on character.

AIDS, like Stonewall, is yet another "public" event that calls White forth. Just as the autobiographical form imposed a sort of chronology that was absent from the two earlier, atemporal novels, many of the late stories impose a plot on what was merely a chronicle. Not, of course, that White or anyone else has an answer to why he and his friends are sick or have died. But something is now riding on the memories that surge forward, if only the necessity of remembering them *now*. The story, so to speak, is built in, and it is called "Before and After."

Many, if not all, gay writers have told this story since the epidemic began — Andrew Holleran has been virtually paralyzed by it — but White has been a comparative latecomer. Not generally given to nostalgia, he has been (until recently) uninterested in the pathetic possibilities of AIDS, the loss of freedom, sexual joy, friendship, youth. But then, these were never the subject of his earlier fictions either. (The past was always something to be escaped.) Nevertheless, now that his life seems destined to a swift end he can see its shape. With the shape, certain new emotions come out, just as a certain character came out in the autobiographical novels. Those emotions include pity, forgiveness, and good humor. The old White, pre-AIDS, was furious at everyone, most of all himself; and his recollections tended to settle old scores. In stories like "Cinnamon Skin," "Watermarked," "Pyrography," and "Reprise" (all from *Skinned Alive*), the figures who betrayed, abandoned, or simply let him down come back like shriven penitents.[29]

In some of the other stories in this collection, he does something he has rarely attempted, moves out of the first-person narrative voice, that rueful, self-correcting arrogant ingratiating "I," to a more objective third-person. In some of these late stories, many though not all about AIDS, there are men who are not only *not* Edmund White, but who don't even *resemble* Edmund White. I think of Mark in "Palace Days," a superannuated party boy who now runs the Bunyonettes, "a gay travel agency that arranged all-male tours. Forty gay guys would float down the Nile from Aswan to Luxor, impressing the Egyptians with their muscles and mustaches and shocking them with their pink short shorts and

filmy, drawstring *après-piscine* harem pants" (174). Or of Ray in "An Oracle,"
the younger half of a male couple whose older half (George) has recently died of
AIDS. Ray is sweet, serious, a beauty, who has been kept by the more forceful
George for years, and not quite approved of it: "George saw him obviously as a
sort of superior home entertainment center—stylish, electric. Ray didn't like to
stare into this reflection, he who'd won the Bellefontaine spelling bee and written one hundred and twenty closely reasoned pages on anomie. He saw that
without noticing it he'd drifted into the joking, irresponsible, anguished half-
world of the gay sophisticate who always knows what Sondheim has up his
sleeve, who might delay his first spring visit to the island until he's worked on
those forearms two more weeks, who feels confident Europe is as extinct as
a dead star and all the heat and life for the planet must radiate from New
York . . ." (122).

In both kinds of stories, the first- and third-person, I sense a new tone, as of
someone walking very softly among ruins, careful to see and remember and not
to knock anything down. The barely concealed fury that animated so much of
his earlier writing, and which manifested itself in memorable, unfair cameos of
his father, his sister, and a long string of gay male hysterics, has apparently died
down. He can still, of course, open a motive with a flick of his scalpel. Describing Ray's first job in New York as a manuscript reader for Grove Press, White
casually deflates Ray's provinciality: "Since he'd read little except the classics in
school, his standards were impossibly high, and since his acquaintanceship till
now had included only Ohio farmers, Chicago intellectuals and Toronto gay
liberationists, his grasp of the potential market for any particular book was
skewed" (120). But the story sets itself a kinder task: feeling its way into this lost
man, who is not just solemn, but "ironic" and "human." The very first line is
heartbreaking in what it does not say: "After George died, Ray went through a
long period of uncertainty" (112). White is not so quick as he might once have
been to give a lashing of sarcasm to Ray's "uncertainty," but takes it seriously, as
if he were Ray himself carefully choosing a word for his troubled solitude.

The stories that seem like memoirs (whether they are so or not is unimportant, their tone is so rueful and retrospective) are similarly soft. The Edmund
White character in "Pyrography," for instance, is the same old one we've met
before in *A Boy's Own Story* or *The Beautiful Room Is Empty*: scared, queer,
eager to please. But the story (about a camping trip with two straight friends)
does not revolve around his inadequacies. Indeed it doesn't really revolve
around anything at all: it's a watercolor of that now-distant moment, with as
seemingly little "point" as Hemingway's "Big Two-Hearted River."[30] "Watermarked" is a generous tribute to a first boyfriend, Randall, which follows him
from his attempts to be an actor in New York through a bad patch of drugs and
alcohol to sobriety and love with Saul. "Reprise" is perhaps the most touching,
a short vignette about "Jim Grady," a boy he'd met and had sex with as an

adolescent who reappears forty years later in Paris. Never close—Jim's life turned out to be a stifled one by most standards—he and White nonetheless fall into bed together: "On his trip to Paris I slept with him just that first time in his hotel room; as we kissed, he removed his smudged, taped welfare glasses and revealed his darting young blue eyes. He undressed my sagging body and embraced my thirty-six-inch waist and bared his own body, considerably slimmer but just as much a ruin with its warts and wattles and long white hair. And yet, when he hitched me into his embrace and said, 'Hey,' I felt fourteen again" (172).

As this touching, funny passage suggests, one of the wonderful surprises in recent gay literature has been White's emergence from the dungeon of his deficiencies. While he is still quick to point out failings, and to talk about them with unsparing wit, he seems to have relaxed. It was odd to notice in *Skinned Alive* that some of the tales of failure that float through the earlier books could be given a faster, funnier spin. "Cinnamon Skin," for instance, tells the story of a trip White made with his father and stepmother to Acapulco in the fifties, and of his seduction of a Mexican musician at their hotel. In *Nocturnes* the event appears briefly but inconclusively as a "photograph" from the narrator's sexual past:

> An Indian, on his break at last, rises from the piano and leads me out of the bar to the end of the pier. We sit on the bench. He takes my hand. With the help of my bilingual dictionary, rich in claret leather, he haltingly assembles a plan for our escape—tomorrow night, the boat expectant under a gardenia moon gone yellow, and then a plunge through parting spray to a village where his mother, at first as wooden as his devotion, then as efficient as my beauty, awaits us on the white beach, her shoulders wrapped in a pink, stirring rebozo. . . . For some reason I look around and see my father sauntering out toward us, drunkenly smiling at the tropical stars, undoubtedly searching for the Southern Cross. "Daddy," I say, rising with magnificent aplomb. "I'd like you to meet a friend of mine. Pablo. Yes, Pablo. This is Daddy."
>
> "Back to bed, son. Off you go. Pablo, how about a jazz rendition of 'Smoke Gets In Your Eyes'?" My father masterfully guides the poor man back to the bar. (56–57)

In *Nocturnes* this brief recollection is left to hang trembling on the edge of significance. Pablo is simply another of the long train of men the narrator has loved or desired in vain. The point is that the past is merely a collection of bright pebbles like this (and the pebbles are given rhetorical shape in White's jeweled vocabulary: rebozo, gardenia moon). "Like Isis," he writes, "I fly up and down this long river, my brother, searching for the parts of your broken body that I might piece it together again . . ." (57). Memory is a literal re-membering—but one that fails to reanimate.

The story told in "Cinnamon Skin" is (in Forster's terms) a *plot*. That is, the incident with Pablo is both the climax of White's reminiscence and a reason for it. Indeed, it is amazing to see now what White first "left out." (I am speaking, I realize, as though the stories were simply interchangeable, which of course they are not.) In "Cinnamon Skin" Pablo is still a musician, but the teenaged White has become an active seducer: "The man who had accompanied Libertad's daughter on the piano was a jowly Indian in his late thirties. Perhaps he smiled at me knowingly or held my hand a second too long when we were introduced, but I honestly can't remember his giving me the slightest sign of being interested in me. And yet I became determined to seduce him" (269). The process of seduction is elaborately explained—a marvelous wince-making description of White dousing himself with aftershave and posing naked in front of his mirror looking anxiously at his "chest, belly button, penis."

The aftermath is a comically botched assignation in which Pablo first goes to the wrong room, then (in the right one) fucks poor White with mechanical contempt:

> He didn't kiss me. He pulled my underpants down, spit on his wide, stubby cock, and pushed it up my ass. He didn't hold me in his arms. My ass hurt like hell. I wondered if I'd get blood or shit on the sheets. He was lying on top of me, pushing my face and chest into the mattress. He plunged in and out. It felt like I was going to shit and I hoped I would be able to hold it in. I was afraid I'd smell and repulse him. He smelled of old sweat. His fat belly felt cold as it pressed against my back. He breathed a bit harder, then abruptly stopped his movements. He pulled out and stood up. He must have ejaculated. It was in me now. He headed for the bathroom, switched on the harsh light, washed his penis in the bowl, and dried it off with one of the two small white towels that the maid brought every day. He had to stand on tiptoe to wash his cock properly in the bowl. (271–72)

It is not only the staccato Hemingway prose that seems new. The whole story is, because it has become a plot: the plot to seduce, the Feydeau farce of mistaken rooms, the comic irony of the boy's getting exactly what he wants and finding it exactly what he doesn't.

Even more different is what follows. As a tag to the memoir of this long-ago trip, White appends an epilogue unlike any he would have permitted himself in earlier work:

> Recently I was in Mexico City to interview Maria Felix, an old Mexican movie star. She kept me waiting a full twenty-four hours while she washed her hair (as she explained). I wandered around the city, still in ruins from a recent earth-

quake. The beautiful town of two million had grown into a filthy urban sprawl of slums where twenty-four million people now lived and milled around and starved. . . . I walked and walked, and I cried as I went, my body streaked by passing headlights. I felt that we'd been idiots back then, Dad and Kay and I, but we'd been full of hope and we'd come to a beautiful Art Deco hotel, the Palacio Nacional, and we'd admired the castle in Chapultepec Park and the fashionable people strolling up and down the Reforma. We'd been driving in Daddy's big Cadillac, Kay was outfitted in her wonderfully tailored Hattie Carnegie suit, with the lapel watch Daddy had given her dangling from the braided white and yellow gold brooch studded with lapis lazuli. Now they were both dead, and the city was dirty and crumbling, and the man I was travelling with was sero-positive, and so was I. Mexico's hopes seemed as dashed as mine, and all the goofy innocence of that first thrilling trip abroad had died, my boyhood hopes for love and romance faded, just as the blue in Kay's lapis had lost its intensity year after year, until it ended up as white and small as a blind eye. (272–73)

This too, if not a plot exactly, is nevertheless a gesture toward conventional conclusion. (*"Où sont les neiges d'antan?"*) Indeed, the story can be thought of as itself exemplifying the old and new strands of White's career. The description of his father's casual brutality ("God damn it, Kay, shut your goddam mouth" [260]) and Kay's casual racism ("Kay encouraged me to wave at the tiny, bare-foot Indians walking along the highway in their bright costumes . . ." [263–64]) all recall the White of earlier work (especially *A Boy's Own Story*). How horrible, stifling, hateful their world is. How precisely, unforgivingly it is rendered. So are the embarrassing details — from which one wants to avert one's eyes — of White's own unappealing sissidom ("I was ashamed of my recently acquired height, cracking voice, and first pubic hairs, and I posed in front of the foggy bathroom mirror with a towel turban around my head and my penis pushed back and concealed between my legs" [263]).

But the introduction and epilogue are kinder. When the teenage White invents preposterous stories about himself — that he was really English — the accent is "so obviously fabricated and snobbish that it eventually provoked a smile" (256). In earlier work the same self-invention would have provoked hostility and disgust. And by the end, in a turn as unexpected as it is touching, the familiar figures of White's fiction — horrible bullying father, dizzy stepmother, sissy son — become hopeful and full of "goofy innocence." They are not malicious, but ignorant: "idiots." The ridiculous Cadillac which was earlier the very symbol of the ugly American — "new, massive," and so pointlessly huge "I could stretch out full length, slightly nauseated from the cigars that my father chain-smoked and his interminable monologues about the difference between stocks and bonds" [257] — is now "Daddy's big Cadillac," and it is hard not to hear in that phrase a longing for the ridiculous security both afforded.

While White has always written about the past — his *only* topic is memory — he has formerly been at pains to purge from his memoirs any hint of sentimentality or nostalgia. (This has been in itself a brave as well as a perverse choice, for surely he has as much cause for weeping as anyone.) Here, he gives them voice. And it is impossible to read these final paragraphs without being moved. In many of the reminiscences in *Skinned Alive,* as in *Our Paris* and some of the AIDS stories, pathos begins to peer out. Before, he could talk about the shame of sex and snobbery with ease, but pathos was always the dirtiest secret in the darkest corner. Here, this too comes out of the closet.

One doesn't usually think of Edmund White as an alarming writer, but he seems one to me. Beneath the elegant prose and raconteur's charm, I always hear a haunted nervousness amounting to terror. He is always the mystified Prince of the Island in *Forgetting Elena* who makes hesitant fearful love to Elena: "Even if what we're doing is quite customary, I'm certain I'm not pursuing it in the right way. I'm wrong, it's wrong, this will come out badly." The supersubtle apprehensiveness is both his greatest gift as a writer, allowing him to register the tiniest twinges of irony and remorse, and (to me) his greatest liability. He has really just one story, the story of being wrong. Let me give a few examples.

In *A Boy's Own Story,* the narrator has fallen in love with yet another straight unavailable boy, the most "popular" boy in his school who nonetheless shares atheism and a liking for "philosophy" with the narrator. In this scene, the young White is sleeping over at Tom's house, and they're in that stage of adolescent romance when friendship seems everything. They are bursting with ideas and feelings: "The big dark house creaked around us as we lay on our separate beds in zany positions and talked and talked our way into the inner recesses of the night, those dim lands so tender to the couple." One of the things they talk about is friendship itself: "how it was as intense as love, better than love, a kind of love. I told Tom my father had said friendships don't last, they wear out and must be replaced every decade as we grow older — but I reported this heresy (which I'd invented; my poor father had no friends to discard) only so that Tom and I might denounce it and pledge to each other our eternal fidelity. 'Jesus,' Tom said, 'those guys are so damn *cynical!* Jeez . . .'" (116).

The passage is of no particular importance but reveals White at work in a characteristic way. The writer is ironizing an earlier self whose motives are shrewdly, but unfairly reduced to machination and deceit. Thus, he invents his father's cynical line "only so that Tom and I might denounce it and pledge to each other our eternal fidelity." The underlying message in this scene (which can stand for many of White's comic/grotesque scenes of amorous failure) is this:

the homosexual boy is always scheming, never direct; and even worse, his scheming is undignified and ridiculous. At no point in this brief description is there any hint that the young White was ever taken in by that blather about friendship being "better than love, a kind of love" or that he felt the longing with which those two wishful stillborn clauses ache.

One can defend the passage by saying that, after all, it is written in the voice and person of a self-hating gay teenager, that indeed his doubts and shames are the point of the story. This is true, but my objection isn't that the younger White is self-hating, but that the older one is unforgiving—unforgiving and, worse, *wise*. There is no escaping his automatic reduction of youthful love to a single discreditable motive. From his superior (defensive) viewpoint, he tells this story as if completely confident that he knows what his younger self was doing during those long talky nights with Tom; he's certain that what he wanted was to seduce. The result for me is painfully mixed. I cannot help admiring the brilliant vignette and sharp-edged language; but the foregone conclusions about the scene seem unfair, even agonizing.

In part White's automatic self-depreciation is modern good manners. We are far too well bred to attempt self-defense or panegyric, and take "apology" not in Newman's sense, but our own stammering apologetic one. (It is hard to imagine a contemporary artist imitating Wagner's crow of triumph in *My Life* about the fiendish cleverness with which he had combined the three themes of the *Meistersinger* Overture!) Indeed, we tell *our* story with a kind of brutality we would not inflict on anyone else. Not surprisingly, White himself has given memorable expression to this idea. In describing his family's dysfunction—wife abandoned by husband, children by father, and all miserable—White sums up his sister's version of self-blame like this: "No wonder honesty came to mean for my sister saying only the most damaging things against herself. If she *began* by admitting defeat, then something was possible: sincerity perhaps, or at least the avoidance of appearing ludicrous" (75). But this is exactly what White himself does, how *he* gets out of the moral jam of being, or feeling, "wrong." He, too, "begins by admitting defeat" and thus achieves "sincerity . . . or at least the avoidance of appearing ludicrous." He, too, makes himself look good by making himself look bad first. Never does he permit his confessors—that is, his readers—to make the discoveries themselves, however, but always gets there first to make sure the scene of the crime is sufficiently bleak and bloody. As a result, what looked so bracingly upright at first comes to seem a species of cowardice, even arrogance. He will not risk (or he disdains) the novelist's ultimate abandonment of a fictional character to the caprice and vindictiveness of a reader, and in this respect seems less a novelist than a memoirist or essayist.

For instance, a few pages after the "Tom" episode, there is a brilliant description of White pretending to himself he's fallen in love with "Helen," a beautiful girl at his school, and of writing her a letter in purple prose telling her so. "That night I wrote her a letter. I chose a special yellow parchment, a spidery pen point and black ink. . . . I sat down with great formality at my desk and composed the missive, first in pencil on scratch paper. If I reproduced it (I still have the pencil draft) you'd laugh at me or we would laugh together at the prissy diction and the high-flown sentiment. What would be harder to convey is how much it meant to me, how it read to me back then. I offered her my love and allegiance while admitting I knew how unworthy of her I was" (135).

This is a fascinating passage. Perhaps it would indeed be hard to convey his adolescent worship of Helen, but not because the letter would give the wrong idea. Indeed, wouldn't such a hideously embarrassing document give exactly the right idea of hopeless love? Why then has he spared himself, under the pretense of sparing *us?* Is it his writer's vanity? The fear that we would not approve the flights of goopy rhetoric? But then, why has he kept the pencil draft? There is, in other words, a somewhat fraudulent though sadistic honesty to his self-batterings — and they last through much of his career.

Accompanying it, indeed making it possible, is that marvelous style, a marriage (as David Bergman says) of Christopher Isherwood and Vladimir Nabokov.[31] For example, here is a description of Tom again, full of the most ravishing language. He and White and Tom's father are out on a sailboat. White is, of course, hopeless at sailing ("I knew I was in the way") and he assumes Mr. Wellington regards him with "disapproval," "holding his judgment in reserve." Both are watching the beautiful Tom, and White suddenly knows that, despite his obvious heterosexuality, he and Mr. Wellington are alike. The conceit allows White to tell his love, as if the father's presence permitted what would otherwise be forbidden to him alone, but the freedom is decidedly reined in:

Here was this boy, laughing and blonded by the sun and smooth-skinned, his whole body straining up as he reached to cleat something so that his T-shirt parted company with his dirty, sagging jeans and we — the father and I — could see Tom's muscles like forked lightning on his taut stomach; here was this boy so handsome and free and well liked and here were we flanking him, looking up at him, at the torso flowering out of the humble calyx of his jeans. It seemed to me then that beauty is the highest good, the one thing we all want to be or have or, failing that, destroy, and that all the world's virtues are nothing but the world's spleen and deceit. The ugly, the old, the rich and the accomplished speak of invisible virtues — of character and wisdom and power and skill — because they lack the visible ones, that ridiculous down under the lower lip that can't decide to be a beard, those prehensile bare feet racing down the sleek deck, big hands too heavy for slender arms, the sweep of lashes over faded lapis-lazuli eyes, lips deep red, the windblown hair intricate as Velásquez's rendering of lace. (124)

This is not prose you or I could write. Neither is it the prose a sixteen-year-old boy could write, but that scarcely matters. Tom disappears into a kind of verbal glory, like the tiny Host in a huge baroque monstrance. He is far less interesting than the language used to describe him. Even if the passage is meant to evoke Tom's sexual power over the narrator, it fails: the details of his body ("muscles like forked lightning on his taut stomach," "big hands too heavy for slender arms") have erotic potential but little erotic effect. One's heart beats faster for the clauses and caesuras than for Tom.

What is riding on White's description? What was riding on the younger White's desire? To whom do these phrases matter? All these are questions I find myself asking as I read this remarkable passage, just as I asked them as I read the description of sex on the piers in the late-seventies New York. The gorgeous prose belongs not to the boy who was so ineptly in love, but to an older, smarter, safer man whose first and last love was always language. The words *themselves* are the point — to use 'calyx' at all! to flank it with 'humble' and 'jeans' on either side! It is the English language that is the hero of this sentence and of White's fiction. His style, "this glorious image I've made, sustained like a baldachino on points of shadow" (*Nocturnes,* 5), exists to support the elaborate façade of playfulness that constitutes both the "character" of the story-teller and the story he tells. Yet although "I" is in every sentence of the four novels, though the stories are always about him, we know nothing that he doesn't permit us to see and doesn't carefully arrange. We "see" depths of self-abnegation and horror, but see them through falsely candid eyes, and are never permitted to glimpse the statue from the back.

He may be, then, our best writer of novels without being our best novelist. Or it may be that his best fiction is not to be found in either of the early novels, or in the two autobiographical ones, but in the short stories of his later career where he dares to imagine characters different from himself, or to show pity for those battered first editions of himself. It is in these, I think, that he risks the final distancing of fiction, the cutting a character loose from its nurse's leading-strings.

Such a cutting loose is extremely difficult in first-person narratives, where the temptation to make oneself look "good" (even by making oneself look "bad" first) usually proves irresistible. It can, however, be done. For example, in *Great Expectations,* the adult Pip tries to control our perception of himself, and does so in a very Whitean way, by "saying only the most damaging things" about himself and thinking them "honest." But far more than White, Dickens is able to present Pip as one character among others. He does this by constructing scenes in which Pip speaks with another character at length and is not interrupted by his adult self. But above all, he does it with *plot*. Plot, while seeming superficial, gives *Great Expectations* more profound resources than those of wit and voice, which are the mere superego of fiction. Plot conveys symbolic meanings which shed more light on Pip than Pip ever could, no matter how intelligent, humorous, and remorseful he might be.

The great scene in chapter 39, when Pip's convict-benefactor Magwitch emerges out of a storm at the dead of night, does more than "explain" the source of Pip's "expectations"; and Pip's horror of him goes beyond mere snobbish discomfiture at having such a "father," beyond even Pip's fear of losing the disdainful Estella. His is a terror of recognition, the recognition that this beaten, stubborn, murderous man is himself. *He* doesn't know it, Dickens does; and the scene — so melodramatic and so structurally sound — makes us know it as well. Nor can I imagine that any purely essayistic style, no matter how brilliant, could do what this richly symbolic encounter does, precisely because the essay dwells too much in the light of conscious awareness. The reader's profound illumination may exceed even Dickens's own intention. For consider: if the horrifying convict Magwitch is to be allowed (as he is) to prove tranquil, even wise, perhaps his symbolic son Pip can, too — and this in the teeth of the official self-lacerating intention of the first-person narrator and his endless iterations of guilt. And it is *plot* that allows us to come to this conviction, which is far deeper than Pip's, or Dickens's, own.

"My plots are rather primitive," White confessed to Jordan Egrably in the *Paris Review*. Would that they were! No one would care if his plots were primitive so long as they functioned *as* plots. (Henry James delights the reader partly because of the combination of cast-iron melodrama and gilded rhetoric.) But he is more "interested in controlling the mood" and to this extent fails to give me the gorgeous, obvious lies that tell the truth by profound indirections.

White's fiction, despite his reputation for aestheticism and playfulness, always strikes me as fundamentally serious, even (for all its charm) slightly grim. (*He* is the one who is "eccentric, patient, scrupulous," not the reader he so disingenuously flatters in *A Boy's Own Story*.) While his manner may be whimsical (associations, puns, fantasies), the whimsy is always tied firmly to the ground. Scene after scene, the smiling clever story is the same: How I fooled myself! How ridiculous I am! How impossible it is to overcome the lovelessness of an unhappy youth! Indeed, it is not White's mendacity but his honesty that finally makes me impatient with him. I am impatient not because the message is sad, but because its manner is. I miss the electric charge of passionate willfulness; and his substitute — an unresentful acceptance of limitation and loss — is so plainly "wise" that my own treacherous heart feels cheated. It does not see itself in this temperate mirror.

At the same time, especially as I have grown older and more temperate myself, I find a new ability to like what I do not love, and a personal reminiscence will close this long self-doubting chapter.

Last winter, when I began reading *Skinned Alive* for this book, I opened the first story with my usual uncharitable misgivings. But as I read "Pyrography," with its open-ended depiction of a single moment from an irrecoverable and possibly meaningless past, I found myself strangely moved. After so many other works of gay fiction, after tragic hectoring from *Narrow Rooms* or *Giovanni's Room,* after romantic pathos from *Dancer from the Dance,* after grim gray novels of life on the Lower East Side or chirpy upbeat novels of life on the Upper East Side, I was simply happy to be in White's company again, the company of a writer who had so little design on me — except of course the one imperious, nonnegotiable demand that I be amused. I felt toward him then as toward a friend with whom I had quarreled long ago. But time had passed, and having reached some accommodation with my own limitations, and also with his, I woke suddenly to the recognition that for that moment I wanted to be nowhere else; for that moment I wanted to hear no other voice, read no other book. I magnanimously forgave him for being so wise and disillusioned, and for so steadily refusing, from beginning to end of his distinguished career, to treat himself as a hero. In that moment I began to see that I had disliked him when young because he did not treat *me* as one either, any more than he exaggerated the world-historical importance of gay liberation. Now that I am past the age of such self-aggrandizement, his wit has become a pleasant bitterness, austere in lamentation.

In fact — *pace* David Bergman, my dear friend and his — I now think the only thing lacking in Edmund White is "betrayal": the ecstatic betrayal of fiction.

AFTERWORD

Of Walter Pater's essays on the Renaissance in *Appreciations,* Oscar Wilde insouciantly wrote: "Mr. Pater's essays became to me 'the golden book of spirit and sense, the holy writ of beauty.' They are still this to me. It is possible of course that I may exaggerate about them. I certainly hope that I do; for where there is no exaggeration there is no love, and where there is no love there is no understanding. It is only about things that do not interest one, that one can give a really unbiassed opinion; and this is no doubt the reason why an unbiassed opinion is always absolutely valueless."[1]

Having delivered myself of so many hopelessly biased opinions of my own, it is time (namely: too late) to make the usual apologies.

I have tried to "cover" gay male fiction: a difficult task which has become an impossible one as gay fiction has become more prolific and available — more written, and more read. It used to be that a bimonthly trip to the Glad Day Bookstore in Boston was sufficient to keep one up-to-date on what was being written. No longer. Hundreds of gay books of one sort or another come out every year. I could not, and have not, read them all. And even of the books I have read and enjoyed, I have left out much more than I included. In one sense, the exclusion was simply pragmatic, and must be accepted on the grounds that discussion of a few representative books was my only hope of covering gay fiction in any way at all. But furthermore, the kind of coverage I had in mind was not that of, say, a literary history but that of literary criticism. My book does not aim to do literary archaeology, and I am sure that my many mistakes of judgment will be corrected by scholars who are doing such work.

My task was simpler in one sense, and much harder in another. I tried to make sense of an already fairly large body of fiction, discern as well as I could its major branches, and convey to the reader what seemed particularly worth read-ing, what one should read *first*. What I have written is, in that sense, a "canon." By "canon" I mean that, though I may have left out some books that will seem canonical a hundred years hence, I do not think that the ones I have included (even those I dislike) will be absent from such a list. Whether for subject or style, the books I discuss struck me and strike me still as central to the project of gay fiction in the postwar period.

Are these the only good gay books? Of course not. For one thing, I have discussed at most two dozen works. There are plenty more where they came from, as I indicate in the Appendix that follows this Afterword. Second, many of the works I do discuss here are atypical: most of James Purdy's novels are neither as gay nor as overtly sexual as *Narrow Rooms*; Williams's gay stories (though among his very best) are at most a twelfth of his output. Third, certain works by the same author vary so much in quality from each other that one scarcely knows how to judge the author. Is Andrew Holleran to be judged as the author of *Nights in Aruba* or of *Dancer from the Dance*? Finally, even though I find *A Single Man,* for example, a better novel than any of Edmund White's, White on the whole must be considered a more significant gay author if only because he has written so often, so well, and so completely on this topic.

There are many authors I have not mentioned, or mentioned only in passing, who could easily have taken a place in my "canon." Some of Allan Gurganus's short stories (such as "Adult Art" and "Forced Use") are as good as anything in Tennessee Williams.[2] Philip Gambone's short-story collection *The Language We Use Up Here* tells the stories I always want David Leavitt to tell and does so with greater self-irony and charm.[3] My choices were made on personal taste and history. But I chose them also because they were useful in illustrating certain permanent questions about gay life. Though there were many other books that emerged from the ghetto, I suspect most would have fallen either onto the Kramer or the Holleran side of the debate on the value of ghetto life, which I have characterized as the "life of desire." And while *Faggots* is hardly my favor-ite book about the gay ghetto, it is important enough to remain a thorn in gay liberation's flesh twenty years after its publication.

I have said I chose my books for subject or style; but I still want to make a distinction between books that have something to say, those that are merely pretty, and those that are both substantial and beautiful. Thus, I find David Leavitt's novels interesting mainly for their subject matter. Leavitt's were among the very first stories and novels to think through the question of gay assimila-tion, especially assimilation into the formerly off-limits territory of one's birth family. On the other hand (as I have made obvious) I find the novels *qua* novels clunky, earnest, and a bit dull. Edmund White's writing is the exact opposite of Leavitt's—he can turn a sentence on a dime—but he has usually left me cold (though, as I admit in my essay on him, that "coldness" has come to seem refreshing to me, especially in the wake of more overheated fictions).

And finally, the reader will be able to divine the handful of books that strike me as being both substantial and artistically successful: Williams's short stories, Isherwood's *A Single Man,* Vidal's *Myra Breckinridge,* Holleran's *Dancer from the Dance,* Mordden's short stories, Bartlett's *Ready to Catch Him Should He Fall,* Purdy's *Narrow Rooms* and *Eustace Chisolm and the Works.* These are none of them perfect books; nor am I so foolish as to wish that I could be exiled to some desert island with these alone. I like to hate Larry Kramer (and goodness knows he likes to *be* hated); I like arguing with James Baldwin and Dale Peck; I like the narcotic beauty of Michael Cunningham. I would not wish to live without Delany's *The Mad Man* or the even sexier and more troubling *Hogg* and *Equinox.*

But luckily, the literature available to interested readers (gay or straight) is not limited, as this book is, by personal blindness and the need to bring things within a brief compass. There are hundreds of interesting, beautiful, subtle works "by, for, and about gay men" that are now in every good library and bookstore in the country. Twenty-five years ago, when I was coming out, they were not there. As a reminder to myself of what I have left out, and as a signpost for the interested reader, I include a list of other books that have accompanied and made possible a fortunate gay life.

Not all of these books are necessarily highbrow or even respectable. Like Edmund White and Neil Bartlett, I find myself quite unable to isolate sexual, even pornographic, fiction from supposedly unerotic and "serious" fiction. My model in this respect is a fascinating character we meet in White's *The Beautiful Room Is Empty,* Lou, a thirty-year-old gay man who befriends the adolescent White. He is a kind of gay man one meets less often nowadays, but who occupied an important place in the development of gay consciousness. A "sexual formalist," he "disliked a spasm of delight much as he disliked any sudden visitation of feeling." He sees homosexuality as a crime and himself as a determined, even proud criminal. His shelf of books reflects this. "He ended up with a small canon of books about himself — John Rechy's *City of Night,* which was just appearing chapter by chapter in magazines, the few isolated scraps of William Burroughs he could find in print, Jean Genet's *Our Lady of the Flowers.* In these books he saw his own darkness reflected. He appreciated that in them there was no trace of American optimism. He also liked that these pages were devoted to 'sexy fairies' and that every page could cost the reader some come."[4] I suppose I am a bit like Lou myself, both in my sexual "formalism" and in my liking for books which have cost me some come. In the following brief list of books, I have included a few whose seminal cover charge I have willingly paid.

I have included also a few titles that fall into a category I call "Gay 202" literature: books written by and for, but not necessarily about, gay men. These books, which one wants warily to call examples of "gay sensibility," are nonetheless central to my experience of gay life, and a reminder of the witty codes gay men have devised over the years to make themselves known to each other, if not to the larger world.

MORE GAY FICTION:

AN APPENDIX

Terry Andrews, *The Story of Harold* (New York: Holt, Rinehart and Winston, 1974). This is an indescribably perverse story about a children's-book author, the married man he is in love with (and whips), the man's blind son, and a bum who wants to be set on fire; by a pseudonymous author whose identity remains speculative.

Neil Bartlett, *The House on Brooke Street* (New York: Dutton, 1997). Bartlett's second novel is not as good as *Ready to Catch Him,* but explores the same romantic territory of loss, shame, and imagination.

Bruce Benderson, *Used* (New York: Dutton, 1984). This splendid novel takes seriously what Dennis Cooper only plays with.

Christopher Bram, *Surprising Myself* (New York: Donald I. Fine, 1987); *In Memory of Angel Clare* (New York: Donald I. Fine, 1989). Bram is like a less romantic Neil Bartlett, in the sense that he imagines gay characters living in "pregay" times. I've always been a bit underwhelmed by the novels, but impressed by the subjects.

William Burroughs, *The Wild Boys* (New York: Grove Press, 1971). Is this a gay novel? There is certainly a lot of rectal mucus floating around in it; and like Dennis Cooper, Burroughs captures some essential part of male perversity.

William Carney, *The Real Thing* (New York: G. P. Putnam's Sons, 1968). This 1968 novel is the most elegantly written S and M novel in gay fiction.

Willa Cather, "Paul's Case: A Study in Temperament," in Cather, *Collected Short Fiction* (Lincoln: University of Nebraska Press, 1965). This 1906 short story by a lesbian writer never uses the word homosexual and yet can be read by a modern gay man with instant recognition.

John Cheever, *Falconer* (New York: Ballantine, 1977). Cheever was finally outed by his daughter, Susan, after his death, but there can't have been many readers who were surprised, after this very Cheeverian novel of prison love.

Christopher Coe, *I Look Divine* (New York: Ticknor and Fields, 1987); *Such Times* (New York: Harcourt Brace and Company, 1993). Beautiful, sad reports from a dandy in the age of clones, and of AIDS.

Sam Dallessandro, *The Zombie Pit* (Freedom, CA: The Crossing Press, 1989). This collection of short stories by a writer who died far too young (of AIDS) is my favorite example of affectless postmodern L.A. love.

Guy Davenport, *The Cardiff Team* (New York: New Directions, 1996). Davenport's refined style and enormous learning make these stories of adolescent desire (and desire for adolescents) dangerously attractive.

Robert Ferro, *The Family of Max Desir* (New York: Dutton, 1983); *Second Son* (New York: Crown, 1988). Ferro makes an interesting contrast with David Leavitt. In Leavitt, the family's story takes over the gay son's. Ferro is more exciting to me because he takes the risk of showing the centrality and power of the gay son within his family.

John Fox, *The Boys on the Rock* (New York: St. Martin's, 1984). An unpretentious coming-out story, set winningly in the context of Eugene McCarthy's unsuccessful presidential campaign in 1968. Fox, like Sam Dallessandro, is a casualty of the AIDS epidemic whose loss I particularly regret.

Philip Gambone, *The Language We Use Up Here* (New York: Dutton, 1991). Gambone's stories of adult gay men coming to terms with waning love and waxing lust are funny, unpretentious, and honest.

Barry Gifford, *Landscape with Traveller: The Pillow Book of Francis Reeves* (New York: E. P. Dutton, 1980). This is the only book by a nongay writer in my list; perhaps the only book not by its author. This "pillow book" claims to be journal entries of a middle-aged gay man, in love with a younger straight one but unhysterical about it. From what I understand, Gifford is that younger straight man, and his book either reproduces "Francis Reeves's" journal or imagines it. Either way, *Landscape with Traveller* is a strange *hommage* from a heterosexual man to a homosexual one. *Sui generis,* and not to be missed.

Robert Glück, *Jack the Modernist* (New York: Sea Horse, 1985). Glück deserved more space in my book than I gave him. A representative of what has been somewhat grandly called the "new narrative" school of fiction, Glück writes highly intelligent, unpredictable stories about urban (not necessarily gay) life.

Michael Grumley, *Life Drawing* (New York: Grove Weidenfeld, 1991). Edmund White points out in his foreword to *Life Drawing* that we rarely read books by handsome men. This is one. Grumley was Robert Ferro's lover, but is less well known as a writer. *Life Drawing* is worth reading, however, and quite different from Ferro's work. Less a coming-out story than a coming-of-age story, it is about a gay Huck Finn finally consummating his love with Jim.

Allan Gurganus: "Adult Art," in *Men on Men 2: Best New Gay Fiction,* ed. with intro. by George Stambolian (New York: Plume, 1988); "Forced Use," in *The Faber Book of Gay Short Fiction,* ed. Edmund White (London: Faber and Faber, 1991). Tennessee Williams would have loved these two stories of homosexual lust.

Kevin Killian, *Shy* (Freedom, CA: The Crossing Press, 1989); *Bedrooms Have Windows* (New York: Amethyst Press, 1989). Killian holds down the East Coast headquarters of the "new narrative" firm. His sardonic stories of waifs on drugs are a little less chilly than Dennis Cooper's.

Stephen McCauley, *The Object of My Affection* (New York: Washington Square Press, 1988). Like the novels of David Leavitt, McCauley's are reader-friendly and welcoming. I find them alternately smarmy and bratty, but most readers like them better than I do.

James McCourt, *Mawrdew Czgowchwz* (New York: Farrar Straus and Giroux, 1974). McCourt is one of the few gay writers to persevere in a lofty and disdainful dandyism; and his novel about the great singer Mawrdew Czgowchwz is an *objet de culte* among opera queens and other gay men. Boyd McDonald would not have liked it in the least.

Men on Men series, edited by George Stambolian and David Bergman. George Stambolian began editing this series of short-story anthologies in 1986, and continued editing them until his 1991 death from AIDS, when it was taken over by David Bergman. Many of the best gay writers in America appeared here first, and many already established authors continue to be published here. As of late 1997, there are six books in the series.

Men on Men: Best New Gay Fiction, ed. with intro. by George Stambolian (New York: Plume, 1986).

Men on Men 2: Best New Gay Fiction, ed. with intro. by George Stambolian (New York: Plume, 1988).

Men on Men 3: Best New Gay Fiction, ed. with intro. by George Stambolian (New York: Plume, 1990).

Men on Men 4: Best New Gay Fiction, ed. George Stambolian, intro. by Felice Picano, afterword by Andrew Holleran (New York: Plume, 1992).

Men on Men 5: Best New Gay Fiction, ed. with intro. by David Bergman (New York: Plume Penguin, 1994).

Men on Men 6: Best New Gay Fiction, ed. with intro. by David Bergman (New York: Plume Penguin, 1996).

Mark Merlis, *American Studies* (New York: Penguin, 1996). The best gay novel of the past few years: hot, unsentimental, and unexpected. Who would have thought a *roman à clef* about Professor F. O. Matthiessen would be this good?

Robert Patrick, *Temple Slave* (New York: Richard Kasak, 1994). An over-the-top memoir of the sixties theater (and gay) scene in New York. Funny and nostalgic.

David Plante, *The Foreigner* (New York: E. P. Dutton, 1986). David Plante is a highly regarded serious novelist whose charm I have so far resisted. This Jamesian story of a gay American abroad comes the closest to overcoming my resistance.

James Purdy, *Garments the Living Wear* (San Francisco: City Lights, 1989). Anything whatever by Purdy can be astonishing. This is his AIDS novel — sort of. Curious readers should also seek out his short story collection *63, Dream Palace: Selected Stories 1956–1987* (Santa Rosa: Black Sparrow Press, 1991).

John Rechy, *City of Night* (New York: Grove Press, 1963); *The Sexual Outlaw: A Documentary* (New York: Grove Press, 1977). Classic works of gay fiction that leave me cold, despite the fact that they are sexually relentless. Like Purdy, Rechy may be an acquired taste, especially if you like your gay fiction driven, unhappy, and religiose.

Paul Russell, *The Salt Point* (New York: Dutton, 1990); *Boys of Life* (New York: Dutton, 1991). Sad tales with a nihilistic edge: *petit Guignol,* so to speak.

Vikram Seth, *The Golden Gate* (New York: Random House, 1987). A "novel in verse," *The Golden Gate* is what *Tales of the City* would be if it were turned into a sonnet sequence: witty, casual, inclusive — though unexpectedly poignant.

Matthew Stadler, *Landscape: Memory* (New York: Charles Scribner's Sons, 1990); *The Dissolution of Nicholas Dee* (New York: Charles Scribner's Sons, 1993). James Purdy, who likes almost no other gay writers, admires Matthew Stadler, a young novelist whose indescribable works are less clotted than Purdy's but just as odd. I predict a series of unnerving, beautiful books from him.

George Whitmore, *The Confessions of Danny Slocum* (New York: St. Martin's Press, 1980). George Whitmore was one of the less well known members of the "Violet Quill" group of gay writers in seventies New York. His neglect may be partly due to his unflattering pictures of gay life in that time. *Danny Slocum* dares to take on the sexual license of the ghetto — despite his last name, Danny has a problem with *premature* ejaculation — and does so without recourse to Larry Kramer's jeremiads.

NONCE, GENRE, AND ONE-HANDED BOOKS

E. F. Benson, *Make Way for Lucia* (New York: Crowell, 1977). One of at least three gay sons of a late-Victorian archbishop of Canterbury, E. F. Benson was a prolific author who hit his stride in six novels about the terminally snobbish and social-climbing "Lucia." *Make Way for Lucia* (the title given to the one-volume republication of these six novels) is Gay 202 literature — books not about gay men, but read primarily *by* them. The series does, however, include a marvelously prissy gay man of a certain age, his butch, hockey-playing sisters, a frighteningly avant garde lesbian painter, and what would seem to be a caricature of Henry James in the unbelievably courtly Mr. Wyse.

Thomas M. Disch, *On Wings of Song* (New York: St. Martin's, 1979). A charming allegory, lightly handled: what if, not homosexuality, but singing were forbidden? Disch is also a writer of edgy science fiction and a splendid poetry critic. His collection of reviews, *The Castle of Indolence* (New York: Picador, 1995) is not only perceptive, but also makes me laugh out loud.

Flesh and the Word series, edited by John Preston and Michael Lowenthal. Dirty stories by the first unabashed pornographer in gay fiction, John Preston; and, after Preston's death from AIDS, by his talented protégé Michael Lowenthal. The series numbers four books, with more in the offing.

Flesh and the Word: An Anthology of Erotic Writing, ed. with intro. by John Preston (New York: Plume, 1992).

Flesh and the Word 2: An Anthology of Erotic Writing, ed. with intro. by John Preston (New York: Plume, 1993).

Flesh and the Word 3: An Anthology of Gay Erotic Writing, ed. with intro. by John Preston with Michael Lowenthal (New York: Plume, 1995).

Flesh and the Word 4: Gay Erotic Confessionals, ed. with intro. by Michael Lowenthal (New York: Plume, 1997).

Joseph Hansen: The Dave Brandstetter Mysteries. Hard-boiled L.A. murder mysteries with a gay hero who breaks every stereotype. Here are some representative titles: *Fadeout* (New York: Harper and Row, 1970); *Death Claims* (New York: Harper, 1973); *The Man Everybody Was Afraid Of* (New York: Holt, Rinehart and Winston, 1978); *Skinflick* (New York: Holt, 1979); *Gravedigger* (New York: Holt, 1982).

Tom Hardy, *The Green Hotel* (Kukuihaele, HI: Omniun, 1987). Dirty stories, but the eponymous story, told by an unnamed older man about the sailor and Marine who once shared a hotel room, would not be out of place in Isherwood, Williams, or Bartlett.

Michael Nava: The Henry Rios mysteries. More L.A. detective stories, but unlike Dave Brandstetter, the son of a rich insurance executive, Henry Rios is a reluctant American success story, uneasily balancing his Chicano family, his gay lovers, his law degree, and his drinking problem. These are first-rate mysteries, but I always suspect that Nava will one day write a big gay novel outside this genre. Some of his best mysteries are *The Little Death* (Boston: Alyson, 1986); *Goldenboy* (Boston: Alyson, 1988); and *The Death of Friends* (New York: Putnam, 1996).

Aaron Travis, *The Flesh Fables* (S. Norwalk, CT: Fire Island Press, 1990). The most superbly demented dirty stories imaginable. "Blue Light" has already attained classic status.

NOTES

INTRODUCTION: FIVE HOUSES OF GAY FICTION

1. Reed Woodhouse, "Five Houses of Gay Fiction," *Harvard Gay and Lesbian Review* 1: 1 (Winter 1994), 1.

2. Dennis Cooper, *Frisk* (New York: Grove Weidenfeld, 1991), 69.

3. Flannery O'Connor, *Mystery and Manners: Occasional Prose,* ed. Sally and Robert Fitzgerald (London and Boston: Faber and Faber, 1972), 103–4.

4. Quoted in Constantine P. Cavafy, *The Complete Poems of Cavafy* (expanded edition), trans. Rae Dalven, with an introduction by W. H. Auden (New York and London: Harvest, 1976), 288.

5. Alan Dershowitz, *The Vanishing American Jew: In Search of Jewish Identity for the Next Century* (Boston: Little, Brown, 1997); Randall Kennedy, "My Race Problem — And Ours," *Atlantic Monthly,* May 1997, 55–66; and Daniel Harris, *The Rise and Fall of Gay Culture* (New York: Hyperion, 1997).

6. David Leavitt, "The Term Paper Artist," in *Arkansas: Three Novellas* (New York: Houghton Mifflin, 1997).

7. Christopher Isherwood, *A Single Man* (New York: Farrar, Straus, and Giroux, 1964), 27–28.

8. David Leavitt, Introduction to *The Penguin Book of Gay Short Stories* (New York: Viking, 1994), xxvi.

9. Milan Kundera, *Testaments Betrayed* (New York: HarperCollins, 1995), 91–92.

10. Frank Browning, *A Queer Geography: Journeys Toward a Sexual Self* (New York: Crown, 1996). See especially chap. 2, "Genius Loci," 51–98.

11. Edmund White, *The Beautiful Room Is Empty* (New York: Knopf, 1988), 226.

12. Edmund White, "Skinned Alive," in *Skinned Alive* (New York: Vintage, 1996), 56.

13. Orlando Patterson, *Freedom* (New York: Basic Books, 1991). See especially chap. 3, "The Greek Origins of Freedom," 47–63.

14. W. H. Auden, "Robert Frost," in *The Dyer's Hand* (New York: Vintage, 1968), 353.

1. FROM THE CLOSET TO THE THEATER

1. James Baldwin, *Giovanni's Room* (New York: Laurel, 1988), 77, 87. All subsequent citations are from this edition and will be given parenthetically within the text.

2. Fritz Peters, *Finistère* (New York: Farrar, Straus and Co., 1951).

3. Camille Paglia, *Sexual Personae: Art and Decadence from Nefertiti to Emily Dickinson* (New Haven: Yale University Press, 1990), 196.

4. T. S. Eliot, *Selected Essays* (London: Faber and Faber, 1969), 145.

5. Narcissism is a charge frequently brought against gay men. See Edmund Bergler, *Principles of Self-Damage* (1959), quoted in Patrick Higgins, *A Queer Reader* (New York: The New Press, 1993), 125: "The homosexual does not take this second and decisive unconscious step [of "active reversal"]. Because of his exaggerated narcissism, he cannot accept the partial victory of active reversal, but must instead reject the whole disappointing sex." Bergler's prose is as opaque as his thought: "Naive observers assume that the homosexual is 'attracted' to other men; actually, men merely represent defensive allies in his continuing unconscious battle to establish the preeminence of the penis and to negate his masochistic attachment to mother." Etc., etc.

6. W. H. Auden, *A Certain World: A Commonplace Book* (New York: Viking, 1974), 304 (entry on "Pleasure").

7. Tennessee Williams, *Collected Stories,* intro. Gore Vidal (New York: New Directions, 1985), 570. Subsequent citations from the short stories are from this edition and will be given parenthetically within the text.

8. Gore Vidal, "Introduction" to Williams, *Collected Stories,* xxiii.

9. Frank O'Connor, *The Lonely Voice* (Cleveland: World, 1963).

10. Vidal, "Introduction," xxiii–xxiv.

11. Donald Spoto, *The Kindness of Strangers: The Life of Tennessee Williams* (Boston: Little, Brown, 1985), 319.

12. John M. Clum, "'Something Cloudy, Something Clear': Homophobic Discourse in Tennessee Williams," *South Atlantic Quarterly* 88: 1 (Winter 1989), 161–79.

13. Such as Edward A. Sklepowitch, "In Pursuit of the Lyric Quarry: The Image of the Homosexual in Tennessee Williams' Prose Fiction," in *Tennessee Williams: A Tribute,* ed. Jack Tharpe (Jackson: University Press of Mississippi, 1977).

14. "Intimations," quoted in Clum, "'Something Cloudy.'"

15. Williams himself was perfectly aware that he was not a good poet: In "An Open Response to Tom Buckley" (who had interviewed him hostilely in an earlier issue), Williams wrote: "Baby, I'm not a poet . . . Plays are my vocation . . . I can write a conventional and graceful lyric, but I know I'm not a poet of any consequence whatsoever." *Atlantic Monthly,* January 1971, 34–35.

16. Clum, " 'Something Cloudy,' " 170.

17. Vidal, "Introduction," xx.

18. Clum, " 'Something Cloudy,' " 168.

19. Ibid., 166.

20. Ibid., 168.

21. Clum's slur against Williams's "little treatise on mystery" is on 168; the slur against Mr. Krupper's unaccountable attraction to "beautiful (of course) young men" is on 166.

22. William Blake, "To Thomas Butts," in *Selected Poems of William Blake,* intro. Basil De Sélincourt (London: Oxford University, 1968). This splendid piece of rhetoric ends:

> Now I a fourfold vision see
> And a fourfold vision is given to me;
> 'Tis fourfold in my supreme delight,
> And threefold in soft Beulah's night,
> And twofold always. — May God us keep
> From single vision, and Newton's sleep!

23. Randall Jarrell, in an appreciative essay on Kipling's short stories, says: "their reader feels, 'You can write better stories than Kipling's but not better Kipling stories.' This kingdom of theirs is a strange, disquieting, but quite wonderful place, as if some of the Douanier Rousseau's subjects had been repainted by Degas. If we cannot make the very greatest claims for the stories, it would be absurd not to make great ones: as long as readers enjoy style and skill, originality and imagination—in a word, genius—they will take delight in Kipling's stories." I think one could substitute "Williams" for Kipling in this passage. Randall Jarrell, "The English in England," in *Kipling, Auden & Co.: Essays and Reviews 1935–1964* (New York: Farrar, Straus and Giroux), 346.

2. SEXUAL DANDYISM AND THE LEGACY OF OSCAR WILDE

1. Oscar Wilde, *The Picture of Dorian Gray* (Harmondsworth, UK: Penguin, 1949), 124.

2. Oscar Wilde, *The Importance of Being Earnest,* in *Three Plays,* intro. H. Montgomery Hyde (London: Eyre Methuen, 1981).

3. Harold Bloom, "Doctor Samuel Johnson, The Canonical Critic," in *The West-ern Canon: The Books and School of the Ages* (New York: Harcourt Brace, 1994), 183–202.

4. "Woman Warrior: Sexual Philosopher Camille Paglia Jousts with the Politically Correct," cover story, *New York*, March 4, 1991.

5. Gore Vidal, *Myra Breckinridge* (New York: Vintage, 1986), 3. All subsequent citations are from this edition and will be given parenthetically within the text.

6. Camille Paglia, *Sexual Personae: Art and Decadence from Nefertiti to Emily Dickinson* (New Haven: Yale University Press, 1990), 38.

7. Camille Paglia, "No Law in the Arena," in *Vamps and Tramps: New Essays* (New York: Vintage, 1994), 93.

8. For a good account of Wilde's sublime impudence, see Richard Ellmann, *Oscar Wilde* (New York: Knopf, 1988).

9. Liam Hudson and Bernadine Jacot, *The Way Men Think: Intellect, Intimacy, and the Erotic Imagination* (New Haven: Yale University Press, 1991), viii.

10. Paglia, *Sexual Personae*, 428. The citations within Paglia are from Baudelaire.

11. Wilde, *The Importance of Being Earnest*, Act 2.

12. Paglia, *Sexual Personae*, 220: "Patrick Dennis' *Auntie Mame* (1955) is the American *Alice in Wonderland* and in my view more interesting and important than any 'serious' novel after World War II."

13. Diana Vreeland, *DV* (New York: Vintage, 1985), 129. The tale of her disap-pointment at discovering only cold tea in the flask goes like this: "It was a heart-breaker. It was so letting down. I think it was the single most anticlimactic moment of my life. Cold tea!"

14. *Straight to Hell*, ed. Boyd McDonald. Both Vidal and William S. Burroughs apparently wrote letters to Boyd McDonald proclaiming their interest in *STH*. Their one-word encomium was used as an advertisement for the magazine. As I recall, it ran *in toto*: " 'Fascinating.' Gore Vidal. 'Fascinating.' William S. Burroughs."

15. The anthologies of *STH* continue to be published (by Fidelity Publishing, Inc., of Boston), and will presumably continue until McDonald's large backlog of letters is finally exhausted, or until the editors run out of suitably monosyllabic titles. The number of books in the series stands now at thirteen, according to Fidelity's French Wall.

Information about McDonald and *Straight to Hell* is hard to come by. Two long interviews, both in the Boston *Guide* (February 1988 and November 1993), provide much of the information which I have used in this essay.

It is very hard to determine exactly when *Straight to Hell* came into existence. It originated as a sort of club for gay men interested in foreskins, but (as Boyd re-ported) quickly transformed itself into a journal of more general interest. But be-cause *STH* was, especially at the beginning, essentially *samizdat* literature, typed and mimeo'd by hand and circulated somewhat clandestinely, exact publishing his-tory is impossible.

The earliest number I have seen (number 3) dates from 1973. It is still in typed, mimeo'd form: neat but not as elegant as the later "chapbook" editions. This astonishing issue nevertheless shows Boyd already at his most impudent. In this passage, for instance, McDonald sounds like a homegrown (and funnier) Michel Foucault — several years, let it be remembered, before Foucault's works were translated into English: "Homosexuals are both born and made but there are no born 'straights.' There are men who live a 'straight' life but it is a chosen way of life, like living on the East Side. It is social, not natural . . ." (2).

A second gives a typically sardonic comment on the concept of "predatory" homosexuals. " 'The New York Times' reports that homosexuals 'prey' upon teenage boys in Times Square. One way these helpless innocents could protect themselves from homosexual advances would be to stop showing their pricks and saying 'What's it worth to you?' or 'Do you want to suck my dick?' It would help, also, if the boys did not loiter about caressing and fondling their groins, arranging their pricks in their pants to display soft-ons or stare down at their hard-ons to call attention to them" (3).

I am indebted to the Rare Books and Manuscripts Division of the New York Public Library for unearthing these precious relics of the early seventies, which form part of the enormous International Gay Information Center Archives, located at the Library.

16. Boyd's unflattering comments on ballet and opera occur in *The Guide to the Gay Northeast* (Boston: Fidelity Publishing), February 1988, 14. Thom Gunn's approval was made public in an interview in the San Francisco *Sentinel* (a gay newspaper), which McDonald quoted in *Straight to Hell*, no. 44: "Personally, I have been far more influenced by the wit and style of *The Manhattan Review of Unnatural Acts* than I have been by the tiresome campiness of Ronald Firbank, who is usually taken as one of the chief exemplars of the aforementioned gay sensibility." Boyd adds: "As I don't know from poetry, I enquired about Thom Gunn, an Englishman now living in San Francisco. A professor who is an *STH* subscriber assures me that Gunn is highly regarded."

17. *Christopher Street,* the first upscale glossy magazine for gay and lesbian readers, published its first issue in July 1976, just in time for the American Bicentennial.

18. "The Man in the Nylon Jockstrap," *Straight to Hell,* no. 47 (1980), 23: "Babs strode up to the Chairman, placed her bare right shoulder (for the top of her frock was brassiere-like, such as Kim Novak wore to the 1979 Academy Awards) against his chest, swooned back like Loretta Young with Tyrone Power so that the Chairman was forced to catch her fall, and gasped, 'Possess me, you who already possesses so substantial a percentage of the corporate securities. I too want to be publicly held, like common stock.' "

19. The following discussion of a representative issue refers to *Straight to Hell,* no. 45 (1979).

20. "Remembering Boyd McDonald," *The Guide* 13: 11 (November 1993), 20–

21, 19. McDonald's opinion about the distinction between "homosexuality" and "gayness" is taken from the last interview he gave, published at the time of his death.

21. Boyd McDonald, interview in *The Guide*, November 1993, 21. The reference is to Randy Shilts, *Conduct Unbecoming: Lesbians and Gays in the U.S. Military* (New York: St. Martin's Press, 1993).

22. *Smut: An S.T.H. Chap-book*, ed. Boyd McDonald, intro. Mitzel (New York: Gay Presses of New York, 1984), 189.

23. A good example of the quality of Firbank's salaciousness, which I must admit makes me laugh out loud, can be seen in the poem written by "the Hon. 'Eddy' Monteith": "And here was a sweet thing suggested by an old Nursery Rhyme, 'Loves, have you Heard?':

> 'Loves, have you heard about the rabbits??
> They have such odd fantastic habits. . . .
> Oh, Children . . . ! I daren't disclose to You
> The licentious things *some* rabbits do.' "

The Flower Beneath the Foot, in Ronald Firbank, *Five Novels,* with an introduction by Osbert Sitwell (New York: New Directions, 1981), 41.

24. Herman Tarnower, *The Complete Scarsdale Medical Diet: Plus Dr. Tarnower's Lifetime Keep-Slim Program* (New York: Rawson, Wade, 1978). A more queenly response to the shooting of Dr. Tarnower was given by a colleague of mine at the Concord Academy, where I taught for a brief shining semester in 1981. This man was primarily thrilled not that Tarnower had been shot, but that he had been shot by the *headmistress of the Madeira School.* The world of private schools being a small and dreary one, Mrs. Harris's justified act of vengeance inspired him. He has not yet, so far as I know, taken the law into his own hands, however.

25. "Eating Stuff in Grocery," *Raunch,* ed. Boyd McDonald (Boston: Fidelity, 1990), 85.

26. Though these lines appear in Oliver Goldsmith's "The Traveller, or A Prospect of Society," they are thought to have been written by his friend Samuel Johnson. See *The Poems of Thomas Gray, William Collins, and Oliver Goldsmith,* ed. Roger Lonsdale (London: Longman, 1969), 656 n.

27. *The Guide,* November 1993, 22.

3. IMMODESTY AND IMMOLATION

1. A classic statement of this point of view is made by David Leavitt, Introduction to the *Penguin Book of Gay Short Stories* (New York: Viking, 1994), xv–xxviii.

2. Liam Hudson and Bernadine Jacot, *The Way Men Think: Intellect, Intimacy, and the Erotic Imagination* (New Haven: Yale University Press, 1991), "Male

Vices," 118–35, refers to some of the statistical evidence for the overwhelming gender imbalance in every kind of sexual crime from rape to child molestation, obscene phone calls, self-exposure, and necrophilia.

3. See Chapter 1, "The Prohibitionists," in Andrew Sullivan, *Virtually Normal: An Argument about Homosexuality* (New York: Knopf, 1995), especially 29–30.

4. Cf. Paglia, *Sexual Personae: Art and Decadence from Nefertiti to Emily Dickinson* (New Haven: Yale University Press, 1990), 14–15: "I agree with Sade that we have the right to thwart nature's procreative compulsions, through sodomy or abortion. Male homosexuality may be the most valorous of attempts to evade the femme fatale and to defeat nature. By turning away from the Medusan mother, whether in honor or detestation of her, the male homosexual is one of the great forgers of absolutist western identity. But of course nature has won, as she always does, by making disease the price of promiscuous sex."

5. James Purdy, interview with Fred Barron, *Penthouse*, July 1974.

6. In chapter 35 of Henry James, *The Portrait of a Lady* (Harmondsworth, UK: Penguin, 1986), 401.

7. Paglia's rhapsody on gay-male "hybris" can be found on p. 100 of *Sexual Personae*.

8. Elisabeth Badinter, *XY: On Masculine Identity* (New York: Columbia University Press, 1995), 56.

9. Hudson and Jacot, *The Way Men Think,* 40. Ralph Greenson, the analyst to whom they refer, reported his finding in the *International Journal of Psycho-Analysis* 49 (1968), 370. He would seem to agree with Elisabeth Badinter about the difficulty and necessity of a boy's separating himself from his mother.

10. Ibid., in two chapters: "The Male Wound" (37–58) and "Male Vices" (118–35).

11. Dennis Cooper, *Frisk* (New York: Grove Weidenfeld, 1991), 123. Subsequent citations are taken from this edition and will be given parenthetically in the text.

12. Paglia, *Sexual Personae,* 247: "Serial or sex murder, like fetishism, is a perversion of male intelligence. It is a criminal abstraction, masculine in its deranged egotism and orderliness. It is the asocial equivalent of philosophy, mathematics, and music. There is no female Mozart because there is no female Jack the Ripper."

13. *Basic Training: San Francisco Style,* 1992.

14. James Purdy, *Narrow Rooms,* with an introduction by Paul Binding (London: GMP, 1985), 61. Subsequent citations are taken from this edition and will be given parenthetically in the text.

15. Badinter discusses homosexual initiations into manhood in *XY*, Chapter 3, "It Is Man Who Engenders Man."

16. Novalis's opinion is quoted by Mario Praz in the introductory essay to *Three Gothic Novels* (*The Castle of Otranto, Vathek, Frankenstein*), ed. Peter Fairclough (Harmondsworth, UK: Penguin, 1968), 11.

4. THE LIFE OF DESIRE IN 1978

1. See Neil Miller, *Out of the Past: Gay and Lesbian History from 1869 to the Present* (New York: Vintage, 1995); and Martin Duberman, *Stonewall* (New York: Dutton, 1993). See also Ronald Bayer, *Homosexuality and American Psychiatry: The Politics of Diagnosis* (New York: Basic Books, 1981), 176, 178.

2. Samuel R. Delany, *The Mad Man* (New York: Rhinoceros, 1996), 185.

3. The title of one in a series of long, funny, and unnerving essays by Charley Shively. Boston's *Fag Rag* was an early liberationist newspaper. See Miller, *Out of the Past,* 419.

4. Some hostile reviews included Martin Duberman's in *The New Republic,* January 6, 1979, 30–32; Barbara G. Harrison's "Love on the Seedy Side," *Washington Post Book World,* December 17, 1978, 4; and John Lahr's "Camp Tales," which explicitly compares and contrasts *Faggots* and *Dancer from the Dance: New York Times Book Review,* January 14, 1979, 39–40.

5. Larry Kramer, *Faggots* (New York: Plume, 1987), 16. Subsequent citations are taken from this edition and will be given parenthetically in the text.

6. Alexander Pope, *The Dunciad,* in *The Poems of Alexander Pope: A One-Volume Edition of the Twickenham Text with Selected Annotations,* ed. John Butt (New Haven: Yale University Press, 1966), 785–86. Pope's and Warburton's mock-scholarly note on this incident may clarify the passage: "The strange story following which may be taken for a fiction of the Poet, is justified by a true relation in Spon's Voyages. Vaillant (who wrote the History of the Syrian Kings as it is to be found on medals) coming from the Levant, where he had been collecting various Coins, and being pursued by a Corsaire of Sallee, swallowed down twenty gold medals. A sudden Bourasque freed him from the Rover, and he got to land with them in his belly. On his road to Avignon he met two Physicians, of whom he demanded assistance. One advis'd Purgations, the other Vomits. In this uncertainty he took neither, but pursued his way to Lyons, where he found his ancient friend, the famous Physician and Antiquary Dufour, to whom he related his adventures. Dufour first ask'd him *whether the Medals were of the highest Empire?* He assur'd him they were. Dufour was ravish'd with the hope of possessing such a treasure, he bargain'd with him on the spot for the most curious of them, and was to recover them at his own expence." The application to Pope's own society is somewhat remote. "Annius" may be "Sir Andrew Fountaine, purchaser of antiques for the museums of the wealthy" (according to the Twickenham editors), while "Mummius" may be Lord Sandwich, "virtuoso and President of the Egyptian Club."

7. Paglia's exclamation at the dissimilarity of the sexes is found on p. 27 of *Sexual Personae: Art and Decadence from Nefertiti to Emily Dickinson* (New Haven: Yale University Press, 1990).

8. Andrew Holleran, *Dancer from the Dance* (New York: Plume, 1986), 146. Subsequent citations are taken from this edition and will be given parenthetically in the text.

9. Gatsby's "count of enchanted objects" occurs in F. Scott Fitzgerald, *The Great Gatsby*, with preface and notes by Matthew J. Bruccoli (New York: Scribner Paperback Fiction Edition, 1995), 98.

10. In Miller, *Out of the Past*, 448, we meet a man whose experience of life before and after AIDS seems similar to my own: "The thirtyish owner of a small Boston computer firm exemplified many of the dilemmas of gay men of the period — and some of the solutions. Until AIDS arrived, this man had led a comfortable life. He didn't have a lover, but he and his closest friend spent many an evening at the Bird Sanctuary along the Charles River, where anonymous sex with other men was easily available. But when, within a period of two months, his two closest friends were both diagnosed with AIDS, he realized he couldn't lead his life as before. . . . Before AIDS, he said, 'the future was always bright. Things were always looking up.' Now he was asking the question 'How should a man live?' . . . For people his age, he noted, 'Sex was such a big part of our identity. You have to redefine things. I had a fairly comfortable self-image and lifestyle that has been radically altered. As it turns out, the things I have changed to are a lot more enjoyable.' Still, he said, 'I am in mourning. . . . I hate having things taken away from me.' "

11. William Shakespeare, *Antony and Cleopatra*. The sneer about a "gypsy's lust" is in 1.1; Enobarbus's mocking advice in 1.2; and Cleopatra's reverie about the dead Antony in 5.2.

12. Perhaps also apropos is the "southern" correspondent's comment in the final sheaf of letters: "*The greatest drug of all, my dear, was not one of those pills in so many colors that you took over the years. . . . It was the city, darling, it was the city, unreal city, the city itself. And do you see why I had to leave? As Santayana said, dear, artists are unhappy because they are not interested in happiness; they live for beauty. God, was that steaming, loathsome city beautiful!!!*" (244; italics Holleran's). Malone is, in this sense, an "artist," for he has lived for beauty, not happiness. Note the triple exclamation points, hyperanimated brow-raisers which save this passage from being too heavy.

13. Edmund White, "Skinned Alive" in *Skinned Alive* (New York: Vintage, 1996), 56.

14. Randall Jarrell, *Poetry and the Age* (New York: Ecco, 1980), 121.

15. William Hazlitt, "On Dryden and Pope," *Lectures on the English Poets* (with *The Spirit of the Age: Or Contemporary Portraits*), introduction by Catherine Macdonald Maclean (New York: Dutton, Everyman's Library, 1967), 72.

16. Andrew Holleran, "The Sense of Sin," in *Wrestling with the Angel: Faith and Religion in the Lives of Gay Men*, ed. Brian Bouldrey (New York: Riverhead, 1995), 83.

17. See for example, George Santayana, "War Shrines," in *Soliloquies in England and Later Soliloquies*, with new introduction by Ralph Ross (Ann Arbor: University of Michigan Press, 1967). "How charming is divine philosophy, when it is really divine, when it descends to earth from a higher sphere, and loves the things of earth without needing or collecting them! What the gay Aristippus said of his mistress: I

possess, I am not possessed, every spirit should say of an experience that ruffles it like a breeze playing on the summer sea. A thousand ships sail over it in vain, and the worst of tempests is in a teapot. This once acknowledged and inwardly digested, life and happiness can honestly begin. Nature is innocently fond of puffing herself out, spreading her peacock feathers, and saying, What a fine bird am I! And so she is; to rave against this vanity would be to imitate it. On the contrary, the secret of a merry carnival is that Lent is at hand. Having virtually renounced our follies, we are for the first time able to enjoy them with a free heart in their ephemeral purity" (97).

This advice, beautifully phrased as it is, always strikes me as just a little monk-ish — despite Santayana's customary playfulness. Santayana admitted to his protégé Daniel Cory that he had been homosexual while an undergraduate at Harvard, implying that this interest had passed with maturity. His best modern biographer, John McCormick, rightly suspects that this was a feint, for Santayana spent much of his adult life in the company of well-known homosexuals, including the Anglo-American novelist Howard Sturgis, whose house Queen's Acre Santayana visited when in England. See Daniel Cory, *Santayana: The Later Years; A Portrait with Letters* (New York: Braziller, 1963); and John McCormick, *George Santayana: A Biography* (New York: Knopf, 1987). But while it is unlikely that the philosopher entirely recovered from his case of youthful homosexuality, how much he acted on it later in life remains unclear. Another essay from the *Soliloquies in England,* "Friend-ships," almost addresses the subject but skips away from it at the last minute. I nonetheless remember reading it when *I* was an undergraduate, and taking comfort from what I rightly guessed to be an indirect defense of homosexual love.

5. VIRTUALLY NORMAL, AND VICE-VERSA

1. David Leavitt, Introduction to *The Penguin Book of Gay Short Stories,* ed. David Leavitt and Mark Mitchell (New York: Viking, 1994), xv–xxviii.

2. John Preston's series about action-hero Alex Kane (published between 1984 and 1987) includes *Sweet Dreams, Golden Years, Deadly Lies, Stolen Moments, Secret Dancers,* and *Lethal Secrets.* All are published by Alyson Press, Boston.

3. Leavitt, "Territory," *The New Yorker,* May 31, 1982, 34.

4. The argument between Stephen Spender and David Leavitt concerned Spend-er's 1951 autobiography *World within World* and Leavitt's *soi-disant* homage to it, *While England Sleeps* (1993). When Spender objected to what he took to be the plagiarism of his work by Leavitt, Leavitt responded with an essay in the *New York Times Magazine,* "Did I Plagiarize His Life?" (*New York Times Magazine,* April 3, 1994, 36). Spender's response to this was published in the *New York Times Book Review* (September 4, 1994): "My Life Is Mine; It Is Not David Leavitt's."

While Spender does seem unnecessarily defensive and upset about what he calls Leavitt's "pornographic" sex scenes, Leavitt strikes this reader as a spoiled brat getting his first spanking. The incident has so impressed itself on Leavitt's mind that it receives fictional treatment in his new novella *The Term Paper Artist.* Under the guise of a postmodern self-referentiality, Leavitt is able in this story to assert his innocence yet again.

5. David Leavitt, *The Term Paper Artist* in *Arkansas: Three Novellas* (Boston, Houghton Mifflin, 1997), 21–22.

6. Leavitt, Introduction, *Penguin Book of Gay Short Stories,* xxviii.

7. Ibid., "Yes, writers might constantly be distracted by the sight of pretty boys behind breakfast counters; they could afford to be distracted; a work of literature cannot" (xix).

8. David Leavitt, *The Lost Language of Cranes* (New York: Bantam, 1987), 29–30. Subsequent citations are taken from this edition and will be cited parenthetically in the text.

9. Christopher Isherwood, *A Single Man* (New York: Farrar, Straus and Giroux, 1964), 23, 40. Subsequent citations are taken from this edition and will be cited parenthetically in the text.

10. Isherwood's involvement in Vedanta is thoroughly and amusingly remembered in his *My Guru and His Disciple* (New York: Farrar, Straus and Giroux, 1980).

11. Montaigne, "On Experience," *The Complete Essays of Montaigne,* translated by Donald M. Frame (Stanford: Stanford University Press, 1982), 856.

12. Tennessee Williams, too, remembers this period in southern California with affection. See his memoir/story "The Mattress by the Tomato Patch" in *Collected Stories.* In it he imagines the daydreams of his landlady Olga, a middle-aged woman full of life and lust: "She sees royal palm trees and the white clocktower of downtown Santa Monica, and possibly says to herself, Well, I guess I'll have a hot barbecue and a cold beer for lunch at the Wop's stand on Muscle Beach and I'll see if Tiger is there, and if he isn't, I'll catch the five o'clock bus to L.A. and take in a good movie, and after that I'll walk over to Olivera Street and have some tamales with chili and two or three bottles of Carta Blanca and come back out to the beach on the nine o'clock bus. That will be after sundown, and three miles east of the beach, they turn the lights out in the bus (because of the wartime blackout), and Olga will have chosen a good seat-companion near the back of the bus, a sailor who's done two hitches and knows the scoop, so when the lights go out, her knees will divide and his will follow suit and the traveling dusk will hum with the gossamer wings of Eros. She'll nudge him when the bus slows toward the corner of Wilshire and Ocean. They'll get off there and wander hand-in-hand into the booming shadows of Palisades Park, which Olga knows like a favorite book never tired of. All along that enormously tall cliff, under royal palms and over the Pacific, are little summer houses and trellised arbors with beaches where sudden acquaintances burst into prodigal flower." Williams, *Collected Stories* (New York: New Directions, 1985), 363–64.

13. In keeping with this peculiarly strenuous "intimacy" is a remark Isherwood

made on the "Tonight" program of the BBC in 1977, quoted in *Cue* (London), no. 139. The subject is "being a homosexual." "It depends so much on the kind of person you are, doesn't it? I mean, if you dislike feeling you're in a minority, if you dislike a certain amount of persecution, if you dislike, in other words, the predicament which the homosexual is in, even in very civilised countries like this one (England) — then, of course, it's not for you. But if you're rather aggressive, and if you don't mind being in the minority, and if it even stimulates you in some way — then I think it's quite bracing."

Isherwood's attitude strikes me as the quintessence of pre-Stonewall gay liberation: a private liberation based on self-respect rather than legislation or social change. Being gay *does* mean being persecuted, but on the other hand, some people — himself, presumably — rather *enjoy* the opportunity to fight back. Isherwood talks here of homosexuality as if it were a dangerous and exciting adventure — like sky-diving — not a humiliating weakness that needs to be nurtured and protected.

Although I am very glad to be living in a later time than Isherwood, a time when laws in my state at least *do* protect gay men and lesbians from the grossest forms of discrimination, I nonetheless honor not only Isherwood's bravery, but his scrappiness. His attitude seems remarkably similar to that of Boyd McDonald, another pre-Stonewall faggot. A post-Stonewall version of the same thing will be seen in Ethan Mordden's "tales of gay Manhattan." In all three, what I most admire is the unsentimental, but quite undespairing acknowledgment that one is in a minority and thus in a vulnerable position. At the same time, *because* one is in this minority, one actually has various advantages: an ironic perspective and (as here) the chance for a good fight. As Boyd McDonald put it, "Homosexuality has a lot to offer some guys." The implication (as in Isherwood) is that other guys *don't* know, or don't deserve, what homosexuality "has to offer."

6. HOMEWARD BOUND

1. *Hometowns: Gay Men Write about Where They Belong,* ed. John Preston (New York: Dutton, 1991); Samuel R. Delany, *Atlantis: Three Tales* (Hanover, NH: Wesleyan University Press, 1995); Mark Doty, *Atlantis* (New York: HarperCollins, 1995); Philip Gambone, *The Language We Use Up Here* (New York: Dutton, 1991); Frank Browning, *A Queer Geography* (New York: Crown, 1996).

2. Armistead Maupin, *Tales of the City* (New York: Harper and Row, 1978). The entire series of six novels has been compiled as *28 Barbary Lane: A Tales of the City Omnibus* (New York: Harper and Row, 1990).

3. Michael Cunningham interview with Reed Woodhouse, December 21, 1991.

4. Michael Cunningham, *A Home at the End of the World* (New York: Farrar, Straus and Giroux, 1990), 343. Subsequent citations are taken from this edition and will be cited parenthetically in the text.

5. Mordden's most recent continuation of the "Buddies" series, *Some Men Are Lookers* (New York: St. Martin's Press, 1997), reveals this problem very clearly. *Some Men Are Lookers* describes, in a series of interlocked stories, the break-up of one of the series' long-term couples: the waiflike Little Kiwi and Dennis Savage, Bud's best friend. At the same time Mordden continues to explore his favorite questions of who and what is gay, introducing an assortment of new, though familiar characters to test his hypothesis (e.g., the married man, the "straight gay," the drag queen, and so on). But the collection is unable, I think, to contain the two kinds of tale he is telling in it: the tale of the death of friendship and love on the one hand, and the tale of witty urban matchmaking and flirtation on the other. Further, the all-important charm of the whimsical, childlike Little Kiwi (as of his younger sidekick, Cosgrove) now seems wearisome and unconvincing. I found myself impatiently asking why anyone would put up with the two youths' terminal ditziness. Even as a *fantasy* of "family," the group Mordden presents seems simply incredible: a group of middle-aged men pretending they are still twenty-five, and a pair of younger men in their twenties pretending they are still eight. For the first time in my reading of Mordden, I felt squeamish, as if I were watching kiddie porn.

6. In 1962, Irving Bieber wrote an influential book (*Homosexuality: A Psychoanalytic Study*) based on all of two hundred gay men, which, predictably, "found that the cause was Mother," as Patrick Higgins tartly puts it in his introduction to *A Queer Reader* (New York: The New Press, 1993), 12.

7. The gay novelist Joseph Olshan wondered: "Why must Cunningham insist on taking the reader through one unsavory sexual act after another?" (Joseph Olshan, "Two Trips through the Minefields of Emotions," *Chicago Tribune Book Review*, November 4, 1990, 8). His squeamishness is unaccountable, given the almost maidenly propriety of all of Cunningham's characters. Envy, I suspect, motivated him. Certainly his own novel, *Nightswimmer* (New York: Simon and Schuster, 1994), left me longing for *A Home at the End of the World*.

8. Murger's phrase appears at the top of Act 4 in the Ricordi score of *La Bohème*, English translation by William Grist and Percy Pinkerton (Melville, NY: Belwin Mills, n.d.), 229.

9. *The New Yorker*, July 25, 1988.

10. Cunningham interview with Reed Woodhouse.

11. Allan Hollinghurst, *The Swimming-Pool Library* (New York: Random House, 1988).

12. Interview with Reed Woodhouse.

13. Richard Eder, "Squaring a Triangle," *Los Angeles Times Book Review*, November 11, 1990, 3.

14. Sir John Hawkins recalled Johnson's delight in this sort of cut-and-thrust conversation: "I have heard Johnson assert *that a tavern chair was the throne of human felicity*. 'As soon,' said he, 'as I enter the door of a tavern I experience an oblivion of care and a freedom from solicitude: . . . I dogmatize and am contradicted,

and in this conflict of opinions and sentiments I find delight.' " Quoted in John Wain, *Samuel Johnson* (New York: Viking, 1975), 239–40.

15. Michael Schwartz, "Ethan Mordden," in *Contemporary Gay American Novelists: A Bio-Bibliographical Critical Sourcebook,* ed. Emmanuel S. Nelson (Westport and London: Greenwood, 1993), 282–90.

16. Ethan Mordden, "Sliding into Home," in *Buddies* (New York: St. Martin's Press, 1986), 232.

17. The phrase "a place at the table" was coined by Bruce Bawer in his book of that name (New York: Poseidon, 1993).

18. See Elisabeth Badinter, *XY: On the Masculine Identity* (New York: Columbia University Press, 1995).

19. Ethan Mordden, *Buddies,* 88–89. Subsequent citations from this and *Everybody Loves You* (New York: St. Martin's Press, 1988) will be given parenthetically in the text as *B* and *ELY.*

20. A very interesting story, "Interview with the Drag Queen," in *I've a Feeling We're Not in Kansas Anymore: Tales from Gay Manhattan* (New York: St. Martin's Press, 1985), shows Mordden's interest in, and insight into, this perennial gay impersonation.

21. *One Last Waltz* appeared in 1986 (New York: St. Martin's Press).

22. "The Homogay" is in Mordden's first collection, *I've A Feeling We're Not in Kansas Anymore;* "Rope" is in *Buddies.*

23. From Alan Barnett's *The Body and Its Dangers* (New York: St. Martin's Press, 1990).

24. A more extended defense of the Pines and of Mordden's own fiction, can be found in "Sliding into Home" (*Buddies,* 231): "So we all got into sweaters and hooded sweatshirts — Dennis Savage had to outfit Dave somewhat; we wouldn't let him on the beach out of uniform — and we put Bauhaus on his leash, and off we went to the water's edge where the hard sand is, and there we made Dave turn back to gaze upon the strip of lights that comprises what may be the only gay colony in the history of the world. You say, 'What of the Grove?', but the Grove was founded back in the days of the haunted homosexual, of the loving war of queen and hustler, when to be homosexual was to be faggot, queer, bent — Franklin Pangborn or Lucius Beebe, instead of . . . well, for instance, reader: you. The Grove is not gay. The Pines, for all its attitude and casually frantic code of behavior, is gay. And as we regarded it, now in its blasted morale of chaste amusements, of the no-fault cruising of look-but-don't-touch and the survivor mentality that hits those who have simply lived to be thirty-five, we began to tell Dave of its days of glory. Of riding the ferry in a bracing air of anticipation, being able to throw off our covers and be; or of heading for Tea, a whole house in force, just to see who our people were, who we are; or of meeting, some weekend, someone's older friend, who would unveil forgotten mysteries of the pre-Stonewall days. Liberty, self-knowledge, anthropology: culture. Our place, in our time."

25. *The Boys in the Band* by Mart Crowley (1968) was one of the first modern plays to be openly gay. Despite its maudlin melodrama, it plays surprisingly well, even now, and was accorded a rather successful revival on Broadway in 1996.

26. Cf. John Jay Chapman on "President Eliot" (of Harvard) in *The Selected Writings of John Jay Chapman,* ed. with an introduction by Jacques Barzun (New York: Minerva, 1957), 217: "Every generation is a secret society, and has incommunicable enthusiasms, tastes and interests which are a mystery both to its predecessors and to posterity."

27. Neil Miller, *Out of the Past: Gay and Lesbian History from 1869 to the Present* (New York: Vintage, 1995), 448.

7. A WEDDING AND THREE FUNERALS

1. The works mentioned in this and subsequent paragraphs are listed here in alphabetical order.

Alan Barnett, "The *Times* As It Knows Us," in *The Body and Its Dangers* (New York: St. Martin's Press, 1990).

Tim Barrus, *Genocide: The Anthology* (Stanford, CT: Knights Press, 1988).

Mark Doty, *Turtle, Swan* (Boston: Godine, 1987); *Bethlehem in Broad Daylight* (Boston: Godine, 1991); *My Alexandria* (Urbana: University of Illinois Press, 1993); and *Atlantis* (New York: HarperPerennial, 1995). *Heaven's Coast* (New York: HarperCollins), a prose memoir of his lover Wally Roberts's death, appeared in 1996.

Jack Fritscher, *Some Dance to Remember* (Stanford, CT: Knights Press, 1990).

Thom Gunn, *The Man with Night Sweats* (New York: Farrar, Straus and Giroux, 1992).

William Hoffman, *As Is* (New York: Vintage, 1985).

Andrew Holleran, "Friends at Evening," *Men on Men: Best New Gay Fiction,* edited and with an introduction by George Stambolian (New York: Plume, 1986). See also his most recent novel, *The Beauty of Men* (New York: William Morrow, 1996).

Larry Kramer, *The Normal Heart* (New York: New American Library, 1985).

Tony Kushner, *Angels in America: A Gay Fantasia on National Themes* (New York: Theatre Communications Group, 1995).

Longtime Companion (1990).

Adam Mars-Jones, "Slim," in Edmund White and Mars-Jones, *The Darker Proof: Stories from a Crisis* (New York: Plume, 1988).

Paul Monette, *Love Alone* (New York: St. Martin's, 1988).

Oscar Moore, *A Matter of Life and Sex* (New York: Plume, 1993).

Ethan Mordden, *How Long Has This Been Going On?* (New York: Villard, 1995).

Parting Glances (1991).

Felice Picano, *Like People in History* (New York: Viking Penguin, 1995).

Sarah Schulman, *People in Trouble* (New York: Dutton, 1990).

Edmund White, "Palace Days," "An Oracle," and "Running on Empty" in *The Darker Proof: Stories from a Crisis* by Edmund White and Adam Mars-Jones (New York: Plume, 1988). These stories were later published, with other stories, in Edmund White, *Skinned Alive* (New York: Vintage, 1995).

2. Andrew Holleran, "Reading and Writing," *Ground Zero* (New York: William Morrow, 1988), 12.

3. Alan Barnett in conversation with Michael Denneny: "Bearing Witness in the Age of AIDS," *Harvard Gay and Lesbian Review* 4:2 (Spring 1997).

4. Ibid.

5. Joe Keenan's brilliant Wodehouse-like farces include *Blue Heaven* (New York: Penguin, 1988) and *Putting on the Ritz* (New York: Viking Penguin, 1991). Paul Rudnick's play *Jeffrey* appeared in 1994. His comic film reviews collected in *If You Ask Me,* supposedly by "Libby Gelman-Waxner," appeared the same year (New York: Fawcett Columbine, 1994).

6. Mr. Sleary, the word-slurring circus owner in *Hard Times,* delivers the moral of that book as follows: "Don't be croth with uth poor vagabondth. People mutht be amuthed. They can't be alwayth a-learning, nor yet they can't be alwayth a-working, they ain't made for it. You *mutht* have uth, Thquire. Do the withe thing and the kind thing too, and make the betht of uth, not the wurtht!" Charles Dickens, *Hard Times,* with an afterword by Charles Shapiro (New York: Signet, 1961), 287.

7. Neil Bartlett in *Christopher Street,* November 11, 1991, 25.

8. Paul Monette, *Love Alone: 18 Elegies for Rog* (New York: St. Martin's Press, 1988), xi.

9. Vladimir Nabokov, *Strong Opinions* (New York: McGraw-Hill, 1973), 66: "My advice to a budding literary critic would be as follows. Learn to distinguish banality. Remember that mediocrity thrives on 'ideas.' Beware of the modish message. Ask yourself if the symbol you have detected is not your own footprint. I ignore allegories. By all means place the 'how' above the 'what' but do not let it be confused with the 'so what.' Rely on the sudden erection of your small dorsal hairs. Do not drag in Freud at this point. All the rest depends on personal talent." Intimidating advice which I have tried, at least, to follow in this book.

10. Wilfred Owen, quoted in Monette, *Love Alone,* xi.

11. Samuel R. Delany, *The Mad Man* (New York: Rhinoceros, 1996), 5. Subsequent citations are taken from this edition and will be given parenthetically in the text.

12. Though not by Steven F. Kruger, *AIDS Narratives: Gender and Sexuality, Fiction and Science* (New York: Garland, 1996).

13. John Weir, *The Irreversible Decline of Eddie Socket* (New York: Harper and

Row, 1989), 3. Subsequent citations are taken from this edition and will be given parenthetically in the text.

14. Dale Peck, *Martin and John* (New York: HarperPerennial, 1994), 220–21. Subsequent citations are taken from this edition and will be given parenthetically in the text.

15. Stephen McCauley, *The Object of My Affection* (New York: Washington Square Press, 1988).

16. Christopher Bram, *In Memory of Angel Clare* (New York: Plume, 1990).

17. Harold Brodkey, "To My Readers," *The New Yorker,* June 21, 1993, 80–82. His essay eventually became *This Wild Darkness: The Story of My Death* (New York: Henry Holt, 1996).

18. Yeats's line about "the place of excrement" is in his late poem "Crazy Jane Talks with the Bishop."

19. Samuel Delany, "Coming/Out," in *Boys Like Us: Gay Writers Tell Their Coming Out Stories,* ed. Patrick Merla (New York: Avon, 1997), 25.

20. This false prediction is recorded in J. E. Austen-Leigh, *A Memoir of Jane Austen* (Oxford, 1926), 157.

21. Vito Russo, review of *Longtime Companion* in *The Advocate,* May 8, 1990, 53.

22. Rafael Campo, "Age 5 Born with AIDS," anthologized in *Things Shaped in Passing: More "Poets for Life" Writing from the AIDS Pandemic,* ed. Michael Klein and Richard McCann (New York: Persea, 1997).

23. Christopher Davis, *Valley of the Shadow* (New York: St. Martin's Press, 1988), 116. Subsequent citations are taken from this edition and will be given parenthetically in the text.

24. His editor was Michael Denneny, the dean of gay editors.

25. Jack Fritscher, *Some Dance to Remember,* 8.

26. David Feinberg, *Eighty-Sixed* (New York: Penguin, 1990).

27. Bruce Benderson, *User* (New York: Dutton, 1994).

28. Andrew Holleran, *Nights in Aruba* (New York: William Morrow, 1983), and *The Beauty of Men* (New York: William Morrow, 1996).

29. Tim Long, "The Keeper of Structures," The Dale Peck Interview. In *VIEWS* (cybermagazine), Guru Communications, Inc., Virtual Community Network.

30. See for example Sonata in F, Hob. XVI/47. Haydn, *Sämtliche Klaviersonaten,* Band 3, edited by Christa Landon (Wien: Wiener Urtext Edition, 1973).

31. *Martin and John* (New York: HarperPerennial, 1994), 113. Subsequent citations are taken from this edition and will be given parenthetically in the text.

32. Peck, in the interview cited above in which he deplored the accusation of being "anti-narrative," spoke of how he "adores" Hemingway's "incredibly clean prose line."

33. Peck himself confesses frequently, even automatically, to "not knowing." Here are some random examples: "Sometimes I feel that my mother is less a person than

an idea in my head. But when I tell someone about her I'm always asked, Why'd she stay? Why'd she take it? And she becomes real again, a person. Like my father, like Susan, like any man I meet and sleep with once and never see again. I have to admit I don't know why she took it. And that's where this story stops, I think. That's where it fails" (30); "I don't think we were ever quite aware of how we depended on him, but he filled a space in our lives, the space created by Justin's death" (56); "I think about screaming, but don't" (126); "I want to ask him again, Where did you come from, why did you come here? But I have no idea what he'd say to theat" (134); "Sometimes I only understand people through objects" (209); "I don't know if I should go to him or stay back" (135); "all at once I realized I knew as little about Martin — and about myself — as I did about this Johnson" (185); "I wanted to say something, but I didn't know what" (188); "And I didn't know what to think" (217).

34. Alfred, Lord Tennyson, *In Memoriam A.H.H.,* in *Tennyson's Poems,* edited with an introduction by Mildred M. Bozman (London: Dent/Everyman's Library, 1965).

8. BOY'S LIFE

1. Thom Gunn, *The Occasions of Poetry: Essays in Criticism and Autobiography,* expanded edition, edited and with an introduction by Clive Wilmer (San Francisco: North Point, 1985), 129. The whole essay on Robert Duncan is well worth reading.

2. Alan Hollinghurst, *The Swimming-Pool Library* (New York: Random House, 1988), 216.

3. Neil Bartlett, *Ready to Catch Him Should He Fall* (New York: Dutton, 1990), 310. Subsequent citations are taken from this edition and will be given parenthetically in the text.

4. Tennessee Williams, "Hard Candy," *Collected Stories* (New York: New Directions, 1985), 338.

5. Neil Bartlett, untitled talk at a conference at the University of Sussex, edited and printed in *Critical Quarterly* 37:4 (Winter 1995), 66–68.

6. Ibid.

7. The whole question of gay visibility, and of gay culture, is brilliantly opened by Bartlett in the preface to his play *Night After Night* (London: Methuen Drama, 1993), 3: "Some people think that performers in the theatre mean what they say, and only what they say. According to this theory, gay people only really started to appear on stage in Britain in the late 1960s and 'gay theatre' is a series of plays in which people talk about the 'theme' or 'subject' of homosexuality. Before that (so the theory goes), all we had was a few tortured ancestors — the frightened or frightening queens of *The Vortex, The Green Bay Tree,* the Britten operas, *Cat On A Hot Tin Roof.* . . . This version of history chooses to forget that gay people were there all the time, occupying a central place in the manufacture of all our nights out — stage

managing, dressing, selling the tickets, directing, designing, composing and chore-ographing the most popular shows in town. One particular kind of artist has always worked right in the heart of the West End: the chorus boy. Applauded, desirable, skilful, athletic, he contradicted and contradicts every stereotype of a gay person. The strange thing is that he does it without saying a word, and whilst dancing his way through lyrics and plots that have, or ought to have, absolutely nothing to do with the reality of our lives. This conundrum persists: thousands of people go to see shows every night and have no idea that they are watching their fantasies being acted out by gay people, while gay people still know what they have always known, that shows which 'say' nothing about us can still be some of the most powerful and exciting vehicles of our pleasures and our griefs."

8. Robert Duncan, "Sonnet" ("Now there is a Love of which Dante does not speak unkindly"), in *Roots and Branches* (New York: New Directions, 1969), 122. The final stanza runs:

> Sharpening their vision, Dante says, like a man
>   seeking to thread a needle,
> They try the eyes of other men
> Towards that eye of the needle
>   Love has appointed there
> For a joining that is not easy.

9. Bartlett, untitled talk.

10. Virgil's farewell to Dante occurs in *Purgatorio,* Canto 27.

11. Frank Browning, *A Queer Geography: Journeys toward a Sexual Self* (New York: Crown, 1996), 4.

12. Edmund White, *The Burning Library: Essays,* ed. David Bergman (New York: Knopf, 1994), 89–94.

13. Edmund White, *States of Desire: Travels in Gay America* (New York: Plume, 1983), xvii–xix.

14. Edmund White, Foreword to *The Faber Book of Gay Short Fiction* (London: Faber and Faber, 1991), ix.

15. Edmund White, "The Joy of Gay Lit," *Out* magazine, September 1997, 112.

9. WHITE LIES

1. W. H. Auden, "American Poetry," in *The Dyer's Hand* (New York: Vintage, 1968), 366.

2. "The *Paris Review* Interview" (with Jordan Egrably) in Edmund White, *The Burning Library: Essays,* ed. David Bergman (New York: Knopf, 1994), 262.

3. "Thank *God* for Stephen Sondheim!" is a line attributed to some mythical

(certainly undying) "East Side Queen" in Edmund White, *States of Desire: Travels in Gay America* (New York: Plume, 1991), 262.

4. Edmund White and Hubert Sorin, *Our Paris* (New York: Knopf, 1994), xv.

5. David Bergman, Introduction to White, *The Burning Library,* xii.

6. Oscar White, *The Importance of Being Earnest,* Act 1.

7. Edmund White, *A Boy's Own Story* (New York: Dutton, 1982), 83–84. Subsequent citations will be to this edition and will be given parenthetically in the text.

8. Edmund White, *Nocturnes for the King of Naples* (New York: St. Martin's, 1978), 90. Subsequent citations will be to this edition and will be given parenthetically in the text.

9. Johnson, *Preface to Shakespeare,* in Samuel Johnson, *Rasselas, Poems, and Selected Prose,* 3d ed., edited with an introduction and notes by Bertrand H. Bronson (San Francisco: Rinehart, 1971), 263.

10. Oscar Wilde, *The Decay of Lying,* in *The Artist as Critic: Critical Writings of Oscar Wilde,* ed. Richard Ellmann (Chicago: Phoenix, 1982), 290–319. See especially p. 292.

11. "The *Paris Review* Interview," 259.

12. Ibid., 264.

13. Ibid. "Vladimir Nabokov is my favorite writer" (248); or: "When you finish reading a book like *Lolita* you feel that there's nothing more wonderful in the whole world than writing a novel" (243).

14. Edmund White, *Forgetting Elena* (New York: Vintage, 1994), 42. Subsequent citations will be to this edition and will be given parenthetically in the text.

15. David Bergman, "Edmund White," in *Contemporary Gay American Novelists: A Bio-Bibliographical Critical Sourcebook,* ed. Emmanuel S. Nelson (Westport and London: Greenwood, 1993), 390.

16. White, *States of Desire,* 339–40.

17. The Madonna of the Mule-mill and the Blue Gesù are both stage-props in *Concerning the Eccentricities of Cardinal Pirelli* in Ronald Firbank, *Five Novels* (New York: New Directions, 1981).

18. Firbank, quoted in Brigid Brophy, *Prancing Novelists* (New York: Harper and Row, 1973), 402.

19. Firbank, *The Flower beneath the Foot,* in *Five Novels,* 36.

20. Roland Barthes, *On Racine,* trans. Richard Howard (New York: Hill and Wang, 1964), 38.

21. David Bergman, *Gaiety Transfigured* (Madison and London: University of Wisconsin Press, 1991), 194–95.

22. Flannery O'Connor, *Mystery and Manners: Occasional Prose,* selected and edited by Sally and Robert Fitzgerald (London: Faber and Faber, 1972), 67–68. "One of the most common and saddest spectacles is that of a person of really fine sensibility and acute psychological perception trying to write fiction by using these qualities alone. This type of writer will put down one intensely emotional or keenly perceptive sentence after the other, and the result will be complete dullness."

23. Samuel Johnson, *Lives of the Poets* ("Milton") in *Rasselas, Poems and Selected Prose,* 335.

24. The phrase "The Age of Anxiety" is of course a title of W. H. Auden's "baroque eclogue" written between 1944 and 1946. It was later used as the sobriquet by the intermittently gay Leonard Bernstein in his Symphony no. 2.

25. White, *States of Desire,* 340–41.

26. E. M. Forster, *Aspects of the Novel* (New York: Harvest, 1954), 86.

27. Edmund White, *The Beautiful Room Is Empty* (New York: Knopf, 1988), 147. Subsequent citations will be to this edition and will be given parenthetically in the text.

28. The nasty phrase "injustice collector" was a favorite of the psychiatrist Edmund Bergler (1899–1962). See Edmund Bergler and Joost A. M. Meerloo, "The Injustice Collector," in *Justice and Injustice* (New York: Grune and Stratton, 1963), 20–35.

29. Edmund White, *Skinned Alive* (New York: Vintage, 1996). Citations to the short stories in this collection will be given parenthetically in the text.

30. Ernest Hemingway, *"Big Two-Hearted River,"* a story in two parts, is in Ernest Hemingway, *In Our Time* (New York: Charles Scribner, 1925).

31. Edmund White, *The Burning Library: Essays,* ed. with introduction by David Bergman (New York: Knopf, 1994), xvii.

AFTERWORD

1. "Mr. Pater's Last Volume," in Oscar Wilde, *The Artist as Critic: Critical Writings of Oscar Wilde,* ed. Richard Ellmann (Chicago: Phoenix, 1982), 229–30.

2. Allan Gurganus, "Adult Art," in *Men on Men 2: Best New Gay Fiction,* ed. George Stambolian (New York: Plume, 1988); "Forced Use," in *The Faber Book of Gay Short Fiction,* ed. Edmund White (London: Faber and Faber, 1991).

3. Philip Gambone, *The Language We Use Up Here* (New York: Dutton, 1991).

4. Edmund White, *The Beautiful Room Is Empty* (New York: Knopf, 1988), 135, 140–41.

INDEX